THE OXFORD MINIDICTIONARY OF QUOTATIONS

THE OXFORD MINIDICTIONARY OF QUOTATIONS

Oxford New York
OXFORD UNIVERSITY PRESS
1983

Oxford University Press, Walton Street, Oxford OX2 6DP

London Glasgow New York Toronto
Delhi Bombay Calcutta Madras Karachi
Kuala Lumpur Singapore Hong Kong Tokyo
Nairobi Dar es Salaam Cape Town
Melbourne Auckland

and associated companies in
Beirut Berlin Ibadan Mexico City Nicosia

Oxford is a trade mark of Oxford University Press

Library of Congress Cataloging in Publication Data

Main entry under title:

The Oxford minidictionary of quotations.

Derived from the 3rd ed. of the Oxford dictionary of quotations.
Includes index.
1. Quotations. 2. Quotations, English. I. Oxford dictionary of quotations.
PN6080.'96 1983 808.88'2 83-8287

ISBN 0-19-211594-4

British Library Cataloguing in Publication Data

The Oxford minidictionary of quotations.
1. Quotations, English
080 PN6081

ISBN 0-19-211594-4

Printed in Great Britain
at the University Press, Oxford
by Eric Buckley
Printer to the University

PREFACE

THE famous *Oxford Dictionary of Quotations* has, over the forty years since it first appeared, held a unique place among reference works. 'The ultimate cultural reduction . . . the iron rations of Literature in a knapsack' is how Anthony Burgess described the third edition when it was published in 1979. *The Oxford Minidictionary of Quotations* is derived from this most recent edition of *ODQ* for those, with or without knapsacks, who want a book they can fit into their pockets.

In spite of its small format, the dictionary offers nearly 4,000 of the most quoted items from more than 700 authors, writers, wits, philosophers, politicians, and many others. Each quotation is indexed under various key words, to help the user track down half-remembered (or misremembered) phrases. The index may be used, too, to seek out quotations appropriate to a given subject or for a particular occasion.

Traditional proverbs, nursery rhymes, catch-phrases from films, radio, and television, advertising slogans, and the words of popular songs have regretfully been set aside from the present application of the word 'quotation', not least because of the difficulty of establishing authorship in such areas. For items of the first two kinds, the reader will find *The Concise Oxford Dictionary of*

Proverbs and *The Oxford Dictionary of Nursery Rhymes* invaluable.

B. J. PALMER

March 1983

HOW TO USE THE DICTIONARY

THE arrangement is alphabetical by the names of authors; sections such as the Anonymous one, Ballads, the Bible, the Mass in Latin, etc., are included in the alphabetical order.

Under each author, quotations are arranged by the alphabetical order of the titles of the works from which they come: books, plays, poems. These are printed in bold italic type. Titles of pieces (e.g., articles, essays, short stories) that constitute part of a published volume are in bold roman (the volume title having been given in bold italic). Quotations from diaries, letters, speeches, etc., however, are given in chronological order, and normally follow the literary works quoted. Poetry quotations precede prose ones for poets; and vice versa for writers most of whose work was in prose. Quotations cited from biographies or other writers' works are kept to the end under each author; sources are then given conventionally with titles of books or plays in italic (not bold) type. Books of the Bible are presented in canonical order, not alphabetically.

Numerical source references are given for the first line of each quotation, by, e.g., act, scene, and, if appropriate, line number; by chapter or by page or section or verse number. Each quotation without a full source given depends from its immediate predecessor. If no source reference is given at all, the quotation is from the same poem or chapter or whatever as the last preceding named or numbered one.

ACCIUS 170–c.90 B.C.

1 *Oderint, dum metuant.*
Let them hate, so long as they fear.
Atreus. Seneca, *De Ira*, I, 20, 4

DEAN ACHESON 1893–1971

2 Great Britain has lost an Empire and has not yet found a role.
Speech at the Military Academy, West Point, 5 Dec. 1962

LORD ACTON 1834–1902

3 Power tends to corrupt and absolute power corrupts absolutely.
Letter to Bishop Mandell Creighton, 3 Apr. 1887. See *Life and Letters of Mandell Creighton* (1904), i.372. See Napoleon and Adam Smith.

SARAH F. ADAMS 1805–1848

4 Nearer, my God, to thee,
Nearer to thee!
Nearer My God to Thee

JOSEPH ADDISON 1672–1719

5 'Tis not in mortals to command success,
But we'll do more, Sempronius; we'll deserve it.
Cato, I.ii.43

6 What pity is it
That we can die but once to serve our country!
IV.iv 81

7 Thus I live in the world rather as a spectator of mankind than as one of the species.
The Spectator, 1

8 I have often thought, says Sir Roger, it happens very well that Christmas should fall out in the Middle of Winter.
269

9 I value my garden more for being full of blackbirds than of cherries, and very frankly give them fruit for their songs.
477

1 If we may believe our logicians, man is distinguished from all other creatures by the faculty of laughter.
494

2 'We are always doing', says he, 'something for Posterity, but I would fain see Posterity do something for us.'
583

AGATHON 446?–c.401 B.C.

3 Even God cannot change the past.
Aristotle, *Nicomachean Ethics*, VI.2.1139b

ALCUIN c.735–804

4 *Nec audiendi qui solent dicere, Vox populi, vox Dei.*
And those people should not be listened to who keep saying the voice of the people is the voice of God.
Letter to Charlemagne, A.D.800. ***Works***, Epist.127

DEAN ALDRICH 1647–1710

5 If all be true that I do think,
There are five reasons we should drink;
Good wine—a friend—or being dry—
Or lest we should be by and by—
Or any other reason why.
Reasons for Drinking

MRS. ALEXANDER 1818–1895

6 All things bright and beautiful,
All creatures great and small,
All things wise and wonderful,
The Lord God made them all.
All Things Bright and Beautiful (1848)

7 The rich man in his castle,
The poor man at his gate,
God made them, high or lowly,
And order'd their estate.

ABBÉ D'ALLAINVAL 1700–1753

8 *L'embarras des richesses.*
The more alternatives, the more difficult the choice.
Title of comedy, 1726

WILLIAM ALLINGHAM 1828–1889

1 Up the airy mountain,
Down the rushy glen,
We daren't go a-hunting,
For fear of little men.
The Fairies

ST. AMBROSE c.339–397

2 *Si fueris Romae, Romano vivito more;*
Si fueris alibi, vivito sicut ibi.
If you are at Rome live in the Roman style; if you are elsewhere live as they live elsewhere.
Jeremy Taylor, *Ductor Dubitantium*, I.i.5. Usually quoted as 'When in Rome, do as the Romans do'.

KINGSLEY AMIS 1922–

3 More will mean worse.
Encounter, July 1960

BISHOP LANCELOT ANDREWES 1555–1626

4 It was no summer progress. A cold coming they had of it. ... The ways deep, the weather sharp, the days short, the sun farthest off *in solstitio brumali*, the very dead of Winter.
Sermon 15, Of the Nativity (1622)

ANONYMOUS

ENGLISH

5 A Company for carrying on an undertaking of Great Advantage, but no one to know what it is.
The South Sea Company Prospectus, 1711. Cowles, *The Great Swindle* (1963), ch.5

6 Adam
Had 'em.
On the antiquity of Microbes. (Claimed as the shortest poem.)

7 A gentleman haranguing on the perfection of our law, and that it was equally open to the poor and the rich, was answered by another, 'So is the London Tavern'.
Tom Paine's Jests ... (1794), 23. Also attr. to John Horne Tooke.

1 All human beings are born free and equal in dignity and rights.
Universal Declaration of Human Rights (1948), Article 1

2 All present and correct.
King's Regulations (Army). Report of the Orderly Sergeant to the Officer of the Day

3 All this buttoning and unbuttoning.
18th Century suicide note

4 Along the electric wire the message came:
He is not better—he is much the same.
Said to be from a poem on the illness of the Prince of Wales, afterwards Edward VII, often attr. to Alfred Austin.

5 An abomination unto the Lord, but a very present help in time of trouble. [A lie.]
(Cf. Proverbs 12:22; Psalms 46:1)

6 Appeal from Philip drunk to Philip sober.
Valerius Maximus, *Facta ac Dicta Memorabilia* (c. A.D. 32), VI, ii

7 Are we downhearted? No!
Expression much used by British soldiers in 1914-18

8 Be happy while y'er leevin,
For y'er a lang time deid.
Scottish motto for a house. N. & Q. 7 Dec. 1901, 469

9 Dear Sir, Your astonishment's odd:
I am always about in the Quad.
  And that's why the tree
  Will continue to be,
Since observed by Yours faithfully, God.
Reply to Knox's limerick on idealism.

10 From ghoulies and ghosties and long-leggety beasties
And things that go bump in the night,
    Good Lord, deliver us!
Cornish

11 God be in my head,
And in my understanding;
God be in my eyes,
And in my looking;

God be in my mouth,
And in my speaking;

God be in my heart,
And in my thinking;

God be at my end,
And at my departing.
Sarum Missal

1 Happy is that city which in time of peace thinks of war. (Inscription in the armoury of Venice.)
Burton, *Anatomy of Melancholy*, pt.ii, 3, memb.6. See Vegetius.

2 Here's tae us; wha's like us?
Gey few, and they're a' deid.
Scottish Toast, probably of nineteenth-century origin. The first line appears in Crosland, *The Unspeakable Scot* (1902), p.24n. Various versions of the second line are current.

3 'How different, how very different from the home life of our own dear Queen!'
Irvin S. Cobb, *A Laugh a Day*. Comment by a middle-aged British matron at a performance of Cleopatra by Sarah Bernhardt.

4 If God were to take one or other of us, I should go and live in Paris.
Reported in S. Butler, *Notebooks*, ed. G. Keynes and B. Hill, 1951, p.193

5 They're hangin' men an' women there for the wearin' o' the Green.
The Wearin' o' the Green. (Famous street ballad, later added to by Boucicault.)

6 Lizzie Borden took an axe
And gave her mother forty whacks;
When she saw what she had done
She gave her father forty-one!
Lizzie Borden was acquitted of murdering her father and stepmother on 4 Aug. 1892 in Fall River, Massachusetts

Matthew, Mark, Luke, and John,
The Bed be blest that I lie on.
Thomas Ady, *A Candle in the Dark* (1656)

1 Miss Buss and Miss Beale
Cupid's darts do not feel.
How different from us,
Miss Beale and Miss Buss.
Of the Headmistress of the North London Collegiate School and the Principal of the Ladies' College, Cheltenham, c.1884

2 Multiplication is vexation,
Division is as bad;
The Rule of three doth puzzle me,
And Practice drives me mad.
Elizabethan MS. dated 1570

3 Now I lay me down to sleep;
I pray the Lord my soul to keep.
If I should die before I wake,
I pray the Lord my soul to take.
First printed in a late edition of the *New England Primer*, 1781

4 O Death, where is thy sting-a-ling-a-ling,
O Grave, thy victoree?
The bells of Hell go ting-a-ling-a-ling
For you but not for me.
Song popular in the British Army, 1914-18

5 O God, if there be a God, save my soul, if I have a soul!
Prayer of a common soldier before the battle of Blenheim (see *N. & Q.*, clxxiii.264). Quoted in Newman's *Apologia*.

6 Oh my dear fellow, the noise ... and the people!
Of the Battle of Bastogne. Attr. to a Captain Strahan. See Griffin, 'Dialogue with W.H. Auden', *Hudson Review* III, iv, Winter 51, p.583

7 It was resolved, That England was too pure an Air for Slaves to breathe in.
'In the 11th of Elizabeth' (17 Nov. 1568–16 Nov. 1569). Rushworth, *Historical Collections* (1680–1722), II, p.468

8 Please do not shoot the pianist. He is doing his best.
Oscar Wilde, *Impressions of America*. 'Leadville'

9 Please to remember the Fifth of November,
Gunpowder Treason and Plot.
We know no reason why gunpowder treason
Should ever be forgot.
Traditional since 17th cent.

1 Since wars begin in the minds of men, it is in the minds of men that the defences of peace must be constructed.
Constitution of the United Nations Educational, Scientific and Cultural Organisation (1946)

2 Sumer is icumen in,
Lhude sing cuccu!
Groweth sed, and bloweth med,
And springth the wude nu.
Cuckoo Song, c.1250, sung annually at Reading Abbey gateway. First recorded by John Fornset, a monk of Reading Abbey

3 That this house will in no circumstances fight for its King and country.
Motion passed at the Oxford Union, 9 Feb. 1933

4 The almighty dollar is the only object of worship.
Philadelphia Public Ledger, 2 Dec. 1836

5 The eternal triangle.
Book Review in the *Daily Chronicle*, 5 Dec. 1907

6 They come as a boon and a blessing to men,
The Pickwick, the Owl, and the Waverley pen.
dvertisement by MacNiven and Cameron Ltd, Edinburgh and mingham

days hath September,
e, and November;
ave thirty-one,
ruary alone,
nty-eight days clear
each leap year.

heart the keener, courage
ns.
Gordon (1926) from Anglo-

evident, that all men are
owed by their Creator

1 Western wind, when wilt thou blow,
The small rain down can rain?
Christ, if my love were in my arms
And I in my bed again!
Oxford Book of 16th Cent. Verse

2 Whose Finger do you want on the Trigger When the World Situation Is So Delicate?
Headline in the *Daily Mirror*. See H. Cudlipp, *Publish and Be Damned* (1953), p.263

3 Would you like to sin
With Elinor Glyn
On a tiger-skin?
Or would you prefer
to err
with her
on some other fur?
c.1907. A. Glyn, *Elinor Glyn* (1955), pt.II.30

4 You pays your money and you takes your choice.
From a peepshow rhyme. See V.S. Lean, *Collectanea* (1902–4).

FRENCH

5 *Cet animal est très méchant,*
Quand on l'attaque il se défend.
This animal is very bad; when attacked it de
La Ménagerie, by Théodore P.K., 1828

6 *Chevalier sans peur et sans reproche.*
Knight without fear and without bl
Description in contemporary chronicl
1524

7 *Honi soit qui mal y pense*
Evil be to him who evil
Motto of the Order of t
probably on 23 Apr. of 1

8 *La grande phrase reç*
royaliste que le roi

1 *Liberté! Égalité! Fraternité!*
Freedom! Equality! Brotherhood!
Motto of the French Revolution, but of earlier origin

2 *Nous n'irons plus aux bois, les lauriers sont coupés.*
We'll to the woods no more,
The laurels all are cut.
Old nursery rhyme quoted by Banville in *Les Cariatides, les stalactites*. Tr. Housman, *Last Poems*, introductory

3 *Revenons à ces moutons.*
Let us return to our sheep. (Let us get back to the subject.)
Maistre Pierre Pathelin (line 1191). Often quoted as '*Retournons à nos moutons*'

4 *Tout passe, tout casse, tout lasse.*
Everything passes, everything perishes, everything palls.
Cahier, *Quelques six mille proverbes*

GREEK

5 Know thyself.
Inscribed on the temple of Apollo at Delphi. Plato, *Protagoras*, 343 b, ascribes the saying to the Seven Wise Men.

6 Nothing in excess.

7 Whenever God prepares evil for a man, He first damages his mind.
Scholiast on Sophocles, *Antigone*, 622 ff. See Duport.

ITALIAN

8 *Se non è vero, è molto ben trovato.*
If it is not true, it is a happy invention.
Apparently a common saying in the sixteenth century. Found in Giordano Bruno (1585) in the above form.

LATIN

9 *Ad majorem Dei gloriam.*
To the greater glory of God.
Motto of the Society of Jesus

10 *Ave Caesar, morituri te salutant.*
Hail Caesar; those who are about to die salute you.
Gladiators saluting the Roman Emperor. See Suetonius, *Claudius*, 21.

1 *Ave Maria, gratia plena, Dominus tecum: Benedicta tu in mulieribus.*
Hail Mary, full of grace, the Lord is with thee: Blessed art thou among women.
Ave Maria, also known as *The Angelic Salutation*, dating from the 11th cent.

2 *Et in Arcadia ego.*
And I too in Arcadia.
Tomb inscription often depicted in classical paintings. The meaning is disputed.

3 *Gaudeamus igitur,*
Juvenes dum sumus
Post jucundam juventutem,
Post molestam senectutem,
Nos habebit humus.
Let us then rejoice,
While we are young.
After the pleasures of youth
And the tiresomeness of old age
Earth will hold us.
Medieval students' song, traced to 1267, but revised in the 18th cent.

4 *Nemo me impune lacessit.*
No one provokes me with impunity.
Motto of the Crown of Scotland and of all Scottish regiments

5 *Per ardua ad astra.*
Hard and high to the stars!
Motto of the Mulvany family, adopted as official motto of the Royal Flying Corps and still in use as motto of the R.A.F. See P.G. Hering, *Customs and Traditions of the Royal Air Force* (1961).

6 *Post coitum omne animal triste.*
After coition every animal is sad.
Post-classical

7 *Quidquid agas, prudenter agas, et respice finem.*
Whatever you do, do cautiously, and look to the end.
Gesta Romanorum, 103

8 *Sic transit gloria mundi.*
Thus passes the glory of the world.
Spoken during the coronation of a new Pope, while flax is burned. Used at the coronation of Alexander V, Pisa, 7 July 1409, but earlier in origin. See Thomas à Kempis.

1 *Si monumentum requiris, circumspice.*
If you seek for a monument, gaze around.
Inscription in St. Paul's Cathedral, London, attr. to the son of the architect, Sir Christopher Wren.

2 *Te Deum laudamus: Te Dominum confitemur.*
We praise thee, God: we own thee Lord.
Te Deum. Hymn traditionally ascribed to St. Ambrose and St. Augustine in 387, but some modern scholars attribute it to St. Niceta (d.c.414).

3 *Tempora mutantur, et nos mutamur in illis.*
Times change, and we change with them.
Harrison, *Description of Britain* (1577), III, iii, 99. Attributed to the Emperor Lothar I (795-855) in the form *Omnia mutantur, nos et mutamur in illis*

4 *Vox et praeterea nihil.*
A voice and nothing more.
Of a nightingale. See also Plutarch, *Moralia*, 'Sayings of Spartans', 233a.

THOMAS GOLD APPLETON 1812–1884

5 Good Americans, when they die, go to Paris.
O.W. Holmes, *Autocrat of the Breakfast Table*, 6

ARABIAN NIGHTS

6 Who will change old lamps for new ones? ... new lamps for old ones?
The History of Aladdin

Open Sesame!
The History of Ali Baba

ARCHILOCHUS fl. c.650 B.C.

The fox knows many things—the hedgehog one *big* one.
Diehl (ed.), *Anth. Lyr. Gr.*, I, p.241, no.103

[illegible]HIMEDES 287–212 B.C.

[illegible]! (I've got it!)
[illegible] Pollio, *De Architectura*, ix.215

MARQUIS D'ARGENSON 1694–1757

1 *Laisser-faire.*
No interference.
Mémoires, vol.5, p.364.

LUDOVICO ARIOSTO 1474–1533

2 *Natura il fece, e poi roppe la stampa.*
Nature made him, and then broke the mould.
Orlando Furioso, x.84

ARISTOTLE 384–322 B.C.

3 Man is by nature a political animal.
Politics, i.2.1253a

4 Tragedy is thus a representation of an action that is worth serious attention, complete in itself and of some amplitude ... by means of pity and fear bringing about the purgation of such emotions.
Poetics, 6.1449b

5 Poetry is something more philosophical and more worthy of serious attention than history.
9.1451b

6 Probable impossibilities are to be preferred to improbable possibilities.
24.1460a

7 *Amicus Plato, sed magis amica veritas.*
Plato is dear to me, but dearer still is truth.
Greek original ascribed to Aristotle

NEIL A. ARMSTRONG 1930–

8 That's one small step for a man, one giant leap mankind.
On landing on the moon, 21 July 1969

MATTHEW ARNOLD 1822–1888

9 And we forget because we must
And not because we will.
Absence

1 Ah, love, let us be true
To one another!
Dover Beach, l.29

2 And we are here as on a darkling plain
Swept with confused alarms of struggle and flight,
Where ignorant armies clash by night.
l.35

3 Wandering between two worlds, one dead,
The other powerless to be born.
The Grande Chartreuse, l.85

4 Creep into thy narrow bed,
Creep, and let no more be said!
The Last Word

5 Let the long contention cease!
Geese are swans, and swans are geese.
Let them have it how they will!
Thou art tired; best be still.

6 Go, for they call you, Shepherd, from the hill.
The Scholar-Gipsy (1853), l.1

7 Crossing the stripling Thames at Bab-lock-hithe.
l.74

8 Others abide our question. Thou art free.
Shakespeare

9 And that sweet City with her dreaming spires.
Thyrsis, l.19

10 Too quick despairer, wherefore wilt thou go?
l.61

11 Home of lost causes, and forsaken beliefs, and unpopular names, and impossible loyalties! [Oxford.]
Essays in Criticism, First Series (1865), preface

12 Miracles do not happen.
Literature and Dogma, preface to 1883 edition, last words

13 The true meaning of religion is thus not simply morality, but morality touched by emotion.
i, 2

1 Have something to say, and say it as clearly as you can. That is the only secret of style.
G.W.E. Russell, *Collections and Recollections*, ch.13

DR. THOMAS ARNOLD 1795–1842

2 My object will be, if possible, to form Christian men, for Christian boys I can scarcely hope to make.
Letter, in 1828, on appointment to Headmastership of Rugby

3 As for rioting, the old Roman way of dealing with that is always the right one; flog the rank and file, and fling the ringleaders from the Tarpeian rock.
Cornhill Magazine, Aug. 1868

ROGER ASCHAM 1515–1568

4 There is no such whetstone, to sharpen a good wit and encourage a will to learning, as is praise.
The Schoolmaster (1570), 1

H.H. ASQUITH 1852–1928

5 We had better wait and see.
R.Jenkins, *Asquith*, ch.14

SIR JACOB ASTLEY 1579–1652

6 O Lord! thou knowest how busy I must be this day: if I forget thee, do not thou forget me.
Prayer before the Battle of Edgehill. Sir Philip Warwick, *Memoires*, 1701, p.229

SURGEON-CAPTAIN E.L. ATKINSON 1882–1929 and APSLEY CHERRY-GARRARD 1882–1959

7 Hereabouts died a very gallant gentleman, Captain L.E.G. Oates of the Inniskilling Dragoons.
Epitaph on a cairn and cross erected in the Antarctic, November 1912

JOHN AUBREY 1626–1697

8 Sciatica: he cured it, by boiling his buttock.
Brief Lives. Sir Jonas Moore

1 Anno 1670, not far from Cirencester, was an apparition; being demanded whether a good spirit or a bad? returned no answer, but disappeared with a curious perfume and most melodious twang.
***Miscellanies*. Apparitions** (1696)

W.H. AUDEN 1907–1973

2 I'll love you till the ocean
Is folded and hung up to dry
And the seven stars go squawking
Like geese about the sky.
As I Walked Out One Evening

3 O plunge your hands in water,
Plunge them in up to the wrist;
Stare, stare in the basin
And wonder what you've missed.

4 And the crack in the tea-cup opens
A lane to the land of the dead.

5 August for the people and their favourite islands.
Birthday Poem

6 Perfection, of a kind, was what he was after.
Epitaph on a Tyrant

7 When he laughed, respectable senators burst with laughter,
And when he cried the little children died in the streets.

8 Now Ireland has her madness and her weather still,
For poetry makes nothing happen.
In Memory of W.B. Yeats, I

9 Time that is intolerant
Of the brave and innocent,
And indifferent in a week
To a beautiful physique,

Worships language and forgives
Everyone by whom it lives.
III

1 In the deserts of the heart
Let the healing fountain start,
In the prison of his days
Teach the free man how to praise.

2 Lay your sleeping head, my love,
Human on my faithless arm.
Lullaby

3 But in my arms till break of day
Let the living creature lie,
Mortal, guilty, but to me
The entirely beautiful.

4 Look, stranger, on this island now.
On This Island

5 Harrow the house of the dead; look shining at
New styles of architecture, a change of heart.
Petition

6 Hunger allows no choice
To the citizen or the police;
We must love one another or die.
September 1, 1939

7 Private faces in public places
Are wiser and nicer
Than public faces in private places.
Collected Poems, 11 *1927–1932, Shorts*

8 To the man-in-the-street, who, I'm sorry to say,
  Is a keen observer of life,
The word 'Intellectual' suggests straight away
  A man who's untrue to his wife.
IV *1939-47, Shorts*

9 Tomorrow for the young the poets exploding like bombs.
Spain 1937

10 History to the defeated
May say Alas but cannot help nor pardon.

11 The sky is darkening like a stain;
Something is going to fall like rain,
  And it won't be flowers.
The Witnesses (1932 poem)

ÉMILE AUGIER 1820–1889

1 *La nostalgie de la boue!*
Longing to be back in the mud!
Le Mariage d'Olympe, I.i

ST. AUGUSTINE 354–430

2 *Da mihi castitatem et continentiam, sed noli modo.*
Give me chastity and continency—but not yet!
Confessions, bk.viii, ch.7

3 *Tolle lege, tolle lege.*
Take up and read, take up and read.
ch.12

4 *Imperas nobis continentiam.*
You impose continency upon us.
bk.x, ch.29

5 *Salus extra ecclesiam non est.*
There is no salvation outside the church.
De Bapt. IV, c.xvii.24. See St. Cyprian.

6 *Dilige et quod vis fac.*
Love and do what you will.
(Often quoted as *Ama et fac quod vis.*)
In Epist. Joann. Tractatus, vii, 8

7 *Cum dilectione hominum et odio vitiorum.*
With love for mankind and hatred of sins.
Often quoted in the form: Love the sinner but hate the sin. ***Opera Omnia***, vol.II. col.962, letter 211. Migne's *Patrologiae* (1845), vol.XXXIII

8 *Roma locuta est; causa finita est.*
Rome has spoken; the case is concluded.
Sermons, bk.i

EMPEROR AUGUSTUS 63 B.C.–A.D. 14

9 I inherited it brick and left it marble.
Suetonius, *Divus Augustus*, 28. Of the city of Rome.

JANE AUSTEN 1775–1817

10 The sooner every party breaks up the better. [Mr. Woodhouse.]
Emma, ch.25

1 One has no great hopes from Birmingham. I always say there is something direful in the sound. [Mrs. Elton.]
ch.36

2 There certainly are not so many men of large fortune in the world, as there are pretty women to deserve them.
Mansfield Park, ch.1

3 A large income is the best recipe for happiness I ever heard of. It certainly may secure all the myrtle and turkey part of it.
ch.22

4 Let other pens dwell on guilt and misery.
ch.48

5 Oh! who can ever be tired of Bath?
Northanger Abbey, ch.10

6 A woman especially, if she have the misfortune of knowing any thing, should conceal it as well as she can.
ch.14

7 From politics, it was an easy step to silence.

8 My sore throats are always worse than anyone's. [Mary Musgrove.]
Persuasion, ch.18

9 All the privilege I claim for my own sex ... is that of loving longest, when existence or when hope is gone. [Anne.]
ch.23

10 It is a truth universally acknowledged, that a single man in possession of a good fortune, must be in want of a wife.
Pride and Prejudice, ch.1

11 May I ask whether these pleasing attentions proceed from the impulse of the moment, or are the result of previous study? [Mr. Bennet.]
ch.14

12 For what do we live, but to make sport for our neighbours, and laugh at them in our turn? [Mr. Bennet.]
ch.57

1 'I am afraid,' replied Elinor, 'that the pleasantness of an employment does not always evince its propriety.'
Sense and Sensibility, ch.13

2 Where so many hours have been spent in convincing myself that I am right, is there not some reason to fear I may be wrong?
ch.31

CHARLES BABBAGE 1792–1871

3 Every moment dies a man,
Every moment one and one-sixteenth is born.
See *New Scientist*, 4 Dec. 1958, p.1428. Unpublished letter to Tennyson, whose *Vision of Sin* this parodies.

FRANCIS BACON 1561–1626

4 All good moral philosophy is but an handmaid to religion.
Advancement of Learning, II.xxii.14

5 Silence is the virtue of fools.
De Dignitate et Augmentis Scientiarum, I, vi, 31. Antitheta, 6 (ed. 1640, tr. Gilbert Watts)

6 A little philosophy inclineth man's mind to atheism, but depth in philosophy bringeth men's minds about to religion.
Essays. 16. **Atheism**

7 There is no excellent beauty that hath not some strangeness in the proportion.
43. **Of Beauty**

8 If the hill will not come to Mahomet, Mahomet will go to the hill. (Proverbially, 'If the mountain will not ... ')
12. **Boldness**

9 A wise man will make more opportunities than he finds.
52. **Of Ceremonies and Respects**

10 Men fear death as children fear to go in the dark; and as that natural fear in children is increased with tales, so is the other.
2. **Of Death**

1 It is as natural to die as to be born; and to a little infant, perhaps, the one is as painful as the other.

2 If a man look sharply, and attentively, he shall see Fortune: for though she be blind, yet she is not invisible.
40. **Of Fortune**

3 God Almighty first planted a garden; and, indeed, it is the purest of human pleasures.
46. **Of Gardens**

4 It is a strange desire to seek power and to lose liberty.
11. **Of Great Place**

5 He that hath wife and children hath given hostages to fortune; for they are impediments to great enterprises, either of virtue or mischief.
8. **Of Marriage and Single Life.** See Lucan.

6 Wives are young men's mistresses, companions for middle age, and old men's nurses.

7 He was reputed one of the wise men that made answer to the question when a man should marry? 'A young man not yet, an elder man not at all.'

8 Children sweeten labours, but they make misfortunes more bitter.
7. **Of Parents and Children**

9 Revenge is a kind of wild justice.
4. **Of Revenge**

10 Money is like muck, not good except it be spread.
15. **Of Seditions and Troubles**

11 Some books are to be tasted, others to be swallowed, and some few to be chewed and digested; that is, some books are to be read only in parts; others to be read but not curiously; and some few to be read wholly, and with diligence and attention.
50. **Of Studies**

12 Reading maketh a full man; conference a ready man; and writing an exact man.

13 There is a superstition in avoiding superstition.
17. **Of Superstition**

1 Travel, in the younger sort, is a part of education; in the elder, a part of experience.
18. **Of Travel**

2 What is truth? said jesting Pilate; and would not stay for an answer.
1. **Of Truth.** See St. John 18:38.

3 Opportunity makes a thief.
Letter to the Earl of Essex, 1598

4 *Quod enim mavult homo verum esse, id potius credit.*
For what a man would like to be true, that he more readily believes.
Novum Oganum, bk.I, Aphor.49.

5 *Magna ista scientiarum mater.*
That great mother of sciences.
80. [Of natural philosophy]

6 *Nam et ipsa scientia potestas est.*
Knowledge itself is power.
Religious Meditations. **Of Heresies**

WALTER BAGEHOT 1826–1877

7 If he were a horse, nobody would buy him; with that eye no one could answer for his temper.
Biographical Studies. Essay II, **Lord Brougham**

8 The Sovereign has, under a constitutional monarchy such as ours, three rights—the right to be consulted, the right to encourage, the right to warn.
The English Constitution (1867), 3. **The Monarchy** (continued)

9 A constitutional statesman is in general a man of common opinion and uncommon abilities.
Historical Essays. **The Character of Sir Robert Peel**

10 One of the greatest pains to human nature is the pain of a new idea.
Physics and Politics, No.v

BRUCE BAIRNSFATHER 1888–1959

11 Well, if you knows of a better 'ole, go to it.
Fragments from France, No.1 (1915)

MICHAEL BAKUNIN 1814–1876

1 *Die Lust der Zerstörung ist zugleich eine schaffende Lust!*
The urge for destruction is also a creative urge!
'Die Reaktion in Deutschland' in *Jahrbuch für Wissenschaft und Kunst* (1842), under the pseudonym 'Jules Elysard'

2 From each according to his faculties, to each according to his needs; that is what we wish sincerely and energetically.
Declaration signed by forty-seven anarchists on trial after the failure of their uprising at Lyons in 1870. See Marx.

STANLEY BALDWIN 1867–1947

3 A lot of hard-faced men who look as if they had done very well out of the war.
Of the House of Commons returned after the election of 1918. J.M. Keynes, *Economic Consequences of the Peace*, Ch.5; and see Middlemass and Barnes, *Baldwin*, p.72n.

4 My lips are not yet unsealed.
10 Dec. 1935, speech on the Abyssinian crisis. Usually quoted as 'My lips are sealed.'

BALLADS

5 'What gat ye to your dinner, Lord Randal, my Son?
What gat ye to your dinner, my handsome young man?'
'I gat eels boil'd in broo'; mother, make my bed soon,
For I'm weary wi' hunting, and fain wald lie down.'
Lord Randal

6 When captains couragious whom death could not daunte,
Did march to the seige of the city of Gaunt.
Mary Ambree

7 Yestreen the Queen had four Maries,
The night she'll hae but three;
There was Marie Seaton, and Marie Beaton,
And Marie Carmichael, and me.
The Queen's Maries

8 'I saw the new moon late yestreen
Wi' the auld moon in her arm;

And if we gang to sea master,
  I fear we'll come to harm.'
Sir Patrick Spens

1 O waly, waly, up the bank,
  And waly, waly, doun the brae,
And waly, waly, yon burn-side,
  Where I and my Love wont to gae!
Waly, Waly

2 'Tom Pearse, Tom Pearse, lend me your grey mare,
All along, down along, out along, lee.
For I want for to go to Widdicombe Fair,
Wi' Bill Brewer, Jan Stewer, Peter Gurney, Peter Davey, Dan'l Whiddon, Harry Hawk,
Old Uncle Tom Cobbleigh and all.'
Widdicombe Fair

RICHARD BANCROFT 1544–1610

3 Where Christ erecteth his Church, the devil in the same churchyard will have his chapel.
Sermon at Paul's Cross, 9 Feb. 1588

PHINEAS T. BARNUM 1810–1891

4 There's a sucker born every minute.
Attr.

J.M. BARRIE 1860–1937

5 His Lordship may compel us to be equal upstairs, but there will never be equality in the servants' hall.
The Admirable Crichton, I

6 When the first baby laughed for the first time, the laugh broke into a thousand pieces and they all went skipping about, and that was the beginning of fairies.
Peter Pan, I

7 Every time a child says 'I don't believe in fairies' there is a little fairy somewhere that falls down dead.

8 To die will be an awfully big adventure.
III

9 It's a sort of bloom on a woman. If you have it [charm], you don't need to have anything else; and if you

don't have it, it doesn't much matter what else you have.
***What Every Woman Knows*, I**

1 There are few more impressive sights in the world than a Scotsman on the make.
II

BERNARD M. BARUCH 1870–1965

2 Let us not be deceived—we are today in the midst of a cold war.
Speech before South Carolina Legislature, 16 Apr. 1947. Mr. Baruch said the expression 'cold war' was suggested to him by H.B. Swope, former editor of the New York *World*.

THOMAS BASTARD 1566–1618

3 Age is deformed, youth unkind,
We scorn their bodies, they our mind.
Chrestoleros (1598), Bk.7, Epigram 9

CHARLES BAUDELAIRE 1821–1867

4 *Hypocrite lecteur,—mon semblable,—mon frère.*
Hypocrite reader—my likeness—my brother.
Les Fleurs du Mal*, *Préface

5 *Là, tout n'est qu'ordre et beauté,*
Luxe, calme et volupté.
Everything there is simply order and beauty, luxury, peace and sensual indulgence.
liii, **L'Invitation au Voyage**

PIERRE-AUGUSTIN CARON DE BEAUMARCHAIS 1732–1799

6 *Aujourd'hui ce qui ne vaut pas la peine d'être dit, on le chante.*
Today if something is not worth saying, people sing it.
***Le Barbier de Séville*, I.ii**

7 *Je me presse de rire de tout, de peur d'être obligé d'en pleurer.*
I make myself laugh at everything, for fear of having to weep.

1 *Boire sans soif et faire l'amour en tout temps, madame, il n'y a que ça qui nous distingue des autres bêtes.*
Drinking when we are not thirsty and making love all year round, madam; that is all there is to distinguish us from other animals.
Le Mariage de Figaro, II.xxi

2 *Parce que vous êtes un grand seigneur, vous vous croyez un grand génie! ... Vous vous êtes donné la peine de naître, et rien de plus.*
Because you are a great lord, you believe yourself to be a great genius! ... You took the trouble to be born, but no more.

FRANCIS BEAUMONT 1584–1616 and JOHN FLETCHER 1579–1625

(see also under FLETCHER)

3 You are no better than you should be.
The Coxcomb, IV.iii

4 I care not two-pence.

5 It is always good
When a man has two irons in the fire.
The Faithful Friends, I.ii (attr.)

6 Those have most power to hurt us, that we love.
The Maid's Tragedy, V.iv

7 Kiss till the cow comes home.
The Scornful Lady, II.ii

SAMUEL BECKETT 1906–

8 *Estragon:* Let's go.
Vladimir: We can't.
Estragon: Why not?
Vladimir: We're waiting for Godot.
Waiting for Godot (1954), I

THOMAS BECON 1512–1567

9 For when the wine is in, the wit is out.
Catechism, 375

SIR THOMAS BEECHAM 1879–1961

1 A musicologist is a man who can read music but can't hear it.
H. Proctor-Gregg, *Beecham Remembered* (1976), p.154

2 In the first movement alone, I took note of six pregnancies and at least four miscarriages. [Of Bruckner's 7th Symphony.]
Oral trad.

MAX BEERBOHM 1872–1956

3 Most women are not so young as they are painted.
A Defence of Cosmetics

4 To give an accurate and exhaustive account of that period would need a far less brilliant pen than mine.
1880

5 I was a modest, good-humoured boy. It is Oxford that has made me insufferable.
More. **Going back to School**

6 Zuleika, on a desert island, would have spent most of her time in looking for a man's foot-print.
Zuleika Dobson, ch.2

7 The dullard's envy of brilliant men is always assuaged by the suspicion that they will come to a bad end.
ch.4

8 Only the insane take themselves quite seriously.
Lord David Cecil, *Max* (1964), ch.2

LUDWIG VAN BEETHOVEN 1770–1827

9 *Muss es sein? Es muss sein.*
Must it be? It must be.
Epigraph to String Quartet in F Major, Opus 135

MRS. APHRA BEHN 1640–1689

10 Faith, Sir, we are here to-day, and gone to-morrow.
The Lucky Chance, IV

HILAIRE BELLOC 1870–1953

1 Child! do not throw this book about;
Refrain from the unholy pleasure
Of cutting all the pictures out!
Preserve it as your chiefest treasure.
Bad Child's Book of Beasts, dedication

2 The Dromedary is a cheerful bird:
I cannot say the same about the Kurd.
The Dromedary

3 I shoot the Hippopotamus
With bullets made of platinum,
Because if I use leaden ones
His hide is sure to flatten 'em.
The Hippopotamus

4 Mothers of large families (who claim to common sense)
Will find a Tiger well repay the trouble and expense.
The Tiger

5 The chief defect of Henry King
Was chewing little bits of string.
Cautionary Tales. **Henry King**

6 Physicians of the utmost fame
Were called at once, but when they came
They answered, as they took their fees,
'There is no cure for this disease.'

7 'Oh, my friends, be warned by me,
That breakfast, dinner, lunch, and tea
Are all the human frame requires ... '
With that the wretched child expires.

8 And always keep a hold of Nurse
For fear of finding something worse.
Jim

9 We had intended you to be
The next Prime Minister but three.
Lord Lundy

10 But as it is! ... My language fails!
Go out and govern New South Wales.

11 Matilda told such Dreadful Lies,
It made one Gasp and Stretch one's Eyes;

Her Aunt, who, from her Earliest Youth,
Had kept a Strict Regard for Truth,
Attempted to Believe Matilda:
The effort very nearly killed her.
Matilda

1 The moon on my left and the dawn on my right.
My brother, good morning: my sister, good night.
The Early Morning

2 I said to Heart, 'How goes it?' Heart replied:
'Right as a Ribstone Pippin!' But it lied.
***Epigrams.* The False Heart**

3 When I am dead, I hope it may be said:
'His sins were scarlet, but his books were read.'
On his Books

4 The accursed power which stands on Privilege
(And goes with Women, and Champagne, and Bridge)
Broke—and Democracy resumed her reign:
(Which goes with Bridge, and Women and Champagne).
On a Great Election

5 I am a sundial, and I make a botch
Of what is done far better by a watch.
On a Sundial

6 Remote and ineffectual Don
That dared attack my Chesterton.
Lines to a Don

7 Lord Finchley tried to mend the Electric Light
Himself. It struck him dead: and serve him right!
It is the business of the wealthy man
To give employment to the artisan.
Lord Finchley

8 The nuisance of the tropics is
The sheer necessity of fizz.
The Modern Traveller **(1898), iv**

9 Whatever happens, we have got
The Maxim Gun, and they have not.
vi

10 Oh! let us never, never doubt
What nobody is sure about!
***More Beasts for Worse Children.* The Microbe**

1 Like many of the upper class
He liked the sound of broken glass.
***New Cautionary Tales*. About John**

2 When I am living in the Midlands
That are sodden and unkind ...
The great hills of the South Country
Come back into my mind.
The South Country

3 Do you remember an Inn,
Miranda?
Tarantella

4 The fleas that tease in the high Pyrenees.

P.-L. B. DU BELLOY 1725–1775

5 *Plus je vis d'étrangers, plus j'aimai ma patrie.*
The more foreigners I saw, the more I loved my homeland.
Le Siège de Calais (1765), II.iii

JULIEN BENDA 1868–1956

6 *La trahison des clercs.*
The intellectuals' betrayal.
Title of book (1927)

STEPHEN VINCENT BENÉT 1898–1943

7 Bury my heart at Wounded Knee.
American Names

ARNOLD BENNETT 1867-1931

8 Journalists say a thing that they know isn't true, in that hope that if they keep on saying it long enough it will be true.
The Title, Act II

JEREMY BENTHAM 1748–1832

9 The greatest happiness of the greatest number is the foundation of morals and legislation.
***The Commonplace Book*.** See Hutcheson.

1 Prose is when all the lines except the last go on to the end.
Poetry is when some of them fall short of it.
M. St.J. Packe, *Life of John Stuart Mill*, bk.I, ch.ii

EDMUND CLERIHEW BENTLEY 1875–1956

2 The art of Biography
Is different from Geography.
Geography is about maps,
But Biography is about chaps.
Biography for Beginners

3 Sir Humphrey Davy
Abominated gravy.
He lived in the odium
Of having discovered Sodium.

4 John Stuart Mill
By a mighty effort of will
Overcame his natural bonhomie
And wrote 'Principles of Political Economy'.

5 Sir Christopher Wren
Said, 'I am going to dine with some men.
If anybody calls
Say I am designing St Paul's.'

6 George the Third
Ought never to have occurred.
One can only wonder
At so grotesque a blunder.
More Biography

LORD CHARLES BERESFORD 1846–1919

7 Very sorry can't come. Lie follows by post.
Telegram to the Prince of Wales after an eleventh-hour summons to dine. R. Nevill, *The World of Fashion 1837–1922* (1923), ch 5. See Proust.

BISHOP BERKELEY 1685–1753

8 [Tar water] is of a nature so mild and benign ... as to warm without heating, to cheer but not inebriate.
Siris, par.217

BERNARD OF CHARTRES d. c.1130

1 We are like dwarfs on the shoulders of giants, so that we can see more than they, and things at a greater distance.
John of Salisbury, *Metalogicon* (1159), bk.III.ch.iv. See also R.K. Merton, *On the Shoulders of Giants* (1965).

LORD BERNERS 1883–1950

2 He's always backing into the limelight.
Oral tradition, of T.E. Lawrence

THEOBALD VON BETHMANN HOLLWEG 1856–1921

3 Just for a word—'neutrality', a word which in wartime has so often been disregarded, just for a scrap of paper—Great Britain is going to make war.
To Sir Edward Goschen, 4 Aug. 1914

SIR JOHN BETJEMAN 1906–

4 Oh! chintzy, chintzy cheeriness,
Half dead and half alive!
Death in Leamington

5 Old men who never cheated, never doubted,
Communicated monthly, sit and stare
At the new suburb stretched beyond the run-way
Where a young man lands hatless from the air.
Death of King George V

6 You ask me what it is I do. Well actually, you know,
I'm partly a liaison man and partly P.R.O.
Essentially I integrate the current export drive
And basically I'm viable from ten o'clock till five.
Executive

7 Phone for the fish-knives, Norman,
As Cook is a little unnerved;
You kiddies have crumpled the serviettes
And I must have things daintily served.
How to Get On in Society

8 Milk and then just as it comes dear?
I'm afraid the preserve's full of stones;
Beg pardon, I'm soiling the doileys
With afternoon tea-cakes and scones.

1 Oh wasn't it naughty of Smudges?
Oh, Mummy, I'm sick with disgust.
She threw me in front of the judges
And my silly old collarbone's bust.
Hunter Trials

2 In the Garden City Café with its murals on the wall
Before a talk on 'Sex and Civics' I meditated on the Fall.
Huxley Hall

3 But, gracious Lord, whate'er shall be,
Don't let anyone bomb me.
In Westminster Abbey

4 Think of what our Nation stands for,
Books from Boots' and country lanes,
Free speech, free passes, class distinction,
Democracy and proper drains.

5 And my childish wave of pity, seeing children carrying down
Sheaves of drooping dandelions to the courts of Kentish Town.
Parliament Hill Fields

6 Come, friendly bombs, and fall on Slough
It isn't fit for humans now.
Slough

7 Miss Joan Hunter Dunn, Miss Joan Hunter Dunn,
How mad I am, sad I am, glad that you won.
A Subaltern's Love Song

8 Oh! strongly adorable tennis-girl's hand!

9 *Ghastly Good Taste*, or *A Depressing Story of the Rise and Fall of English Architecture*.
Book title (1933)

ANEURIN BEVAN 1897–1960

10 The Tory Party ... So far as I am concerned they are lower than vermin.
Speech at Manchester, 4 July 1948

11 You will send a Foreign Minister, whoever he may be, naked into the conference chamber.
M. Foot, *Aneurin Bevan*, vol. ii (1973), ch 15. Speech at Labour Party Conference, 3 Oct. 1957, against unilateral nuclear disarmament.

ERNEST BEVIN 1881–1951

1 My [foreign] policy is to be able to take a ticket at Victoria Station and go anywhere I damn well please.
Spectator, 20 Apr. 1951

2 If you open that Pandora's Box you never know what Trojan 'orses will jump out.
On the Council of Europe. Sir Roderick Barclay, *Ernest Bevin and the Foreign Office* (1975), p.67

THE BIBLE

OLD TESTAMENT

3 In the beginning God created the heaven and the earth.
Genesis 1:1

4 And God said, Let there be light: and there was light.
3

5 And the evening and the morning were the first day.
5

6 And God saw that it was good.
10

7 Male and female created he them.
27

8 Be fruitful, and multiply, and replenish the earth, and subdue it.
28

9 But of the tree of the knowledge of good and evil, thou shalt not eat of it.
2:17

10 And the rib, which the Lord God had taken from man, made he a woman.
22

11 Bone of my bones, and flesh of my flesh.
23

12 And they sewed fig leaves together, and made themselves aprons [breeches in Genevan Bible, 1560].
And they heard the voice of the Lord God walking in the garden in the cool of the day.
3:7

1 In sorrow thou shalt bring forth children.
16

2 In the sweat of thy face shalt thou eat bread.
19

3 For dust thou art, and unto dust shalt thou return.

4 Am I my brother's keeper?
4:9

5 And the Lord set a mark upon Cain.
15

6 The land of Nod, on the east of Eden.
16

7 There were giants in the earth in those days.
6:4

8 I do set my bow in the cloud, and it shall be for a token of a covenant between me and the earth.
9:13

9 Nimrod the mighty hunter before the Lord.
10:9

10 But his wife looked back from behind him, and she became a pillar of salt.
19:26

11 Behold behind him a ram caught in a thicket by his horns.
22:13

12 Esau selleth his birthright for a mess of potage.
Heading to chapter 25 in Genevan Bible

13 Behold, Esau my brother is a hairy man, and I am a smooth man.
27:11

14 And he dreamed, and behold a ladder set up on the earth, and the top of it reached to heaven: and behold the angels of God ascending and descending on it.
28:12

15 Mizpah; for he said, The Lord watch between me and thee, when we are absent one from another.
31:49

1 Now Israel loved Joseph more than all his children, because he was the son of his old age; and he made him a coat of many colours.
37:3

2 Behold, this dreamer cometh.
19

3 Jacob saw that there was corn in Egypt.
42:1

4 Bring down my gray hairs with sorrow to the grave.
38

5 Ye shall eat the fat of the land.
45:18

6 I have been a stranger in a strange land.
Exodus 2:22. See Exodus 18:3.

7 Behold, the bush burned with fire, and the bush was not consumed.
3:2

8 A land flowing with milk and honey.
8

9 Let my people go.
7:16

10 And the Lord went before them by day in a pillar of a cloud, to lead them the way; and by night in a pillar of fire, to give them light.
13:21

11 Life for life,
Eye for eye, tooth for tooth, hand for hand, foot for foot.
21:23

12 Thou shalt not suffer a witch to live.
22:18

13 Thou shalt not seethe a kid in his mother's milk.
23:19

14 A stiffnecked people.
33:3

15 There shall no man see me and live.
20

1 Thou shalt love thy neighbour as thyself.
Leviticus 19:18. See Matt. 19:19.

2 The Lord bless thee, and keep thee:
The Lord make his face shine upon thee, and be gracious unto thee:
The Lord lift up his countenance upon thee, and give thee peace.
Numbers 6:24

3 The men which Moses sent to spy out the land.
13:16

4 What hath God wrought!
23:23. Quoted by Samuel Morse in the first electric telegraph message, Washington, 24 May 1844

5 Be sure your sin will find you out.
32:23

6 Hear, O Israel: The Lord our God is one Lord.
Deuteronomy 6:4

7 For the Lord thy God is a jealous God.
15

8 A dreamer of dreams.
13:1

9 The wife of thy bosom.
6

10 Thou shalt not muzzle the ox when he treadeth out the corn.
25:4

11 Cursed be he that removeth his neighbour's landmark.
27:17

12 I have set before you life and death, blessing and cursing: therefore choose life that both thou and thy seed may live.
30:19

13 Be strong and of a good courage; be not afraid, neither be thou dismayed: for the Lord thy God is with thee, whithersoever thou goest.
Joshua 1:9

14 Hewers of wood and drawers of water.
9:21

1 She brought forth butter in a lordly dish. [Jael.]
Judges 5:25

2 The Lord is with thee, thou mighty man of valour.
6:12

3 Faint, yet pursuing.
8:4

4 Out of the eater came forth meat, and out of the strong came forth sweetness.
14:14

5 He smote them hip and thigh.
15:8

6 With the jawbone of an ass.
16

7 Intreat me not to leave thee, or to return from following after thee: for whither thou goest, I will go; and where thou lodgest, I will lodge: thy people shall be my people, and thy God my God.
Ruth 1:16

8 Speak, Lord; for thy servant heareth.
1 Samuel 3:9

9 Quit yourselves like men, and fight.
4:9

10 God save the king.
10:24

11 A man after his own heart.
13:14

12 I did but taste a little honey with the end of the rod that was in mine hand, and, lo, I must die.
14:43

13 Agag came unto him delicately.
15:32

14 Now he was ruddy, and withal of a beautiful countenance, and goodly to look to.
16:12

15 God hath delivered him into mine hand.
23:7

1 Behold, I have played the fool, and have erred exceedingly. [Saul.]
26:21

2 Tell it not in Gath, publish it not in the streets of Askelon.
2 Samuel 1:19

3 Saul and Jonathan were lovely and pleasant in their lives, and in their death they were not divided.
23

4 How are the mighty fallen in the midst of the battle!
25

5 Thy love to me was wonderful, passing the love of women.
26

6 The poor man had nothing, save one little ewe lamb.
12:3

7 Would God I had died for thee, O Absalom, my son, my son!
18:33

8 By my God have I leaped over a wall.
22:30

9 Behold, the half was not told me.
1 Kings 10:7

10 The navy of Tharshish, bringing gold, and silver, ivory, and apes, and peacocks.
22

11 My father hath chastised you with whips, but I will chastise you with scorpions.
12:11

12 There ariseth a little cloud out of the sea, like a man's hand.
18:44

13 A still small voice.
19:12

14 Feed him with bread of affliction and with water of affliction, until I come in peace.
22:27

1 A certain man drew a bow at a venture.
34

2 There is death in the pot.
2 Kings 4:40

3 Is thy servant a dog, that he should do this great thing?
8:13

4 The driving is like the driving of Jehu, the son of Nimshi; for he driveth furiously.
9:20

5 He died in a good old age, full of days, riches, and honour.
1 Chronicles 29:28

6 The man whom the king delighteth to honour.
Esther 6:6

7 The Lord gave, and the Lord hath taken away; blessed be the name of the Lord.
Job 1:21

8 Curse God, and die.
2:9

9 There the wicked cease from troubling, and there the weary be at rest.
3:17

10 Man is born unto trouble, as the sparks fly upward.
5:7

11 No doubt but ye are the people, and wisdom shall die with you.
12:2

12 Man that is born of a woman is of few days, and full of trouble.
He cometh forth like a flower, and is cut down: he fleeth also as a shadow, and continueth not.
14:1

13 Miserable comforters are ye all.
16:2

14 I am escaped with the skin of my teeth.
19:20

15 Oh that my words were now written! oh that they were printed in a book!
23

1 I know that my redeemer liveth, and that he shall stand at the latter day upon the earth.
25

2 The price of wisdom is above rubies.
28:18

3 I am a brother to dragons, and a companion to owls.
30:29

4 My desire is ... that mine adversary had written a book.
31:35

5 Gird up now thy loins like a man.
38:3

6 When the morning stars sang together, and all the sons of God shouted for joy.
7

7 He saith among the trumpets, Ha, ha; and he smelleth the battle afar off, the thunder of the captains, and the shouting.
39:25

8 Canst thou draw out leviathan with an hook?
41:1

For psalms in the Book of Common Prayer see PRAYER BOOK.

9 For whom the Lord loveth he correcteth.
Proverbs 3:12

10 Her ways are ways of pleasantness, and all her paths are peace.
17

11 Get wisdom: and with all thy getting get understanding.
4:7

12 Go to the ant thou sluggard; consider her ways, and be wise.
6:6

13 Yet a little sleep, a little slumber, a little folding of the hands to sleep.
10. See Prov. 24:33

14 He goeth after her straightway, as an ox goeth to the slaughter.
7:22

1 Stolen waters are sweet.
9:17

2 A wise son maketh a glad father.
10:1

3 The destruction of the poor is their poverty.
15

4 A virtuous woman is a crown to her husband.
12:4

5 The tender mercies of the wicked are cruel.
10

6 Hope deferred maketh the heart sick.
13:12

7 The way of transgressors is hard.
15

8 He that spareth his rod hateth his son.
24

9 A soft answer turneth away wrath.
15:1

10 A merry heart maketh a cheerful countenance.
13

11 Better is a dinner of herbs where love is, than a stalled ox and hatred therewith.
17. Better is a mess of pottage with love, than a fat ox with evil will. (Matthew's Bible, 1535).

12 Pride goeth before destruction, and an haughty spirit before a fall.
16:18

13 There is a friend that sticketh closer than a brother.
18:24

14 Wine is a mocker, strong drink is raging.
20:1

15 Train up a child in the way he should go: and when he is old, he will not depart from it.
22:6

16 Look not thou upon the wine when it is red.
23:31

1 Heap coals of fire upon his head.
25:21

2 As cold waters to a thirsty soul, so is good news from a far country.
25

3 Answer a fool according to his folly, lest he be wise in his own conceit.
26:5

4 As a dog returneth to his vomit, so a fool returneth to his folly.
11

5 The slothful man saith, There is a lion in the way: a lion is in the streets.
13

6 The wicked flee when no man pursueth.
28:1

7 The way of an eagle in the air; the way of a serpent upon a rock; the way of a ship in the midst of the sea; and the way of a man with a maid.
30:19

8 Who can find a virtuous woman? for her price is far above rubies.
31:10

9 Her children arise up, and call her blessed.
28

10 Vanity of vanities, saith the Preacher, vanity of vanities; all is vanity.
Ecclesiastes 1:2

11 There is no new thing under the sun.
9

12 *All is vanity and vexation of spirit.*
14

13 He that increaseth knowledge increaseth sorrow.
18

14 To every thing there is a season, and a time to every purpose under the heaven:
A time to be born, and a time to die; a time to plant, and a time to pluck up that which is planted.
3:1

1 A time to love, and a time to hate; a time of war, and a time of peace.
8

2 The sleep of a labouring man is sweet.
5:12

3 As the crackling of thorns under a pot, so is the laughter of a fool.
7:6

4 One man among a thousand have I found; but a woman among all those have I not found.
28

5 There is no discharge in that war.
8:8

6 A living dog is better than a dead lion.
9:4

7 Eat thy bread with joy, and drink thy wine with a merry heart.
7

8 Whatsoever thy hand findeth to do, do it with thy might.
10

9 The race is not to the swift, nor the battle to the strong.
11

10 He that diggeth a pit shall fall into it.
10:8

11 Woe to thee, O land, when thy king is a child!
16

12 Wine maketh merry: but money answereth all things.
19

13 Cast thy bread upon the waters: for thou shalt find it after many days.
11:1

14 Remember now thy Creator in the days of thy youth.
12:1

15 Or ever the silver cord be loosed, or the golden bowl be broken.
6

1 Of making many books there is no end; and much study
is a weariness of the flesh.
12

2 I am black, but comely, O ye daughters of Jerusalem.
Song of Solomon 1:5

3 I am the rose of Sharon, and the lily of the valleys.
2:1

4 His banner over me was love.
4

5 Stay me with flagons, comfort me with apples: for I am
sick of love.
5

6 Rise up, my love, my fair one, and come away.
For, lo, the winter is past, the rain is over and gone;
The flowers appear on the earth; the time of the singing
of birds is come, and the voice of the turtle is heard in
our land.
2:10

7 Take us the foxes, the little foxes, that spoil the vines.
15

8 Behold, thou art fair, my love; behold, thou art fair; thou
hast doves' eyes within thy locks.
4:1

9 Thy lips are like a thread of scarlet.
3

10 Thy two breasts are like two young roes that are twins,
which feed among the lilies.
5

11 Many waters cannot quench love, neither can the floods
drown it.
8:7

12 Though your sins be as scarlet, they shall be as white as
snow.
Isaiah 1:18

13 They shall beat their swords into plowshares, and their
spears into pruninghooks: nation shall not lift up sword
against nation, neither shall they learn war any more.
2:4

1 What mean ye that ye beat my people to pieces, and grind the faces of the poor?
3:15

2 Woe unto them that join house to house, that lay field to field, till there be no place.
5:8

3 Woe unto them that rise up early in the morning, that they may follow strong drink.
11

4 Holy, holy, holy, is the Lord of hosts: the whole earth is full of his glory.
6:3

5 Woe is me! for I am undone; because I am a man of unclean lips, and I dwell in the midst of a people of unclean lips.
5

6 Whom shall I send, and who will go for us? Then said I, Here am I; send me.
8

7 Then said I, Lord, how long?
11

8 Wizards that peep and that mutter.
8:19

9 The people that walked in darkness have seen a great light.
9:2

10 For unto us a child is born, unto us a son is given: and the government shall be upon his shoulder: and his name shall be called Wonderful, Counsellor, The mighty God, The everlasting Father, The Prince of Peace.
6

11 And there shall come forth a rod out of the stem of Jesse.
11:1

12 The wolf also shall dwell with the lamb, and the leopard shall lie down with the kid; and the calf and the young lion and the fatling together; and a little child shall lead them.
6

1 Dragons in their pleasant palaces.
13:22

2 How art thou fallen from heaven, O Lucifer, son of the morning!
14:12

3 Watchman, what of the night?
21:11

4 Let us eat and drink; for to morrow we shall die.
22:13. See Eccl. 8:15, Luke 12:19, and 1 Cor. 15:32.

5 Line upon line; here a little, and there a little.
28:10

6 We have made a covenant with death, and with hell are we at agreement.
15

7 The desert shall rejoice, and blossom as the rose.
35:1

8 Sorrow and sighing shall flee away.
10

9 Set thine house in order.
38:1

10 Comfort ye, comfort ye my people.
40:1

11 Every valley shall be exalted, and every mountain and hill shall be made low: and the crooked shall be made straight, and the rough places plain:
And the glory of the Lord shall be revealed, and all flesh shall see it together: for the mouth of the Lord hath spoken it.
4

12 He shall feed his flock like a shepherd: he shall gather the lambs with his arm, and carry them in his bosom, and shall gently lead those that are with young.
11

13 There is no peace, saith the Lord, unto the wicked.
48:22

14 How beautiful upon the mountains are the feet of him that bringeth good tidings, that publisheth peace.
52:7

1 For they shall see eye to eye, when the Lord shall bring again Zion.
8

2 He is despised and rejected of men; a man of sorrows, and acquainted with grief.
53:3

3 All we like sheep have gone astray; we have turned every one to his own way; and the Lord hath laid on him the iniquity of us all.
6

4 He is brought as a lamb to the slaughter.
7

5 Seek ye the Lord while he may be found, call ye upon him while he is near.
55:6

6 To bind up the brokenhearted, to proclaim liberty to the captives, and the opening of the prison to them that are bound.
61:1

7 Who is this that cometh from Edom, with dyed garments from Bozrah?
63:1

8 I am holier than thou.
65:5

9 For, behold, I create new heavens and a new earth.
17

10 Saying, Peace, peace; when there is no peace.
Jeremiah 6:14

11 Is there no balm in Gilead?
8:22

12 Can the Ethiopian change his skin, or the leopard his spots?
13:23

13 The heart is deceitful above all things, and desperately wicked.
17:9

14 Behold, and see if there be any sorrow like unto my sorrow.
Lamentations 1:12

1 The wormwood and the gall.
3:19

2 It is good for a man that he bear the yoke in his youth.
27

3 As is the mother, so is her daughter.
Ezekiel 16:44

4 The fathers have eaten sour grapes, and the children's teeth are set on edge.
18:2

5 When the wicked man turneth away from his wickedness that he hath committed, and doeth that which is lawful and right, he shall save his soul alive.
27

6 The valley which was full of bones.
37:1

7 Can these bones live?
3

8 Cast into the midst of a burning fiery furnace.
Daniel 3:6

9 And this is the writing that was written, MENE, MENE, TEKEL, UPHARSIN.
5:25

10 According to the law of the Medes and Persians, which altereth not.
6:8

11 They have sown the wind, and they shall reap the whirlwind.
Hosea 8:7

12 I will restore to you the years that the locust hath eaten, the cankerworm, and the caterpillar, and the palmer-worm.
Joel 2:25

13 Your sons and your daughters shall prophesy, your old men shall dream dreams, your young men shall see visions.
28

14 Beat your plowshares into swords, and your pruning-hooks into spears.
3:10

1 Multitudes, multitudes in the valley of decision.
14

2 They shall sit every man under his vine, and under his fig tree.
Micah 4:4

APOCRYPHA

3 I shall light a candle of understanding in thine heart, which shall not be put out.
2 Esdras 14:25

4 We will fall into the hands of the Lord, and not into the hands of men.
Ecclesiasticus 2:18

5 Judge none blessed before his death.
11:28

6 He that toucheth pitch shall be defiled therewith.
13:1

7 Leave off first for manners' sake.
31:17

8 Wine is as good as life to a man, if it be drunk moderately.
27

9 He that sinneth before his Maker, Let him fall into the hand of the physician.
38:15

10 Let us now praise famous men, and our fathers that begat us.
44:1

11 And some there be, which have no memorial.
9

12 Their name liveth for evermore.
14

13 When he was at the last gasp.
2 Maccabees 7:9

NEW TESTAMENT

14 There came wise men from the east to Jerusalem, Saying, Where is he that is born King of the Jews? for we have seen his star in the east, and are come to worship him.
St. Matthew 2:1

1 They presented unto him gifts; gold, and frankincense, and myrrh.
11

2 The voice of one crying in the wilderness, Prepare ye the way of the Lord, make his paths straight.
3:3. See Isaiah 40:3.

3 O generation of vipers, who hath warned you to flee from the wrath to come?
7

4 This is my beloved Son, in whom I am well pleased.
17

5 Man shall not live by bread alone, but by every word that proceedeth out of the mouth of God.
4:4. See Deut. 8:3.

6 Thou shalt not tempt the Lord thy God.
7 and Deut. 6:16

7 Follow me, and I will make you fishers of men.
19

8 Blessed are the poor in spirit: for theirs is the kingdom of heaven.
Blessed are they that mourn: for they shall be comforted.
Blessed are the meek: for they shall inherit the earth.
Blessed are they which do hunger and thirst after righteousness: for they shall be filled.
Blessed are the merciful: for they shall obtain mercy.
Blessed are the pure in heart: for they shall see God.
Blessed are the peacemakers: for they shall be called the children of God.
5:3

9 Ye are the salt of the earth.
13

10 Let your light so shine before men, that they may see your good works.
16

11 I am come not to destroy, but to fulfil.
17

12 Let your communication be Yea, yea; Nay, nay.
37

1 Whosoever shall smite thee on thy right cheek, turn to him the other also.
39

2 He maketh his sun to rise on the evil and on the good, and sendeth rain on the just and on the unjust.
45

3 Be ye therefore perfect, even as your Father which is in heaven is perfect.
48

4 When thou doest alms, let not thy left hand know what thy right hand doeth.
6:3

5 After this manner therefore pray ye: Our Father which art in heaven, Hallowed be thy name.
Thy kingdom come. Thy will be done in earth, as it is in heaven.
Give us this day our daily bread.
And forgive us our debts, as we forgive our debtors.
And lead us not into temptation, but deliver us from evil:
For thine is the kingdom, and the power, and the glory, for ever. Amen.
9 and Luke 11:2

6 Lay not up for yourselves treasures upon earth, where moth and rust doth corrupt, and where thieves break through and steal:
But lay up for yourselves treasures in heaven.
19

7 Where your treasure is, there will your heart be also.
21

8 No man can serve two masters ... Ye cannot serve God and mammon.
24

9 Consider the lilies of the field, how they grow; they toil not, neither do they spin.
28

10 Solomon in all his glory was not arrayed like one of these.
29

1 Take therefore no thought for the morrow: for the morrow shall take thought for the things of itself. Sufficient unto the day is the evil thereof.
34

2 Judge not, that ye be not judged.
7:1. See Luke 6:37.

3 Why beholdest thou the mote that is in thy brother's eye, but considerest not the beam that is in thine own eye?
3

4 Neither cast ye your pearls before swine.
6

5 Ask, and it shall be given you; seek, and ye shall find; knock, and it shall be opened unto you.
7

6 If his son ask bread, will he give him a stone?
9

7 Therefore all things whatsoever ye would that men should do to you, do ye even so to them.
12

8 Wide is the gate, and broad is the way, that leadeth to destruction.
13

9 Strait is the gate, and narrow is the way, which leadeth unto life.
14

10 Beware of false prophets, which come to you in sheep's clothing, but inwardly they are ravening wolves.
15

11 Do men gather grapes of thorns, or figs of thistles?
16

12 *By their fruits* ye shall know them.
20

13 I say to this man, Go, and he goeth; and to another, Come, and he cometh; and to my servant, Do this, and he doeth it.
8:9

14 There shall be weeping and gnashing of teeth.
12

1 The foxes have holes, and the birds of the air have nests; but the Son of man hath not where to lay his head.
20

2 Let the dead bury their dead.
22

3 Why eateth your Master with publicans and sinners?
9:11

4 I am not come to call the righteous, but sinners to repentance.
13

5 Neither do men put new wine into old bottles.
17

6 Thy faith hath made thee whole.
22

7 The maid is not dead, but sleepeth.
24

8 When ye depart out of that house or city, shake off the dust of your feet.
10:14

9 Be ye therefore wise as serpents, and harmless as doves.
16

10 Are not two sparrows sold for a farthing? and one of them shall not fall on the ground without your Father.
29. See Luke 12:6.

11 The very hairs of your head are all numbered.
30

12 I came not to send peace, but a sword.
34

13 He that findeth his life shall lose it: and he that loseth his life for my sake shall find it.
39

14 What went ye out into the wilderness to see? A reed shaken with the wind?
11:7

15 Come unto me, all ye that labour and are heavy laden, and I will give you rest.
28

1 For my yoke is easy, and my burden is light.
30

2 He that is not with me is against me.
12:30 and Luke 11:23

3 He findeth it empty, swept, and garnished.
44

4 Some seeds fell by the wayside.
13:4

5 The kingdom of heaven is like to a grain of mustard seed.
31

6 One pearl of great price.
46

7 A prophet is not without honour, save in his own country, and in his own house.
57

8 If the blind lead the blind, both shall fall into the ditch.
15:14

9 The signs of the times.
16:3

10 Thou art Peter, and upon this rock I will build my church; and the gates of hell shall not prevail against it.
18

11 Get thee behind me, Satan.
23

12 What is a man profited, if he shall gain the whole world, and lose his own soul?
26 and Mark 8:36

13 Except ye be converted, and become as little children, ye shall not enter into the kingdom of heaven.
18:3

14 Whoso shall *offend* one of these little ones which believe *in me*, it were better for him that a millstone were hanged about his neck, and that he were drowned in the depth of the sea.
6. See Luke 17:2.

15 If thine eye offend thee, pluck it out, and cast it from thee.
9

1 For where two or three are gathered together in my name, there am I in the midst of them.
20

2 What therefore God hath joined together, let not man put asunder.
19:6

3 Go and sell that thou hast, and give to the poor, and thou shalt have treasure in heaven.
21

4 It is easier for a camel to go through the eye of a needle, than for a rich man to enter into the kingdom of God.
24. See Luke 10:25.

5 With men this is impossible; but with God all things are possible.
26

6 But many that are first shall be last; and the last shall be first.
30

7 Which have borne the burden and heat of the day.
20:12

8 My house shall be called the house of prayer; but ye have made it a den of thieves.
21:13 and Isaiah. 56:7

9 For many are called, but few are chosen.
22:14

10 Render therefore unto Caesar the things which are Caesar's; and unto God the things that are God's.
21

11 For in the resurrection they neither marry, nor are given in marriage.
30

12 Blind guides, which strain at a gnat, and swallow a camel.
23:24

13 Ye are like unto whited sepulchres.
27

14 Ye shall hear of wars and rumours of wars.
24:6

1 For nation shall rise against nation, and kingdom against kingdom.
7

2 The abomination of desolation.
15 and Daniel 12:11

3 Wheresoever the carcase is, there will the eagles be gathered together.
28

4 Heaven and earth shall pass away, but my words shall not pass away.
35

5 Watch therefore: for ye know not what hour your Lord doth come.
42

6 Well done, thou good and faithful servant.
25:21

7 Unto every one that hath shall be given, and he shall have abundance: but from him that hath not shall be taken away even that which he hath.
29

8 And he shall set the sheep on his right hand, but the goats on the left.
33

9 For I was an hungred, and ye gave me meat: I was thirsty and ye gave me drink: I was a stranger, and ye took me in: Naked, and ye clothed me: I was sick, and ye visited me: I was in prison, and ye came unto me.
35

10 Inasmuch as ye have done it unto one of the least of these my brethren, ye have done it unto me.
40

11 *They* covenanted with him for thirty pieces of silver.
26:15

12 Jesus took bread, and blessed it, and brake it, and gave it to the disciples, and said, Take, eat; this is my body.
26

13 This night, before the cock crow, thou shalt deny me thrice.
34

1 If it be possible, let this cup pass from me.
39

2 What, could ye not watch with me one hour?
40

3 Watch and pray, that ye enter not into temptation: the spirit indeed is willing but the flesh is weak.
41

4 All they that take the sword shall perish with the sword.
52

5 He saved others; himself he cannot save.
27:42

6 Eli, Eli, lama sabachthani? ... My God, my God, why hast thou forsaken me?
46. See Psalms 22:1.

7 And, lo, I am with you alway, even unto the end of the world.
28:20

8 The sabbath was made for man, and not man for the sabbath.
St. Mark 2:27

9 If a house be divided against itself, that house cannot stand.
3:25

10 He that hath ears to hear, let him hear.
4:9

11 My name is Legion: for we are many.
5:9

12 Clothed, and in his right mind.
15

13 Lord, I believe; help thou mine unbelief.
9:24

14 Suffer the little children to come unto me, and forbid them not: for of such is the kingdom of God.
10:14

15 Hail, thou art highly favoured, the Lord is with thee: blessed art thou among women.
St. Luke 1:28

1 My soul doth magnify the Lord.
46

2 He hath put down the mighty from their seats, and exalted them of low degree.
He hath filled the hungry with good things; and the rich he hath sent empty away.
52

3 She brought forth her firstborn son, and wrapped him in swaddling clothes, and laid him in a manger; because there was no room for them in the inn.
2:7

4 Shepherds abiding in the field, keeping watch over their flock by night.
And, lo, the angel of the Lord came upon them, and the glory of the Lord shone round about them: and they were sore afraid.
8

5 Behold, I bring you good tidings of great joy.
10

6 Glory to God in the highest, and on earth peace, good will toward men.
14

7 Lord, now lettest thou thy servant depart in peace, according to thy word.
29

8 Wist ye not that I must be about my Father's business?
49

9 Physician, heal thyself.
4:23

10 Love your enemies, do good to them which hate you.
6:27

11 Give, and *it shall* be given unto you.
38

12 Her sins, which are many, are forgiven; for she loved much.
7:47

13 No man, having put his hand to the plough, and looking back, is fit for the kingdom of God.
9:62

1 For the labourer is worthy of his hire.
10:7

2 A certain man went down from Jerusalem to Jericho, and fell among thieves.
30

3 He passed by on the other side.
31

4 Go, and do thou likewise.
37

5 But Martha was cumbered about much serving.
40

6 He taketh from him all his armour wherein he trusted.
11:22

7 No man, when he hath lighted a candle, putteth it in a secret place, neither under a bushel.
33

8 Woe unto you, lawyers!
52

9 Thou fool, this night thy soul shall be required of thee.
12:20

10 Friend, go up higher.
14:10

11 For whosoever exalteth himself shall be abased; and he that humbleth himself shall be exalted.
11 and Matthew 23:12

12 Bring in hither the poor, and the maimed, and the halt, and the blind.
21

13 Rejoice with me; for I have found my sheep which was lost.
15:6

14 Joy shall be in heaven over one sinner that repenteth, more than over ninety and nine just persons, which need no repentance.
7

15 Wasted his substance with riotous living.
13

1 Father, I have sinned against heaven, and before thee,
And am no more worthy to be called thy son.
18

2 Bring hither the fatted calf, and kill it.
23

3 This my son was dead, and is alive again; he was lost, and is found.
24

4 I cannot dig; to beg I am ashamed.
16:3

5 The crumbs which fell from the rich man's table.
21. See Matthew 15:27.

6 And it came to pass that the beggar died, and was carried by the angels into Abraham's bosom.
22

7 Between us and you there is a great gulf fixed.
26

8 The kingdom of God is within you.
17:21

9 God, I thank thee, that I am not as other men are.
18:11

10 God be merciful to me a sinner.
13

11 In your patience possess ye your souls.
21:19

12 Nevertheless, not my will, but thine, be done.
22:42

13 Father, forgive them: for they know not what they do.
23:34

14 Father, *into* thy hands I commend my spirit.
46. See Psalms 31:6.

15 In the beginning was the Word, and the Word was with God, and the Word was God.
St. John 1:1

16 And the light shineth in darkness; and the darkness comprehended it not.
5

1 That was the true Light, which lighteth every man that cometh into the world.
9

2 He came unto his own, and his own received him not.
11

3 And the Word was made flesh, and dwelt among us.
14

4 He it is, who coming after me is preferred before me, whose shoe's latchet I am not worthy to unloose.
27

5 Behold the Lamb of God, which taketh away the sin of the world.
29

6 The wind bloweth where it listeth.
3:8

7 God so loved the world, that he gave his only begotten Son, that whosoever believeth in him should not perish, but have everlasting life.
16

8 Rise, take up thy bed, and walk.
5:8

9 He that is without sin among you, let him first cast a stone at her.
8:7

10 Neither do I condemn thee: go, and sin no more.
11

11 The truth shall make you free.
32

12 There is no truth in him. When he speaketh a lie, he speaketh of his own: for he is a liar, and the father of it.
44

13 The night cometh, when no man can work.
9:4

14 I am the good shepherd.
10:11

15 I am the resurrection, and the life.
11:25

1 Jesus wept.
35

2 It is expedient for us, that one man should die for the people, and that the whole nation perish not.
50

3 The poor always ye have with you.
12:8

4 Let not your heart be troubled.
14:1

5 In my Father's house are many mansions.
2

6 I am the way, the truth, and the life: no man cometh unto the Father, but by me.
6

7 Greater love hath no man than this, that a man lay down his life for his friends.
15:13

8 Pilate saith unto him, What is truth?
18:38

9 Now Barabbas was a robber.
40

10 What I have written I have written.
19:22

11 It is finished.
30

12 Touch me not.
20:17

13 Blessed are they that have not seen, and yet have believed.
29

14 And suddenly there came a sound from heaven as of a rushing mighty wind.
Acts of the Apostles 2:2

15 Silver and gold have I none; but such as I have give I thee.
3:6

16 Walking, and leaping, and praising God.
8

1 Breathing out threatenings and slaughter.
9:1

2 Saul, Saul, why persecutest thou me?
4

3 It is hard for thee to kick against the pricks.
5

4 God is no respecter of persons.
10:34. See Romans 2:11.

5 Come over into Macedonia, and help us.
16:9

6 What must I do to be saved?
30

7 Certain lewd fellows of the baser sort.
17:5

8 Those that have turned the world upside down.
6

9 I found an altar with this inscription, TO THE UNKNOWN GOD.
23

10 For in him we live, and move, and have our being.
28

11 Great is Diana of the Ephesians.
19:34

12 It is more blessed to give than to receive.
20:35

13 A citizen of no mean city.
21:39

14 Hast thou appealed unto Caesar? unto Caesar shalt thou go.
25:12

15 Much learning doth make thee mad.
26:24

16 Almost thou persuadest me to be a Christian.
28

17 Who against hope believed in hope.
Romans 4:18

1 Shall we continue in sin, that grace may abound?
6:1

2 Death hath no more dominion.
9

3 The wages of sin is death.
23

4 For the good that I would I do not: but the evil which I would not, that I do.
7:19. See Ovid.

5 All things work for good to them that love God.
8:28

6 For I am persuaded, that neither death, nor life, nor angels, nor principalities, nor powers, nor things present, nor things to come,
Nor height, nor depth, nor any other creature, shall be able to separate us from the love of God, which is in Christ Jesus our Lord.
38

7 Present your bodies a living sacrifice, holy, acceptable unto God.
12:1

8 Vengeance is mine; I will repay, saith the Lord.
19

9 Overcome evil with good.
21

10 The powers that be are ordained of God.
13:1

11 Let us put on the armour of light.
12

12 Doubtful disputations.
14:1

13 Salute one another with an holy kiss.
16:16

14 Your body is the temple of the Holy Ghost.
1 Corinthians 6:19

15 It is better to marry than to burn.
7:9

1 I am made all things to all men.
9:22

2 All things are lawful for me, but all things are not expedient.
10:23

3 For the earth is the Lord's, and the fulness thereof.
26. See Psalms 24:1.

4 If a man have long hair, it is a shame unto him.
But if a woman have long hair, it is a glory to her.
11:14

5 Though I speak with the tongues of men and of angels, and have not charity, I am become as sounding brass, or a tinkling cymbal.
13:1

6 Though I have all faith, so that I could remove mountains, and have not charity, I am nothing.
2

7 Charity suffereth long, and is kind; charity envieth not; charity vaunteth not itself, is not puffed up.
4

8 Beareth all things, believeth all things, hopeth all things, endureth all things.
7

9 For we know in part, and we prophesy in part.
9

10 When I was a child, I spake as a child, I understood as a child, I thought as a child: but when I became a man, I put away childish things.
11

11 For now we see through a glass, darkly.
12

12 And now abideth faith, hope, charity, these three; but the greatest of these is charity.
13

13 Let all things be done decently and in order.
14:40

14 But now is Christ risen from the dead, and become the firstfruits of them that slept.
15:20

1 The last enemy that shall be destroyed is death.
26

2 Evil communications corrupt good manners.
33

3 The first man is of the earth, earthy.
47

4 The trumpet shall sound, and the dead shall be raised incorruptible, and we shall be changed.
52

5 O death, where is thy sting? O grave, where is thy victory?
55

6 Quit you like men, be strong.
16:13

7 The letter killeth, but the spirit giveth life.
2 Corinthians 3:6

8 A house not made with hands.
5:1

9 God loveth a cheerful giver.
9:7

10 For ye suffer fools gladly, seeing ye yourselves are wise.
19

11 There was given to me a thorn in the flesh.
12:7

12 Be not deceived; God is not mocked: for whatsoever a man soweth, that shall he also reap.
Galatians 6:7

13 Ye see how large a letter I have written unto you with mine own hand.
11

14 Carried about with every wind of doctrine.
Ephesians 4:14

15 We are members one of another.
25

16 Be ye angry and sin not: let not the sun go down upon your wrath.
26

1 Put on the whole armour of God.
6:11

2 For we wrestle not against flesh and blood, but against principalities, against powers, against the rulers of the darkness of this world, against spiritual wickedness in high places.
12

3 Stand therefore, having your loins girt about with truth, and having on the breastplate of righteousness.
14

4 Rejoice in the Lord alway: and again I say, Rejoice.
Philippians 4:4

5 The peace of God, which passeth all understanding, shall keep your hearts and minds through Christ Jesus.
7

6 Whatsoever things are true, whatsoever things are honest, whatsoever things are just, whatsoever things are pure, whatsoever things are lovely, whatsoever things are of good report; if there be any virtue and if there be any praise, think on these things.
8

7 I can do all things through Christ which strengtheneth me.
13

8 Luke, the beloved physician.
Colossians 4:14

9 If any would not work, neither should he eat.
2 Thessalonians 3:10

10 I suffer not a woman to teach, nor to usurp authority over the man, but to be in silence.
1 Timothy 2:12

11 Not given to wine, no striker, not greedy of filthy lucre.
3:3

12 Old wives' fables.
4:7

13 Use a little wine for thy stomach's sake.
5:23

1 For we brought nothing into this world, and it is certain we can carry nothing out.
6:7

2 The love of money is the root of all evil.
10

3 I have fought a good fight, I have finished my course, I have kept the faith.
2 Timothy 4:7

4 Unto the pure all things are pure.
Titus 1:15

5 Without shedding of blood is no remission.
Hebrews 9:22

6 It is a fearful thing to fall into the hands of the living God.
10:31

7 Faith is the substance of things hoped for, the evidence of things not seen.
11:1

8 We also are compassed about with so great a cloud of witnesses.
12:1

9 Let us run with patience the race that is set before us.

10 Whom the Lord loveth he chasteneth.
6

11 Be not forgetful to entertain strangers: for thereby some have entertained angels unawares.
13:2

12 For here have we no continuing city.
14

13 Faith without works is dead.
James 2:20

14 Ye have heard of the patience of Job.
5:11

15 Let your yea be yea; and your nay, nay.
12

16 All flesh is as grass, and all the glory of man as the flower of grass.
1 Peter 1:24. See Isaiah 40:6.

1 But ye are a chosen generation, a royal priesthood, an holy nation, a peculiar people.
2:9

2 Giving honour unto the wife, as unto the weaker vessel.
3:7

3 Charity shall cover the multitude of sins.
4:8

4 Your adversary the devil, as a roaring lion, walketh about, seeking whom he may devour.
5:8

5 He that loveth not knoweth not God; for God is love.
1 John 4:8

6 Perfect love casteth out fear.
18

7 If a man say, I love God, and hateth his brother, he is a liar: for he that loveth not his brother whom he hath seen, how can he love God whom he hath not seen?
20

8 I am Alpha and Omega, the beginning and the ending, saith the Lord.
Revelation 1:8

9 Be thou faithful unto death, and I will give thee a crown of life.
2:10

10 Behold, I stand at the door, and knock.
3:20

11 Holy, holy, holy, Lord God Almighty, which was, and is, and is to come.
4:8

12 Behold a pale horse: and his name that sat on him was Death.
6:8

13 God shall wipe away all tears from their eyes.
7:17

14 And when he had opened the seventh seal, there was silence in heaven about the space of half an hour.
8:1

1 And the sea gave up the dead which were in it.
20:13

2 And I saw a new heaven and a new earth: for the first heaven and the first earth were passed away; and there was no more sea.
21:1

3 There shall be no more death, neither sorrow, nor crying, neither shall there be any more pain.
4

4 Amen. Even so, come, Lord Jesus.
22:20

VULGATE

5 *Dominus illuminatio mea.*
The Lord is the source of my light.
Psalm 26:1 (A.V. Psalm 27:1)

6 *Beatus vir qui timet Dominum!*
Happy is the man who fears the Lord.
111:1 (A.V. Psalm 112:1)

7 *Non nobis, Domine, non nobis; sed nomini tuo da gloriam.*
Not unto us, Lord, not unto us; but to thy name give glory.
113:(9) (A.V. Psalm 115:1)

8 *De profundis clamavi ad te, Domine.*
Up from the depths I have cried to thee, Lord.
129:1 (A.V. Psalm 130:1)

9 *Vanitas vanitatum, dixit Ecclesiastes; vanitas vanitatum, et omnia vanitas.*
Vanity of vanities, said the preacher; vanity of vanities, and everything is vanity.
Ecclesiastes 1:2

10 *Magnificat anima mea Dominum.*
My soul doth magnify the Lord. [Tr. Book of Common Prayer]
Ev. S. Luc. 1:46

11 *Nunc dimittis servum tuum, Domine, secundum verbum tuum in pace.*
Lord, now lettest thou thy servant depart in peace: according to thy word. [Tr. Book of Common Prayer]
2:29

1 *Pax Vobis.*
Peace be unto you.
24:36

2 *Quo vadis?*
Where are you going?
Ev. S. Joann. 16:5

3 *Ecce homo.*
Behold the man.
19:5

4 *Consummatum est.*
It is achieved.
30

5 *Noli me tangere.*
Do not touch me.
20:17

6 *Magna est veritas, et praevalet.*
Great is truth, and it prevails.
3 Esdr. 4:41

ISAAC BICKERSTAFFE 1735?–1812?

7 There was a jolly miller once,
  Lived on the river Dee;
He worked and sang from morn till night;
  No lark more blithe than he.
Love in a Village (1762), I.v

8 I care for nobody, not I,
  If no one cares for me.

9 In every port he finds a wife.
Thomas and Sally (1761), ii

REVD. E.H. BICKERSTETH 1825–1906

10 Peace, perfect peace, in this dark world of sin?
Songs in the House of Pilgrimage (1875)

JOSH BILLINGS (HENRY WHEELER SHAW) 1818–1885

11 Thrice is he armed that hath his quarrel just,
But four times he who gets his blow in fust.
Josh Billings, his Sayings (1865). See Shakespeare, ***Henry IV, Pt.2***, III.ii.

LAURENCE BINYON 1869–1943

1 They shall grow not old, as we that are left grow old:
Age shall not weary them, nor the years condemn.
At the going down of the sun and in the morning
We will remember them.
Poems For the Fallen

EARL OF BIRKENHEAD (F.E. SMITH) 1872–1930

2 We have the highest authority for believing that the meek shall inherit the Earth; though I have never found any particular corroboration of this aphorism in the records of Somerset House.
Contemporary Personalities (1924). **Marquess Curzon**

3 Nature has no cure for this sort of madness [Bolshevism], though I have known a legacy from a rich relative work wonders.
Law, Life and Letters (1927), ii. ch.19

4 The world continues to offer glittering prizes to those who have stout hearts and sharp swords.
Rectorial Address, Glasgow University, 7 Nov. 1923

PRINCE BISMARCK 1815–1898

5 *Die Politik ist die Lehre von Möglichen.*
Politics is the art of the possible.
In conversation with Meyer von Waldeck, 11 Aug. 1867

SIR WILLIAM BLACKSTONE 1723–1780

6 That the king can do no wrong, is a necessary and fundamental principle of the English constitution.
Commentaries on the Laws of England, bk. iii.17

7 It is better that ten guilty persons escape than one innocent suffer.
iv.27

WILLIAM BLAKE 1757–1827

8 To see a World in a Grain of Sand,
And a Heaven in a Wild Flower,
Hold Infinity in the palm of your hand,
And Eternity in an hour.
Auguries of Innocence, 1

1 A Robin Redbreast in a Cage
Puts all Heaven in a Rage.
5

2 The Vision of Christ that thou dost see
Is my vision's greatest enemy.
Thine has a great hook nose like thine,
Mine has a snub nose like to mine.
The Everlasting Gospel, a, l.1

3 And did those feet in ancient time
Walk upon England's mountains green?
Milton, preface

4 And did the Countenance Divine
Shine forth upon our clouded hills?
And was Jerusalem builded here
Among these dark Satanic mills?

Bring me my bow of burning gold!
Bring me my arrows of desire!
Bring me my spear! O clouds, unfold!
Bring me my chariot of fire!

I will not cease from Mental Fight,
Nor shall my Sword sleep in my hand,
Till we have built Jerusalem,
In England's green & pleasant Land.

5 Mock on, mock on, Voltaire, Rousseau;
Mock on, mock on, 'tis all in vain!
You throw the sand against the wind,
And the wind blows it back again.
MS. Notebooks, 1800-03, p.7

6 Great things are done when men and mountains meet;
This is not done by jostling in the street.
p.43

7 Tyger! Tyger! burning bright
In the forests of the night,
What immortal hand or eye
Could frame thy fearful symmetry?
Songs of Experience, **The Tyger**

8 Did he who made the Lamb make thee?

1 Love seeketh not itself to please,
Nor for itself hath any care,
But for another gives its ease,
And builds a Heaven in Hell's despair.
The Clod and the Pebble

2 Love seeketh only Self to please,
To bind another to its delight,
Joys in another's loss of ease,
And builds a Hell in Heaven's despite.

3 Little Lamb, who made thee?
Dost thou know who made thee?
***Songs of Innocence*, The Lamb**

4 My mother bore me in the southern wild,
And I am black, but O! my soul is white;
White as an angel is the English child,
But I am black, as if bereav'd of light.
The Little Black Boy

5 For Mercy has a human heart,
Pity a human face,
And Love, the human form divine,
And Peace, the human dress.
The Divine Image

6 Can I see another's woe,
And not be in sorrow too?
On Another's Sorrow

7 Energy is Eternal Delight.
***The Marriage of Heaven and Hell*: The Voice of the Devil**

8 The reason Milton wrote in fetters when he wrote of Angels and God, and at liberty when of Devils and Hell, is because he was a true Poet, and of the Devil's party without knowing it.
(note)

9 The road of excess leads to the palace of wisdom.
Proverbs of Hell

10 A fool sees not the same tree that a wise man sees.

11 Eternity is in love with the productions of time.

12 If the fool would persist in his folly he would become wise.

1 The tigers of wrath are wiser than the horses of instruction.

2 Damn braces. Bless relaxes.

3 Sooner murder an infant in its cradle than nurse unacted desires.

4 I was in a printing house in Hell, and saw the method in which knowledge is transmitted from generation to generation.
A Memorable Fancy, pl.12–13

5 If the doors of perception were cleansed everything would appear as it is, infinite.
pl.14

LESLEY BLANCH 1907–

6 She was an Amazon. Her whole life was spent riding at breakneck speed along the wilder shores of love.
The Wilder Shores of Love, 2. **Jane Digby El Mezrab**

PHILIP PAUL BLISS 1838–1876

7 Hold the fort, for I am coming.
The Charm. **Ho, My Comrades, See the Signal!**

BOETHIUS c.480–c.524

8 *Nam in omni adversitate fortunae infelicissimum genus est infortunii, fuisse felicem.*
For in every ill-turn of fortune the most unhappy sort of misfortune is to have been happy.
Consolation of Philosophy, bk.ii, prose 4

HUMPHREY BOGART 1899–1957

9 If she can stand it I can. Play it!
Casablanca (1942), script by Julius J. Epstein, Philip G. Epstein, Howard Koch. Often quoted as 'Play it again, Sam'.

JOHN B. BOGART 1845–1921

10 When a dog bites a man that is not news, but when a man bites a dog that is news.
Oral tradition: also attr. Charles Dana and Amos Cummings

SIR DAVID BONE 1874–1959

1 It's 'Damn you, Jack—I'm all right!' with you chaps.
The Brassbounder (1910), ch.3

DANIEL J. BOORSTIN 1914–

2 The celebrity is a person who is known for his well-knownness.
The Image (1961), ch.2, **From Hero to Celebrity: The Human Pseudo-event,** pt.iii

3 A best-seller was a book which somehow sold well simply because it was selling well.
ch.4, **From Shapes to Shadows: Dissolving Forms,** pt.viii

CESARE BORGIA 1476–1507

4 *Aut Caesar, aut nihil.*
Caesar or nothing.
Motto

GEORGE BORROW 1803–1881

5 There's night and day, brother, both sweet things; sun, moon, and stars, brother, all sweet things; there's likewise a wind on the heath. Life is very sweet, brother; who would wish to die?
Lavengro, ch.25

6 Youth will be served, every dog has his day, and mine has been a fine one.
ch.92

MARÉCHAL BOSQUET 1810–1861

7 *C'est magnifique, mais ce n'est pas la guerre.*
It is magnificent, but it is not war.
Remark on the charge of the Light Brigade, 1854

JOHN COLLINS BOSSIDY 1860–1928

8 And this is good old Boston,
  The home of the bean and the cod,
Where the Lowells talk only to Cabots,
  And the Cabots talk only to God.
Toast at Holy Cross Alumni dinner, 1910

JACQUES-BÉNIGNE BOSSUET 1627–1704

1 *L'Angleterre, ah, la perfide Angleterre.*
England, ah, faithless England.
Premier Sermon pour La Fête de la Circoncision de Notre Seigneur

JAMES BOSWELL 1740–1795

2 Most vices may be committed very genteelly: a man may debauch his friend's wife genteelly: he may cheat at cards genteelly.
Life of Johnson, vol.ii, p.340. 6 Apr. 1775

DION BOUCICAULT 1820?–1890

3 Men talk of killing time, while time quietly kills them.
London Assurance (1841), II.i

ANTOINE BOULAY DE LA MEURTHE 1761–1840

4 *C'est pire qu'un crime, c'est une faute.*
It is worse than a crime, it is a blunder.
On hearing of the execution of the Duc d'Enghien, 1804

LORD BOWEN 1835–1894

5 The rain it raineth on the just
And also on the unjust fella:
But chiefly on the just, because
The unjust steals the just's umbrella.
Walter Sichel, *Sands of Time*.

6 On a metaphysician: A blind man in a dark room—looking for a black hat—which isn't there.
Attr. See *N. & Q.*, clxxxii.153.

E.E. BOWEN 1836–1901

7 Forty years on, when afar and asunder
Parted are those who are singing to-day.
Forty Years On. Harrow School Song

JOHN BRADFORD 1510?–1555

8 But for the grace of God there goes John Bradford.
D.N.B. Exclamation on seeing some criminals taken to execution.

F.H. BRADLEY 1846–1924

1 The secret of happiness is to admire without desiring. And that is not happiness.
Aphorisms (1930), 33

ANNE BRADSTREET 1612–1672

2 I am obnoxious to each carping tongue,
Who sayes my hand a needle better fits.
The Prologue

JOHN BRAHAM 1774?–1856

3 England, home and beauty.
The Americans (1811). Song, **The Death of Nelson**

HARRY BRAISTED nineteenth century

4 If you want to win her hand,
Let the maiden understand
That she's not the only pebble on the beach.
You're Not the Only Pebble on the Beach

ERNEST BRAMAH 1868–1942

5 It is a mark of insincerity of purpose to spend one's time in looking for the sacred Emperor in the low-class tea-shops.
***The Wallet of Kai Lung*. Transmutation of Ling**

6 However entrancing it is to wander unchecked through a garden of bright images, are we not enticing your mind from another subject of almost equal importance?
***Kai Lung's Golden Hours*. Story of Hien**

REVD. JAMES BRAMSTON 1694?–1744

7 What's not destroy'd by Time's devouring hand?
Where's Troy, and where's the Maypole in the Strand?
The Art of Politicks (1729), l.71

BERTOLT BRECHT 1898–1956

8 *Erst kommt das Fressen, dann kommt die Moral.*
First comes fodder, then comes morality.
***Die Dreigroschenoper*, II**, finale

1 Andrea: *Unglücklich das Land, das keine Helden hat! ...* Galileo: *Nein, unglücklich das Land, das Helden nötig hat.*
Andrea: Unhappy the land that has no heroes.
Galileo: No, unhappy the land that needs heroes.
Leben des Galilei, sc.13

NICHOLAS BRETON 1545?–1626?

2 We rise with the lark and go to bed with the lamb.
The Court and Country, par.8

ROBERT BRIDGES 1844–1930

3 When men were all asleep the snow came flying,
In large white flakes falling on the city brown.
London Snow

4 Whither, O splendid ship, thy white sails crowding,
Leaning across the bosom of the urgent West?
A Passer-By

JOHN BRIGHT 1811–1889

5 The angel of death has been abroad throughout the land; you may almost hear the beating of his wings.
House of Commons, 23 Feb. 1855

6 England is the mother of Parliaments.
Birmingham, 18 Jan. 1865

ANTHELME BRILLAT-SAVARIN 1755–1826

7 *Dis-moi ce que tu manges, je te dirai ce que tu es.*
Tell me what you eat and I will tell you what you are.
Physiologie du Goût (1825), **Aphorismes ... pour servir de prolégomènes ...** iv. See Feuerbach.

CHARLOTTE BRONTË 1816–1855

8 Reader, I married him.
Jane Eyre, ch.38

EMILY BRONTË 1818–1848

9 No coward soul is mine,
No trembler in the world's storm-troubled sphere.
Last Lines

1 Cold in the earth—and fifteen wild Decembers,
From those brown hills, have melted into spring.
Remembrance

RUPERT BROOKE 1887–1915

2 Blow out, you bugles, over the rich Dead!
The Dead

3 These laid the world away; poured out the red
Sweet wine of youth.

4 Their sons, they gave, their immortality.

5 The cool kindliness of sheets, that soon
Smooth away trouble.
The Great Lover

6 The benison of hot water.

7 But somewhere, beyond space and time,
Is wetter water, slimier slime!
Heaven

8 Unkempt about those hedges blows
An English unofficial rose.
The Old Vicarage, Grantchester

9 God! I will pack, and take a train,
And get me to England once again!

10 For Cambridge people rarely smile,
Being urban, squat, and packed with guile.

11 Stands the Church clock at ten to three?
And is there honey still for tea?

12 Now, God be thanked Who has matched us with His hour,
And caught our youth, and wakened us from sleeping.
Peace

13 If I should die, think only this of me:
That there's some corner of a foreign field
That is for ever England.
The Soldier

14 And laughter, learnt of friends; and gentleness,
In hearts at peace, under an English heaven.

JOHN BROWN 1715–1766

1 Altogether upon the high horse.
Letter to Garrick, 27 Oct. 1765

THOMAS BROWN 1663–1704

2 I do not love you, Dr Fell,
But why I cannot tell;
But this I know full well,
I do not love you, Dr Fell.
Works (1719), vol.IV, p.113. See Martial.

T.E. BROWN 1830–1897

3 A garden is a lovesome thing, God wot!
My Garden

CECIL BROWNE

4 But not so odd
As those who choose
A Jewish God,
But spurn the Jews.
Reply to Ewer

SIR THOMAS BROWNE 1605–1682

5 Dreams out of the ivory gate, and visions before midnight.
On Dreams

6 There is another man within me, that's angry with me, rebukes, commands, and dastards me.
Religio Medici (1643), pt.i, 7

7 We all labour against our own cure, for death is the cure of all diseases.
pt.ii, 9

8 For the world, I count it not an inn, but an hospital, and a place, not to live, but to die in.
11

9 There is surely a piece of divinity in us.

10 Old mortality, the ruins of forgotten times.
Urn Burial (1658), Epistle Dedicatory

1 What song the Syrens sang, or what name Achilles assumed when he hid himself among women, though puzzling questions, are not beyond all conjecture.
ch. 5

2 Man is a noble animal, splendid in ashes, and pompous in the grave.

SIR WILLIAM BROWNE 1692–1774

3 The King to Oxford sent a troop of horse,
For Tories own no argument but force:
With equal skill to Cambridge books he sent,
For Whigs admit no force but argument.
Reply to Trapp's epigram. Nichols' *Literary Anecdotes*, vol.III, p.330

ELIZABETH BARRETT BROWNING 1806–1861

4 What was he doing, the great god Pan,
Down in the reeds by the river?
A Musical Instrument

5 How do I love thee? Let me count the ways.
Sonnets from the Portuguese, 43

ROBERT BROWNING 1812–1889

6 I feel for the common chord again ...
The C Major of this life.
Abt Vogler, xii

7 Ah, but a man's reach should exceed his grasp,
Or what's a heaven for?
Andrea del Sarto, l.97

8 Not verse now, only prose!
By the Fireside, ii

9 Oh, the little more, and how much it is!
And the little less, and what worlds away!
xxxix

10 We loved, sir—used to meet:
How sad and bad and mad it was—
But then, how it was sweet!
Confessions

1 He said, 'What's time? Leave Now for dogs and apes!
   Man has Forever.'
A Grammarian's Funeral, l.83

2 That low man goes on adding one to one,
   His hundred's soon hit;
This high man, aiming at a million,
   Misses an unit.
l.117

3 Oh, to be in England
Now that April's there.
Home-Thoughts, from Abroad

4 That's the wise thrush; he sings each song twice over,
Lest you should think he never could recapture
The first fine careless rapture!

5 I sprang to the stirrup, and Joris, and he;
I galloped, Dirck galloped, we galloped all three.
How they brought the Good News from Ghent to Aix

6 Escape me?
Never—
Beloved!
Life in a Love

7 Just for a handful of silver he left us,
   Just for a riband to stick in his coat.
The Lost Leader

8 Shakespeare was of us, Milton was for us,
Burns, Shelley, were with us—they watch from their graves!

9 Never glad confident morning again!

10 Ah, did you once see Shelley plain,
   And did he stop and speak to you
And did you speak to him again?
   How strange it seems, and new!
Memorabilia

11 That's my last Duchess painted on the wall,
Looking as if she were alive.
My Last Duchess, l.1

1 She had
A heart—how shall I say?—too soon made glad,
Too easily impressed; she liked whate'er
She looked on, and her looks went everywhere.
1.21

2 Never the time and the place
And the loved one all together!
Never the Time and the Place

3 It was roses, roses, all the way.
The Patriot

4 Anything like the sound of a rat
Makes my heart go pit-a-pat!
The Pied Piper of Hamelin, st. iv

5 'Come in!'—the Mayor cried, looking bigger:
And in did come the strangest figure!
v

6 God's in his heaven.
All's right with the world!
Pippa Passes, pt.I, l.228

7 Who fished the murex up?
What porridge had John Keats?
Popularity

8 And all night long we have not stirred,
And yet God has not said a word!
Porphyria's Lover

9 Fear death?—to feel the fog in my throat,
The mist in my face.
Prospice

10 Grow old along with me!
The best is yet to be.
Rabbi ben Ezra, i

11 O lyric Love, half-angel and half-bird
And all a wonder and a wild desire.
The Ring and the Book, bk.i, l.1391

12 Gr-r-r- there go, my heart's abhorrence!
Water your damned flower-pots, do!
Soliloquy of the Spanish Cloister

1 What of soul was left, I wonder, when the kissing had to stop?
A Toccata of Galuppi's, xiv

2 Dear dead women, with such hair, too—what's become of all the gold
Used to hang and brush their bosoms? I feel chilly and grown old.
xv

3 I pluck the rose
And love it more than tongue can speak—
Then the good minute goes.
Two in the Campagna, 10

4 What's become of Waring
Since he gave us all the slip?
Waring, I.i

BEAU BRUMMELL 1778–1840

5 I always like to have the morning well-aired before I get up.
Charles Macfarlane, *Reminiscences of a Literary Life*, 27

WILLIAM CULLEN BRYANT 1794–1878

6 They seemed
Like old companions in adversity.
A Winter Piece, l.26

GEORGE VILLIERS, SECOND DUKE OF BUCKINGHAM 1628–1687

7 The world is made up for the most part of fools and knaves.
To Mr. Clifford, on his Humane Reason

8 Ay, now the plot thickens very much upon us.
The Rehearsal (1671), III.ii

COMTE DE BUFFON 1707–1788

9 *Ces choses sont hors de l'homme, le style est l'homme même.*

These things [subject matter] are external to the man; style is the man.
Discours sur le Style, address given to the Académie française 25 Aug. 1753

1 *Le génie n'est qu'une plus grande aptitude à la patience.*
Genius is only a greater aptitude for patience.
Hérault de Séchelles, *Voyage à Montbar* (1803), p.15

PROF. ARTHUR BULLER 1874–1944

2 There was a young lady named Bright,
Whose speed was far faster than light;
  She set out one day
  In a relative way,
And returned home the previous night.
Punch, 19 Dec. 1923

COUNT VON BÜLOW 1849–1929

3 *Wir verlangen auch unseren Platz an der Sonne.*
We also demand our own place in the sun.
Reichstag, 6 Dec. 1897

EDWARD GEORGE BULWER-LYTTON, BARON LYTTON 1803–1873

4 Beneath the rule of men entirely great
The pen is mightier than the sword.
Richelieu (1838), II.ii

5 There is no man so friendless but what he can find a friend sincere enough to tell him disagreeable truths.
What Will He Do With It? (1858), bk.iii, ch.15 (heading)

ALFRED BUNN 1796?–1860

6 Alice, where art thou?
Song

7 I dreamt that I dwelt in marble halls.
The Bohemian Girl, Act II

JOHN BUNYAN 1628–1688

8 As I walk'd through the wilderness of this world.
The Pilgrim's Progress (1678), pt.i

1 The name of the slough was Despond.

2 The valley of Humiliation.

3 It beareth the name of Vanity-Fair, because the town where 'tis kept, is lighter than vanity.
See Psalms 62:9

4 Hanging is too good for him, said Mr Cruelty.

5 A man that could look no way but downward, with a muckrake in his hand.
pt.ii

6 He that is down needs fear no fall,
He that is low no pride.
Shepherd Boy's Song

7 An ornament to her profession.

8 Who would true valour see,
Let him come hither.

9 My sword, I give to him that shall succeed me in my pilgrimage, and my courage and skill to him that can get it.

10 So he passed over, and the trumpets sounded for him on the other side. [Mr. Valiant-for-Truth.]

GELETT BURGESS 1866–1951

11 I never saw a Purple Cow,
I never hope to see one;
But I can tell you, anyhow,
I'd rather see than be one!
***Burgess Nonsense Book*. The Purple Cow**

12 Ah, yes! I wrote the 'Purple Cow'—
I'm sorry, now, I wrote it!
But I can tell you anyhow,
I'll kill you if you quote it!

DEAN BURGON 1813–1888

13 Match me such marvel save in Eastern clime,
A rose-red city 'half as old as Time'!
Petra (1845). See Rogers.

EDMUND BURKE 1729–1797

1 In all disputes between them and their rulers, the presumption is at least upon a par in favour of the people.
Thoughts on the Cause of the Present Discontents (1770)

2 We must soften into a credulity below the milkiness of infancy to think all men virtuous. We must be tainted with a malignity truly diabolical, to believe all the world to be equally wicked and corrupt.

3 So to be patriots, as not to forget we are gentlemen.

4 To tax and to please, no more than to love and to be wise, is not given to men.
Speech on American Taxation (1774)

5 Your representative owes you, not his industry only, but his judgement; and he betrays, instead of serving you, if he sacrifices it to your opinion.
Speech to the Electors of Bristol, 3 Nov. 1774

6 You choose a member indeed; but when you have chosen him, he is not member of Bristol, but he is a member of *parliament*.

7 The use of force alone is but *temporary*. It may subdue for a moment; but it does not remove the necessity of subduing again; and a nation is not governed, which is perpetually to be conquered.
Speech on Conciliation with America (22 Mar. 1775)

8 I do not know the method of drawing up an indictment against an whole people.

9 Moderation, in a case like this, is a sort of treason.
Letter to the Sheriffs of Bristol (1777)

10 The people are the masters.
Speech on the Economical Reform, 11 Feb. 1780

11 Applaud us when we run; console us when we fall; cheer us when we recover; but let us pass on—for God's sake, let us pass on!
Speech at Bristol previous to the Election, 1780

12 Your governor stimulates a rapacious and licentious soldiery to the personal search of women.
Speech on Fox's East India Bill, 1 Dec. 1783 (Of Warren Hastings in India)

1 The people never give up their liberties but under some delusion.
Speech at County Meeting of Buckinghamshire, 1784

2 An event has happened, upon which it is difficult to speak, and impossible to be silent.
Impeachment of Warren Hastings, 5 May 1789

3 People will not look forward to posterity, who never look backward to their ancestors.
Reflections on the Revolution in France (1790)

4 I thought ten thousand swords must have leaped from their scabbards to avenge even a look that threatened her with insult.
Of Queen Marie Antoinette

5 Superstition is the religion of feeble minds.

6 Somebody had said, that a king may make a nobleman, but he cannot make a gentleman.
Letter to Wm. Smith, 29 Jan. 1795

7 The storm has gone over me; and I lie like one of those old oaks which the late hurricane has scattered about me ... I am torn up by the roots, and lie prostrate on the earth!
A Letter to a Noble Lord (1796)

8 And having looked to government for bread, on the very first scarcity they will turn and bite the hand that fed them.
Thoughts and Details on Scarcity (1797)

JOHN BURNS 1858–1943

9 I have seen the Mississippi. That is muddy water. I have seen the St Lawrence. That is crystal water. But the Thames is liquid history.
Oral trad.

ROBERT BURNS 1759–1796

10 Then gently scan your brother man,
   Still gentler sister woman;
Tho' they may gang a kennin wrang,
   To step aside is human.
Address to the Unco Guid

1 But to see her was to love her,
Love but her, and love for ever.
Ae Fond Kiss

2 Had we never lov'd sae kindly,
Had we never lov'd sae blindly,
Never met—or never parted,
We had ne'er been broken-hearted.

3 Should auld acquaintance be forgot,
  And never brought to mind?
Auld Lang Syne

4 We'll tak a cup o' kindness yet,
  For auld lang syne.

5 Freedom and Whisky gang thegither!
The Author's Earnest Cry and Prayer, xxxi

6 Bonnie wee thing, cannie wee thing,
  Lovely wee thing, wert thou mine,
I wad wear thee in my bosom,
  Lest my jewel I should tine.
The Bonnie Wee Thing

7 Gin a body meet a body
  Coming through the rye;
Gin a body kiss a body,
  Need a body cry?
Coming Through the Rye (taken from an old song, ***The Bob-tailed Lass***)

8 I wasna fou, but just had plenty.
Death and Dr. Hornbook, iii

9 Flow gently, sweet Afton, among thy green braes,
Flow gently, I'll sing thee a song in thy praise.
Flow gently, sweet Afton

10 The rank is but the guinea's stamp,
  The man's the gowd for a' that!
For a' that and a' that

11 A man's a man for a' that.

12 Go fetch to me a pint o' wine,
An' fill it in a silver tassie.
Go Fetch to Me a Pint

1 John Anderson my jo, John,
When we were first acquent,
Your locks were like the raven,
Your bonny brow was brent.
John Anderson My Jo

2 Some have meat and cannot eat,
Some cannot eat that want it:
But we have meat and we can eat,
Sae let the Lord be thankit.
The Kirkudbright Grace. (Also known as the Selkirk Grace.)

3 I once was a maid, tho' I cannot tell when,
And still my delight is in proper young men.
Love and Liberty—A Cantata, l.57

4 Man's inhumanity to man
Makes countless thousands mourn!
Man was made to Mourn

5 My heart's in the Highlands, my heart is not here;
My heart's in the Highlands a-chasing the deer.
My Heart's in the Highlands

6 O, my Luve's like a red red rose
That's newly sprung in June.
My Love is like a Red Red Rose

7 The wan moon sets behind the white wave,
And time is setting with me, Oh.
Open the door to me, Oh

8 The mair they talk I'm kent the better.
The Poet's Welcome (to his bastard child)

9 Scots, wha hae wi' Wallace bled,
Scots, wham Bruce has aften led.
Scots, Wha Hae (Robert Bruce's March to Bannockburn)

10 While we sit bousing at the nappy,
And getting fou and unco happy.
Tam o' Shanter, l.10

11 O wad some Pow'r the giftie gie us
To see oursels as others see us!
To a Louse

12 Wee, sleekit, cow'rin', tim'rous beastie,
O what a panic's in thy breastie!
To a Mouse

1 The best laid schemes o' mice an' men
Gang aft a-gley.

2 Tho' father and mither and a' should gae mad,
O whistle, and I'll come to you, my lad.
Whistle, and I'll come to you, my Lad

3 Ye banks and braes o' bonny Doon,
How can ye bloom sae fresh and fair?
How can ye chant, ye little birds,
And I sae weary fu' o' care?
Ye Banks and Braes o' Bonny Doon

ROBERT BURTON 1577–1640

4 Like watermen, that row one way and look another.
***Anatomy of Melancholy.* Democritus to the Reader**

5 *Hinc quam sit calamus saevior ense patet.*
From this it is clear how much the pen is worse than the sword.
pt.i, 2, memb.4, subsect.4

6 Every thing, saith Epictetus, hath two handles, the one to be held by, the other not.
pt.ii, 3, memb.3

7 England is a paradise for women, and hell for horses: Italy a paradise for horses, hell for women, as the diverb goes.
pt.iii, 3, memb.1, subsect.2

8 Be not solitary, be not idle.
final words

HERMANN BUSENBAUM 1600–1668

9 *Cum finis est licitus, etiam media sunt licita.*
The end justifies the means.
***Medulla Theologiae Moralis* (1650)**

COMTE DE BUSSY-RABUTIN 1618–1693

10 *L'amour vient de l'aveuglement,*
L'amitié de la connaissance.
Love comes from blindness, friendship from knowledge.
***Histoire Amoureuse des Gaules.* Maximes d'Amour, pt.I**

1 *L'absence est à l'amour ce qu'est au feu le vent;*
Il éteint le petit, il allume le grand.
Absence is to love what wind is to fire; it extinguishes the small, it enkindles the great.
pt.II. See Francis de Sales and La Rochefaucauld.

2 *Comme vous savez, Dieu est d'ordinaire pour les gros escadrons contre les petits.*
As you know, God is usually on the side of the big squadrons against the small.
Letter to the Comte de Limoges, 18 Oct. 1677. Cf. Tacitus, *Histories*, iv. 17

NICHOLAS MURRAY BUTLER 1862–1947

3 An expert is one who knows more and more about less and less.
attr. to a Commencement Address. Columbia University

SAMUEL BUTLER 1612–1680

4 Compound for sins, they are inclin'd to
By damning those they have no mind to.
Hudibras, pt.I, c.1, l.213

5 For in what stupid age or nation
Was marriage ever out of fashion?
pt.III, c.1, l.817

6 What makes all doctrines plain and clear?
About two hundred pounds a year.
And that which was prov'd true before,
Prove false again? Two hundred more.
l.1277

7 He that complies against his will,
Is of his own opinion still.
c.3, l.547

8 The best of all our actions tend
To the preposterousest end.
***Genuine Remains:* Satire upon the Weakness and Misery of Man,** l.41

9 All love at first, like generous wine,
Ferments and frets until 'tis fine;

But when 'tis settled on the lee,
And from th' impurer matter free,
Becomes the richer still the older,
And proves the pleasanter the colder.
Miscellaneous Thoughts

SAMUEL BUTLER 1835–1902

1 Genius ... has been defined as a supreme capacity for taking trouble ... It might be more fitly described as a supreme capacity for getting its possessors into pains of all kinds, and keeping them therein so long as the genius remains.
Note Books, selected and edited by H. Festing Jones (1912), ch.XI

2 An honest God's the noblest work of man.
Further extracts from the Note Books, selected and edited by A. Bartholomew (1934), p.26. See Ingersoll and Pope, *Essay on Man.*

3 'Man wants but little here below' but likes that little good—and not too long in coming.
p.61. See Goldsmith and E. Young.

4 My Lord, I do not believe. Help thou mine unbelief.
Note Books, selected and edited by G. Keynes and B. Hill (1951), p.284

5 They would have been equally horrified at hearing the Christian religion doubted, and at seeing it practised.
The Way of All Flesh, ch.15

6 The advantage of doing one's praising for oneself is that one can lay it on so thick and exactly in the right places.
ch.34

7 There's many a good tune played on an old fiddle.
ch.61

8 'Tis better to have loved and lost, than never to have lost at all.
ch.77. See Tennyson, *In Memoriam.*

9 O God! Oh Montreal!
Psalm of Montreal

10 It was very good of God to let Carlyle and Mrs Carlyle marry one another and so make only two people miserable instead of four, besides being very amusing.
Letter to Miss Savage, 21 Nov. 1884

WILLIAM BUTLER 1535–1618

1 Doubtless God could have made a better berry [strawberry], but doubtless God never did.
Walton, *Compleat Angler*, pt.i, ch.5

JOHN BYROM 1692–1763

2 Strange! that such high dispute shou'd be
'Twixt Tweedledum and Tweedledee.
Epigram on the Feuds between Handel and Bononcini

3 God bless the King, I mean the Faith's Defender;
God bless—no harm in blessing—the Pretender;
But who Pretender is, or who is King,
God bless us all—that's quite another thing.
To an Officer in the Army

LORD BYRON 1788–1824

4 His heart was one of those which most enamour us,
Wax to receive, and marble to retain.
Beppo, st.34

5 The nursery still leaps out in all they utter—
Besides, they always smell of bread and butter.
st.39

6 Mark! where his carnage and his conquests cease!
He makes a solitude, and calls it—peace!
The Bride of Abydos, c.II.st.20. See Tacitus.

7 Hereditary bondsmen! know ye not
Who would be free themselves must strike the blow?
Childe Harold's Pilgrimage, c.II.st.76

8 On with the dance! let joy be unconfined;
    No sleep till morn, when Youth and Pleasure meet
To chase the glowing Hours with flying feet.
c.III.st.12

9 Yet, Freedom! yet thy banner, torn, but flying,
Streams like the thunder-storm *against* the wind.
c.IV.st.98

10 *There* were his young barbarians all at play,
There was their Dacian mother— he, their sire,
Butcher'd to make a Roman holiday.
st.141

1 While stands the Coliseum, Rome shall stand;
When falls the Coliseum, Rome shall fall;
And when Rome falls—the World.
st.145

2 Roll on, thou deep and dark blue Ocean— roll!
st.179

3 The Assyrian came down like the wolf on the fold,
And his cohorts were gleaming in purple and gold.
Destruction of Sennacherib

4 For the Angel of Death spread his wings on the blast,
And breathed in the face of the foe as he pass'd.

5 What men call gallantry, and gods adultery,
Is much more common where the climate's sultry.
Don Juan, c.I.st.63

6 A little still she strove, and much repented,
And whispering 'I will ne'er consent'— consented.
st.117

7 Man's love is of man's life a thing apart,
'Tis woman's whole existence.
st.194

8 Let us have wine and women, mirth and laughter,
Sermons and soda-water the day after.
c.II.st.178

9 Marriage from love, like vinegar from wine—
A sad, sour, sober beverage—by time
Is sharpen'd from its high celestial flavour,
Down to a very homely household savour.
c.III.st.5

10 The isles of Greece, the isles of Greece!
Where burning Sappho loved and sung.
st.86, 1

11 The mountains look on Marathon—
And Marathon looks on the sea;
And musing there an hour alone,
I dream'd that Greece might still be free.
3

12 For what is left the poet here?
For Greeks a blush—for Greece a tear.
6

1 And if I laugh at any mortal thing,
'Tis that I may not weep.
c.IV.st.4

2 Merely innocent flirtation,
Not quite adultery, but adulteration.
c.XII.st.63

3 The English winter—ending in July,
To recommence in August.
c.XIII.st.42

4 'Tis strange—but true; for truth is always strange;
Stranger than fiction.
c.XIV.st.101

5 With just enough of learning to misquote.
English Bards and Scotch Reviewers, l.66

6 Though women are angels, yet wedlock's the devil.
***Hours of Idleness.* To Eliza**

7 Who killed John Keats?
'I,' says the Quarterly,
So savage and Tartarly;
''Twas one of my feats.'
John Keats

8 Maid of Athens, ere we part,
Give, oh give me back my heart!
Or, since that has left my breast,
Keep it now, and take the rest!
Maid of Athens

9 She walks in beauty, like the night
Of cloudless climes and starry skies;
And all that's best of dark and bright
Meet in her aspect and her eyes.
She Walks in Beauty

10 So, we'll go no more a roving
So late into the night,
Though the heart be still as loving,
And the moon be still as bright.
So, We'll Go No More a Roving

11 Though the night was made for loving,
And the day returns too soon,

Yet we'll go no more a-roving
By the light of the moon.

1 You should have a softer pillow than my heart.
To his wife. E.C. Mayne, ed., *The Life and Letters of Anne Isabella, Lady Noel Byron*, ch.11

2 Love in this part of the world is no sinecure.
Letter to John Murray from Venice, 27 Dec. 1816

3 I awoke one morning and found myself famous.
(Referring to the instantaneous success of *Childe Harold*). Moore, *Life of Byron*, I, 347.

JAMES BRANCH CABELL 1879–1958

4 The optimist proclaims that we live in the best of all possible worlds; and the pessimist fears this is true.
The Silver Stallion, bk.iv, ch.26

AUGUSTUS CAESAR

see AUGUSTUS

JULIUS CAESAR 102?–44 B.C.

5 *Gallia est omnis divisa in partes tres.*
Gaul as a whole is divided into three parts.
De Bello Gallico, I.i

6 *Et tu, Brute?*
You too Brutus?
Oral trad. See Philemon Holland, trans., Suetonius, *Historie of Twelve Caesars* (1606).

7 *Veni, vidi, vici.*
I came, I saw, I conquered.
Suetonius, *Divus Julius*, xxxvii.2

8 The die is cast.
xxxii. At the crossing of the Rubicon

9 Caesar's wife must be above suspicion.
Oral trad. See Plutarch, *Lives*, Julius Caesar, x.6.

CALLIMACHUS c.305–c.240 B.C.

10 A great book is like great evil.
Fragments, ed. R. Pfeiffer, 465

CHARLES ALEXANDRE DE CALONNE 1734–1802

1 *Madame, si c'est possible, c'est fait; impossible? cela se fera.*
Madam, if a thing is possible, consider it done; the impossible? that will be done.
J. Michelet, *Histoire de la Révolution Française* (1847), vol.I, pt.ii, sect 8. Better known as the U.S. Armed Forces slogan, 'The difficult we do immediately; the impossible takes a little longer'.

C.S. CALVERLEY 1831–1884

2 The farmer's daughter hath soft brown hair;
(*Butter and eggs and a pound of cheese*)
And I met with a ballad, I can't say where,
Which wholly consisted of lines like these.
Ballad

3 O Beer! O Hodgson, Guinness, Allsopp, Bass!
Names that should be on every infant's tongue!
Beer

4 I cannot sing the old songs now!
It is not that I deem them low;
'Tis that I can't remember how
They go.
Changed. See Claribel.

5 A bare-legg'd beggarly son of a gun.
The Cock and the Bull

6 Life is with such all beer and skittles;
They are not difficult to please
About their victuals.
Contentment

7 Sweet, when the morn is grey;
Sweet, when they've cleared away
Lunch; and at close of day
Possibly sweetest.
Ode to Tobacco

8 I have a liking old
For thee, though manifold
Stories, I know, are told
Not to thy credit.

GENERAL CAMBRONNE 1770–1842

1 *La Garde meurt, mais ne se rend pas.*
The Guards die but do not surrender.
Attr. to Cambronne when called upon to surrender at Waterloo. Cambronne denied the saying at a banquet at Nantes, 19 Sept. 1830

2 *Merde!*
Said to be Cambronne's actual reply to the call to surrender: euphemistically known as '*Le mot de Cambronne*'.

WILLIAM CAMDEN 1551–1623

3 Betwixt the stirrup and the ground
Mercy I asked, mercy I found.
Remains. Epitaph for a Man Killed by Falling from His Horse

BARON CAMPBELL 1779–1861

4 I proposed to bring a Bill into parliament to deprive an author who publishes a book without an Index of the privilege of copyright.
Lives of the Chief Justices, preface to vol.iii, which included an index to the previously published vols.

MRS. PATRICK CAMPBELL 1865–1940

5 I don't mind where people make love, so long as they don't do it in the street and frighten the horses.
Oral tradition

6 Marriage is the result of the longing for the deep, deep peace of the double bed after the hurly-burly of the chaise-longue.
Oral tradition

ROY CAMPBELL 1901–1957

7 You praise the firm restraint with which they write—
I'm with you there, of course:
They use the snaffle and the curb all right,
But where's the bloody horse?
On Some South African Novelists

1 South Africa, renowned both far and wide
For politics and little else beside.
The Wayzgoose (1928)

THOMAS CAMPBELL 1777–1844

2 O leave this barren spot to me!
Spare, woodman, spare the beechen tree.
The Beech-Tree's Petition

3 'Tis the sunset of life gives me mystical lore,
And coming events cast their shadows before.
Lochiel's Warning

4 A chieftain to the Highlands bound
Cries, 'Boatman, do not tarry!
And I'll give thee a silver pound
To row us o'er the ferry.'
Lord Ullin's Daughter

5 'Tis distance lends enchantment to the view,
And robes the mountain in its azure hue.
Pleasures of Hope, pt.i, l.7

6 Now Barabbas was a publisher.
Often attributed to Byron

THOMAS CAMPION 1567–1620

7 There is a garden in her face,
Where roses and white lilies grow.
Fourth Book of Airs, vii. Also attr. Richard Alison.

8 There cherries grow, which none may buy
Till 'Cherry ripe' themselves do cry.

GEORGE CANNING 1770–1827

9 A steady patriot of the world alone,
The friend of every country but his own. [The Jacobin.]
New Morality, l.113

10 But of all plagues, good Heaven, thy wrath can send,
Save me, oh, save me, from the candid friend.
l.207

DOMENICO CARACCIOLO 1715–1789

1 *Il y a en Angleterre soixante sectes religieuses différentes, et une seule sauce.*
In England there are sixty different religions, and only one sauce.
Attr. *N. & Q.*, Dec. 1968

HENRY CAREY 1693?–1743

2 Of all the girls that are so smart
 There's none like pretty Sally,
She is the darling of my heart,
 And she lives in our alley.
Sally in our Alley

JANE WELSH CARLYLE 1801–1866

3 I am not at all the sort of person you and I took me for.
Letter to Thomas Carlyle, 7 May 1822

THOMAS CARLYLE 1795–1881

4 A well-written Life is almost as rare as a well-spent one.
Critical and Miscellaneous Essays, vol.i. **Richter**

5 The three great elements of modern civilization, Gunpowder, Printing, and the Protestant Religion.
State of German Literature. See Bacon, *Novum Organum, bk.I, aphor. 129*

6 In epochs when cash payment has become the sole nexus of man to man.
vol.iv. **Chartism,** ch.6

7 'Genius' (which means transcendent capacity of taking trouble, first of all).
Frederick the Great, bk.iv, ch.3. See Buffon.

8 Happy the people whose annals are blank in history-books!
bk.xvi, ch.1

9 A whiff of grapeshot.
History of the French Revolution, pt.I, bk.v, ch.3

10 The seagreen Incorruptible. [Robespierre.]
pt.II, bk.iv, ch.4

1 The history of the world is but the biography of great men.
Heroes and Hero-Worship, i. **The Hero as Divinity**

2 Respectable Professors of the Dismal Science. [Political Economy.]
Latter-Day Pamphlets, No.1. **The Present Time**

3 Man is a tool-using animal.
Sartor Resartus, bk.i, ch.5

4 The folly of that impossible precept, 'Know thyself'; till it be translated into this partially possible one, 'Know what thou canst work at'.
bk.ii, ch.7

5 If Jesus Christ were to come to-day, people would not even crucify him. They would ask him to dinner, and hear what he had to say, and make fun of it.
D.A. Wilson, *Carlyle at his Zenith*

6 Macaulay is well for a while, but one wouldn't *live* under Niagara.
R.M. Milnes, *Notebook*, 1838

ANDREW CARNEGIE 1835–1919

7 The man who dies ... rich dies disgraced.
North American Review, June 1889, **'The Gospel of Wealth'**, pt.I

JULIA A. CARNEY 1823–1908

8 Little drops of water,
  Little grains of sand,
Make the mighty ocean
  And the beauteous land.
Little Things

JOSEPH EDWARDS CARPENTER 1813–1885

9 What are the wild waves saying
  Sister, the whole day long.
What are the Wild Waves Saying?

LEWIS CARROLL 1832–1898

10 What I tell you three times is true.
The Hunting of the Snark, Fit 1. **The Landing**

1 He would answer to 'Hi!' or to any loud cry,
  Such as 'Fry me!' or 'Fritter-my-wig!'

2 But oh, beamish nephew, beware of the day,
  If your Snark be a Boojum! For then
You will softly and suddenly vanish away,
  And never be met with again!
Fit 3. **The Baker's Tale**

3 They sought it with thimbles, they sought it with care;
  They pursued it with forks and hope;
They threatened its life with a railway-share;
  They charmed it with smiles and soap.
Fit 5. **The Beaver's Lesson**

4 He thought he saw an Elephant,
  That practised on a fife:
He looked again, and found it was
  A letter from his wife.
'At length I realize,' he said,
  'The bitterness of life!'
Sylvie and Bruno, ch.5

5 He thought he saw a Rattlesnake
  That questioned him in Greek,
He looked again and found it was
  The Middle of Next Week.
'The one thing I regret,' he said,
  'Is that it cannot speak!'
ch.6

6 He thought he saw a Banker's Clerk
  Descending from the bus:
He looked again, and found it was
  A Hippopotamus:
'If this should *stay to dine*,' he said,
  'There won't be much for us.'
ch.7

7 'What is the use of a book', thought Alice, 'without pictures or conversations?'
Alice's Adventures in Wonderland, ch.1

8 'Curiouser and curiouser!' cried Alice.
ch.2

1 How doth the little crocodile
Improve his shining tail,
And pour the waters of the Nile
On every golden scale!
See Watts.

2 Oh my dear paws! Oh my fur and whiskers!
ch.4

3 'You are old, Father William,' the young man said,
'And your hair has become very white;
And yet you incessantly stand on your head—
Do you think, at your age, it is right?'
ch.5. See Southey.

4 'I have answered three questions, and that is enough.'

5 'I shall sit here,' he said, 'on and off, for days and days.'
ch.6

6 He only does it to annoy,
Because he knows it teases.

7 'It was the *best* butter.'
ch.7

8 Twinkle, twinkle, little bat!
How I wonder what you're at!
Up above the world you fly!
Like a teatray in the sky.
See Taylor.

9 Take care of the sense, and the sounds will take care of themselves.
ch.9

10 I only took the regular course ... the different branches of Arithmetic—Ambition, Distraction, Uglification and Derision.

11 'That's the reason they're called lessons,' the Gryphon remarked: 'because they lessen from day to day.'

12 'Will you walk a little faster?' said a whiting to a snail,
'There's a porpoise close behind us, and he's treading on my tail.'
ch.10

13 Will you, won't you, will you, won't you, will you join the dance?

1 'Tis the voice of the lobster; I heard him declare,
'You have baked me too brown, I must sugar my hair.'

See Watts.

2 Soup of the evening, beautiful Soup!

3 'Begin at the beginning,' the King said, gravely, 'and go on till you come to the end: then stop.'

ch.11

4 'Twas brillig, and the slithy toves
Did gyre and gimble in the wabe;
All mimsy were the borogoves,
And the mome raths outgrabe.

Through the Looking-Glass, ch.1

5 'And hast thou slain the Jabberwock?
Come to my arms, my beamish boy!
O frabjous day! Callooh! Callay!'
He chortled in his joy.

6 Curtsey while you're thinking what to say. It saves time.

ch.2

7 Speak in French when you can't think of the English for a thing.

8 Now, *here*, you see, it takes all the running *you* can do, to keep in the same place.

9 'Contrariwise,' continued Tweedledee, 'if it was so, it might be; and if it were so, it would be: but as it isn't, it ain't. That's logic.'

ch.4

10 'If seven maids with seven mops
Swept it for half a year,
Do you suppose,' the Walrus said,
'That they could get it clear?'
'I doubt it,' said the Carpenter,
And shed a bitter tear.

11 'The time has come,' the Walrus said,
'To talk of many things:
Of shoes—and ships—and sealing wax—
Of cabbages—and kings—
And why the sea is boiling hot—
And whether pigs have wings.'

1 'Let's fight till six, and then have dinner,' said Tweedledum.

2 The rule is, jam to-morrow and jam yesterday—but never jam to-day.
ch.5

3 Why, sometimes I've believed as many as six impossible things before breakfast.

4 They gave it me,—for an un-birthday present.
ch.6

5 'When *I* use a word,' Humpty Dumpty said in a rather scornful tone, 'it means just what I choose it to mean—neither more nor less.'

6 'The question is,' said Humpty Dumpty, 'which is to be master—that's all.'

7 You see it's like a portmanteau—there are two meanings packed up into one word.

8 He's an Anglo-Saxon Messenger—and those are Anglo-Saxon attitudes.
ch.7

9 It's as large as life, and twice as natural!

10 I am fond of children (except boys).
Letter to Kathleen Eschwege. S.D. Collingwood, *The Life and Letters of Lewis Carroll* (1898), p.416

PHOEBE CARY 1824–1871

11 And though hard be the task,
'Keep a stiff upper lip'.
Keep a Stiff Upper Lip

L. CASSIUS LONGINUS RAVILLA
late 2nd cent. B.C.

12 *Cui bono?*
To whose profit?
Cicero, *pro Rosc. Am.* XXX.84 and *Pro Milone* XII.32

THE ELDER CATO, THE CENSOR 234–149 B.C

13 *Delenda est Carthago.*
Carthage must be destroyed.
Pliny the Elder, *Naturalis Historia*, xv.18.74

CATULLUS 87–54? B.C.

1 *Passer mortuus est meae puellae.*
My lady's sparrow is dead.
Carmina, iii

2 *Vivamus, mea Lesbia, atque amemus,*
Rumoresque senum severiorum
Omnes unius aestimemus assis.
My sweetest Lesbia let us live and love,
And though the sager sort our deeds reprove,
Let us not weigh them.
v. Tr. Campion, *A Book of Airs*, i.

3 *Da mi basia mille, deinde centum,*
Dein mille altera, dein secunda centum,
Deinde usque altera mille, deinde centum.
Give me a thousand kisses, then a hundred, then another thousand, then a second hundred, then yet another thousand, then a hundred.

4 *Nam risu inepto res ineptior nulla est.*
For there is nothing sillier than a silly laugh.
xxxix

5 *Odi et amo: quare id faciam, fortasse requiris.*
Nescio, sed fieri sentio et excrucior.
I hate and I love: why I do so you may well ask. I do not know, but I feel it happen and am in agony.
lxxxv

CONSTANTINE CAVAFY 1863–1933

6 What shall become of us without any barbarians?
Those people were a kind of solution.
Expecting the Barbarians

EDITH CAVELL 1865–1915

7 Standing, as I do, in the view of God and eternity I realize that patriotism is not enough. I must have no hatred or bitterness towards anyone.
Spoken to the chaplain who attended her before her execution by firing squad, 12 Oct. 1915. *The Times*, 23 Oct. 1915

ROBERT CECIL See SALISBURY

THOMAS OF CELANO c.1190–1260

1 *Dies irae, dies illa,*
Solvet saeclum in favilla.
That day, the day of wrath, will turn the universe to ashes.
Dies irae, 1. Attr. Printed in Missal, Mass for the Dead

2 *Tuba mirum sparget sonum*
Per sepulchra regionum,
Coget omnes ante thronum.

Mors stupebit et natura.
The trumpet will fling out a wonderful sound through the tombs of all regions, it will drive everyone before the throne. Death will be aghast and so will nature.
7

MRS. CENTLIVRE 1667?–1723

3 The real Simon Pure.
A Bold Stroke for a Wife, V.i

MIGUEL DE CERVANTES 1547–1616

4 *El Caballero de la Triste Figura.*
The Knight of the Doleful Countenance.
Don Quixote, pt.i, ch.19

5 *La mejor salsa del mundo es el hambre.*
Hunger is the best sauce in the world.
pt.ii, ch.5

6 *Dos linages sólos hay en el mundo, como decía una abuela mía, que son el tenir y el no tenir.*
There are only two families in the world, as a grandmother of mine used to say: the haves and the have-nots.
ch.20

7 *Digo, paciencia y barajar.*
What I say is, patience, and shuffle the cards.
ch.23

PATRICK REGINALD CHALMERS 1872–1942

8 What's lost upon the roundabouts we pulls up on the swings!
Green Days and Blue Days: **Roundabouts and Swings**

JOSEPH CHAMBERLAIN 1836–1914

1 We are not downhearted. The only trouble is, we cannot understand what is happening to our neighbours.
Smethwick, 18 Jan. 1906

NEVILLE CHAMBERLAIN 1869–1940

2 In war, whichever side may call itself the victor, there are no winners, but all are losers.
Kettering, 3 July 1938

3 How horrible, fantastic, incredible, it is that we should be digging trenches and trying on gas-masks here because of a quarrel in a far-away country between people of whom we know nothing.
(Of Germany's annexation of the Sudetenland.) Radio broadcast, 27 Sept. 1938. K.Feiling, *Life of Neville Chamberlain*, bk.iv, ch.28

4 I believe it is peace for our time ... peace with honour.
After Munich Agreement. 30 Sept. 1938. See Disraeli.

HADDON CHAMBERS 1860–1921

5 The long arm of coincidence.
Captain Swift (1888), Act II

NICOLAS-SÉBASTIEN CHAMFORT 1741–1794

6 *Des qualités trop supérieures rendent souvent un homme moins propre à la société. On ne va pas au marché avec des lingots; on y va avec de l'argent ou de la petite monnaie.*
Qualities too elevated often unfit a man for society. We don't take ingots with us to market; we take silver or nsmall change.
Maximes et Pensées (1796), ch.3

7 *L'amour, tel qu'il existe dans la société, n'est que l'échange de deux fantaisies et le contact de deux épidermes.*
Love, in the form in which it exists in society, is nothing but the exchange of two fantasies and the superficial contact of two bodies.
ch.6

RAYMOND CHANDLER 1888–1959

1 When in doubt have a man come through a door with a gun in his hand.
The Simple Art of Murder (1950), preface, referring to the policy of light crime fiction magazines

2 Down these mean streets a man must go who is not himself mean; who is neither tarnished nor afraid.
The Simple Art of Murder

GEORGE CHAPMAN 1559?–1634?

3 Speed his plough.
Bussy D'Ambois, I.i

4 I am ashamed the law is such an ass.
Revenge for Honour, III.ii

KING CHARLES II 1630–1685

5 Let not poor Nelly starve.
Burnet, *History of My Own Time*, vol.II, bk.iii, ch.17

6 He had been, he said, an unconscionable time dying; but he hoped that they would excuse it.
Macaulay, *Hist. England*, 1849, vol.i, ch.4, p.437

PIERRE CHARRON 1541–1603

7 *La vraye science et le vray étude de l'homme, c'est l'homme.*
The true science and study of man is man.
De la Sagesse (1601), bk.I, ch.i

EARL OF CHATHAM See WILLIAM PITT

GEOFFREY CHAUCER 1340?–1400

All references are to *The Works of Geoffrey Chaucer*, ed. F.N. Robinson, 2nd edition (1957)

8 Whan that Aprill with his shoures soote
The droghte of March hath perced to the roote.
The Canterbury Tales, **General Prologue,** l.1

9 He was a verray, parfit gentil knyght.
l.72

1 He was as fressh as is the month of May.
l.92

2 And Frenssh she spak ful faire and fetisly,
After the scole of Stratford atte Bowe,
For Frenssh of Parys was to hire unknowe.
l.122

3 A Clerk ther was of Oxenford also,
That unto logyk hadde longe ygo.
l.285

4 And gladly wolde he lerne and gladly teche.
l.308

5 Nowher so bisy a man as he ther nas,
And yet he semed bisier than he was.
l.321

6 She was a worthy womman al hir lyve:
Housbondes at chirche dore she hadde fyve.
l.459

7 If gold ruste, what shall iren do?
l.500

8 The smylere with the knyf under the cloke.
The Knight's Tale, l.1999

9 And what is bettre than wisedoom? Womman. And what is bettre than a good womman? Nothyng.
The Tale of Melibee, l.1107

10 Whan that the month in which the world bigan,
That highte March, whan God first maked man.
The Nun's Priest's Tale, l.3187

11 Mordre wol out, that se we day by day.
l.4241

12 So was *hir joly whistle* wel ywet.
The Reeve's Tale, l.4155

13 Yblessed be god that I have wedded fyve!
Welcome the sixte, whan that evere he shal.
The Wife of Bath's Prologue, l.44

14 The bacon was nat fet for hem, I trowe,
That som men han in Essex at Dunmowe.
l.217

1 But, Lord Crist! whan that it remembreth me
Upon my yowthe, and on my jolitee,
It tikleth me aboute myn herte roote.
Unto this day it dooth myn herte boote
That I have had my world as in my tyme.
l.469

2 And she was fayr as is the rose in May.
The Legend of Cleopatra, l.613

3 Farewel my bok, and my devocioun!
***The Legend of Good Women,* The Prologue,** l.39

4 Thou shalt make castels thanne in Spayne,
And dreme of joye, all but in vayne.
The Romaunt of the Rose, l.2573

5 It is nought good a slepyng hound to wake.
Troilus and Criseyde, iii, l.764

6 Oon ere it herde, at tothir out it wente.
iv, l.434

7 For tyme ylost may nought recovered be.
l.1283

8 Go, litel bok, go, litel myn tragedye.
v, l.1786

9 O yonge, fresshe folkes, he or she.
l.1835

10 Flee fro the prees, and dwelle with sothfastnesse.
Truth: Balade de Bon Conseyle, l.1

ANTON CHEKHOV 1860–1904

11 People don't notice whether it's winter or summer when they're happy. If I lived in Moscow I don't think I'd care what the weather was like.
Three Sisters, II

12 When a woman isn't beautiful, people always say, 'You have lovely eyes, you have lovely hair.'
Uncle Vanya, III

EARL OF CHESTERFIELD 1694–1773

13 In my mind, there is nothing so illiberal and so ill-bred, as audible laughter.
***Advice to his Son.* Graces, Laughter.** See Catullus.

1 There is a Spanish proverb, which says very justly, Tell me whom you live with, and I will tell you who you are.
Letter to his son, 9 Oct. 1747

2 Do as you would be done by is the surest method that I know of pleasing.
16 Oct. 1747

3 I recommend you to take care of the minutes: for hours will take care of themselves.
6 Nov. 1747

4 Wear your learning, like your watch in a private pocket: and do not merely pull it out and strike it; merely to show that you have one.
22 Feb. 1748

5 It must be owned, that the Graces do not seem to be natives of Great Britain; and I doubt, the best of us here have more of rough than polished diamond.
18 Nov. 1748

6 Idleness is only the refuge of weak minds.
20 July 1749

7 Is it possible to love such a man? No. The utmost I can do for him is to consider him as a respectable Hottentot. [Lord Lyttelton.]
28 Feb. 1751

8 A chapter of accidents.
16 Feb. 1753

9 Religion is by no means a proper subject of conversation in a mixed company.
Undated Letter to his Godson, No.112

10 Cunning is the dark sanctuary of incapacity.
Letters from a Celebrated Nobleman to his Heir (1783)

G.K. CHESTERTON 1874–1936

11 Talk about the pews and steeples
    And the cash that goes therewith!
But the souls of Christian peoples ...
        Chuck it, Smith!
Antichrist, or the Reunion of Christendom

1 I tell you naught for your comfort,
Yea, naught for your desire,
Save that the sky grows darker yet
And the sea rises higher.
Ballad of the White Horse, bk.i

2 For the great Gaels of Ireland
Are the men that God made mad,
For all their wars are merry,
And all their songs are sad.
bk.ii

3 Because it is only Christian men
Guard even heathen things.
bk.iii

4 When fishes flew and forests walked
And figs grew upon thorn,
Some moment when the moon was blood
Then surely I was born.
The Donkey

5 The devil's walking parody
On all four-footed things.

6 Fools! For I also had my hour;
One far fierce hour and sweet:
There was a shout about my ears,
And palms before my feet.

7 They died to save their country and they only saved the world.
The English Graves

8 Strong gongs groaning as the guns boom far,
Don John of Austria is going to the war.
Lepanto

9 Before the Roman came to Rye or out to Severn strode,
The rolling English drunkard made the rolling English road.
The Rolling English Road

10 The night we went to Birmingham by way of Beachy Head.

1 Smile at us, pay us, pass us; but do not quite forget.
For we are the people of England, that never have spoken yet.
The Secret People

2 God made the wicked Grocer
For a mystery and a sign.
That men might shun the awful shops
And go to inns to dine.
Song Against Grocers

3 And Noah he often said to his wife when he sat down to dine,
'I don't care where the water goes if it doesn't get into the wine.'
Wine and Water

4 One sees great things from the valley; only small things from the peak.
The Hammer of God

5 The artistic temperament is a disease that afflicts amateurs.
Heretics (1905), ch.17

6 The human race, to which so many of my readers belong.
The Napoleon of Notting Hill, ch.1

7 The Christian ideal has not been tried and found wanting. It has been found difficult; and left untried.
What's Wrong with the World (1910), i.5. **The Unfinished Temple**

8 If a thing is worth doing, it is worth doing badly.
iv.14. **Folly and Female Education**

PROFESSOR NOAM CHOMSKY 1928–

9 Colourless green ideas sleep furiously.
An example of a sentence which, though grammatically acceptable, is without meaning. *Syntactic Structures* (1957), 2.3

CHUANG TSE 4th–3rd cent. B.C.

10 I do not know whether I was then a man dreaming I was a butterfly, or whether I am now a butterfly dreaming I am a man.
H.A. Giles, *Chuang Tse*, ch.2

CHARLES CHURCHILL 1731–1764

1 Be England what she will,
With all her faults, she is my country still.
The Farewell, l.27. See Cowper.

2 Just to the windward of the law.
The Ghost, bk.iii, l.56

3 Keep up appearances; there lies the test;
The world will give thee credit for the rest.
Night, l.311

4 Who often, but without success, have pray'd
For apt Alliteration's artful aid.
The Prophecy of Famine, l.85

LORD RANDOLPH CHURCHILL 1849–1894

5 Ulster will fight; Ulster will be right.
Letter, 7 May 1886

6 I never could make out what those damned dots meant. [Decimal points.]
W.S. Churchill, *Lord Randolph Churchill*, vol.ii, p.184

WINSTON CHURCHILL 1874–1965

7 It cannot in the opinion of His Majesty's Government be classified as slavery in the extreme acceptance of the word without some risk of terminological inexactitude.
House of Commons, 22 Feb. 1906

8 I cannot forecast to you the action of Russia. It is a riddle wrapped in a mystery inside an enigma.
Broadcast talk, 1 Oct. 1939

9 I have nothing to offer but blood, toil, tears and sweat.
House of Commons, 13 May 1940

10 We shall go on to the end, we shall fight in France, we shall fight on the seas and oceans, we shall fight with growing confidence and growing strength in the air, we shall defend our island, whatever the cost may be, we shall fight on the beaches, we shall fight on the landing grounds, we shall fight in the fields and in the streets, we shall fight in the hills; we shall never surrender.
4 June 1940

1 Let us therefore brace ourselves to our duties and so bear ourselves that if the British Empire and its Commonwealth last for a thousand years men will still say, 'This was their finest hour'.
18 June 1940

2 Never in the field of human conflict was so much owed by so many to so few.
20 Aug. 1940

3 Give us the tools, and we will finish the job.
Radio Broadcast, 9 Feb. 1941

4 When I warned them [the French Government] that Britain would fight on alone whatever they did, their Generals told their Prime Minister and his divided Cabinet: 'In three weeks England will have her neck wrung like a chicken.'
Some chicken! Some neck!
To the Canadian Parliament, 30 Dec. 1941

5 This is not the end. It is not even the beginning of the end. But it is, perhaps, the end of the beginning.
Mansion House, 10 Nov. 1942. (Of the Battle of Egypt.)

6 An iron curtain has descended across the Continent.
Address at Westminster College, Fulton, U.S.A., 5 Mar. 1946

7 Democracy is the worst form of Government except all those other forms that have been tried from time to time.
House of Commons, 11 Nov. 1947

8 To jaw-jaw is better than to war-war.
Washington, 26 June 1954

9 It was the nation and the race dwelling all round the globe that had the lion's heart. I had the luck to be called upon to give the roar.
Speech at Palace of Westminster on his 80th birthday, 30 Nov. 1954

10 It is a good thing for an uneducated man to read books of quotations.
My Early Life (1930), ch.9

11 In war, resolution; in defeat, defiance; in victory, magnanimity; in peace, goodwill.
Epigram after the Great War, 1914–18. Later used as the 'Moral of the Work' in each volume of ***The Second World War***

1 When you have to kill a man it costs nothing to be polite.
(On the ceremonial form of the declaration of war against Japan, 8 Dec. 1941.) vol.iii, ***The Grand Alliance*** (1950), p.543

2 In defeat, unbeatable; in victory, unbearable.
(Of Viscount Montgomery.) Edward Marsh, *Ambrosia and Small Beer*, ch.5

3 This is the sort of English up with which I will not put.
Attr. comment against clumsy avoidance of a preposition at the end of a sentence. E. Gowers, *Plain Words*, ch.9, 'Troubles with Prepositions', i

COLLEY CIBBER 1671–1757

4 What! now your fire's gone, you would knock me down with the butt-end, would you?
The Refusal, Act I

5 Off with his head—so much for Buckingham.
Richard III (adapted from Shakespeare), IV.iii

6 Stolen sweets are best.
The Rival Fools, Act I

CICERO 106–43 B.C.

7 There is nothing so absurd but some philosopher has said it.
De Divinatione, ii.58

8 *Salus populi suprema est lex.*
The good of the people is the chief law.
De Legibus, III.iii.8

9 *Numquam se minus otiosum esse quam cum otiosus, nec minus solum quam cum solus esset.*
Never less idle than when wholly idle, nor less alone than when wholly alone.
De Officiis, III.i.1

10 *O tempora, O mores!*
Oh, the times! Oh, the manners!
In Catilinam, I.i.1

11 *Civis Romanus sum.*
I am a Roman citizen.
In Verrem, V.lvii.147

1 *Nervos belli, pecuniam infinitam.*
The sinews of war, unlimited money.
Philippic, V.ii.5

JOHN CLARE 1793–1864

2 When badgers fight then everyone's a foe.
Badger

3 He could not die when the trees were green,
For he loved the time too well.
The Dying Child

4 They took me from my wife, and to save trouble
I wed again, and made the error double.
The Exiles

5 A quiet, pilfering, unprotected race.
Gypsies

6 I am—yet what I am, none cares or knows;
My friends forsake me like a memory lost:
I am the self-consumer of my woes.
I Am

7 Dear Sir,—I am in a Madhouse and quite forget your name or who you are.
Letter, 1860

CLARIBEL (MRS. C.A. BARNARD) 1840–1869

8 I cannot sing the old songs
I sang long years ago,
For heart and voice would fail me,
And foolish tears would flow.
Fireside Thoughts

JOHN CLARKE fl. 1639

9 Home is home, though it be never so homely.
Paraemiologia Anglo-Latina (1639)

KARL VON CLAUSEWITZ 1780–1831

10 *Der Krieg ist nichts als eine Fortsetzung der politischen Verkehrs mit Einmischung anderer Mittel.*

War is nothing but the continuation of politics with the admixture of other means.

Vom Kriege (memorial edn. 1952), p.888, commonly rendered in the form 'War is the continuation of politics by other means'.

GEORGES CLEMENCEAU 1841–1929

1 *Quatorze? Le bon Dieu n'a que dix.*
Fourteen? The good Lord has only ten.

Attr. comment on hearing of Woodrow Wilson's Fourteen Points (1918)

2 War is much too serious a thing to be left to the military.

Attr. Also attr. Talleyrand and Briand. See, e.g., John Bailey, *Letters and Diaries* (1935), p.176.

LORD CLIVE 1725–1774

3 By God, Mr Chairman, at this moment I stand astonished at my own moderation!

Reply during Parliamentary cross-examination, 1773

ARTHUR HUGH CLOUGH 1819–1861

4 But for his funeral train which the bridegroom sees in the distance,
Would he so joyfully, think you, fall in with the marriage-procession?

Amours de Voyage, c.III.vi

5 Good, too, Logic, of course; in itself, but not in fine weather.

The Bothie of Tober-na-Vuolich, ii

6 How pleasant it is to have money, heigh ho!
How pleasant it is to have money.

Dipsychus, sc.v

7 Thou shalt have one God only; who
Would be at the expense of two?

The Latest Decalogue

8 Thou shalt not kill; but need'st not strive
Officiously to keep alive.

9 Do not adultery commit;
Advantage rarely comes of it.

1 Thou shalt not steal; an empty feat,
When it's so lucrative to cheat.

2 Thou shalt not covet; but tradition
Approves all forms of competition.

3 Say not the struggle naught availeth.
Say Not the Struggle Naught Availeth

4 If hopes were dupes, fears may be liars.

5 But westward, look, the land is bright.

6 That out of sight is out of mind
Is true of most we leave behind.
***Songs in Absence,* That Out of Sight**

7 What shall we do without you? Think where we are. Carlyle has led us all out into the desert, and he has left us there.
Parting words to Emerson, 15 July 1848. See E.E. Hale, *James Russell Lowell and his Friends* (1889), ch.19.

WILLIAM COBBETT 1762–1835

8 But what is to be the fate of the great wen [London] of all? The monster, called ... 'the metropolis of the empire'?
Rural Rides

JEAN COCTEAU 1889–1963

9 *Victor Hugo ... un fou qui se croyait Victor Hugo.*
Victor Hugo ... A madman who thought he was Victor Hugo.
See ***Opium***, 1930 ed., p.77

SIR EDWARD COKE 1552–1634

10 For a man's house is his castle, *et domus sua cuique est tutissimum refugium.*
***Institutes: Commentary upon Littleton.* Third Institute,** cap.73

11 They [corporations] cannot commit treason, nor be outlawed, nor excommunicate, for they have no souls.
Sutton's Hospital Case, 10 Rep.32b

SAMUEL TAYLOR COLERIDGE 1772–1834

1 It is an ancient Mariner,
And he stoppeth one of three.
'By thy long grey beard and glittering eye,
Now wherefore stopp'st thou me?'
The Ancient Mariner, pt.i

2 He holds him with his glittering eye.

3 The Wedding-Guest here beat his breast,
For he heard the loud bassoon.

4 'Why look'st thou so?'—With my cross-bow
I shot the Albatross.

5 As idle as a painted ship
Upon a painted ocean.
pt.ii

6 Water, water, every where,
And all the boards did shrink;
Water, water, every where.
Nor any drop to drink.

7 'I fear thee, ancient Mariner!
I fear thy skinny hand!
And thou art long, and lank, and brown,
As is the ribbed sea-sand.'
pt.iv

8 Alone, alone, all, all alone,
Alone on a wide wide sea!
And never a saint took pity on
My soul in agony.

9 And a thousand thousand slimy things
Lived on; and so did I.

10 Oh Sleep! it is a gentle thing,
Beloved from pole to pole.
pt.v

11 Like one, that on a lonesome road
Doth walk in fear and dread,
And having once turned round walks on,
And turns no more his head;

Because he knows, a frightful fiend
Doth close behind him tread.
pt.vi

1 He prayeth best, who loveth best
All things both great and small;
For the dear God who loveth us,
He made and loveth all.
pt.vii

2 A sadder and a wiser man,
He rose the morrow morn.

3 What is an Epigram? a dwarfish whole,
Its body brevity, and wit its soul.
Epigram

4 Swans sing before they die—'twere no bad thing,
Did certain persons die before they sing.
Epigram on a Volunteer Singer

5 At this moment he was unfortunately called out by a person on business from Porlock.
Kubla Khan, Preliminary note

6 In Xanadu did Kubla Khan
A stately pleasure-dome decree:
Where Alph, the sacred river, ran
Through caverns measureless to man
   Down to a sunless sea.

7 A savage place! as holy and enchanted
As e'er beneath a waning moon was haunted
By woman wailing for her demon-lover!

8 And 'mid this tumult Kubla heard from far
Ancestral voices prophesying war!

9 A damsel with a dulcimer
In a vision once I saw.

10 Weave a circle round him thrice,
And close your eyes with holy dread,
For he on honey-dew hath fed,
And drunk the milk of Paradise.

11 He who begins by loving Christianity better than Truth

will proceed by loving his own sect or church better than Christianity, and end by loving himself better than all.

Aids to Reflection: Moral and Religious Aphorisms, XXV

1 That willing suspension of disbelief for the moment, which constitutes poetic faith.

Biographia Literaria, ch.14

2 Summer has set in with its usual severity.

Quoted in Lamb's letter to V. Novello, 9 May 1826

3 Prose = words in their best order;—poetry = the *best* words in the best order.

Table Talk, 12 July 1827

4 The man's desire is for the woman; but the woman's desire is rarely other than for the desire of the man.

23 July 1827

5 In politics, what begins in fear usually ends in folly.

5 Oct. 1830

ADMIRAL COLLINGWOOD 1750–1810

6 Now, gentlemen, let us do something today which the world may talk of hereafter.

Said before the Battle of Trafalgar, 21 Oct. 1805. G.L. Newnham Collingwood, ed., *Correspondence and Memoir of Lord Collingwood*

R.G. COLLINGWOOD 1889–1943

7 Perfect freedom is reserved for the man who lives by his own work, and in that work does what he wants to do.

Speculum Mentis, Prologue

MORTIMER COLLINS 1827–1876

8 A man is as old as he's feeling,
A woman as old as she looks.

The Unknown Quantity

WILLIAM COLLINS 1721–1759

9 To fair Fidele's grassy tomb
Soft maids and village hinds shall bring

Each opening sweet of earliest bloom,
And rifle all the breathing spring.
Dirge in Cymbeline

GEORGE COLMAN 1732–1794

1 Love and a cottage! Eh, Fanny! Ah, give me indifference and a coach and six!
The Clandestine Marriage, I.ii

GEORGE COLMAN THE YOUNGER 1762–1836

2 Oh, London is a fine town,
A very famous city,
Where all the streets are paved with gold,
And all the maidens pretty.
The Heir at Law (1797), I.ii

3 Not to be sneezed at.
II.i

4 Says he, 'I am a handsome man, but I'm a gay deceiver.'
Love Laughs at Locksmiths (1808), Act II

CHARLES CALEB COLTON 1780?–1832

5 When you have nothing to say, say nothing.
Lacon (1820), vol.i, No.183

6 Man is an embodied paradox, a bundle of contradictions.
No.408

WILLIAM CONGREVE 1670–1729

7 She lays it on with a trowel.
The Double Dealer (1694), III.x

8 See how love and murder will out.
IV.vi

9 I know that's a secret, for it's whispered every where.
Love for Love (1695), III.iii

10 Music has charms to sooth a savage breast.
The Mourning Bride (1697), I.i

1 Heav'n has no rage, like love to hatred turn'd,
Nor Hell a fury, like a woman scorn'd.
III.viii

2 I always take blushing either for a sign of guilt, or of ill breeding.
The Way of the World (1700), I.ix

3 A little disdain is not amiss; a little scorn is alluring.
III.v

4 I nauseate walking; 'tis a country diversion, I loathe the country.
IV.iv

5 Let us be as strange as if we had been married a great while, and as well-bred as if we were not married at all.
v

6 I may by degrees dwindle into a wife.

JAMES M. CONNELL 1852–1929

7 Tho' cowards flinch and traitors sneer,
We'll keep the red flag flying here.
The Red Flag (1889), in H.E. Piggot, *Songs that made History*, ch.6

CYRIL CONNOLLY 1903–1974

8 She [the artist's wife] will know that there is no more sombre enemy of good art than the pram in the hall.
Enemies of Promise (1938), pt.II. **The Charlock's Shade,** ch.xiv

9 There is no fury like an ex-wife searching for a new lover.
The Unquiet Grave (1944), Part I. **Ecce Gubernator**

10 Imprisoned in every fat man a thin one is wildly signalling to be let out.
Part II. **Te Palinure Petens.** See Orwell.

11 It is closing time in the gardens of the West.
'Comment', *Horizon*, Nos. 120–1, Dec. 1949–Jan. 1950. (Final Issue)

JOSEPH CONRAD 1857–1924

12 Mistah Kurtz—he dead.
The Heart of Darkness (1902), ch.3

1 The terrorist and the policeman both come from the same basket.
The Secret Agent (1907), ch.4

EMPEROR CONSTANTINE 288?–337

2 *In hoc signo vinces.*
In this sign shalt thou conquer.
Eusebius, *Life of Constantine*, i.28

ELIZA COOK 1818–1889

3 I love it, I love it; and who shall dare
To chide me for loving that old arm-chair?
The Old Arm-chair

CALVIN COOLIDGE 1872–1933

4 He said he was against it.
On being asked what had been said by a clergyman who preached on sin

BISHOP RICHARD CORBET 1582–1635

5 Farewell, rewards and Fairies,
  Good housewives now may say,
For now foul sluts in dairies
  Do fare as well as they.
The Fairies' Farewell

PIERRE CORNEILLE 1606–1684

6 *Un premier mouvement ne fut jamais un crime.*
A first impulse was never a crime.
Horace (1640), V.iii

FRANCES CORNFORD 1886–1960

7 Whoso maintains that I am humbled now
  (Who wait the Awful Day) is still a liar;
I hope to meet my Maker brow to brow
  And find my own the higher.
Epitaph for a Reviewer

1 O fat white woman whom nobody loves,
Why do you walk through the fields in gloves ...
Missing so much and so much?
To a Fat Lady Seen from a Train

F.M. CORNFORD 1874–1943

2 Every public action which is not customary, either is wrong or, if it is right, is a dangerous precedent. It follows that nothing should ever be done for the first time.
Microcosmographia Academica, vii

MME CORNUEL 1605–1694

3 *Il n'y a point de héros pour son valet de chambre.*
No man is a hero to his valet.
Lettres de Mlle Aïssé, xii, 13 août, 1728

WILLIAM CORY 1823–1892

4 Jolly boating weather,
And a hay harvest breeze.
Eton Boating Song

5 Swing, swing together
With your body between your knees.

6 Nothing in life shall sever
The chain that is round us now.

7 They told me, Heraclitus, they told me you were dead,
They brought me bitter news to hear and bitter tears to shed.
Heraclitus. Translation of Callimachus, *Epigrams*, 2

8 Your chilly stars I can forgo,
This warm kind world is all I know.
Mimnermus in Church

ÉMILE COUÉ 1857–1926

9 *Tous les jours, à tous points de vue, je vais de mieux en mieux.*
Every day, in every way, I am getting better and better.
Formula in his clinic at Nancy

NOËL COWARD 1899–1973

1 Very flat, Norfolk.
Private Lives, I

2 Extraordinary how potent cheap music is.

3 Certain women should be struck regularly, like gongs.
III

4 Mad dogs and Englishmen go out in the mid-day sun.
Mad Dogs and Englishmen

5 Don't put your daughter on the stage, Missis Worthington.
Mrs. Worthington

ABRAHAM COWLEY 1618–1667

6 Love in her sunny eyes does basking play;
Love walks the pleasant mazes of her hair.
The Change

7 In all her outward parts Love's always seen;
But, oh, he never went within.

8 God the first garden made, and the first city Cain.
The Garden

WILLIAM COWPER 1731–1800

9 Beware of desp'rate steps. The darkest day
(Live till tomorrow) will have pass'd away.
The Needless Alarm, l.132

10 God moves in a mysterious way
His wonders to perform.
Olney Hymns, 35

11 Toll for the brave—
The brave! that are no more.
On the Loss of the Royal George

12 Winks hard, and talks of darkness at noon-day.
The Progress of Error, l.451

13 Thou god of our idolatry, the press.
l.461

14 God made the country, and man made the town.
The Task, bk.i, **The Sofa,** l.749

1 England, with all thy faults, I love thee still—
My country!

bk.ii, **The Timepiece,** l.206. See Charles Churchill.

2 Variety's the very spice of life,
That gives it all its flavour.

l.606

3 How various his employments, whom the world
Calls idle.

bk.iii, **The Garden,** l.352

4 The cups,
That cheer but not inebriate.

bk.iv, **The Winter Evening,** l.37. See Berkeley.

5 I am monarch of all I survey,
My right there is none to dispute.

Verses Supposed to be Written by Alexander Selkirk

ARCHBISHOP CRANMER 1489–1556

6 This was the hand that wrote it, therefore it shall suffer first punishment.

At the stake, 21 March 1556. Green, *Short History of The English People*, p.367

RICHARD CRASHAW 1612?–1649

7 By all the eagle in thee, all the dove.

The Flaming Heart upon the Book of Saint Teresa, l.95

8 Love, thou art absolute sole Lord
Of life and death.

Hymn to the Name & Honour of the Admirable Saint Teresa, l.1

9 Lo here a little volume, but large book.

Prayer ... prefixed to a little Prayer-book

10 It is love's great artillery
Which here contracts itself and comes to lie
Close couch'd in your white bosom.

11 Whoe'er she be,
That not impossible she
That shall command my heart and me.

Wishes to his supposed Mistress

BISHOP MANDELL CREIGHTON 1843–1901

1 No people do so much harm as those who go about doing good.
Life (1904), vol.ii, p.503

SIR RANULPHE CREWE 1558–1646

2 And yet time hath his revolution; there must be a period and an end to all temporal things.
Oxford Peerage Case, 1625. See *D.N.B.*

3 Where is Bohun, where's Mowbray, where's Mortimer? Nay, which is more and most of all, where is Plantagenet? They are entombed in the urns and sepulchres of mortality.

OLIVER CROMWELL 1599–1658

4 The plain russet-coated captain that knows what he fights for and loves what he knows.
Letter of Sept. 1643. Carlyle, *Letters and Speeches of Oliver Cromwell*

5 I beseech you, in the bowels of Christ, think it possible you may be mistaken.
Letter to the General Assembly of the Church of Scotland, 3 Aug. 1650

6 Mr Lely, I desire you would use all your skill to paint my picture truly like me, and not flatter me at all; but remark all these roughnesses, pimples, warts, and everything as you see me, otherwise I will never pay a farthing for it.
Walpole, *Anecdotes of Painting*, ch.12

7 Take away that fool's bauble, the mace.
At the dismissal of the Rump Parliament, 20 Apr. 1653. Bulstrode Whitelock, *Memorials* (1682), p.554. Often quoted as 'Take away these baubles'.

8 You have sat too long here for any good you have been doing. Depart, I say, and let us have done with you. In the name of God, go!
Addressing the Rump Parliament, 20 Apr. 1653. See Bulstrode Whitelock, p.544.

9 My design is to make what haste I can to be gone.
Last words. Morley, *Life*, v, ch.10

BISHOP RICHARD CUMBERLAND 1631–1718

1 It is better to wear out than to rust out.
G. Horne, *The Duty of Contending for the Faith*

E.E. CUMMINGS 1894–1962

2 listen: there's a hell
of a good universe next door; let's go.
pity this busy monster, manunkind

ALLAN CUNNINGHAM 1784–1842

3 A wet sheet and a flowing sea,
A wind that follows fast
And fills the white and rustling sail
And bends the gallant mast.
A Wet Sheet and a Flowing Sea

JOHN PHILPOT CURRAN 1750–1817

4 The condition upon which God hath given liberty to man is eternal vigilance.
Speech on the Right of Election of Lord Mayor of Dublin, 10 July 1790

ST. CYPRIAN d. 258

5 *Habere non potest Deum patrem qui ecclesiam non habet matrem.*
He cannot have God for his father who has not the church for his mother.
De Cath. Eccl. Unitate, vi. See St. Augustine.

DANTE 1265–1321

6 *Nel mezzo del cammin di nostra vita.*
In the middle of the road of our life.
Divina Commedia (ed. Sinclair, 1971). **Inferno,** i.1

7 *LASCIATE OGNI SPERANZA VOI CH'ENTRATE!*
Abandon all hope, you who enter!
iii.1. Inscription at the entrance to Hell

1 *Il gran rifiuto.*
The great refusal.
60

DANTON 1759–1794

2 *De l'audace, et encore de l'audace, et toujours de l'audace!*
Boldness, and again boldness, and always boldness!
Speech to the Legislative Committee of General Defence, 2 Sept. 1792. *Le Moniteur*, 4 Sept. 1792

GEORGE DARLEY 1795–1846

3 O blest unfabled Incense Tree,
That burns in glorious Araby.
Nepenthe, l.147

CHARLES DARWIN 1809–1882

4 I have called this principle, by which each slight variation, if useful, is preserved, by the term of Natural Selection.
On the Origin of Species (1859), ch.3

5 What a book a devil's chaplain might write on the clumsy, wasteful, blundering, low, and horribly cruel works of nature!
Letter to J.D. Hooker, 13 July 1856

CHARLES DAVENANT 1656–1714

6 Custom, that unwritten law,
By which the people keep even kings in awe.
Circe, II.iii

SIR WILLIAM DAVENANT 1606–1668

7 In ev'ry grave make room, make room!
The world's at an end, and we come, we come.
The Law against Lovers, III.i

JOHN DAVIDSON 1857–1909

8 A runnable stag, a kingly crop.
A Runnable Stag

SIR JOHN DAVIES 1569–1626

1 Wedlock, indeed, hath oft compared been
To public feasts where meet a public rout,
Where they that are without would fain go in
And they that are within would fain go out.
A Contention Betwixt a Wife, a Widow, and a Maid for Precedence, l.193

2 And to conclude, I know myself a man,
Which is a proud and yet a wretched thing.
Nosce Teipsum, xlv

W.H. DAVIES 1870–1940

3 It was the Rainbow gave thee birth,
And left thee all her lovely hues.
The Kingfisher

4 What is this life if, full of care,
We have no time to stand and stare?
Leisure

STEPHEN DECATUR 1779–1820

5 Our country! In her intercourse with foreign nations, may she always be in the right; but our country, right or wrong.
Decatur's Toast (1816). See A.S. Mackenzie, *Life of Decatur*, ch.xiv.

CHARLES DE GAULLE 1890–1970

6 *On ne peut pas rassembler à froid un pays qui compte 265 spécialités de fromages.*
Nobody can simply bring together a country that has 265 kinds of cheese.
Speech after the *recul* of the R.P.P. at the elections of 1951

THOMAS DEKKER 1570?–1641?

7 Golden slumbers kiss your eyes,
Smiles awake you when you rise.
Patient Grissil, Act IV.ii

WALTER DE LA MARE 1873–1956

1 Oh, no man knows
Through what wild centuries
Roves back the rose.
All That's Past

2 He is crazed with the spell of far Arabia,
They have stolen his wits away.
Arabia

3 When I lie where shades of darkness
Shall no more assail mine eyes.
Fare Well, i

4 Look thy last on all things lovely,
Every hour.
iii

5 Nought but vast sorrow was there—
The sweet cheat gone.
The Ghost

6 'Is there anybody there?' said the traveller,
Knocking on the moonlit door.
The Listeners

7 'Tell them I came, and no one answered,
That I kept my word,' he said.

8 Slowly, silently, now the moon
Walks the night in her silver shoon.
Silver

C.J. DENNIS 1876–1938

9 Me name is Mud.
The Sentimental Bloke: A Spring Song, st.2 (1916)

JOHN DENNIS 1657–1734

10 A man who could make so vile a pun would not scruple to pick a pocket.
The Gentleman's Magazine (1781), p.324 (Edit. note)

11 Damn them! They will not let my play run, but they steal my thunder!
W.S. Walsh, *Handy-book of Literary Curiosities*

THOMAS DE QUINCEY 1785–1859

1 A duller spectacle this earth of ours has not to show than a rainy Sunday in London.
***Confessions of an English Opium Eater*, pt.ii, The Pleasures of Opium**

2 Murder Considered as One of the Fine Arts.
Essay

DESCARTES 1596–1650

3 *Cogito, ergo sum.*
I think, therefore I am.
Le Discours de la Méthode

PHILIPPE NÉRICAULT called DESTOUCHES 1680–1754

4 *Les absents ont toujours tort.*
The absent are always in the wrong.
***L'Obstacle imprévu*, I.vi**

SERGE DIAGHILEV 1872–1929

5 *Étonne-moi.*
Astonish me.
Said to Jean Cocteau in 1912. *The Journals of Jean Cocteau*, 1

CHARLES DIBDIN 1745–1814

6 Here, a sheer hulk, lies poor Tom Bowling,
The darling of our crew.
Tom Bowling

7 Faithful, below, he did his duty;
But now he's gone aloft.

THOMAS DIBDIN 1771–1841

8 Oh! what a snug little Island,
A right little, tight little Island!
The Snug Little Island

CHARLES DICKENS 1812–1870

1 This is a London particular ... A fog, miss.
Bleak House, ch. 3

2 'Not to put too fine a point upon it'—a favourite apology for plain-speaking with Mr Snagsby.
ch.11

3 He wos wery good to me, he wos! [Jo.]

4 O let us love our occupations,
Bless the squire and his relations.
The Chimes, 2nd Quarter

5 'God bless us every one!' said Tiny Tim.
A Christmas Carol, stave 3

6 'I am a lone lorn creetur',' were Mrs Gummidge's words, ... 'and everythink goes contrairy with me.'
David Copperfield, ch.3

7 Barkis is willin'.
ch.5

8 Annual income twenty pounds, annual expenditure nineteen nineteen six, result happiness. Annual income twenty pounds, annual expenditure twenty pounds ought and six, result misery. [Mr. Micawber.]
ch. 12

9 I am well aware that I am the 'umblest person going. ... My mother is likewise a very 'umble person. We live in a numble abode. [Uriah Heep.]
ch.16

10 The mistake was made of putting some of the trouble out of King Charles's head into my head. [Mr. Dick.]
ch.17

11 I only ask for information. [Miss Rosa Dartle.]
ch.20

12 'People can't die, along the coast,' said Mr Peggotty, 'except when the tide's pretty nigh out. They can't be born, unless it's pretty nigh in—not properly born, till flood. He's a going out with the tide.'
ch.30

13 'When found, make a note of.' [Captain Cuttle.]
Dombey and Son, ch.15

1 You don't object to an aged parent, I hope? [Wemmick.]
Great Expectations, ch.25

2 Papa, potatoes, poultry, prunes, and prism, are all very good words for the lips: especially prunes and prism. [Mrs. General.]
Little Dorrit, bk.ii, ch.5

3 With affection beaming in one eye, and calculation shining out of the other. [Mrs. Todgers.]
Martin Chuzzlewit, ch.8

4 He'd make a lovely corpse. [Mrs. Gamp.]
ch.25

5 We never knows wot's hidden in each other's hearts; and if we had glass winders there, we'd need keep the shutters up, some on us, I do assure you! [Mrs Gamp.]
ch.29

6 A lane was made; and Mrs Hominy, with the aristocratic stalk, the pocket handkerchief, the clasped hands, and the classical cap, came slowly up it, in a procession of one.
ch.34

7 The words she spoke of Mrs Harris, lambs could not forgive ... nor worms forget. [Mrs. Gamp.]
ch.49

8 As she frequently remarked when she made any such mistake, it would be all the same a hundred years hence. [Mrs. Squeers.]
Nicholas Nickleby, ch.9

9 What's the demd total? [Mr Mantalini.]
ch.21

10 Language was not powerful enough to describe the infant phenomenon.
ch.23

11 All is gas and gaiters. [The Gentleman in the Small-clothes.]
ch.49

12 Oliver Twist has asked for more! [Bumble.]
Oliver Twist, ch.2

1 'If the law supposes that,' said Mr Bumble ... 'the law is a ass—a idiot.'
ch.51. See Chapman.

2 The question [with Mr. Podsnap] about everything was, would it bring a blush into the cheek of the young person?
Our Mutual Friend, bk.1, ch.11

3 He'd be sharper than a serpent's tooth, if he wasn't as dull as ditch water. [Fanny Cleaver.]
bk.iii, ch.10

4 Kent, sir—everybody knows Kent—apples, cherries, hops, and women. [Jingle.]
Pickwick Papers, ch.2

5 I wants to make your flesh creep. [The Fat Boy.]
ch.8

6 'But suppose there are two mobs?' suggested Mr Snodgrass. 'Shout with the largest,' replied Mr Pickwick.
ch.13

7 Battledore and shuttlecock's a wery good game, vhen you an't the shuttlecock and two lawyers the battledores, in which case it gets too excitin' to be pleasant.
ch.20

8 Mr Weller's knowledge of London was extensive and peculiar.

9 Be wery careful o' vidders all your life. [Mr. Weller.]

10 'You must not tell us what the soldier, or any other man, said, sir,' interposed the judge; 'it's not evidence.'
ch.34

11 Oh Sammy, Sammy, vy worn't there a alleybi! [Mr. Weller.]

12 Miss Bolo ... went straight home, in a flood of tears and a Sedan chair.
ch.35

13 Anythin' for a quiet life, as the man said wen he took the sitivation at the lighthouse. [Sam Weller.]
ch.43

1 A smattering of everything, and a knowledge of nothing. [Minerva House.]
Sketches by Boz, **Tales,** ch.3. **Sentiment**

2 It was the best of times, it was the worst of times, it was the age of wisdom, it was the age of foolishness, it was the epoch of belief, it was the epoch of incredulity, it was the season of Light, it was the season of Darkness, it was the spring of hope, it was the winter of despair, we had everything before us, we had nothing before us, we were all going direct to Heaven, we were all going direct the other way.
A Tale of Two Cities, bk.i, ch.1

3 It is a far, far better thing that I do, than I have ever done; it is a far, far better rest that I go to, than I have ever known. [Sydney Carton's thoughts on the scaffold.]
bk.iii, ch.15

EMILY DICKINSON 1830–1886

4 Because I could not stop for Death—
He kindly stopped for me—
The Carriage held but just Ourselves—
And Immortality.
Because I could not stop for Death

5 The Bustle in a House
The Morning after Death
Is solemnest of industries
Enacted upon Earth.
The Bustle in a House

6 My life closed twice before its close;
It yet remains to see
If Immortality unveil
A third event to me.
My life closed twice before its close

7 Parting is all we know of heaven
And all we need of hell.

8 Success is counted sweetest
By those who ne'er succeed.
Success is counted sweetest

1 This quiet Dust was Gentlemen and Ladies
And Lads and Girls—
Was laughter and ability and Sighing,
And Frocks and Curls.
This quiet Dust was Gentlemen and Ladies

DENIS DIDEROT 1713–1784

2 *L'esprit de l'escalier.*
Staircase wit.
An untranslatable phrase, the meaning of which is that one only thinks on one's way downstairs of the smart retort one might have made in the drawing-room. ***Paradoxe sur le Comédien***

DIONYSIUS OF HALICARNASSUS fl. 30–7 B.C.

3 History is philosophy from examples.
Ars Rhetorica, xi.2

BENJAMIN DISRAELI 1804–1881

4 Though I sit down now, the time will come when you will hear me.
Maiden speech, 7 Dec. 1837. Meynell, *Disraeli*, i.43

5 The Continent will not suffer England to be the workshop of the world.
House of Commons, 15 Mar. 1838

6 Thus you have a starving population, an absentee aristocracy, and an alien Church, and in addition the weakest executive in the world. That is the Irish Question.
16 Feb. 1844

7 He [Sir C. Wood] has to learn that petulance is not sarcasm, and that insolence is not invective.
16 Dec. 1852

8 England does not love coalitions.

9 Is man an ape or an angel? Now I am on the side of the angels.
Meeting of Society for Increasing Endowments of Small Livings in the Diocese of Oxford, 25 Nov. 1864

1 You behold a range of exhausted volcanoes. (Of the Treasury Bench.)
Manchester, 3 Apr. 1872

2 Lord Salisbury and myself have brought you back peace—but a peace I hope with honour.
House of Commons, 16 July 1878. The phrase 'peace with honour' had been used by Lord John Russell in a speech at Greenock, 19 Sept, 1853.

3 A sophistical rhetorician, inebriated with the exuberance of his own verbosity. (Gladstone.)
At Banquet in Riding School, Knightsbridge, 17 July 1878

4 Everyone likes flattery; and when you come to Royalty you should lay it on with a trowel.
G.W.E. Russell, *Collections and Recollections*, ch.23 (To Matthew Arnold)

5 His Christianity was muscular.
Endymion (1880), ch.14

6 Every woman should marry—and no man.
Lothair (1870), ch.30

7 'I rather like bad wine,' said Mr Mountchesney; 'one gets so bored with good wine.'
Sybil (1845), bk.i, ch.1

8 Little things affect little minds.
bk.iii, ch.2

9 I was told that the Privileged and the People formed Two Nations.
bk.iv, ch.8

10 There are three kinds of lies: lies, damned lies and statistics.
Attr. Mark Twain, *Autobiography*, I.246

AELIUS DONATUS fl. 4th cent. A.D.

11 *Pereant, inquit, qui ante nos nostra dixerunt.*
Confound those who have said our remarks before us.
St. Jerome, *Commentary on Ecclesiastes*, 1. Migne, *Patrologiae Lat. Cursus*, 23.390

JOHN DONNE 1571?–1631

12 All other things, to their destruction draw,
Only our love hath no decay;

This, no to-morrow hath, nor yesterday,
Running it never runs from us away,
But truly keeps his first, last, everlasting day.
The Anniversary

1 Come live with me, and be my love,
And we will some new pleasures prove
Of golden sands, and crystal brooks,
With silken lines, and silver hooks.
The Bait. See also Marlow.

2 The day breaks not, it is my heart.
Break of Day (Attr. also to John Dowland)

3 For God's sake hold your tongue, and let me love.
The Canonization

4 No Spring, nor Summer beauty hath such grace,
As I have seen in one Autumnal face.
Elegies, No.9. **The Autumnal**

5 By our first strange and fatal interview
By all desires which thereof did ensue.
No.16. **On His Mistress**

6 We easily know
By this these angels from an evil sprite,
Those set our hairs, but these our flesh upright.
No.19. **Going to Bed**

7 Licence my roving hands, and let them go,
Before, behind, between, above, below.
O my America! my new-found-land,
My kingdom, safliest when with one man mann'd.

8 So must pure lovers' souls descend
T'affections, and to faculties,
Which sense may reach and apprehend,
Else a great Prince in prison lies.
The Extasy

9 I wonder by my troth, what thou, and I
Did, till we lov'd? were we not wean'd till then?
But suck'd on country pleasures, childishly?
Or snorted we in the Seven Sleepers den?
The Good-Morrow

1 At the round earth's imagined corners, blow
Your trumpets, Angels, and arise, arise.
Holy Sonnets (2), vii

2 Death be not proud, though some have called thee
Mighty and dreadful, for thou art not so.
x

3 One short sleep past, we wake eternally,
And death shall be no more; death, thou shalt die.

4 What if this present were the world's last night?
xiii

5 Batter my heart, three person'd God; for, you
As yet but knock, breathe, shine, and seek to mend.
xiv

6 Sir, more than kisses, letters mingle souls.
***Letters to Severall Personages,* To Sir Henry Wotton**

7 I long to talk with some old lover's ghost,
Who died before the god of love was born.
Love's Deity

8 Nature's great masterpiece, an Elephant,
The only harmless great thing.
Progress of the Soul, xxxix

9 Sweetest love, I do not go,
For weariness of thee.
Song

10 Go, and catch a falling star,
Get with child a mandrake root,
Tell me, where all past years are,
Or who cleft the Devil's foot.
Song, Go and Catch a Falling Star

11 And swear
No where
Lives a woman true and fair.

12 Though she were true, when you met her,
And last, till you write your letter,
Yet she
Will be
False, ere I come, to two, or three.

1 Busy old fool, unruly Sun,
Why dost thou thus,
Through windows, and through curtains call on us?
The Sun Rising

2 This bed thy centre is, these walls thy sphere.

3 Send me not this, nor that, t'increase my store,
But swear thou think'st I love thee, and no more.
The Token

4 I am two fools, I know,
For loving, and for saying so
In whining Poetry.
The Triple Fool

5 I have done one braver thing
Than all the Worthies did,
And yet a braver thence doth spring,
Which is, to keep that hid.
The Undertaking

6 But I do nothing upon my self, and yet I am mine own *Executioner*.
***Devotions upon Emergent Occasions.* Meditation XII**

7 No man is an *Island*, entire of it self.
Meditation XVII

8 Any man's *death* diminishes *me*, because I am involved in *Mankind*; And therefore never send to know for whom the *bell* tolls; It tolls for *thee*.

9 Poor intricated soul! Riddling, perplexed, labyrinthical soul!
LXXX Sermons (1640), xlviii, 25 Jan. 1628/9

LORD ALFRED DOUGLAS 1870–1945

10 I am the Love that dare not speak its name.
Two Loves

ERNEST DOWSON 1867–1900

11 I have forgot much, Cynara! gone with the wind.
Non Sum Qualis Eram

12 I have been faithful to thee, Cynara! in my fashion.

1 They are not long, the days of wine and roses.
Vitae Summa Brevis

SIR ARTHUR CONAN DOYLE 1859–1930

2 The more featureless and commonplace a crime is, the more difficult is it to bring it home.
***The Adventures of Sherlock Holmes.* The Boscombe Valley Mystery**

3 It is quite a three-pipe problem.
The Red-Headed League

4 I have nothing to do to-day. My practice is never very absorbing.

5 You see, but you do not observe.
Scandal in Bohemia

6 It is a capital mistake to theorize before one has data.

7 You know my methods, Watson.
***The Memoirs of Sherlock Holmes.* The Crooked Man**

8 'Excellent!' I [Dr. Watson] cried. 'Elementary,' said he [Holmes].

9 He [Professor Moriarty] is the Napoleon of crime.
The Final Problem

10 'The dog did nothing in the night-time.'
'That was the curious incident,' remarked Sherlock Holmes.
Silver Blaze

11 There is a spirituality about the face, however ... which the typewriter does not generate. The lady is a musician.
***The Return of Sherlock Holmes.* The Solitary Cyclist**

12 There is but one step from the grotesque to the horrible.
***His Last Bow.* Wisteria Lodge**

13 An experience of women which extends over many nations and three separate continents.
The Sign of Four

14 How often have I said to you that when you have eliminated the impossible, whatever remains, *however improbable*, must be the truth?

1 The vocabulary of 'Bradshaw' is nervous and terse, but limited.
The Valley of Fear

2 Mediocrity knows nothing higher than itself, but talent instantly recognizes genius.

SIR FRANCIS DRAKE 1540?–1596

3 There must be a beginning of any great matter, but the continuing unto the end until it be thoroughly finished yields the true glory.
Dispatch to Sir Francis Walsingham, 17 May 1587. Navy Records Society, vol. XI (1898), p.134

4 There is plenty of time to win this game, and to thrash the Spaniards too.
Attr. D.N.B.

5 I remember Drake, in the vaunting style of a soldier, would call the Enterprise the singeing of the King of Spain's Beard. [Of the expedition to Cadiz, 1587.]
Bacon, *Considerations touching a War with Spain* (*Harleian Misc.* 1745, vol.v, p.85, col.1)

6 I must have the gentleman to haul and draw with the mariner, and the mariner with the gentleman.
Corbett, *Drake and the Tudor Navy*, i.249

MICHAEL DRAYTON 1562–1631

7 Fair stood the wind for France
When we our sails advance,
Nor now to prove our chance
Longer will tarry.
To the Cambro-Britons. Agincourt

8 Since there's no help, come let us kiss and part.
Sonnets, lxi

THOMAS DRUMMOND 1797–1840

9 Property has its duties as well as its rights.
Letter to the Earl of Donoughmore, 22 May 1838

JOHN DRYDEN 1631–1700

1 In pious times, ere priestcraft did begin,
Before polygamy was made a sin.
Absalom and Achitophel, pt.i, l.1

2 Scatter'd his Maker's image through the land.
l.10

3 God's pampered people, whom, debauched with ease,
No king could govern nor no God could please.
l.47

4 A fiery soul, which working out its way,
Fretted the pigmy body to decay.
l.156

5 Great wits are sure to madness near alli'd,
And thin partitions do their bounds divide.
l.163

6 And all to leave what with his toil he won
To that unfeather'd two-legged thing, a son.
l.169

7 A man so various that he seem'd to be
Not one, but all mankind's epitome.
Stiff in opinions, always in the wrong;
Was everything by starts, and nothing long:
But, in the course of one revolving moon,
Was chemist, fiddler, statesman, and buffoon.
l.545

8 Railing and praising were his usual themes;
And both (to show his judgement) in extremes.
l.555

9 During his office treason was no crime,
The sons of Belial had a glorious time.
l.597

10 None but the brave deserves the fair.
Alexander's Feast, l.15

11 Errors, like straws, upon the surface flow;
He who would search for pearls must dive below.
All for Love, Prologue

1 I am as free as nature first made man,
Ere the base laws of servitude began,
When wild in woods the noble savage ran.
The Conquest of Granada, pt.i, I.i

2 Thou strong seducer, opportunity!
pt.ii, IV.iii

3 Bold knaves thrive without one grain of sense,
But good men starve for want of impudence.
Epilogue to Constantine the Great

4 Here lies my wife: here let her lie!
Now she's at rest, and so am I.
Epitaph Intended for Dryden's Wife

5 Either be wholly slaves or wholly free.
The Hind and the Panther, pt.ii, l.285

6 Fairest Isle, all isles excelling,
Seat of pleasures, and of loves;
Venus here will choose her dwelling,
And forsake her Cyprian groves.
King Arthur, V. **Song of Venus**

7 I am to be married within these three days; married past redemption.
Marriage à la Mode, I.i

8 Like pilgrims to th' appointed place we tend;
The world's an inn, and death the journey's end.
Palamon and Arcite, bk.iii, l.887

9 From harmony, from heavenly harmony
This universal frame began.
A Song for St. Cecilia's Day, i

10 There is a pleasure sure,
In being mad, which none but madmen know!
The Spanish Friar, I.i

ALEXANDER DUBCEK 1921–

11 Communism with a human face.
Attr. A resolution by the party group in the Ministry of Foreign Affairs, in 1968, referred to Czechoslovak foreign policy acquiring 'its own defined face'. *Rudé právo*, 14 Mar. 1968

MME DU DEFFAND 1697–1780

1 *La distance n'y fait rien; il n'y a que le premier pas qui coûte.*

The distance is nothing; it is only the first step that is difficult.

Commenting on the legend that St. Denis, carrying his head in his hands, walked two leagues. Letter to d'Alembert, 7 July 1763

GEORGE DUFFIELD 1818–1888

2 Stand up!—stand up for Jesus!

***The Psalmist*, Stand Up, Stand Up for Jesus**

ALEXANDRE DUMAS 1802–1870

3 *Cherchons la femme.*

Let us look for the woman.

Les Mohicans de Paris, *passim* (*Cherchez la femme.* Attributed to Joseph Fouche)

4 *Tous pour un, un pour tous.*

All for one, one for all.

Les Trois Mousquetiers, passim

GENERAL DUMOURIEZ 1739–1823

5 *Les courtisans qui l'entourent n'ont rien oublié et n'ont rien appris.*

The courtiers who surround him have forgotten nothing and learnt nothing.

Of Louis XVIII, at the time of the Declaration of Verona, Sept. 1795. *Examen.* Later used by Napoleon on his return from Elba. See Talleyrand.

WILLIAM DUNBAR 1465?–1530?

6 *Timor mortis conturbat me.*

Lament for the Makaris

7 London, thou art of townes *A per se.*

London, l.1

8 London, thou art the flower of cities all!
Gemme of all joy, jasper of jocunditie.

l.16

JOHN DUNNING, BARON ASHBURTON 1731–1783

1 The influence of the Crown has increased, is increasing, and ought to be diminished.
Motion passed in the House of Commons, 1780

JAMES DUPORT 1606–1679

2 *Quem Jupiter vult perdere, dementat prius.*
Whom God would destroy He first sends mad.
Homeri Gnomologia (1660), p.282. See Anon.

RICHARD DUPPA 1770–1831

3 In language, the ignorant have prescribed laws to the learned.
Maxims (1830), 252

JOHN DYER fl. 1714

4 And he that will this health deny,
Down among the dead men let him lie.
Toast: Here's a Health to the King

MARIA EDGEWORTH 1767–1849

5 Well! some people talk of morality, and some of religion, but give me a little snug property.
The Absentee, ch.2

THOMAS ALVA EDISON 1847–1931

6 Genius is one per cent inspiration and ninety-nine per cent perspiration.
Life (1932), ch.24

KING EDWARD VIII 1894–1972

7 I have found it impossible to carry the heavy burden of responsibility and to discharge my duties as King as I would wish to do without the help and support of the woman I love.
Broadcast, 11 Dec. 1936

OLIVER EDWARDS 1711–1791

1 I have tried too in my time to be a philosopher; but, I don't know how, cheerfulness was always breaking in.
Boswell's *Johnson*, 17 Apr. 1778

ALBERT EINSTEIN 1879–1955

2 *Gott würfelt nicht.*
God does not play dice. [Einstein's habitually expressed reaction to the quantum theory.]
B. Hoffman, *Albert Einstein, Creator and Rebel*, ch.10

GEORGE ELIOT 1819–1880

3 I'm not denyin' the women are foolish: God Almighty made 'em to match the men.
Adam Bede (1859), ch. 53

4 Gossip is a sort of smoke that comes from the dirty tobacco-pipes of those who diffuse it: it proves nothing but the bad taste of the smoker.
Daniel Deronda (1874–6), bk.ii, ch.13

5 There is a great deal of unmapped country within us which would have to be taken into account in an explanation of our gusts and storms.
bk.iii, ch.24

6 Half the sorrows of women would be averted if they could repress the speech they know to be useless; nay, the speech they have resolved not to make.
Felix Holt (1866), ch.2

7 A woman, let her be as good as she may, has got to put up with the life her husband makes for her.
Middlemarch (1871–2), ch. 25

8 It was a room where you had no reason for sitting in one place rather than in another.
ch.54

9 The happiest women, like the happiest nations, have no history.
The Mill on the Floss (1860), bk.vi, ch.3

T.S. ELIOT 1888–1965

1 Teach us to care and not to care
Teach us to sit still.
***Ash Wednesday*, 1**

2 Sometimes these cogitations still amaze
The troubled midnight and the noon's repose.
La Figlia Che Piange

3 Time present and time past
Are both perhaps present in time future,
And time future contained in time past.
***Four Quartets*. Burnt Norton, 11**

4 Human kind
Cannot bear very much reality.

5 In my beginning is my end.
East Coker, 11

6 A way of putting it—not very satisfactory:
A periphrastic study in a worn-out poetical fashion.
2

7 What we call the beginning is often the end
And to make an end is to make a beginning.
The end is where we start from.
Little Gidding, 15

8 An old man in a dry month.
Gerontion

9 We are the hollow men
We are the stuffed men
Leaning together
Headpiece filled with straw. Alas!
***The Hollow Men*, 1**

10 *Here we go round the prickly pear*
Prickly pear prickly pear.
5

11 This is the way the world ends
Not with a bang but a whimper.

12 Let us go then, you and I,
When the evening is spread out against the sky
Like a patient etherized upon a table.
The Love Song of J. Alfred Prufrock

1 In the room the women come and go
Talking of Michelangelo.

The yellow fog that rubs its back upon the window-panes.

2 I have measured out my life with coffee spoons.

3 I should have been a pair of ragged claws
Scuttling across the floors of silent seas.

4 I grow old ... I grow old ...
I shall wear the bottoms of my trousers rolled.

5 I have heard the mermaids singing, each to each;
I do not think that they will sing to me.

6 Macavity, Macavity, there's no one like Macavity,
There never was a Cat of such deceitfulness and suavity.
Macavity: The Mystery Cat

7 At whatever time the deed took place—
MACAVITY WASN'T THERE!

8 I am aware of the damp souls of housemaids
Sprouting despondently at area gates.
Morning at the Window

9 Yet we have gone on living,
Living and partly living.
Murder in the Cathedral, pt.I

10 Friendship should be more than biting Time can sever.

11 The last temptation is the greatest treason:
To do the right deed for the wrong reason.

12 The Naming of Cats is a difficult matter,
It isn't just one of your holiday games.
The Naming of Cats

13 The winter evening settles down
With smell of steaks in passageways.
Six o'clock.
The burnt-out ends of smoky days.
Preludes, I

14 April is the cruellest month, breeding
Lilacs out of the dead land.
The Waste Land. 1. **The Burial of the Dead**

1 And I will show you something different from either
Your shadow at morning striding behind you,
Or your shadow at evening rising to meet you
I will show you fear in a handful of dust.

2 A crowd flowed over London Bridge, so many,
I had not thought death had undone so many.

3 When lovely woman stoops to folly and
Paces about her room again, alone,
She smoothes her hair with automatic hand,
And puts a record on the gramophone.
3. **The Fire Sermon.** See Goldsmith.

4 Where the walls
Of Magnus Martyr hold
Inexplicable splendour of Ionian white and gold.

5 A woman drew her long black hair out tight
And fiddled whisper music on those strings.
5. **What the Thunder Said**

6 These fragments have I shored against my ruins.

7 Webster was much possessed by death
And saw the skull beneath the skin.
Whispers of Immortality

8 In the seventeenth century a dissociation of sensibility set in from which we have never recovered.
The Metaphysical Poets

QUEEN ELIZABETH I 1533–1603

9 Anger makes dull men witty, but it keeps them poor.
Bacon, *Apophthegms*, 5

10 *Semper eadem.* (Ever the same.)
Motto

11 I know I have the body of a weak and feeble woman, but I have the heart and stomach of a king, and of a king of England too.
Speech to the Troops at Tilbury on the Approach of the Armada, 1588

12 Must! Is *must* a word to be addressed to princes?
To Robert Cecil, on her death-bed. J.R. Green, *A Short History of the English People*, ch.vii

JOHN ELLERTON 1826–1893

1 The day Thou gavest, Lord, is ended,
The darkness falls at Thy behest.
A Liturgy for Missionary Meetings

JANE ELLIOT 1727–1805

2 I've heard them lilting, at the ewe milking.
Lasses a' lilting, before dawn of day;
But now they are moaning, on ilka green loaning;
The flowers of the forest are a' wede away.
The Flowers of the Forest (1756) (Popular version of the traditional lament for Flodden)

RALPH WALDO EMERSON 1803–1882

3 If the red slayer think he slays,
Or if the slain think he is slain,
They know not well the subtle ways
I keep, and pass, and turn again.
Brahma

4 Here once the embattled farmers stood,
And fired the shot heard round the world.
Hymn Sung at the Completion of the Concord Monument

5 Things are in the saddle,
And ride mankind.
Ode, Inscribed to W.H. Channing

6 Make yourself necessary to someone.
***Conduct of Life*. Considerations by the way**

7 A person seldom falls sick, but the bystanders are animated with a faint hope that he will die.

8 Art is a jealous mistress.
Wealth

9 The only reward of virtue is virtue; the only way to have a friend is to be one.
Essays, vi. **Friendship**

10 There is properly no history; only biography.
i. **History**

1 In skating over thin ice, our safety is in our speed.
vii. **Prudence**

2 A foolish consistency is the hobgoblin of little minds.
ii. **Self-Reliance**

3 To be great is to be misunderstood.

4 What is a weed? A plant whose virtues have not been discovered.
Fortune of the Republic

5 Hitch your wagon to a star.
***Society and Solitude*. Civilization**

6 If a man write a better book, preach a better sermon, or make a better mouse-trap than his neighbour, tho' he build his house in the woods, the world will make a beaten path to his door.
Sarah S.B. Yule, *Borrowings* (1889)

WILLIAM EMPSON 1906–

7 Slowly the poison the whole blood stream fills.
It is not the effort nor the failure tires.
The waste remains, the waste remains and kills.
Missing Dates

FRIEDRICH ENGELS 1820–1895

8 *Der Staat wird nicht 'abgeschaft'*, er stirbt ab.
The State is not 'abolished', *it withers away*.
Anti-Dühring, III.ii

ENNIUS 239–169 B.C.

9 *Unus homo nobis cunctando restituit rem.*
One man by delaying put the state to rights for us.
Annals 12. Cicero, *De Off.*, I, 24, 84

HENRI ESTIENNE 1531–1598

10 *Si jeunesse savoit; si vieillesse pouvoit.*
If youth knew; if age could.
Les Prémices, Épigramme cxci

EUCLID fl. c.300 B.C.

1 *Quod erat demonstrandum*. (trans. from the Greek).
Which was to be proved.

EURIPIDES 480–406 B.C.

2 My tongue swore, but my mind's unsworn.
***Hippolytus*, 612**

ABEL EVANS 1679–1737

3 Lie heavy on him, Earth! for he
Laid many heavy loads on thee!
Epitaph on Sir John Vanbrugh, Architect of Blenheim Palace

GAVIN EWART 1916–

4 Miss Twye was soaping her breasts in the bath
When she heard behind her a meaning laugh
And to her amazement she discovered
A wicked man in the bathroom cupboard.
Miss Twye

WILLIAM NORMAN EWER 1885–1976

5 I gave my life for freedom—This I know:
For those who bade me fight had told me so.
***Five Souls*, 1917**

6 How odd
Of God
To choose
The Jews.
How Odd. See C. Browne.

LUCIUS CARY, VISCOUNT FALKLAND
1610?–1643

7 When it is not necessary to change, it is necessary not to change.
A Speech concerning Episcopacy [delivered 1641]. ***A Discourse of Infallibility*, 1660**

GEORGE FARQUHAR 1678–1707

1 My Lady Bountiful.
The Beaux' Stratagem, I.i

GUY FAWKES 1570–1606

2 A desperate disease requires a dangerous remedy.
6 Nov. 1605. See D.N.B.

GEOFFREY FEARON

3 The 'angry young men' of England.
Times Literary Supplement, 4 Oct. 1957 but see also R. West, *Black Lamb and Grey Falcon* (1941), 'Dalmatia'

EMPEROR FERDINAND I 1503–1564

4 *Fiat justitia et pereat mundus.*
Let justice be done, though the world perish.
Motto. Johannes Manlius, *Locorum Communium Collectanea* (Basle, 1563), II, 290. See Watson.

LUDWIG FEUERBACH 1804–1872

5 *Der Mensch ist, was er isst.*
Man is what he eats.
Advertisement to Moleschott, *Lehre der Nahrungsmittel: Für das Volk* (1850). See Brillat-Savarin.

EUGENE FIELD 1850–1895

6 Wynken, Blynken, and Nod one night
   Sailed off in a wooden shoe—
Sailed on a river of crystal light,
   Into a sea of dew.
Wynken, Blynken, and Nod

7 He played the King as though under momentary apprehension that someone else was about to play the ace.
Of Creston Clarke as King Lear. Attr. to a review in the *Denver Tribune*, c.1880

HENRY FIELDING 1707–1754

8 Oh! The roast beef of England,
And old England's roast beef.
The Grub Street Opera, III.iii

1 He in a few minutes ravished this fair creature, or at least would have ravished her, if she had not, by a timely compliance, prevented him.
Jonathan Wild, bk.iii, ch.7

2 Public schools are the nurseries of all vice and immorality.
Joseph Andrews, bk, iii, ch.5

3 Some folks rail against other folks, because other folks have what some folks would be glad of.
bk.iv, ch.6

4 What is commonly called love, namely the desire of satisfying a voracious appetite with a certain quantity of delicate white human flesh.
Tom Jones, bk.vi, ch.1

5 An amiable weakness.
bk.x, ch.8

CHARLES FITZGEFFREY 1575?–1638

6 And bold and hard adventures t' undertake,
Leaving his country for his country's sake.
Sir Francis Drake (1596), st.213

EDWARD FITZGERALD 1809–1883

7 Awake! for Morning in the Bowl of Night
Has flung the Stone that puts the Stars to Flight.
The Rubáiyát of Omar Khayyám (1859), 1

8 Here with a Loaf of Bread beneath the bough,
A Flask of Wine, a Book of Verse—and Thou
   Beside me singing in the Wilderness—
And Wilderness is Paradise enow.
11

9 They say the Lion and the Lizard keep
The Courts where Jamshyd gloried and drank deep.
17

10 I sometimes think that never blows so red
The Rose as where some buried Caesar bled.
18

1 Lo! some we loved, the loveliest and best
That Time and Fate of all their Vintage prest,
Have drunk their Cup a Round or two before,
And one by one crept silently to Rest.
21

2 Ah, make the most of what we yet may spend,
Before we too into the Dust descend;
Dust into Dust, and under Dust, to lie,
Sans Wine, sans Song, sans Singer, and—sans End!
23

3 Myself when young did eagerly frequent
Doctor and Saint, and heard great argument
About it and about: but evermore
Came out by the same Door as in I went.
27

4 Ah, fill the Cup:—what boots it to repeat
How Time is slipping underneath our Feet:
Unborn TO-MORROW, and dead YESTERDAY,
Why fret about them if TO-DAY be sweet!
37

5 'Tis all a Chequer-board of Nights and Days
Where Destiny with Men for Pieces plays:
Hither and thither moves, and mates, and slays,
And one by one back in the Closet lays.
49

6 The Ball no question makes of Ayes and Noes,
But Here or There as strikes the Player goes;
And He that toss'd you down into the Field,
He knows about it all—HE knows—HE knows!
70 (edn.4)

7 The Moving Finger writes; and, having writ,
Moves on: *nor all thy Piety* nor Wit
Shall lure it back to cancel half a Line,
Nor all thy Tears wash out a Word of it.
51

8 Sold my Reputation for a Song.
93 (edn.4)

9 I often wonder what the Vintners buy
One half so precious as the Goods they sell.
71

1 Ah Love! could thou and I with Fate conspire
To grasp this sorry Scheme of Things entire,
Would not we shatter it to bits—and then
Re-mould it nearer to the Heart's Desire!
73

F. SCOTT FITZGERALD 1896–1940

2 In the real dark night of the soul it is always three o'clock in the morning.
The Crack-Up, ed. E. Wilson (1945), John Peale Bishop, *The Hours*. The phrase 'dark night of the soul' was used as the Spanish title of a work by St. John of the Cross known in English as *The Ascent of Mount Carmel* (1578–80)

3 Let me tell you about the very rich. They are different from you and me.
The Rich Boy. 'Notebooks E' in ***The Crack-Up*** records Ernest Hemingway's rejoinder: 'Yes, they have more money.'

ROBERT FITZSIMMONS 1862–1917

4 The bigger they come, the harder they fall.
Said before his fight with Jefferies in San Francisco, 9 June 1899

JAMES ELROY FLECKER 1884–1915

5 For lust of knowing what should not be known,
We take the Golden Road to Samarkand.
Hassan (1922), V. ii

6 I have seen old ships sail like swans asleep
Beyond that village which men still call Tyre.
The Old Ships (1915)

7 Painted the mid-sea blue or the shore-sea green,
Still patterned with the vine and grapes in gold.

ANDREW FLETCHER OF SALTOUN 1655–1716

8 I knew a very wise man so much of Sir Chr—'s sentiment, that he believed if a man were permitted to make all the ballads, he need not care who should make the laws of a nation.
***Political Works*. Letter to the Marquis of Montrose, and Others** (1703)

JOHN FLETCHER 1579–1625

See also under BEAUMONT

1 Whistle and she'll come to you.
Wit Without Money, IV.iv

2 Charity and beating begins at home.
V.ii

JEAN-PIERRE CLARIS DE FLORIAN 1755–1794

3 *Plaisir d'amour ne dure qu'un moment,*
Chagrin d'amour dure toute la vie.
Love's pleasure lasts but a moment; love's sorrow lasts all through life.
Celestine

JOHN FLORIO 1553?–1625

4 England is the paradise of women, the purgatory of men, and the hell of horses.
Second Frutes (1591)

DR F.J. FOAKES JACKSON 1855–1941

5 It's no use trying to be *clever*—we are all clever here; just try to be *kind*—a little kind.
Said to a recently elected young don at Jesus College, Cambridge. Oral tradition. Noted in A.C. Benson's Commonplace Book

MARSHAL FOCH 1851–1929

6 *Mon centre cède, ma droite recule, situation excellente. J'attaque!*
My centre is giving way, my right is in retreat; situation excellent. I shall attack.
Aston, *Biography of Foch* (1929), ch.13

SAMUEL FOOTE 1720–1777

7 The grand Panjandrum himself, with the little round button at top.
See *Quarterly Review* (1854), 95.516.

8 He is not only dull in himself, but the cause of dullness in others.
Boswell, *Life of Johnson*, ed. Powell, IV, p.178. See Shakespeare, *Henry IV, Pt.2*, I.ii.

MISS C.F. FORBES 1817–1911

1 The sense of being well-dressed gives a feeling of inward tranquillity which religion is powerless to bestow.
Emerson, *Social Aims*

HENRY FORD 1863–1947

2 History is more or less bunk.
Chicago Tribune, 25 May 1916

HOWELL FORGY 1908–

3 Praise the Lord, and pass the ammunition.
Attr. when a Naval Lt., at Pearl Harbor, 7 Dec. 1941

E.M. FORSTER 1879–1970

4 Everything must be like something, so what is this like?
Abinger Harvest (1936), **Our Diversions,** 3 'The Doll Souse', first published 1924

5 Yes—oh dear yes—the novel tells a story.
Aspects of the Novel, ch.2

6 All men are equal—all men, that is to say, who possess umbrellas.
Howard's End, ch.6

7 Personal relations are the important thing for ever and ever, and not this outer life of telegrams and anger.
ch.19

8 Only connect!
ch.22

9 I hate the idea of causes, and if I had to choose between betraying my country and betraying my friend, I hope I should have the guts to betray my country.
Two Cheers for Democracy, pt.2. **What I Believe**

CHARLES FOURIER 1772–1837

10 *L'extension des privilèges des femmes est le principe général de tous progrès sociaux.*

The extension of women's rights is the basic principle of all social progress.
Théorie des Quatre Mouvements (1808), II.iv

ANATOLE FRANCE 1844–1924

1 *La majestueuse égalité des lois, qui interdit au riche comme au pauvre de coucher sous les ponts, de mendier dans les rues et de voler du pain.*
The majestic egalitarianism of the law, which forbids rich and poor alike to sleep under bridges, to beg in the streets, and to steal bread.
Le Lys Rouge (1894), ch.7

FRANCIS I 1494–1547

2 *De toutes choses ne m'est demeuré que l'honneur et la vie qui est saulve.*
Of all I had, only honour and life have been spared.
Letter to his mother after his defeat at Pavia, 1525. *Collection des Documents Inédits sur l'Histoire de France* (1847), I, 129. Usually cited as '*Tout est perdu fors l'honneur*' (All is lost save honour).

ST. FRANCIS DE SALES 1567–1622

3 *Ce sont les grans feux qui s'enflamment au vent, mays les petitz s'esteignent si on ne les y porte a couvert.*
Big fires flare up in a wind, but little ones are blown out unless they are carried in under cover.
Introduction à la vie dévote (1609), pt.III, ch.34

BENJAMIN FRANKLIN 1706–1790

4 Remember, that time is money.
Advice to Young Tradesman (1748)

5 No nation was ever ruined by trade.
***Essays.* Thoughts on Commercial Subjects**

6 The having made a young girl miserable may give you frequent bitter reflection; none of which can attend the making of an old woman happy.
On the Choice of a Mistress (i.e. wife)

1 A little neglect may breed mischief, ... for want of a nail, the shoe was lost; for want of a shoe the horse was lost; and for want of a horse the rider was lost.
Maxims ... Prefixed to ***Poor Richard's Almanack*** (1758)

2 We must indeed all hang together, or, most assuredly, we shall all hang separately.
Remark to John Hancock, at the Signing of the Declaration of Independence, 4 July 1776

3 Man is a tool-making animal.
Boswell, *Life of Johnson*, 7 Apr. 1778

4 Here Skugg
Lies snug
As a bug
In a rug.
Letter to Georgiana Shipley on the death of her squirrel, 26 Sept. 1772

5 There never was a good war, or a bad peace.
Letter to Quincy, 11 Sept. 1783

6 But in this world nothing can be said to be certain, except death and taxes.
Letter to Jean Baptiste Le Roy, 13 Nov. 1789

7 What is the use of a new-born child?
When asked what was the use of a new invention. J. Parton, *Life and Times of Benjamin Franklin* (1864), pt.IV, ch.17

8 *Ça ira.*
That will go its way.
Oral trad. Remark made in Paris, 1776–7, on the American War of Independence. Taken up in the French Revolution and used as the refrain of the song to the tune '*Carillon national*' by 1790.

E.A. FREEMAN 1823–1892

9 History is past politics, and politics is present history.
Methods of Historical Study (1886), p.44

JOHN HOOKHAM FRERE 1769–1846

10 The feather'd race with pinions skim the air—
Not so the mackerel, and still less the bear!
Progress of Man, l.34

ROBERT FROST 1874–1963

1 I have looked down the saddest city lane.
I have passed by the watchman on his beat
And dropped my eyes, unwilling to explain.
Acquainted with the Night

2 'Home is the place where, when you have to go there,
They have to take you in'.
'I should have called it
Something you somehow haven't to deserve.'
The Death of the Hired Man

3 Forgive, O Lord, my little jokes on Thee
And I'll forgive Thy great big one on me.
In the clearing, **Cluster of Faith**

4 Good fences make good neighbours.
North of Boston (1914). **Mending Wall**

5 Two roads diverged in a wood, and I—
I took the one less traveled by,
And that has made all the difference.
The Road Not Taken

6 Whoever it is that leaves him out so late,
When other creatures have gone to stall and bin,
Ought to be told to come and take him in.
The Runaway

7 The woods are lovely, dark, and deep,
But I have promises to keep,
And miles to go before I sleep,
And miles to go before I sleep.
Stopping by Woods on a Snowy Evening

8 To err is human, not to, animal.
The White-tailed Hornet

9 Writing free verse is like playing tennis with the net down.
Address at Milton Academy, Milton, Mass., 17 May 1935

10 Poetry is what gets lost in translation.
Attr.

J.A. FROUDE 1818–1894

11 Wild animals never kill for sport. Man is the only one

to whom the torture and death of his fellow-creatures is amusing in itself.
Oceana (1886), ch.5

CHRISTOPHER FRY 1907–

1 I sometimes think
His critical judgement is so exquisite
It leaves us nothing to admire except his opinion.
The Dark is Light Enough (1954), Act II

2 What, after all,
Is a halo? It's only one more thing to keep clean.
The Lady's Not For Burning (1948), Act I

3 Using words
That are only fit for the Bible.
Act II

4 The moon is nothing
But a circumambulating aphrodisiac
Divinely subsidized to provoke the world
Into a rising birth-rate.
Act III

5 A spade is never so merely a spade as the word
Spade would imply.
Venus Observed (1950), II.i

THOMAS FULLER 1608–1661

6 Worldly wealth he cared not for, desiring only to make both ends meet. [Of Edmund Grindall.]
The History of the Worthies of England (1662), **Worthies of Cumberland**

7 Light (God's eldest daughter) is a principal beauty in building.
The Holy State and the Profane State (1642), bk.iii, ch.7. **Of Building**

8 Anger is one of the sinews of the soul.
ch.8. **Of Anger**

ROSE FYLEMAN 1877–1957

9 There are fairies at the bottom of our garden.
Fairies and Chimneys

REVD. THOMAS GAISFORD 1779–1855

1 Nor can I do better, in conclusion, than impress upon you the study of Greek literature, which not only elevates above the vulgar herd, but leads not infrequently to positions of considerable emolument.
Christmas Day Sermon in the Cathedral, Oxford. Revd. W. Tuckwell, *Reminiscences of Oxford* (2nd edn., 1907), p.124

HUGH GAITSKELL 1906–1963

2 There are some of us who will fight and fight and fight again to save the party we love.
Speech, Labour Party Conference, Scarborough, 5 Oct. 1960

J.K. GALBRAITH 1908–

3 In the affluent society no useful distinction can be made between luxuries and necessaries.
The Affluent Society, ch.21.iv

GALILEO GALILEI 1564–1642

4 *Eppur si muove.*
But it does move.
Attr. to Galileo after his recantation in 1632. The earliest apppearance of the phrase is perhaps in Baretti, *Italian Library* (1757), p.52

GRETA GARBO 1905–

5 I want to be alone.
Grand Hotel (1932), script by William A. Drake.
The phrase had frequently been attributed to Garbo before being used in the film; she seems in fact to have said on various occasions (off screen) 'I want to be left alone' and 'Why don't they leave me alone'.

DAVID GARRICK 1717–1779

6 Kitty, a fair, but frozen maid,
Kindled a flame I still deplore;
The hood-wink'd boy I call'd in aid,
Much of his near approach afraid.
So fatal to my suit before.
A Riddle. *Lady's Magazine*, June 1762

1 Of that there is no manner of doubt—
No probable, possible shadow of doubt—
No possible doubt whatever.

2 Take a pair of sparkling eyes,
Hidden, ever and anon,
In a merciful eclipse.
II

3 When every one is somebodee,
Then no one's anybody.

4 I see no objection to stoutness, in moderation.
Iolanthe (1882), I

5 The Law is the true embodiment
Of everything that's excellent.
It has no kind of fault or flaw,
And I, my Lords, embody the Law.

6 I often think it's comical
How Nature always does contrive
That every boy and every gal,
That's born into the world alive,
Is either a little Liberal,
Or else a little Conservative!
II

7 When in that House MPs divide,
If they've a brain and cerebellum too,
They have to leave that brain outside,
And vote just as their leaders tell 'em to.

8 The House of Peers, throughout the war,
Did nothing in particular,
And did it very well.

9 When you're lying awake with a dismal headache, and repose is taboo'd by anxiety,
I conceive you may use any language you choose to indulge in, without impropriety.

10 A wandering minstrel I—
A thing of shreds and patches,
Of ballads, songs and snatches,
And dreamy lullaby!
The Mikado (1885), I

1 I can trace my ancestry back to a protoplasmal primordial atomic globule. Consequently, my family pride is something in-conceivable.

2 It revolts me, but I do it!

3 I accept refreshment at any hands, however lowly.

4 I've got a little list—I've got a little list
Of society offenders who might well be under ground
And who never would be missed!

5 Three little maids who, all unwary,
Come from a ladies' seminary.

6 Awaiting the sensation of a short, sharp shock,
From a cheap and chippy chopper on a big black block.

7 My object all sublime
I shall achieve in time—
To let the punishment fit the crime.
II

8 Something lingering, with boiling oil in it, I fancy.

9 Merely corroborative detail, intended to give artistic verisimilitude to an otherwise bald and unconvincing narrative.

10 The flowers that bloom in the spring,
Tra la,
Have nothing to do with the case.

11 On a tree by a river a little tom-tit
Sang 'Willow, titwillow, titwillow!'

12 Though the Philistines may jostle, you will rank as an apostle in the high aesthetic band,
If you walk down Piccadilly with a poppy or a lily in your medieval hand.
Patience (1881), I

13 A greenery-yallery, Grosvenor Gallery,
Foot-in-the-grave young man!

14 And I'm never, never sick at sea!
What, never?
No, never!
What, *never*?
Hardly ever!
H.M.S. Pinafore (1878), I

1 I never use a big, big D—

2 When I was a lad I served a term
As office boy to an Attorney's firm.

3 Stick close to your desks and never go to sea,
And you all may be Rulers of the Queen's Navee!

4 I am the very model of a modern Major-General.
The Pirates of Penzance (1879), I

5 When constabulary duty's to be done,
A policeman's lot is not a happy one.
II

6 He combines the manners of a Marquis with the morals of a Methodist.
Ruddigore (1887), I

7 When he's excited he uses language that would make your hair curl.

8 Some word that teems with hidden meaning—like Basingstoke.
II

9 She may very well pass for forty-three
In the dusk with a light behind her!
Trial by Jury (1875)

10 An accepted wit has but to say 'Pass the mustard', and they roar their ribs out!
The Yeoman of the Guard (1888), II

HERMANN GOERING 1893–1946

11 Guns will make us powerful; butter will only make us fat.
Radio Broadcast, summer of 1936, often misquoted as 'Guns before butter'

JOHANN WOLFGANG VON GOETHE 1749–1832

12 *Ich kenne mich auch nicht und Gott soll mich auch davor behüten.*
I do not know myself, and God forbid that I should.
Conversations with Eckermann, 10 Apr. 1829. See Anon.

1 *Entbehren sollst Du! sollst entbehren!*
Das ist der ewige Gesang.
Deny yourself! You must deny yourself!
That is the song that never ends.
Faust, pt.1 (1808). **Studierzimmer**

2 *Meine Ruh' ist hin,*
Mein Herz ist schwer.
My peace is gone,
My heart is heavy.
Gretchen am Spinnrad

3 *Die Tat ist alles, nichts der Ruhm.*
The deed is all, and not the glory.
pt.ii (1832). **Hochgebirg**

4 *Kennst du das Land, wo die Zitronen blühn?*
Know you the land where the lemon-trees bloom?
Wilhelm Meisters Lehrjahre (1795–6), III.i

5 *Kennst du es wohl?*
Dahin! Dahin!
Möcht ich mit dir, o mein Geliebter, ziehn!
Do you know it well? There, there, I would go, O my beloved, with thee!

OLIVER GOLDSMITH 1730–1774

6 Ill fares the land, to hast'ning ills a prey,
Where wealth accumulates, and men decay.
The Deserted Village (1770), l.51

7 But a bold peasantry, their country's pride,
When once destroy'd, can never be supplied.
l.55

8 The loud laugh that spoke the vacant mind.
l.122. See Catullus.

9 Truth from his lips prevail'd with double sway,
And fools, who came to scoff, remain'd to pray.
l.179

10 And still they gaz'd, and still the wonder grew,
That one small head could carry all he knew.
l.215

1 Man wants but little here below,
Nor wants that little long.
Edwin and Angelina, or the Hermit (1766). See E. Young.

2 The man recover'd of the bite,
The dog it was that died.
Elegy on the Death of a Mad Dog

3 Let schoolmasters puzzle their brain,
With grammar, and nonsense, and learning,
Good liquor, I stoutly maintain,
Gives genius a better discerning.
She Stoops to Conquer, I.i, song

4 When lovely woman stoops to folly
And finds too late that men betray,
What charm can soothe her melancholy,
What art can wash her guilt away?
Song from *The Vicar of Wakefield*, ch.29

5 This is Liberty-Hall, gentlemen.
She Stoops to Conquer (1773), II

SAMUEL GOLDWYN 1882–1974

6 You can include me out.
See Zierold, *The Hollywood Tycoons* (1969), ch.3

EDMUND GOSSE 1849–1928

7 A sheep in sheep's clothing.
Of T. Sturge Moore, c.1906. Ferris Greenslet, *Under the Bridge*, ch.12. Also attr. Winston Churchill of Clement Attlee.

CLEMENTINA STIRLING GRAHAM 1782–1877

8 The best way to get the better of temptation is just to yield to it.
Mystifications (1859), Soirée at Mrs Russel's

HARRY GRAHAM 1874–1936

9 'There's been an accident!' they said,
'Your servant's cut in half; he's dead!'
'Indeed!' said Mr Jones, 'and please
Send me the half that's got my keys.'
Ruthless Rhymes for Heartless Homes. Mr. Jones

1 Billy, in one of his nice new sashes,
Fell in the fire and was burnt to ashes;
Now, although the room grows chilly,
I haven't the heart to poke poor Billy.
Tender-Heartedness

KENNETH GRAHAME 1859–1932

2 Believe me, my young friend, there is *nothing*—absolutely nothing—half so much worth doing as simply messing about in boats.
The Wind in the Willows (1908), ch.1

THOMAS GRAY 1716–1771

3 Ruin seize thee, ruthless King!
Confusion on thy banners wait.
The Bard (1757), I.i

4 Youth on the prow, and Pleasure at the helm.
II.ii

5 The curfew tolls the knell of parting day,
The lowing herd wind slowly o'er the lea,
The ploughman homeward plods his weary way,
And leaves the world to darkness and to me.
Elegy in a Country Churchyard (1742–50), 1

6 Beneath those rugged elms, that yew-tree's shade,
Where heaves the turf in many a mouldering heap,
Each in his narrow cell for ever laid,
The rude forefathers of the hamlet sleep.

7 The short and simple annals of the poor.
8

8 The paths of glory lead but to the grave.
9

9 *Full* many a flower is born to blush unseen,
And waste its sweetness on the desert air.
14

10 Some mute inglorious Milton here may rest.
15

11 Far from the madding crowd's ignoble strife.
19

1 They hear a voice in every wind,
And snatch a fearful joy.
Ode on a Distant Prospect of Eton College (1747), l.39

2 Alas, regardless of their doom,
The little victims play!
l.51

3 No more; where ignorance is bliss,
'Tis folly to be wise.
l.99

GRAHAM GREENE 1904–

4 Against the beautiful and the clever and the successful, one can wage a pitiless war, but not against the unattractive.
The Heart of the Matter (1948), bk.1, pt.1, ch.2

5 Any victim demands allegiance.
bk.3, pt.1, ch.1

6 I am a reporter; God exists only for leader-writers.
The Quiet American (1955), pt.I, ch.iv.2

POPE GREGORY THE GREAT c.540–604

7 *Non Angli sed Angeli.*
Not Angles but Angels.
See Bede, *Historia Ecclesiastica*, II.i

STEPHEN GRELLET 1773–1855

8 I expect to pass through this world but once; any good thing therefore that I can do, or any kindness that I can show to any fellow-creature, let me do it now; let me not defer or neglect it, for I shall not pass this way again.
Attr. See John o' London's *Treasure Trove* (1925). Many other claimants to authorship.

JULIAN GRENFELL 1888–1915

9 The naked earth is warm with Spring.
***Into Battle**, The Times*, 27 May 1915

10 And he is deaf, who will not fight
And who dies fighting has increase.

LORD GREY OF FALLODON 1863–1933

1 The lamps are going out all over Europe; we shall not see them lit again in our lifetime.
3 Aug. 1914. ***Twenty-Five Years, 1892–1916*** (1925), vol.ii, ch.18

EARL HAIG 1861–1928

2 Every position must be held to the last man: there must be no retirement. With our backs to the wall, and believing in the justice of our cause, each one of us must fight on to the end.
Order to the British Troops, 12 Apr. 1918

NATHAN HALE 1755–1776

3 I only regret that I have but one life to lose for my country.
Speech before being executed as a spy by the British, 22 Sept. 1776. See Addison.

MRS. SARAH JOSEPHA HALE 1788–1879

4 Mary had a little lamb,
  Its fleece was white as snow,
And everywhere that Mary went
  The lamb was sure to go.
Poems for Our Children (1830). **Mary's Little Lamb**

GEORGE SAVILE, MARQUIS OF HALIFAX 1633–1695

5 When the People contend for their Liberty, they seldom get anything by their Victory but new masters.
Political, Moral, and Miscellaneous Thoughts and Reflections (1750). **Of Prerogative, Power and Liberty**

6 Men are not hanged for stealing horses, but that horses may not be stolen.
Of Punishment

7 He [Halifax] had said he had known many kicked down stairs, but he never knew any kicked up stairs before.
Burnet, *Original Memoirs* (c.1697)

FRIEDRICH HALM 1806–1871

1 *Zwei Seelen und ein Gedanke,*
Zwei Herzen und ein Schlag!
Two souls with but a single thought,
  Two hearts that beat as one.
Der Sohn der Wildnis (1842), Act II *ad fin.* Trans. by Maria Lovell in *Ingomar the Barbarian*

EDMOND HARAUCOURT 1856–1941

2 *Partir c'est mourir un peu.*
To go away is to die a little.
Seul (1891), **Rondel de l'Adieu**

THOMAS HARDY 1840–1928

3 When the Present has latched its postern behind my tremulous stay,
  And the May month flaps its glad green leaves like wings,
Delicate-filmed as new-spun silk, will the neighbours say,
  'He was a man who used to notice such things'?
Afterwards

4 I am the family face;
Flesh perishes, I live on.
Heredity

5 Only a man harrowing clods
  In a slow silent walk.
In Time of 'The Breaking of Nations'

6 Yonder a maid and her wight
  Come whispering by:
War's annals will cloud into night
  Ere their story die.

7 'Yes: that's how we dress when we're ruined,' said she.
The Ruined Maid

8 This is the weather the cuckoo likes,
  And so do I.
Weathers

1 When I set out for Lyonnesse,
A hundred miles away.
When I Set Out For Lyonesse

2 When I came back from Lyonnesse
With magic in my eyes!

MAURICE EVAN HARE 1886–1967

3 There once was a man who said, 'Damn!
It is borne in upon me I am
An engine that moves
In predestinate grooves,
I'm not even a bus, I'm a tram.'
Written, as above, at St. John's College, Oxford, in 1905

SIR JOHN HARINGTON 1561–1612

4 Treason doth never prosper, what's the reason?
For if it prosper, none dare call it treason.
Epigrams (1618), bk.iv, No.5. **Of Treason**

JOEL CHANDLER HARRIS 1848–1908

5 Tar-baby ain't sayin' nuthin', en Brer Fox, he lay low.
Uncle Remus. Legends of the Old Plantation (1881), ch.2. **Tar-Baby Story**

6 Bred en bawn in a brier-patch!
ch.4

BRET HARTE 1836–1902

7 If, of all words of tongue and pen,
The saddest are, 'It might have been,'
More sad are these we daily see:
'It is, but hadn't ought to be!'
Mrs. Judge Jenkins. See Whittier.

8 We are ruined by Chinese cheap labour.
Plain Language from Truthful James (1870)

9 And he smiled a kind of sickly smile, and curled up on the floor,
And the subsequent proceedings interested him no more.
The Society upon the Stanislaus

L.P. HARTLEY 1895–1972

1 The past is a foreign country: they do things differently there.
The Go-Between, Prologue

M. LOUISE HASKINS 1875–1957

2 And I said to the man who stood at the gate of the year: 'Give me a light that I may tread safely into the unknown'. And he replied: 'Go out into the darkness and put your hand into the hand of God. That shall be to you better than light and safer than a known way.'
The Desert (c.1908), Introduction. Quoted by King George VI in a Christmas Broadcast, 25 Dec. 1939, after the lines had been quoted in 'Points from Letters' in *The Times* a few months earlier

REVD. R.S. HAWKER 1803–1875

3 And have they fixed the where and when?
And shall Trelawny die?
Here's twenty thousand Cornish men
Will know the reason why!
Song of the Western Men. The last three lines have existed since the imprisonment by James II, 1688, of the seven Bishops, including Trelawny, Bishop of Bristol.

IAN HAY 1876–1952

4 What do you mean, funny? Funny-peculiar or funny-ha-ha?
The Housemaster (1936), Act III

J. MILTON HAYES 1884–1940

5 There's a one-eyed yellow idol to the north of Khatmandu,
There's a little marble cross below the town;
There's a broken-hearted woman tends the grave of Mad Carew
And the Yellow God forever gazes down.
The Green Eye of the Yellow God (1911)

WILLIAM HAZLITT 1778–1830

6 His worst is better than any other person's best.
English Literature, ch.xiv. **Sir Walter Scott**

1 He [Coleridge] talked on for ever; and you wished him to talk on for ever.
Lectures on the English Poets. Lecture viii, **On the Living Poets**

2 One of the pleasantest things in the world is going on a journey; but I like to go by myself.
Table Talk, xix. **On Going a Journey**

3 The English (it must be owned) are rather a foul-mouthed nation.
xxii. **On Criticism**

4 We can scarcely hate any one that we know.

5 No young man believes he shall ever die.
Uncollected Essays, xviii. **On the Feeling of Immortality in Youth**

EDWARD HEATH 1916–

6 It is the unpleasant and unacceptable face of capitalism but one should not suggest that the whole of British industry consists of practices of this kind.
House of Commons, 15 May 1973

BISHOP REGINALD HEBER 1783–1826

7 Though every prospect pleases,
And only man is vile.
From Greenland's Icy Mountains

G.W.F. HEGEL 1770–1831

8 What experience and history teach is this—that people and governments never have learned anything from history, or acted on principles deduced from it.
Philosophy of History. Introduction

HEINRICH HEINE 1797–1856

9 *Dort, wo man Bücher*
Verbrennt, verbrennt man auch am Ende Menschen.
Wherever books are burned, men also, in the end, are burned.
Almansor (1820–1), l.245

10 *Sie hatten sich beide so herzlich lieb,*
Spitzbübin war sie, er war ein Dieb.

They loved each other beyond belief—
She was a strumpet, he was a thief.

Neue Gedichte (1844), **Romanzen,** I. 'Ein Weib'. Trans. Louis Untermeyer (1938)

1 *Dieu me pardonnera. C'est son métier.*
God will pardon me. It is His trade.

On his deathbed. Attr. Edmond and Charles Goncourt, *Journal*, 23 Feb. 1863

LILLIAN HELLMAN 1905–

2 I cannot and will not cut my conscience to fit this year's fashions.

Letter to the Honourable John S. Wood, Chairman of the House Committee on un-American Activities, 19 May 1952

C.-A. HELVÉTIUS 1715–1771

3 *L'éducation nous faisait ce que nous sommes.*
Education made us what we are.

Discours XXX, ch.30

MRS. HEMANS 1793–1835

4 The boy stood on the burning deck
Whence all but he had fled.

Casabianca

5 The stately homes of England,
How beautiful they stand!

The Homes of England

ERNEST HEMINGWAY 1898–1961

6 But did thee feel the earth move?

For Whom the Bell Tolls (1940), ch.13

W.E. HENLEY 1849–1903

7 Out of the night that covers me,
Black as the Pit from pole to pole,
I thank whatever gods may be
For my unconquerable soul.

Echoes (1888), iv. **Invictus. In Mem. R.T.H.B.**

8 Under the bludgeonings of chance
My head is bloody, but unbowed.

1 I am the master of my fate:
I am the captain of my soul.

2 Madam Life's a piece in bloom
Death goes dogging everywhere;
She's the tenant of the room,
He's the ruffian on the stair.
ix. **To W.R.**

3 What have I done for you,
England, my England?
What is there I would not do,
England, my own?
For England's Sake (1900), iii. **Pro Rege Nostro**

HENRI IV 1553–1610

4 *Paris vaut bien une messe.*
Paris is well worth a mass.
Attr. either to Henri IV or to his minister Sully, in conversation with Henri. *Caquets de l'Accouchée*, 1622

5 The wisest fool in Christendom.
Of James I of England. Also attr. Sully.

PATRICK HENRY 1736–1799

6 Caesar had his Brutus—Charles the First, his Cromwell—and George the Third—('Treason,' cried the Speaker) ... *may profit by their example*. If *this* be treason, make the most of it.
Speech in the Virginia Convention, May 1765. Wirt, *Patrick Henry* (1818), p.65

7 Give me liberty, or give me death!
20 Mar. 1775. Wirt, *Patrick Henry* (1818), p.123

KING HENRY II 1133–1189

8 Will no one revenge me of the injuries I have sustained from one turbulent priest?
Of St. Thomas Becket (Dec. 1170). Oral trad.

HERACLITUS fl. 513 B.C.

9 Everything flows and nothing stays.
Plato, *Cratylus*, 402a

1 You can't step twice into the same river.

A.P. HERBERT 1890–1971

2 Let's find out what everyone is doing,
And then stop everyone from doing it.
Let's Stop Somebody

GEORGE HERBERT 1593–1633

3 He that makes a good war makes a good peace.
***Outlandish Proverbs*, 420**

4 He that lives in hope danceth without musick.
1006

5 I struck the board, and cried, 'No more;
I will abroad.'
***The Temple* (1622). The Collar**

6 But as I rav'd and grew more fierce and wild
At every word,
Methought I heard one calling, 'Child';
And I replied, 'My Lord.'

7 A servant with this clause
Makes drudgery divine;
Who sweeps a room as for Thy laws
Makes that and th' action fine.
The Elixir

8 Who would have thought my shrivel'd heart
Could have recovered greenness?
The Flower

9 Love bade me welcome; yet my soul drew back,
Guilty of dust and sin.
Love

10 When boyes go first to bed,
They step into their voluntarie graves.
Mortification

11 When God at first made man,
Having a glass of blessings standing by;
Let us (said he) pour on him all we can.
The Pulley

1 I would not use a friend as I use Thee.
Unkindness

ROBERT HERRICK 1591–1674

2 Cherry-ripe, ripe, ripe, I cry,
Full and fair ones; come and buy.
Hesperides (1648). **Cherry-Ripe**

3 A sweet disorder in the dress
Kindles in clothes a wantonness.
Delight in Disorder

4 More discontents I never had
Since I was born, than here;
Where I have been, and still am sad,
In this dull Devonshire.
Discontents in Devon

5 Joan as my Lady is as good i' th' dark.
No Difference i' th' Dark

6 Fain would I kiss my Julia's dainty leg,
Which is as white and hairless as an egg.
On Julia's Legs

7 Fair daffodils, we weep to see
You haste away so soon.
To Daffodils

8 Gather ye rosebuds while ye may,
Old Time is still a-flying.
To the Virgins, to Make Much of Time

9 Whenas in silks my Julia goes,
Then, then (methinks) how sweetly flows
That liquefaction of her clothes.
Upon Julia's Clothes

JAMES HERVEY 1714–1758

10 E'en crosses from his sov'reign hand
Are blessings in disguise.
Reflections on a Flower-Garden

LORD HEWART 1870–1943

11 It is not merely of some importance but is of fundamental importance that justice should not only be done,

but should manifestly and undoubtedly be seen to be done.

Rex v. Sussex Justices, 9 Nov. 1923 (King's Bench Reports, 1924, vol.i, p.259)

W.E. HICKSON 1803–1870

1 If at first you don't succeed,
Try, try again.

Try and Try Again

JOE HILL 1879–1914

2 You'll get pie in the sky when you die (That's a lie.)

The Preacher and the Slave

REVD. ROWLAND HILL 1744–1833

3 He did not see any reason why the devil should have all the good tunes.

E.W. Broome, *Rev. Rowland Hill*, vii

HILLEL 'THE ELDER' ?70 B.C.–A.D. 10?

4 If I am not for myself who is for me; and being for my own self what am I? If not now when?

Pirque Aboth. See *Sayings of the Jewish Fathers*, ed. C. Taylor (1877), i. 15.

HIPPOCRATES 5th cent. B.C.

5 The life so short, the craft so long to learn.

Aphorisms, I.i. Trans. Chaucer, *Parliament of Fowls*, l.1. Often quoted in Latin as *Ars longa, vita brevis*. See Seneca, *De Brevitate Vitae* 1.

ADOLF HITLER 1889–1945

6 I go the way that Providence dictates with the assurance of a sleepwalker.

See Alan Bullock, *Hitler, A Study in Tyranny* (1952), ch.7, pt.i.

7 My patience is now at an end.

Speech, 26 Sept. 1938

THOMAS HOBBES 1588–1679

8 The life of man, solitary, poor, nasty, brutish, and short.

Leviathan (1651), pt.i, ch.13

1 I am about to take my last voyage, a great leap in the dark.
Last words. Watkins, *Anecdotes of Men of Learning*

RALPH HODGSON 1871–1962

2 'Twould ring the bells of Heaven
The wildest peal for years,
If Parson lost his senses
And people came to theirs,
And he and they together
Knelt down with angry prayers
For tamed and shabby tigers
And dancing dogs and bears,
And wretched, blind, pit ponies,
And little hunted hares.
The Bells of Heaven

3 Time, you old gypsy man,
  Will you not stay,
Put up your caravan
  Just for one day?
Time, You Old Gypsy Man

HEINRICH HOFFMANN 1809–1894

4 Look at little Johnny there,
Little Johnny Head-In-Air!
Struwwelpeter (1845, translated 1848). **Johnny Head-In-Air**

5 Anything to me is sweeter
Than to see Shock-headed Peter.
Shock-Headed Peter

JAMES HOGG 1770–1835

6 Where the pools are bright and deep
Where the gray trout lies asleep,
Up the river and o'er the lea
That's the way for Billy and me.
A Boy's Song

REVD. JOHN H. HOLMES 1879–1964

1 The universe is not hostile, nor yet is it friendly. It is simply indifferent.
A Sensible Man's View of Religion (1933)

OLIVER WENDELL HOLMES 1809–1894

2 Man wants but little drink below,
But wants that little strong.
A Song of other Days. See Goldsmith and E. Young.

3 Man has his will,—but woman has her way.
The Autocrat of the Breakfast-Table (1858), ch.1

JOHN HOME 1722–1808

4 My name is Norval.
Douglas (1756), II.1

THOMAS HOOD 1799–1845

5 It was the time of roses,
  We plucked them as we passed!
Ballad: It Was Not in the Winter

6 Ben Battle was a soldier bold,
  And used to war's alarms:
But a cannon-ball took off his legs,
  So he laid down his arms!
Faithless Nelly Gray

7 They went and told the sexton, and
  The sexton toll'd the bell.
Faithless Sally Brown

8 I remember, I remember,
The house where I was born.
I Remember

9 He never spoils the child and spares the rod,
But spoils the rod and never spares the child.
The Irish Schoolmaster, xii

10 No sun—no moon!
No morn—no noon
No dawn—no dusk—no proper time of day.
No!

1 No fruits, no flowers, no leaves, no birds,—
November!

2 She stood breast high amid the corn.
Ruth

3 Stitch! stitch! stitch!
In poverty, hunger, and dirt.
The Song of the Shirt (1843)

4 Oh! God! that bread should be so dear,
And flesh and blood so cheap!

ELLEN STURGIS HOOPER 1816–1841

5 I slept, and dreamed that life was Beauty;
I woke, and found that life was Duty.
Beauty and Duty (1840)

ANTHONY HOPE 1863–1933

6 His foe was folly and his weapon wit.
Inscription on the tablet to W.S. Gilbert, Victoria Embankment, London (1915)

LAURENCE HOPE (MRS. M.H. NICOLSON) 1865–1904

7 Pale hands I loved beside the Shalimar,
Where are you now? Who lies beneath your spell?
The Garden of Kama and other Love Lyrics from India (1901). **Pale Hands I Loved**

GERARD MANLEY HOPKINS 1844–1889

8 The world is charged with the grandeur of God.
It will flame out like shining from shook foil.
God's Grandeur

9 O the mind, mind has mountains; cliffs of fall
Frightful, sheer, no-man-fathomed. Hold them cheap
May who ne'er hung there.
No worst, there is None

10 Glory be to God for dappled things.
Pied Beauty

1 All things counter, original, spare, strange;
Whatever is fickle, freckled (who knows how?)

2 Margaret, are you grieving
Over Goldengrove unleaving?
Spring and Fall. To a young child

3 It is the blight man was born for,
It is Margaret you mourn for.

4 Look at the stars! look, look up at the skies!
O look at all the fire-folk sitting in the air!
The Starlight Night

5 Thou art indeed just, Lord, if I contend
With thee; but, sir, so what I plead is just.
Why do sinners' ways prosper? and why must
Disappointment all I endeavour end?
Thou Art Indeed Just, Lord

6 I caught this morning morning's minion, kingdom of daylight's dauphin, dapple-dawn-drawn Falcon.
The Windhover

7 My heart in hiding
Stirred for a bird,—the achieve of, the mastery of the thing!

8 I did say yes
O at lightning and lashed rod;
Thou heardst me truer than tongue confess
Thy terror, O Christ, O God.
The Wreck of the Deutschland, I.2

HORACE 65–8 B.C.

9 *Grammatici certant et adhuc sub iudice lis est.*
Scholars dispute, and the case is still before the courts.
Ars Poetica, 78

10 *Parturient montes, nascetur ridiculus mus.*
Mountains will heave in childbirth, and a silly little mouse will be born.
139

11 *In medias res.*
Into the middle of things.
148

1 *Difficilis, querulus, laudator temporis acti*
Se puero.
Tiresome, complaining, a praiser of the times that were when he was a boy.
173

2 *Indignor quandoque bonus dormitat Homerus.*
I'm aggrieved when sometimes even excellent Homer nods.
359

3 *Nullius addictus iurare in verba magistri.*
Not bound to swear allegiance to any master.
Epistles, I.i.14

4 *Si possis recte, si non, quocumque modo rem.*
If possible honestly, if not, somehow, make money.
66

5 *Naturam expellas furca, tamen usque recurret.*
You may drive out nature with a pitchfork, yet she'll be constantly running back.
x.24

6 *Et semel emissum volat irrevocabile verbum.*
And once sent out a word takes wing irrevocably.
xviii.71

7 *Nam tua res agitur, paries cum proximus ardet.*
For it is your business, when the wall next door catches fire.
84

8 *Atque inter silvas Academi quaerere verum.*
And seek for truth in the groves of Academe.
II.ii.45

9 *Nil desperandum Teucro duce et auspice.*
Teucer shall lead and his star shall preside.
No cause for despair, then.
Odes, I. vii.27. Tr. James Michie

10 *O matre pulchra filia pulchrior.*
What a beautiful mother, and yet more beautiful daughter!
xvi.1

1 *Dulce ridentem Lalagen amabo,*
Dulce loquentem.
I will go on loving Lalage, who laughs so sweetly and talks so sweetly.
xxii.23

2 *Eheu fugaces, Postume, Postume,*
Labuntur anni.
Ah me, Postumus, Postumus, the fleeting years are slipping by.
II.xiv.1

3 *Virginibus puerisque canto.*
I sing to virgin girls and boys.
III.i.1

4 *Dulce et decorum est pro patria mori.*
Lovely and honourable it is to die for one's country.
ii.13

5 *Exegi monumentum aere perennius.*
I have executed a memorial longer lasting than bronze.
xxx.1

6 *Non sum qualis eram bonae*
Sub regno Cinarae.
I am not as I was when dear Cinara was my queen.
IV.i.3

7 *Diffugere nives, redeunt iam gramina campis*
Arboribusque comae.
The snows have dispersed, now grass returns to the fields and leaves to the trees.
vii.1

8 *Dulce est desipere in loco.*
It's lovely to be silly at the right moment.
xii.27

BISHOP SAMUEL HORSLEY 1733–1806

9 In *this* country, my Lords, ... the individual subject ... 'has nothing to do with the laws but to obey them.'
House of Lords, 13 Nov. 1795

A.E. HOUSMAN 1859–1936

1 Loveliest of trees, the cherry now
Is hung with bloom along the bough,
And stands about the woodland ride
Wearing white for Eastertide.

Now of my threescore years and ten,
Twenty will not come again.
A Shropshire Lad (1896), 2

2 Up, lad: when the journey's over
There'll be time enough to sleep.
4. **Reveillé**

3 And naked to the hangman's noose
The morning clocks will ring
A neck God made for other use
Than strangling in a string.
9

4 When I was one-and-twenty
I heard a wise man say,
'Give crowns and pounds and guineas
But not your heart away.'
13

5 But I was one-and-twenty,
No use to talk to me.

6 But why should you as well as I
Perish? gaze not in my eyes.
15

7 Oh, when I was in love with you,
Then I was clean and brave,
And miles around the wonder grew
How well did I behave.
18

8 The garland briefer than a girl's.
19. **To an Athlete Dying Young**

9 In summertime on Bredon
The bells they sound so clear.
21. **Bredon Hill**

1 Here of a Sunday morning
My love and I would lie,
And see the coloured counties,
And hear the larks so high
About us in the sky.

2 'Come all to church, good people,'—
Oh, noisy bells, be dumb;
I hear you, I will come.

3 The lads for the girls and the lads for the liquor are there,
And there with the rest are the lads that will never be old.
23

4 They carry back bright to the coiner the mintage of man,
The lads that will die in their glory and never be old.

5 The goal stands up, the keeper
Stands up to keep the goal.
27

6 On Wenlock Edge the wood's in trouble;
His forest fleece the Wrekin heaves;
The gale, it plies the saplings double,
And thick on Severn snow the leaves.
31

7 You and I must keep from shame
In London streets the Shropshire name.
37

8 Into my heart an air that kills
From yon far country blows:
What are those blue remembered hills,
What spires, what farms are those?

That is the land of lost content,
I see it shining plain,
The happy highways where I went
And cannot come again.
40

9 Shot? so quick, so clean an ending?
Oh that was right, lad, that was brave.
44

Think no more; 'tis only thinking
  Lays lads underground.
49

2 With rue my heart is laden
  For golden friends I had,
For many a rose-lipt maiden
  And many a lightfoot lad.
54

3 Malt does more than Milton can
To justify God's ways to man.
62

4 And down in lovely muck I've lain,
Happy till I woke again.

5 The troubles of our proud and angry dust
  Are from eternity, and shall not fail.
Bear them we can, and if we can we must.
  Shoulder the sky, my lad, and drink your ale.
Last Poems (1922), 9

6 I, a stranger and afraid
In a world I never made.
12

7 The Spartans on the sea-wet rock sat down and combed their hair.
25. **The Oracles**

8 Their shoulders held the sky suspended;
  They stood, and earth's foundations stay;
What God abandoned, these defended,
  And saved the sum of things for pay.
37. **Epitaph on an Army of Mercenaries**

9 Tell me not here, it needs not saying,
  What tune the enchantress plays.
40

10 The cuckoo shouts all day at nothing
  In leafy dells alone;
And traveller's joy beguiles in autumn
  Hearts that have lost their own.

11 They say my verse is sad: no wonder;
  Its narrow measure spans

Tears of eternity, and sorrow,
Not mine, but man's.
More Poems (1936), epigraph

1 Crossing alone the nighted ferry
With the one coin for fee,
Whom, on the wharf of Lethe waiting,
Count you to find? Not me.
23

2 Because I liked you better
Than suits a man to say,
It irked you, and I promised
To throw the thought away.
31

3 Here dead lie we because we did not choose
To live and shame the land from which we sprung.
Life, to be sure, is nothing much to lose;
But young men think it is, and we were young.
36

4 But oh, my two troubles they reave me of rest,
The brains in my head and the heart in my breast.
Collected Poems (1939), **Additional Poems,** 17

5 Oh they're taking him to prison for the colour of his hair.
18

6 O suitably attired in leather boots
Head of a traveller, wherefore seeking whom
Whence by what way how purposed art thou come
To this well-nightingaled vicinity?
Fragment of a Greek Tragedy

7 Reader, behold! this monster wild
Has gobbled up the infant child.
The infant child is not aware
It has been eaten by the bear.
Infant Innocence. Laurence Housman, *A.E.H.* (1937), p.256

8 Gentlemen who use MSS as drunkards use lamp-posts—not to light them on their way but to dissimulate their instability.
M. Manilii Astronomicon Liber Primus (ed.) (1903), introduction, I

JULIA WARD HOWE 1819–1910

1 Mine eyes have seen the glory of the coming of the Lord:
He is trampling out the vintage where the grapes of wrath are stored.
Battle Hymn of the American Republic (Dec. 1861)

MARY HOWITT 1799–1888

2 'Will you walk into my parlour?' said a spider to a fly.
The Spider and the Fly

VICTOR HUGO 1802–1885

3 *On résiste à l'invasion des armées; on ne résiste pas à l'invasion des idées.*
A stand can be made against invasion by an army; no stand can be made against invasion by an idea.
***Histoire d'un Crime,* La Chute, X**

G.W. HUNT 1829–1904

4 We don't want to fight, but, by jingo if we do,
We've got the ships, we've got the men, we've got the money too.
We Don't Want to Fight. Music hall song, 1878

LEIGH HUNT 1784–1859

5 Abou Ben Adhem (may his tribe increase!)
Awoke one night from a deep dream of peace.
Abou Ben Adhem and the Angel

6 Say I'm weary, say I'm sad,
Say that health and wealth have missed me,
Say I'm growing old, but add,
Jenny kissed me.
Rondeau

7 Stolen sweets are always sweeter,
Stolen kisses much completer.
Song of Fairies Robbing an Orchard

8 The two divinest things this world has got,
A lovely woman in a rural spot!
The Story of Rimini, iii, l.257

SIR GERALD HURST 1877–1957

1 One of the mysteries of human conduct is why adult men and women all over England are ready to sign documents which they do not read, at the behest of canvassers whom they do not know, binding them to pay for articles which they do not want, with money which they have not got.
Closed Chapters (1942), p.141

FRANCIS HUTCHESON 1694–1746

2 That action is best, which procures the greatest happiness for the greatest numbers.
Inquiry into the Original of our Ideas of Beauty and Virtue (1725). Treatise II. **Concerning Moral Good and Evil,** sec.3, 8

T.H. HUXLEY 1825–1895

3 I took thought, and invented what I conceived to be the appropriate title of 'agnostic'.
Collected Essays, v. **Agnosticism**

4 It is the customary fate of new truths to begin as heresies and to end as superstitions.
Science and Culture, xii. **The Coming of Age of the Origin of Species**

DOLORES IBÁRRURI 'LA PASIONARIA' 1895–

5 It is better to die on your feet than to live on your knees.
Speech in Paris, 3 Sept. 1936

HENRIK IBSEN 1828–1906

6 The minority is always right.
An Enemy of the People (1882), Act 4

7 You should never have your best trousers on when you turn out to fight for freedom and truth.
Act 5

8 Mother, give me the sun.
Ghosts (1881), Act 3

1 I can just see him. With vine leaves in his hair. Flushed and confident.
Hedda Gabler (1890), Act 2

2 Youth will come here and beat on my door, and force its way in.
The Master Builder (1892), Act 1

3 Take the life-lie away from the average man and straight away you take away his happiness.
The Wild Duck (1884), Act 5

ROBERT G. INGERSOLL 1833–1899

4 An honest God is the noblest work of man.
Gods, pt.1, p.2. See Pope, *Essay on Man.*

CHRISTOPHER ISHERWOOD 1904–

5 The common cormorant or shag
Lays eggs inside a paper bag.
The Common Cormorant

6 I am a camera with its shutter open, quite passive, recording, not thinking.
Goodbye to Berlin, **A Berlin Diary**, Autumn 1930

JACOPONE DA TODI c.1230–1306

7 *Stabat Mater dolorosa,*
Iuxta crucem lacrimosa
Dum pendebat Filius.
There was standing the sorrowing Mother, beside the cross weeping while her Son hung upon it.
Stabat Mater dolorosa. Hymn also ascribed to Pope Innocent III and St. Bonaventure

REVD. RICHARD JAGO 1715–1781

8 With leaden foot time creeps along
While Delia is away.
Absence

HENRY JAMES 1843–1916

9 Live all you can; it's a mistake not to.
The Ambassadors (1903), bk.5, ch.2

1 The black and merciless things that are behind the great possessions.
The Ivory Tower (1917), Notes, p.287

2 Cats and monkeys, monkeys and cats—all human life is there.
The Madonna of the Future (1879)

3 So here it is at last, the distinguished thing. [Of his own death.]
Edith Wharton, *A Backward Glance*, ch.14

WILLIAM JAMES 1842–1910

4 The moral flabbiness born of the bitch-goddess SUCCESS.
Letter to H.G. Wells, 11 Sept. 1906

PRESIDENT THOMAS JEFFERSON 1743–1826

5 The tree of liberty must be refreshed from time to time with the blood of patriots and tyrants. It is its natural manure.
Letter to W.S. Smith, 13 Nov. 1787

6 When a man assumes a public trust, he should consider himself as public property.
Remark to Baron von Humboldt, 1807. Rayner, *Life of Jefferson* (1834), p.356

ST. JEROME c.342–420

7 *Venerationi mihi semper fuit non verbosa rusticitas, sed sancta simplicitas.*
I have revered always not crude verbosity, but holy simplicity.
Letters, 57, xii (*Patrologia Latina* xxii, 579)

JEROME K. JEROME 1859–1927

8 Love is like the measles; we all have to go through it.
The Idle Thoughts of an Idle Fellow (1889). **On Being in Love**

9 I like work: it fascinates me. I can sit and look at it for hours. I love to keep it by me: the idea of getting rid of it nearly breaks my heart.
Three Men in a Boat (1889), ch.15

DOUGLAS JERROLD 1803–1857

1 Love's like the measles—all the worse when it comes late in life.
Wit and Opinions of Douglas Jerrold (1859), **A Philanthropist**

HIRAM JOHNSON 1866–1945

2 The first casualty when war comes is truth.
Speech, U.S. Senate, 1917

PHILANDER CHASE JOHNSON 1866–1939

3 Cheer up, the worst is yet to come.
Shooting Stars. See *Everybody's Magazine*, May 1920.

SAMUEL JOHNSON 1709–1784

4 Sir, we are a nest of singing birds.
Of Pembroke College, Oxford. Boswell, *Life of Johnson* (L.F. Powell's revision of G.B. Hill's edition), vol.i, p.75. 1730

5 It is incident to physicians, I am afraid, beyond all other men, to mistake subsequence for consequence.
Review of Dr. Lucas's *Essay on Waters*. p.91n. 25 Nov. 1734

6 They teach the morals of a whore, and the manners of a dancing master.
Of Lord Chesterfield's *Letters*. p.266. 1754

7 Ignorance, madam, pure ignorance.
When asked by a lady why he defined 'pastern' as the 'knee' of a horse, in his Dictionary. p.293. 1755

8 Lexicographer: a writer of dictionaries, a harmless drudge.
p.296. 1755

9 A man, Sir, should keep his friendship in constant repair.
p.300. 1755

10 Being in a ship is being in a jail, with the chance of being drowned.
p.348. 16 Mar. 1759

11 You may scold a carpenter who has made you a bad table, though you cannot make a table. It is not your trade to make tables.
Of literary criticism. p.409. 25 June 1763

1 The noblest prospect which a Scotchman ever sees, is the high road that leads him to England!
p.425. 6 July 1763

2 Young men have more virtue than old men; they have more generous sentiments in every respect.
p.445. 22 July 1763

3 A woman's preaching is like a dog's walking on his hinder legs. It is not done well; but you are surprised to find it done at all.
p.463. 31 July 1763

4 The triumph of hope over experience.
Of a man who remarried immediately after the death of a wife with whom he had been very unhappy. p.128. 1770

5 Read over your compositions, and where ever you meet with a passage which you think is particularly fine, strike it out.
Quoting a college tutor. p.237. 30 Apr. 1773

6 It is wonderful, when a calculation is made, how little the mind is actually employed in the discharge of any profession.
p.344. 6 Apr. 1775

7 Patriotism is the last refuge of a scoundrel.
p.348. 7 Apr. 1775

8 No man but a blockhead ever wrote, except for money.
vol.iii, p.19. 5 Apr. 1776

9 The grand object of travelling is to see the shores of the Mediterranean.
p.36. 11 Apr. 1776

10 If I had no duties, and no reference to futurity, I would spend my life in driving briskly in a post-chaise with a pretty woman.
p.162. 19 Sept. 1777

11 Depend upon it, Sir, when a man knows he is to be hanged in a fortnight, it concentrates his mind wonderfully.
p.167. 19 Sept. 1777

12 When a man is tired of London, he is tired of life; for there is in London all that life can afford.
p.178. 20 Sept. 1777

1 Claret is the liquor for boys; port for men; but he who aspires to be a hero must drink brandy.
p.381. 7 Apr. 1779

2 Worth seeing? yes; but not worth going to see.
Of the Giant's Causeway. p.410. 12 Oct. 1779

3 I have got no further than this: Every man has a right to utter what he thinks truth, and every other man has a right to knock him down for it.
vol.iv, p.12. 1780

4 Resolve not to be poor: whatever you have, spend less. Poverty is a great enemy to human happiness; it certainly destroys liberty, and it makes some virtues impracticable and others extremely difficult.
p.157. 7 Dec. 1782

5 Sir, I look upon every day to be lost, in which I do not make a new acquaintance.
p.374. Nov. 1784

6 A cucumber should be well sliced, and dressed with pepper and vinegar, and then thrown out, as good for nothing.
5 Oct., p.354

7 What is written without effort is in general read without pleasure.
Johnsonian Miscellanies (1897), vol.ii, p.309

8 Every other author may aspire to praise; the lexicographer can only hope to escape reproach.
Dictionary of the English Language (1775), Preface

9 *Net.* Anything reticulated or decussated at equal distances, with interstices between the intersections.

10 *Oats.* A grain, which in England is generally given to horses, but in Scotland supports the people.

11 *Patron.* Commonly a wretch who supports with insolence, and is paid with flattery.

12 Nothing is more hopeless than a scheme of merriment.
The Idler (1758–60), No.58

13 In the character of his Elegy I rejoice to concur with the common reader.
Lives of the English Poets (1779–81). **Gray**

1 Marriage has many pains, but celibacy has no pleasures.
Rasselas (1759), ch.26

2 Here falling houses thunder on your head,
And here a female atheist talks you dead.
London (1738), l.17

3 The stage but echoes back the public voice.
The drama's laws the drama's patrons give,
For we that live to please, must please to live.
Prologue at the Opening of the Theatre in Drury Lane, 1747

4 Let observation with extensive view,
Survey mankind, from China to Peru.
The Vanity of Human Wishes (1749), l.1

5 He left the name, at which the world grew pale,
To point a moral, or adorn a tale. [Charles XII of Sweden.]
l.219

HANNS JOHST 1890–

6 *Wenn ich Kultur höre ... entsichere ich meinen Browning!*
Whenever I hear the word 'culture' ... I release the safety-catch on my pistol.
Schlageter (1934), I.i. Often attrib. Goering

AL JOLSON 1886–1950

7 You ain't heard nothin' yet, folks.
In the first talking film, *The Jazz Singer*, July 1927

HENRY ARTHUR JONES 1851–1929 and HENRY HERMAN 1832–1894

8 O God! Put back Thy universe and give me yesterday.
The Silver King

BEN JONSON 1573?–1637

9 Thou look'st like Antichrist in that lewd hat.
The Alchemist (1610), IV.vii

10 Queen and huntress, chaste and fair,
Now the sun is laid to sleep,

Seated in thy silver chair,
State in wonted manner keep:
  Hesperus entreats thy light,
Goddess, excellently bright.
Cynthia's Revels (1600), V.iii

1 Alas, all the castles I have, are built with air, thou know'st.
Eastward Ho (1604), II.ii.226

2 Rest in soft peace, and, ask'd say here doth lye
Ben Jonson his best piece of poetrie.
Epigrams (1672), xlv. **On My First Son**

3 Drink to me only with thine eyes,
  And I will pledge with mine;
Or leave a kiss but in the cup,
  And I'll not look for wine.
The Forest (1616), ix. **To Celia**

4 Ramp up my genius, be not retrograde;
But boldly nominate a spade a spade.
The Poetaster (1601), v.i

5 And though thou hadst small Latin, and less Greek.
To the Memory of My Beloved, the Author, Mr. William Shakespeare

6 He was not of an age, but for all time!

7 I loved the man, and do honour his memory, on this side idolatry, as much as any.
Timber, or Discoveries made upon Men and Matter (1641). **De Shakespeare Nostrati. Augustus in Haterium**

8 Have you seen but a bright lily grow,
  Before rude hands have touch'd it?
Have you mark'd but the fall o' the snow
  Before the soil hath smutch'd it? ...
O so white! O so soft! O so sweet is she!
The Underwood (1640). **Celebration of Charis**, iv. **Her Triumph**

9 Come, my Celia, let us prove,
While we can, the sports of love.
Volpone (1605), III.v. See Catullus.

10 Suns, that set, may rise again;
But if once we lose this light,
'Tis with us perpetual night.

JOHN JORTIN 1698–1770

1 *Palmam qui meruit, ferat.*
Let him who has won it bear the palm.
Lusus Poetici (1722): **Ad Ventos.** Adopted as motto by Lord Nelson.

BENJAMIN JOWETT 1817–1893

2 My dear child, you must believe in God in spite of what the clergy tell you.
Private conversation with Margot Asquith, shortly after the near-fatal illness a year before his death. Asquith, *Autobiography*, ch.8

JAMES JOYCE 1882–1941

3 All moanday, tearsday, wailsday, thumpsday, frightday, shatterday.
Finnegans Wake (1939), p.301

4 Ireland is the old sow that eats her farrow.
A Portrait of the Artist as a Young Man (1916), ch.5

5 I fear those big words, Stephen said, which make us so unhappy.
Ulysses (1922). **Nestor**

6 History is a nightmare from which I am trying to awake.

7 Yes I said yes I will Yes.
Penelope, closing words

EMPEROR JULIAN THE APOSTATE c.332–363

8 *Vicisti, Galilaee.*
You have won, Galilean.
Supposed dying words; but a late embellishment of Theodoret, *Hist. Eccles.*, iii.25

DAME JULIAN OF NORWICH 1343–1443

9 Sin is behovely, but all shall be well and all shall be well and all manner of thing shall be well.
Revelations of Divine Love, ch.27

JUVENAL c.60–c.130

1 *Iam pridem Syrus in Tiberim defluxit Orontes*
Et linguam et mores.
The Syrian Orontes has now for long been pouring into the Tiber, with its own language and ways of behaving.
Satires, ii.83

2 *Res angusta domi.*
Straitened circumstances at home.
164

3 *Rara avis in terris nigroque simillima cycno.*
A rare bird on this earth, like nothing so much as a black swan.
vi.165

4 *Sed quis custodiet ipsos*
Custodes?
But who is to guard the guards themselves?
347

5 *Duas tantum res anxius optat,*
Panem et circenses.
Only two things does he worry about or long for—bread and the big match.
x.80. Of the citizen these days.

6 *Orandum est ut sit mens sana in corpore sano.*
You should pray to have a sound mind in a sound body.
356

IMMANUEL KANT 1724–1804

7 *Dieser Imperativ ist kategorisch ... Dieser Imperativ mag der der Sittlichkeit heissen.*
This imperative is Categorical ... This imperative may be called that of Morality.
Grundlegung zur Metaphysik der Sitten, trans. T.K. Abbot, Section II

8 *Handle so, dass du die Menschheit, sowohl in deiner Person, als in der Person eines jeden andern, jederzeit zugleich als Zweck, niemals bloss als Mittel brauchest.*
So act as to treat humanity, whether in thine own person or in that of any other, in every case as an end withal, never as means only.

1 *Aus so krummem Holze, als woraus der Mensch gemacht ist, kann nichts ganz gerades gezimmert werden.*
Out of the crooked timber of humanity no straight thing can ever be made.
Idee zu einer allgemeinen Geschichte in weltbürgerlicher Absicht

ALPHONSE KARR 1808–1890

2 *Plus ça change, plus c'est la même chose.*
The more things change, the more they are the same.
Les Guêpes, Jan. 1849. vi

CHRISTOPH KAUFMANN 1753–1795

3 *Sturm und Drang.*
Storm and stress.
Phrase suggested to F.M. Klinger (1752–1831) as a better title for his play originally called *Der Wirrwarr*

JOHN KEATS 1795–1821

4 A thing of beauty is a joy for ever:
Its loveliness increases; it will never
Pass into nothingness.
Endymion (1818), bk.i, l.1

5 St Agnes' Eve—Ah, bitter chill it was!
The owl, for all his feathers, was a-cold.
The Eve of Saint Agnes, 1

6 The silver, snarling trumpets 'gan to chide.
4

7 And they are gone: aye, ages long ago
These lovers fled away into the storm.
42

8 Ever let the fancy roam,
Pleasure never is at home.
Fancy, l.1

9 Oh, what can ail thee, Knight at arms
  Alone and palely loitering;
The sedge is wither'd from the lake,
  And no birds sing.
La Belle Dame Sans Merci

1 And there I shut her wild, wild eyes
With kisses four.

2 'La belle Dame sans Merci
Hath thee in thrall!'

3 Bards of Passion and of Mirth,
Ye have left your souls on earth!
Have ye souls in heaven too?
Ode

4 Thou still unravish'd bride of quietness,
Thou foster-child of silence and slow time.
Ode on a Grecian Urn

5 Heard melodies are sweet, but those unheard
Are sweeter.

6 'Beauty is truth, truth beauty,'—that is all
Ye know on earth, and all ye need to know.

7 Or if thy mistress some rich anger shows,
Emprison her soft hand and let her rave,
And feed deep, deep upon her peerless eyes.
Ode on Melancholy

8 My heart aches, and a drowsy numbness pains
My sense, as though of hemlock I had drunk.
Ode to a Nightingale

9 O for a beaker full of the warm South,
Full of the true, the blushful Hippocrene,
With beaded bubbles winking at the brim.

10 Fade far away, dissolve, and quite forget
What thou among the leaves hast never known,
The weariness, the fever, and the fret,
Here, where men sit and hear each other groan.

11 Already with thee! tender is the night.

12 The murmurous haunt of flies on summer eves.

13 Now more than ever seems it rich to die,
To cease upon the midnight with no pain.

14 Thou wast not born for death, immortal Bird!
No hungry generations tread thee down.

1 Perhaps the self-same song that found a path
Through the sad heart of Ruth, when sick for home,
She stood in tears amid the alien corn.

2 Forlorn! the very word is like a bell.

3 Was it a vision, or a waking dream?
Fled is that music:—Do I wake or sleep?

4 I had a dove and the sweet dove died;
And I have thought it died of grieving:
O, what could it grieve for? Its feet were tied,
With a silken thread of my own hand's weaving.
Song

5 Much have I travell'd in the realms of gold,
And many goodly states and kingdoms seen.
***Sonnets*. On First Looking into Chapman's Homer**

6 Then felt I like some watcher of the skies
When a new planet swims into his ken;
Or like stout Cortez when with eagle eyes
He star'd at the Pacific—and all his men
Look'd at each other with a wild surmise—
Silent, upon a peak in Darien.

7 To one who has been long in city pent;
'Tis very sweet to look into the fair
And open face of heaven.
To One Who Has Been Long

8 Turn the key deftly in the oiled wards,
And seal the hushed Casket of my Soul.
To Sleep

9 When I have fears that I may cease to be
Before my pen has glean'd my teeming brain.
When I Have Fears

10 Season of mists and mellow fruitfulness,
Close bosom-friend of the maturing sun.
To Autumn

11 Where are the songs of Spring? Ay, where are they?
Think not of them, thou hast thy music too.

12 I am certain of nothing but the holiness of the heart's affections and the truth of imagination—what the

imagination seizes as beauty must be truth—whether it existed before or not.
Letters. To Benjamin Bailey, 22 Nov. 1817

1 Negative Capability, that is, when a man is capable of being in uncertainties, mysteries, doubts, without any irritable reaching after fact and reason.
To G. and T. Keats, 21 Dec. 1817

2 There is nothing stable in the world; uproar's your only music.
To G. and T. Keats, 13 Jan. 1818

3 I wish I could say Tom was any better. His identity presses upon me so all day that I am obliged to go out.
Of his youngest brother. To C.W. Dilke, 21 Sept. 1818

4 Here lies one whose name was writ in water.
Epitaph. Lord Houghton, *Life of Keats*, ii.91

JOHN KEBLE 1792–1866

5 The trivial round, the common task,
Would furnish all we ought to ask.
The Christian Year (1827). **Morning**

THOMAS À KEMPIS See THOMAS

JOHN FITZGERALD KENNEDY 1917–1963

6 And so, my fellow Americans: ask not what your country can do for you—ask what you can do for your country.
Inaugural address, 20 Jan. 1961. Not the first use of this form of words: a similiar exhortation may be found in the funeral oration for John Greenleaf Whittier.

7 All free men, wherever they may live, are citizens of Berlin. And therefore, as a free man, I take pride in the words *Ich bin ein Berliner*.
Speech at City Hall, West Berlin, 26 June 1963

FRANCIS SCOTT KEY 1779–1843

8 'Tis the star-spangled banner; O long may it wave
O'er the land of the free, and the home of the brave!
The Star-Spangled Banner (1814)

BISHOP HENRY KING 1592–1669

1 But hark! My pulse like a soft drum
Beats my approach, tells thee I come.
The Exequy

REVD. MARTIN LUTHER KING 1929–1968

2 A riot is at bottom the language of the unheard.
Chaos or Community (1967), ch.4

3 I have a dream that one day this nation will rise up, live out the true meaning of its creed.
Washington, 27 Aug. 1963. The phrase 'I have a dream' was used by him in other speeches during the summer of that year.

CHARLES KINGSLEY 1819–1875

4 Be good, sweet maid, and let who can be clever;
Do lovely things, not dream them, all day long.
A Farewell. To C.E.G.

5 Do the work that's nearest,
Though it's dull at whiles,
Helping, when we meet them,
Lame dogs over stiles.
Letter to Thomas Hughes

6 'O Mary, go and call the cattle home,
And call the cattle home,
And call the cattle home,
Across the sands of Dee.'
The western wind was wild and dank with foam,
And all alone went she.
The Sands of Dee

7 For men must work, and women must weep.
The Three Fishers

8 I once had a sweet little doll, dears
The prettiest doll in the world;
Her cheeks were so red and so white, dears,
And her hair was so charmingly curled.
Songs from ***The Water Babies*** (1863). **My Little Doll**

9 When all the world is young, lad,
And all the trees are green;

And every goose a swan, lad,
And every lass a queen;
Then hey for boot and horse, lad,
And round the world away:
Young blood must have its course, lad,
And every dog his day.
Young and Old

1 We have used the Bible as if it was a constable's handbook—an opium-dose for keeping beasts of burden patient while they are being overloaded.
***Letters to the Chartists*,** no.2. See Marx.

2 Mrs Bedonebyasyoudid is coming.
The Water Babies (1863), ch.5

3 The loveliest fairy in the world; and her name is Mrs Doasyouwouldbedoneby.

4 More ways of killing a cat than choking her with cream.
Westward Ho! (1855), ch.20

HUGH KINGSMILL 1889–1949

5 What, still alive at twenty-two,
A clean upstanding chap like you?
Sure, if your throat 'tis hard to slit,
Slit your girl's, and swing for it.
***Two Poems after A.E. Housman*,** 1

6 But bacon's not the only thing
That's cured by hanging from a string.

RUDYARD KIPLING 1865–1936

7 Oh, East is East, and West is West, and never the twain shall meet.
The Ballad of East and West

8 Ah! What avails the classic bent
  And what the cultured word,
Against the undoctored incident
  That actually occurred?
The Benefactors.

9 And a woman is only a woman, but a good cigar is a Smoke.
The Betrothed

1 Oh, where are you going to, all you Big Steamers,
With England's own coal, up and down the salt seas?
Big Steamers

2 (Boots—boots—boots—boots—movin' up an' down again!)
Boots

3 These were our children who died for our lands ...
But who shall return us the children?
The Children

4 What should they know of England who only England know?
The English Flag

5 I could not look on Death, which being known,
Men led me to him, blindfold and alone.
Epitaphs of the War. **The Coward**

6 For the female of the species is more deadly than the male.
The Female of the Species

7 Gentleman-rankers out on the spree,
Damned from here to Eternity,
God ha' mercy on such as we,
Baa! Yah! Bah!
Gentleman-Rankers

8 The Glory of the Garden lies in more than meets the eye.
The Glory of the Garden

9 Oh, Adam was a gardener, and God who made him sees
That half a proper gardener's work is done upon his knees.

10 Though I've belted you an' flayed you,
By the livin' Gawd that made you,
You're a better man than I am, Gunga Din!
Gunga Din

11 What is a woman that you forsake her,
And the hearth-fire and the home-acre,
To go with the old grey Widow-maker?
Harp Song of the Dane Women

12 If you can keep your head when all about you
Are losing theirs and blaming it on you.
If—

1 If you can dream—and not make dreams your master.

2 If you can meet with Triumph and Disaster
And treat those two impostors just the same.

3 If you can talk with crowds and keep your virtue,
Or walk with Kings—nor lose the common touch.

4 If you can fill the unforgiving minute
With sixty seconds' worth of distance run,
Yours is the Earth and everything that's in it,
And—which is more—you'll be a Man, my son!

5 There are nine and sixty ways of constructing tribal lays,
And—every—single—one—of—them—is—right!
In the Neolithic Age

6 Then ye returned to your trinkets; then ye contented your souls
With the flannelled fools at the wicket or the muddied oafs at the goals.
The Islanders

7 The Camel's hump is an ugly lump
Which well you may see at the Zoo;
But uglier yet is the Hump we get
From having too little to do.
Just-So Stories **(1902). How the Camel Got His Hump**

8 I keep six honest serving-men
(They taught me all I knew);
Their names are What and Why and When
And How and Where and Who.
I keep six honest serving-men

9 So be warned by my lot (which I know you will not),
An' learn about women from me!
The Ladies

10 For the Colonel's Lady an' Judy O'Grady
Are sisters under their skins!

11 On the road to Mandalay,
Where the flyin'-fishes play,
An' the dawn comes up like thunder outer China 'crost the Bay!
Mandalay

1 And the epitaph drear: 'A Fool lies here who tried to hustle the East.'
The Naulahka (1892), heading of ch.5

2 Brothers and Sisters, I bid you beware
Of giving your heart to a dog to tear.
The Power of the Dog

3 God of our fathers, known of old,
Lord of our far-flung battle-line.
Recessional (1897)

4 The tumult and the shouting dies;
The Captains and the Kings depart.

5 Lord God of Hosts, be with us yet,
Lest we forget—lest we forget!

6 Lo, all our pomp of yesterday
Is one with Nineveh and Tyre!

7 Them that asks no questions isn't told a lie.
Watch the wall, my darling, while the Gentlemen go by!
A Smuggler's Song

8 Each to his choice, and I rejoice
The lot has fallen to me
In a fair ground—in a fair ground—
Yea, Sussex by the sea!
Sussex

9 A fool there was and he made his prayer
(Even as you and I!)
To a rag and a bone and a hank of hair.
The Vampire

10 They shut the road through the woods
Seventy years ago.
The Way Through the Woods

11 Take up the White Man's burden—
Send forth the best ye breed.
The White Man's Burden

12 Good hunting!
The Jungle Book (1894). **Kaa's Hunting**

13 He was a man of infinite-resource-and-sagacity.
Just So Stories (1902). **How the Whale Got His Throat**

1 There lived a Parsee from whose hat the rays of the sun were reflected in more-than-oriental-splendour.
How the Rhinoceros Got His Skin

2 An Elephant's Child—who was full of 'satiable curtiosity.
The Elephant's Child

3 The great grey-green, greasy Limpopo River, all set about with fever-trees.

4 He walked by himself, and all places were alike to him.
The Cat That Walked by Himself

5 The mad all are in God's keeping.
Kim (1901), ch.2

6 She was as immutable as the Hills. But not quite so green.
Plain Tales from the Hills (1888). **Venus Annodomini**

7 Being kissed by a man who didn't wax his moustache was—like eating an egg without salt.
Soldiers Three (1888). **The Gadsbys. Poor Dear Mamma**

8 A Jelly-bellied Flag-flapper.
Stalky & Co. (1899). **The Flag of Their Country**

9 'Tisn't beauty, so to speak, nor good talk necessarily. It's just IT. Some women'll stay in a man's memory if they once walked down a street.
Traffics and Discoveries (1904). **Mrs. Bathurst**

10 Gawd knows, an' 'E won't split on a pal.
Wee Willie Winkie (1888). **Drums of the Fore and Aft**

11 A Soldier of the Great War Known unto God.
Inscription on gravestones above unidentified bodies, chosen by Kipling as literary adviser for the Imperial War Graves Commission, 1919. Gavin Stamp (ed.), *Silent Cities* (1977), p.13

12 Power without responsibility—the prerogative of the harlot throughout the ages.
In conversation with Max Aitken (Lord Beaverbrook); later used by Stanley Baldwin. See Lord Baldwin, Address to The Kipling Society, Oct. 1971.

FRIEDRICH KLOPSTOCK 1724–1803

13 God and I both knew what it meant once; now God alone knows.

C. Lombroso, *The Man of Genius* (1891), pt.I, ch.2. Also attr. to Browning in the form 'When [*Sordello*] was written, God and Robert Browning knew what it meant; now only God knows.'

JOHN KNOX 1505–1572

1 The First Blast of the Trumpet Against the Monstrous Regiment of Women.
Title of Pamphlet, 1558

MGR. RONALD KNOX 1888–1957

2 There once was a man who said 'God
Must think it exceedingly odd
  If he finds that this tree
  Continues to be
When there's no one about in the Quad.'
Attr. Langford Reed, *The Limerick Book*. For answer see Anon.

3 Evangelical vicar, in want of a portable, second-hand font, would dispose, for the same, of a portrait, in frame, of the bishop, elect, of Vermont.
Advertisement placed in a newspaper. See W.S. Baring-Gould, *The Lure of the Limerick*, pt.I, ch.1, n.5.

VICESIMUS KNOX 1752–1821

4 Can anything be more absurd than keeping women in a state of ignorance, and yet so vehemently to insist on their resisting temptation?
See Mary Wollstonecraft, *A Vindication of the Rights of Woman* (1792).

THOMAS KYD 1558?–1594?

5 What outcries pluck me from my naked bed?
The Spanish Tragedy (1592), II.v.1

6 Why then I'll fit you.
IV.i.69

JULES LAFORGUE 1860–1887

7 *Ah! que la vie est quotidienne.*
Oh, what a day-to-day business life is.
Complainte sur certains ennuis (1885)

LADY CAROLINE LAMB 1785–1828

1 Mad, bad, and dangerous to know.
Of Byron, in her journal after their first meeting at a ball in March 1812. See Jenkins, *Lady Caroline Lamb* (1932), ch.6.

CHARLES LAMB 1775–1834

2 The man must have a rare recipe for melancholy, who can be dull in Fleet Street.
The Londoner, in letter to Thomas Manning, 15 Feb. 1802

3 The greatest pleasure I know, is to do a good action by stealth, and to have it found out by accident.
Table Talk by the late Elia. *The Athenaeum*, 4 Jan. 1834

4 I have had playmates, I have had companions,
In my days of childhood, in my joyful school-days,—
All, all are gone, the old familiar faces.
The Old Familiar Faces

5 I do not [know the lady]; but damn her at a venture.
E.V. Lucas, *Charles Lamb* (1905), vol.i, p.320, note

WALTER SAVAGE LANDOR 1775–1864

6 I strove with none; for none was worth my strife;
Nature I loved, and, next to Nature, Art;
I warmed both hands before the fire of life;
It sinks, and I am ready to depart.
Finis

7 Ah, what avails the sceptred race!
Ah, what the form divine!
What every virtue, every grace!
Rose Aylmer, all were thine.
Rose Aylmer

8 Clear writers, like fountains, do not seem so deep as they are; the turbid look the most profound.
Imaginary Conversations (1823). **Southey and Porson**

ANDREW LANG 1844–1912

9 They hear like Ocean on a western beach
The surge and thunder of the Odyssey.
As One That for a Weary Space has Lain

10 If the wild bowler thinks he bowls,
Or if the batsman thinks he's bowled,

They know not, poor misguided souls,
They too shall perish unconsoled.
I am the batsman and the bat,
I am the bowler and the ball,
The umpire, the pavilion cat,
The roller, pitch, and stumps, and all.

Brahma. See Emerson.

JULIA S. LANG 1921–

1 Are you sitting comfortably? Then I'll begin.

Preamble to children's story in *Listen With Mother*, B.B.C. radio programme, from 1950

FREDERICK LANGBRIDGE 1849–1923

2 Two men look out through the same bars:
One sees the mud, and one the stars.

A Cluster of Quiet Thoughts (1896) (Religious Tract Society Publication)

LÂO TSE ?6th cent. B.C.

3 Heaven and Earth are not ruthful;
To them the Ten Thousand Things are but as straw dogs.

Tao-te-ching, 5. Tr. Arthur Waley. (The Ten Thousand Things: all life forms. Straw dogs: sacrificial tokens.)

PHILIP LARKIN 1922–

4 Nothing, like something, happens anywhere.

I Remember, I Remember

5 Why should I let the toad *work*
Squat on my life?

Toads

DUC DE LA ROCHEFOUCAULD 1613–1680

6 *Dans l'adversité de nos meilleurs amis, nous trouvons toujours quelque chose qui ne nous déplaît pas.*
In the misfortune of our best friends, we always find something which is not displeasing to us.

Réflexions ou Maximes Morales (1665), 99

7 *Il y a de bons mariages, mais il n'y en a point de délicieux.*

There are good marriages, but no delightful ones.
Réflexions ou Sentences et Maximes Morales (1678), 113

BISHOP HUGH LATIMER c.1485–1555

1 *Gutta cavat lapidem, non vi sed saepe cadendo.*
The drop of rain maketh a hole in the stone, not by violence, but by oft falling.
7th Sermon preached before Edward VI (1549). See Ovid, *Epistulae ex Ponto*, IV.x.5.

2 Be of good comfort Master Ridley, and play the man. We shall this day light such a candle by God's grace in England, as (I trust) shall never be put out.
16 Oct. 1555. Foxe, *Actes and Monuments* (1562–3), 1570 edn., p.1937

D.H. LAWRENCE 1885–1930

3 To the Puritan all things are impure.
Etruscan Places (1932). Cerveteri

4 Not I, not I, but the wind that blows through me!
Song of a man who has come through

5 Never trust the artist. Trust the tale.
Studies in Classic American Literature (1924), ch.1

EMMA LAZARUS 1849–1887

6 Give me your tired, your poor,
Your huddled masses yearning to breathe free.
The New Colossus

STEPHEN LEACOCK 1869–1944

7 Lord Ronald ... flung himself upon his horse and rode madly off in all directions.
Nonsense Novels (1911). Gertrude the Governess

EDWARD LEAR 1812–1888

8 'How pleasant to know Mr Lear!'
Who has written such volumes of stuff!
Some think him ill-tempered and queer,
But a few think him pleasant enough.
Nonsense Songs (1871), preface

1 Far and few, far and few,
Are the lands where the Jumblies live;
Their heads are green, and their hands are blue,
And they went to sea in a Sieve.
The Jumblies

2 The Owl and the Pussy-Cat went to sea
In a beautiful pea-green boat.
They took some honey, and plenty of money,
Wrapped up in a five-pound note.
The Owl and the Pussy-Cat

3 They dined on mince, and slices of quince,
Which they ate with a runcible spoon;
And hand in hand, on the edge of the sand,
They danced by the light of the moon.

LE CORBUSIER 1887–1965

4 *La maison est une machine à habiter.*
A house is a living-machine.
Vers une architecture (1923), p.ix

ALEXANDRE AUGUSTE LEDRU-ROLLIN 1807–1874

5 *Eh! je suis leur chef, il fallait bien les suivre.*
Ah well! I am their leader, I really ought to follow them!
E. de Mirecourt, *Histoire Contemporaine* no.79, 'Ledru-Rollin' (1857)

HENRY LEE 1756–1818

6 A citizen, first in war, first in peace, and first in the hearts of his countrymen.
Resolutions Adopted by the Congress on the Death of Washington, 19 Dec. 1799

NATHANIEL LEE 1653?–1692

7 When Greeks joined Greeks, then was the tug of war!
The Rival Queens (1677), IV.ii

V.I. LENIN 1870–1924

8 We shall now proceed to construct the socialist order.
Opening words of congress after the capture of the Winter Palace, 26 Oct. 1917, Trotsky, *History of the Russian Revolution*, ch.10

1 Communism is Soviet power plus the electrification of the whole country.
Report at the eighth All-Russia Congress of Soviets on the work of the Council of People's Commissars, 22 Dec. 1920

SPEAKER WILLIAM LENTHALL 1591–1662

2 I have neither eye to see, nor tongue to speak here, but as the House is pleased to direct me.
4 Jan. 1642. Said to Charles I, who had asked if he saw any of the five M.P.s whom the King had ordered to be arrested. Rushworth, *Historical Collections* (1703–08), iv.238

DUC DE LÉVIS 1764–1830

3 *Noblesse oblige.*
Nobility has its obligations.
Maximes et Réflexions, 1812 edn., **Morale,** 'Maximes et Préceptes', lxxiii

LIBERACE 1920–

4 I cried all the way to the bank.
Liberace: An Autobiography, ch.2. After hostile criticism

ABRAHAM LINCOLN 1809–1865

5 You can fool all the people some of the time, and some of the people all the time, but you can not fool all the people all of the time.
Attr. words in a speech at Clinton, 8 Sept. 1858. Attr. also to Phineas Barnum

6 If I could save the Union without freeing any slave, I would do it; and if I could save it by freeing all the slaves, I would do it; and if I could save it by freeing some and leaving others alone, I would also do that.
Letter to Horace Greeley, 22 Aug. 1862

7 With malice toward none; with charity for all.
Second Inaugural Address, 4 Mar. 1865

8 To do all which may achieve and cherish a just and lasting peace among ourselves, and with all nations.

1 The Lord prefers common-looking people. That is why he makes so many of them.
James Morgan, *Our President*, ch.6

MAXIM LITVINOFF 1876–1951

2 Peace is indivisible.
First used publicly 25 Feb. 1920. A.U. Pope, *Maxim Litvinoff*, p.234

LIVY 59 B.C.–A.D. 17 or 64 B.C.–A.D. 12

3 *Vae victis.*
Down with the defeated.
Ab Urbe Condita, 5.48.9. Shouted by Brennus, the Gallic King, who had captured Rome (390 B.C.), but a proverbial cry

FRIEDRICH VON LOGAU 1604–1655

4 *Gottesmühlen mahlen langsam, mahlen aber trefflich klein.*
Though the mills of God grind slowly, yet they grind exceeding small.
Sinngedichte (1653), III.ii.24 (tr. H.W. Longfellow)

HENRY WADSWORTH LONGFELLOW
1807–1882

5 I shot an arrow into the air,
It fell to earth, I knew not where.
The Arrow and the Song

6 The cares that infest the day
Shall fold their tents, like the Arabs,
And as silently steal away.
The Day is Done

7 The shades of night were falling fast,
As through an Alpine village passed
A youth, who bore, 'mid snow and ice,
A banner with the strange device,
Excelsior!
Excelsior

1 A boy's will is the wind's will
And the thoughts of youth are long, long thoughts.
My Lost Youth

2 Listen, my children, and you shall hear
Of the midnight ride of Paul Revere,
On the eighteenth of April in Seventy-five.
Paul Revere's Ride (1861)

3 Tell me not, in mournful numbers,
Life is but an empty dream!
A Psalm of Life

4 Life is real! Life is earnest!
And the grave is not its goal.

5 Lives of great men all remind us
We can make our lives sublime,
And, departing, leave behind us
Footprints on the sands of time.

6 By the shore of Gitche Gumee,
By the shining Big-Sea-Water,
Stood the wigwam of Nokomis,
Daughter of the Moon, Nokomis.
The Song of Hiawatha (1855), iii. **Hiawatha's Childhood**

7 From the waterfall he named her,
Minnehaha, Laughing Water.
iv. **Hiawatha and Mudjekeewis**

8 As unto the bow the cord is,
So unto the man is woman;
Though she bends him, she obeys him,
Though she draws him, yet she follows;
Useless each without the other!
x. **Hiawatha's Wooing**

9 Onaway! Awake, beloved!
xi. **Hiawatha's Wedding-feast**

10 Ships that pass in the night, and speak each other in passing.
Tales of a Wayside Inn, pt.III (1874), **The Theologian's Tale. Elizabeth,** iv

11 Under the spreading chestnut tree
The village smithy stands;

The smith, a mighty man is he,
  With large and sinewy hands.
The Village Blacksmith

1 Something attempted, something done,
  Has earned a night's repose.

2 It was the schooner Hesperus,
  That sailed the wintry sea.
The Wreck of the Hesperus

3 When she was good
She was very, very good,
But when she was bad she was horrid.
B.R.T. Machetta, *Home Life of Longfellow*

ANITA LOOS 1893–1981

4 A girl like I.
Gentlemen Prefer Blondes (1925), *passim*

5 Kissing your hand may make you feel very very good but a diamond and safire bracelet lasts forever.
ch.4

6 Fun is fun but no girl wants to laugh all of the time.

LOUIS XIV 1638–1715

7 *L'État c'est moi.*
I am the State.
Attr. remark before the Parlement de Paris, 13 Apr. 1655. Dulaure, *Histoire de Paris* (1834), vol.6, p.298. Probably apocryphal.

8 *J'ai failli attendre.*
I almost had to wait.
Expression of impatience. Attribution doubted by e.g. E. Fournier, *L'Esprit dans l'Histoire* (4th edn., 1884), ch.xlviii

LOUIS XVIII 1755–1824

9 *Il n'est aucun de vous qui n'ait dans sa giberne le baton du duc de Reggio; c'est à vous à l'en faire sortir.*
There is not one of you who has not in his knapsack the field marshal's baton; it is up to you to bring it out.
Speech to the Saint-Cyr cadets, 9 Aug. 1819. *Moniteur*, 10 Aug. 1819

1 *L'exactitude est la politesse des rois.*
Punctuality is the politeness of kings.
Attr. *Souvenirs de J. Lafitte* (1844), bk.1, ch.3

RICHARD LOVELACE 1618–1658

2 Stone walls do not a prison make
Nor iron bars a cage.
To Althea, From Prison

3 I could not love thee (Dear) so much,
Lov'd I not honour more.
To Lucasta, Going to the Wars

ROBERT LOWE, VISCOUNT SHERBROOKE 1811–1892

4 The Chancellor of the Exchequer ... is intrusted with a certain amount of misery which it is his duty to distribute as fairly as he can.
House of Commons, 11 Apr. 1870

JAMES RUSSELL LOWELL 1819–1891

5 I *don't* believe in princerple,
But O, I *du* in interest.
The Biglow Papers, No.6. **The Pious Editor's Creed**

6 Once to every man and nation comes the moment to decide,
In the strife of Truth with Falsehood, for the good or evil side.
The Present Crisis

7 Truth forever on the scaffold, Wrong forever on the throne.

LUCAN 39–65

8 *Coniunx*
Est mihi, sunt nati: dedimus tot pignora fatis.
I have a wife, I have sons: all of them hostages given to fate.
Works, VII.661

LUCRETIUS 94?–55 B.C.

1 *Nil posse creari*
De nilo.
Nothing can be created out of nothing.
De Rerum Natura, i.155

2 *Suave, mari magno turbantibus aequora ventis,*
E terra magnum alterius spectare laborem.
Lovely it is, when the winds are churning up the waves on the great sea, to gaze out from the land on the great efforts of someone else.
ii.1

MARTIN LUTHER 1483–1546

3 *Hier stehe ich. Ich kann nicht anders.*
Here stand I. I can do no other.
Speech at the Diet of Worms, 18 Apr. 1521

4 *Wer nicht liebt Wein, Weib und Gesang,*
Der bleibt ein Narr sein Leben lang.
Who loves not woman, wine, and song
Remains a fool his whole life long.
Attr. Written in the Luther room in the Wartburg, but no proof exists of its authorship

5 *Ein' feste Burg ist unser Gott,*
Ein' gute Wehr und Waffen.
A safe stronghold our God is still,
A trusty shield and weapon.
Klug'sche Gesangbuch (1529). Tr. Carlyle

JOHN LYLY 1554?–1606

6 Cupid and my Campaspe play'd
At cards for kisses, Cupid paid.
Campaspe (1584), III.v

BARON LYNDHURST 1772–1863

7 Campbell has added another terror to death.
On being assured that he had not yet been included in Lord Campbell's *Lives of the Lord Chancellors*. See E. Bowen-Rowlands, *Seventy-Two Years At the Bar*, ch.10. See Wetherell.

LYSANDER d. 395 B.C.

1 Deceive boys with toys, but men with oaths.
Plutarch, *Lives*, *Lysander*, 8

H.F. LYTE 1793–1847

2 Abide with me; fast falls the eventide;
The darkness deepens; Lord, with me abide.
Abide with Me

3 Change and decay in all around I see;
O Thou, who changest not, abide with me.

LORD MACAULAY 1800–1859

4 And how can man die better
  Than facing fearful odds,
For the ashes of his fathers,
  And the temples of his Gods?
Lays of Ancient Rome (1842). **Horatius,** 27

5 'Now who will stand on either hand,
  And keep the bridge with me?'
29

6 But those behind cried 'Forward!'
  And those before cried 'Back!'
50

7 And even the ranks of Tuscany
  Could scarce forbear to cheer.
60

8 The priest who slew the slayer,
  And shall himself be slain.
The Battle of Lake Regillus, 10

9 His imagination resembled the wings of an ostrich. It enabled him to run, though not to soar.
Essays and Biographies. **John Dryden** (*Edinburgh Review*, Jan. 1828)

10 The gallery in which the reporters sit has become a fourth estate of the realm.
Historical Essays Contributed to the 'Edinburgh Review'. **Hallam's 'Constitutional History'** (Sept. 1828)

1 Every schoolboy knows who imprisoned Montezuma, and who strangled Atahualpa.
Lord Clive (Jan. 1840)

2 There is only one cure for the evils which newly acquired freedom produces; and that is freedom.
***Literary Essays Contributed to the 'Edinburgh Review'*. Milton** (Aug. 1825)

3 If men are to wait for liberty till they become wise and good in slavery, they may indeed wait for ever.

4 We know no spectacle so ridiculous as the British public in one of its periodical fits of morality.
Moore's 'Life Of Lord Byron' (June 1830)

5 The Puritan hated bear-baiting, not because it gave pain to the bear, but because it gave pleasure to the spectators.
***History of England*,** vol.i (1849), ch.2

GENERAL GEORGE B. McCLELLAN 1826–1885

6 All quiet along the Potomac.
Attr. in the American Civil War

DR. JOHN McCRAE 1872–1918

7 In Flanders fields the poppies blow
Between the crosses, row on row,
That mark our place.
***In Flanders Fields*.** Ypres Salient, 3 May 1915

8 If ye break faith with us who die
We shall not sleep, though poppies grow
In Flanders fields.

WILLIAM McGONAGALL 1825–1902

9 Beautiful Railway Bridge of the Silv'ry Tay!
Alas, I am very sorry to say
That ninety lives have been taken away
On the last Sabbath day of 1879,
Which will be remember'd for a very long time.
The Tay Bridge Disaster

MARSHALL McLUHAN 1911–

1 The medium is the message.
Understanding Media (1964), pt.i, ch.1

MARSHAL MACMAHON 1808–1893

2 *J'y suis, j'y reste.*
Here I am, and here I stay.
At the taking of the Malakoff, 8 Sept. 1855. MacMahon later cast doubt on the attribution: '*Je ne crois pas ... avoir donné à ma pensée cette forme lapidaire.*' See Hanoteaux, *Histoire de la France contemporaine*, vol.ii, ch.1, sect.i.

HAROLD MACMILLAN 1894–

3 Let's be frank about it; most of our people have never had it so good.
20 July 1957. 'You Never Had It So Good' was the Democratic Party slogan in the U.S. election campaign of 1952

4 The wind of change is blowing through this continent.
Cape Town, 3 Feb. 1960. The speech was drafted by Sir David Hunt as described by him in *On the Spot: An Ambassador Remembers* (1975)

LEONARD MACNALLY 1752–1820

5 This lass so neat, with smiles so sweet,
Has won my right good-will,
I'd crowns resign to call thee mine,
Sweet lass of Richmond Hill.
The Lass of Richmond Hill. E. Duncan, *Minstrelsy of England* (1905), i.254. Attr. also to W. Upton in *Oxford Song Book*, and to W. Hudson in Baring-Gould, *English Minstrelsie* (1895), iii.54

LOUIS MACNEICE 1907–1963

6 All of London littered with remembered kisses.
Autumn Journal, iv

7 It's no go the merrygoround, it's no go the rickshaw,
All we want is a limousine and a ticket for the peepshow.
Bagpipe Music

8 The glass is falling hour by hour, the glass will fall for ever,
But if you break the bloody glass, you won't hold up the weather.

1 Time was away and somewhere else,
There were two glasses and two chairs
And two people with the one pulse
(Somebody stopped the moving stairs).
Meeting Point

2 The sunlight on the garden
Hardens and grows cold,
We cannot cage the minute
Within its nets of gold,
When all is told
We cannot beg for pardon.
The Sunlight on the Garden

SAMUEL MADDEN 1686–1765

3 Words are men's daughters, but God's sons are things.
Boulter's Monument (1745), l.377

MAGNA CARTA 1215

4 *Nulli vendemus, nulli negabimus aut differemus, rectum aut justitiam.*
To no man will we sell, or deny, or delay, right or justice.
40

JOSEPH DE MAISTRE 1753–1821

5 *Toute nation a le gouvernement qu'elle mérite.*
Every country has the government it deserves.
Lettres et Opuscules Inédits, i, p.215, 15 Aug. 1811

STÉPHANE MALLARMÉ 1842–1898

6 *La chair est triste, hélas! et j'ai lu tous les livres.*
The flesh, alas, is wearied; and I have read all the books there are.
Brise Marin

GEORGE LEIGH MALLORY 1886–1924

7 Because it is there.
Answer to the question 'Why do you want to climb Mt. Everest?'
D. Robertson, *George Mallory* (1969), p.215

THOMAS ROBERT MALTHUS 1766–1834

1 Population, when unchecked, increases in a geometrical ratio. Subsistence only increases in an arithmetical ratio.
The Principle of Population (1798), 1

W.R. MANDALE nineteenth century

2 Up and down the City Road,
In and out the Eagle,
That's the way the money goes—
Pop goes the weasel!
Pop Goes the Weasel

MANILIUS 1st cent. A.D.

3 *Eripuitque Jovi fulmen viresque tonandi.*
And snatched from Jove the lightning shaft and power to thunder.
Astronomica, i.104. Of human intelligence

MRS. MANLEY 1663–1724

4 No time like the present.
The Lost Lover (1696), IV.i

MAO TSE-TUNG 1893–1976

5 Letting a hundred flowers blossom and a hundred schools of thought contend is the policy.
Speech, 2 May 1956. See Roderick MacFarquhar, *Origins of the Cultural Revolution* (1974), vol.1, p.51.

6 Every Communist must grasp the truth, 'Political power grows out of the barrel of a gun.'
Selected Works (Peking, 1961), vol.ii. **Problems of War and Strategy,** ii, 6 Nov. 1938

7 All reactionaries are paper tigers.
vol.iv. **Talk with Anna Louise Strong,** Aug. 1946

WILLIAM LEARNED MARCY 1786–1857

8 To the victor belong the spoils of the enemy.
Parton, *Life of Jackson* (1860), vol.iii, p.378

QUEEN MARIE-ANTOINETTE 1755–1793

1 *Qu'ils mangent de la brioche.*
Let them eat cake.

On being told that her people had no bread. Attributed to Marie-Antoinette, but much older. Rousseau refers in his *Confessions*, 1740, to a similar remark, as a well-known saying.

CHRISTOPHER MARLOWE 1564–1593

2 Why this is hell, nor am I out of it:
Thinkst thou that I who saw the face of God,
And tasted the eternal joys of heaven,
Am not tormented with ten thousand hells
In being deprived of everlasting bliss!

Doctor Faustus (1604), I.iii.76

3 Hell hath no limits nor is circumscrib'd
In one self place, where we are is Hell.

II.i.120

4 All places shall be hell that are not heaven.

125

5 Was this the face that launch'd a thousand ships,
And burnt the topless towers of Ilium?

V.i.97

6 O I'll leap up to my God: who pulls me down?
See see where Christ's blood streams in the firmament.
One drop would save my soul, half a drop, ah my Christ.

ii.138

7 O soul, be changed into little water drops,
And fall into the ocean, ne'er be found:
My God, my God, look not so fierce on me.

179

8 Cut is the branch that might have grown full straight,
And burnèd is Apollo's laurel bough,
That sometime grew within this learned man.

epilogue

9 My men, like satyrs grazing on the lawns,
Shall with their goat feet dance an antic hay.

Edward II (1593), I.i.59

10 I count religion but a childish toy,
And hold there is no sin but ignorance.

The Jew of Malta (c.1592), prologue

1 And, as their wealth increaseth, so enclose
Infinite riches in a little room.
I.i.36

2 As for myself, I walk abroad o' nights
And kill sick people groaning under walls:
Sometimes I go about and poison wells.
II.iii.172

3 *Barnadine:* Thou hast committed—
Barabas: Fornication? But that was in another country: and besides, the wench is dead.
IV.i.40

4 Come live with me, and be my love,
And we will all the pleasures prove,
That valleys, groves, hills and fields,
Woods or steepy mountain yields.
The Passionate Shepherd to his Love. See Donne.

5 From jigging veins of rhyming mother-wits.
Tamburlaine the Great (1590), prologue

6 Is it not passing brave to be a King,
And ride in triumph through Persepolis?
pt.I, l.758

7 Holla, ye pampered Jades of Asia:
What, can ye draw but twenty miles a day?
pt.II, l.3980. See Shakespeare, *Henry IV*, Pt.2, III.iv.

DON MARQUIS 1878–1937

8 toujours gai, archy, toujours gai.
archys life of mehitabel, i. **the life of mehitabel the cat**

CAPTAIN MARRYAT 1792–1848

9 As savage as a bear with a sore head.
The King's Own (1830), ch.26

10 If you please, ma'am, it was a very little one. [The nurse excusing her illegitimate baby.]
Mr. Midshipman Easy (1836), ch.3

11 It's just six of one and half-a-dozen of the other.
The Pirate (1836), ch.4

MARTIAL b. A.D. 43

1 *Non amo te, Sabidi, nec possum dicere quare:*
Hoc tantum possum dicere, non amo te.
I don't love you, Sabidius, and I can't tell you why; all I can tell you is this, that I don't love you.
Epigrammata, I.xxxii

2 *Difficilis facilis, iucundus acerbus es idem:*
Nec tecum possum vivere nec sine te.
Difficult or easy, pleasant or bitter, you are the same you: I cannot live with you—nor without you.
XII.xlvi (xlvii)

3 *Rus in urbe.*
Country in the town.
lvii

ANDREW MARVELL 1621–1678

4 My love is of a birth as rare
As 'tis for object strange and high:
It was begotten by despair
Upon impossibility.
The Definition of Love

5 As lines so loves oblique may well
Themselves in every angle greet
But ours so truly parallel,
Though infinite can never meet.

6 Annihilating all that's made
To a green thought in a green shade.
The Garden, 6

7 Had we but world enough, and time,
This coyness, Lady, were no crime.
To His Coy Mistress

8 My vegetable love should grow
Vaster than empires, and more slow.

9 But at my back I always hear
Time's wingèd chariot hurrying near.
And yonder all before us lie
Deserts of vast eternity.

1 The grave's a fine and private place,
But none I think do there embrace.

KARL MARX 1818–1883

2 A spectre is haunting Europe—The spectre of Communism.
The Communist Manifesto (1848), opening words

3 The workers have nothing to lose in this [revolution] but their chains. They have a world to gain. Workers of the world, unite!
closing words

4 From each according to his abilities, to each according to his needs.
Criticism of the Gotha Programme (1875). See Bakunin.

5 Religion ... is the opium of the people.
Critique of Hegel's Philosophy of Right (1843–4), Introduction. See Kingsley.

6 The philosophers have only interpreted the world in various ways; the point is to change it.
Theses on Feuerbach (1888), xi

7 The class struggle necessarily leads to the dictatorship of the proletariat.
Letter to Weydemeyer 5 Mar. 1852

MARY TUDOR 1516–1558

8 When I am dead and opened, you shall find 'Calais' lying in my heart.
Holinshed, *Chronicles*, iii.1160

JOHN MASEFIELD 1878–1967

9 Quinquireme of Nineveh from distant Ophir
Rowing home to haven in sunny Palestine,
With a cargo of ivory,
And apes and peacocks,
Sandalwood, cedarwood, and sweet white wine.
Cargoes. See 1 Kings, 10

10 Dirty British coaster with a salt-caked smoke stack,
Butting through the Channel in the mad March days,
With a cargo of Tyne coal,
Road-rail, pig-lead,
Firewood, iron-ware, and cheap tin trays.

1 I must down to the seas again, to the lonely sea and the sky,
And all I ask is a tall ship and a star to steer her by.
Sea Fever

2 I must down to the seas again, for the call of the running tide
Is a wild call and a clear call that may not be denied.

3 I must down to the seas again, to the vagrant gypsy life,
To the gull's way and the whale's way where the wind's like a whetted knife;
And all I ask is a merry yarn from a laughing fellow-rover,
And quiet sleep and a sweet dream when the long trick's over.

4 It is good to be out on the road, and going one knows not where,
Going through meadow and village, one knows not whither nor why.
Tewkesbury Road

5 It's a warm wind, the west wind, full of birds' cries;
I never hear the west wind but tears are in my eyes.
For it comes from the west lands, the old brown hills,
And April's in the west wind, and daffodils.
The West Wind

THE MASS IN LATIN

6 *Mea culpa, mea culpa, mea maxima culpa.*
Through my fault, through my fault, through my most grievous fault.

7 *Kyrie eleison, Kyrie eleison, Kyrie eleison.*
Christe eleison, Christe eleison, Christe eleison.
Lord, have mercy upon us.
Christ, have mercy upon us.

8 *Requiem aeternam dona eis, Domine: et lux perpetua luceat eis.*
Grant them eternal rest, O Lord; and let perpetual light shine on them.
[To be said only at Masses for the dead.]

1 *Gloria in excelsis Deo, et in terra pax hominibus bonae voluntatis.*
Glory be to God on high, and on earth peace to men of good will.

2 *Sanctus, sanctus, sanctus, Dominus Deus Sabaoth. Pleni sunt coeli et terra gloria tua. Hosanna in excelsis.*
Holy, holy, holy, Lord God of Hosts. Heaven and earth are full of thy glory. Hosanna in the highest.

3 *Pax Domini sit semper vobiscum.*
The peace of the Lord be always with you.

4 *Agnus Dei, qui tollis peccata mundi, dona nobis pacem.*
Lamb of God, who takest away the sins of the world, give us peace.

5 *Requiescant in pace.*
May they rest in peace.
[In Masses for the dead.]

PHILIP MASSINGER 1583–1640

6 Pray enter
You are learned Europeans and we worse
Than ignorant Americans.
The City Madam (1658), III.iii

7 Serves and fears
The fury of the many-headed monster,
The giddy multitude.
The Unnatural Combat (1639), III.ii

LORD JUSTICE SIR JAMES MATHEW 1830–1908

8 In England, Justice is open to all, like the Ritz hotel.
R.E. Megarry, *Miscellany-at-Law* (1955), p.254. See Anon.

BILL MAULDIN 1921–

9 I feel like a fugitive from th' law of averages.
Up Front (1946), p.39

HUGHES MEARNS 1875–1965

10 As I was going up the stair
I met a man who wasn't there.

He wasn't there again to-day.
I wish, I wish he'd stay away.
The Psychoed

LORD MELBOURNE 1779–1848

1 I like the Garter; there is no damned merit in it.
On the Order of the Garter. H.Dunckley, *Lord Melbourne* (1890)

2 Things have come to a pretty pass when religion is allowed to invade the sphere of private life.
Remark on hearing an evangelical sermon. G.W.E. Russell, *Collections and Recollections*, ch.6

3 Now, is it to lower the price of corn, or isn't it? It is not much matter which we say, but mind, we must all say *the same*.
(At a Cabinet meeting.) Attr. See Bagehot, *The English Constitution*, ch.1.

4 God help the Minister that meddles with art!
Lord David Cecil, *Lord M*, ch.3

5 What I want is men who will support me when I am in the wrong.
ch.4. 'Reply to a politician' who said 'I will support you as long as you are in the right.'

HERMAN MELVILLE 1819–1891

6 Call me Ishmael.
Moby Dick, ch.1, opening words

GILLES MÉNAGE 1613–1692

7 *Comme nous nous entretenions de ce qui pouvait rendre heureux, je lui dis:* Sanitas sanitatum, et omnia sanitas.
While we were discussing what could make one happy, I said to him: *Sanitas sanitatum et omnia sanitas.*
Ménagiana (1693), p.166. Part of a conversation with Jean-Louis Guez de Balzac (1594–1654). See Ecclesiastes, 1.

MENANDER 342/1–293/89 B.C.

8 Whom the gods love dies young.
Dis Exapatōn, fr.4

GEORGE MEREDITH 1828–1909

1 But, as you will! we'll sit contentedly,
And eat our pot of honey on the grave.
Modern Love (1862), xxix

2 In tragic life, God wot,
No villain need be! Passions spin the plot:
We are betrayed by what is false within.
xliii

3 Love, that had robbed us of immortal things,
This little moment mercifully gave,
Where I have seen across the twilight wave
The swan sail with her young beneath her wings.
xlvii

4 Ah, what a dusty answer gets the soul
When hot for certainties in this our life!
l

5 Enter these enchanted woods,
You who dare.
The Woods of Westermain

6 Kissing don't last: cookery do!
The Ordeal of Richard Feverel (1859), ch.28

DIXON LANIER MERRITT 1879–1954

7 A wonderful bird is the pelican,
His bill will hold more than his belican.
He can take in his beak
Food enough for a week,
But I'm damned if I see how the helican.
The Pelican

CHARLOTTE MEW 1869–1928

8 She sleeps up in the attic there
Alone, poor maid. 'Tis but a stair
Betwixt us. Oh! my God! the down,
The soft young down of her, the brown,
The brown of her—her eyes, her hair, her hair!
The Farmer's Bride

JOHN STUART MILL 1806–1873

1 Unearned increment.
Dissertations and Discussions, vol.iv (1876), p.299

2 The liberty of the individual must be thus far limited; he must not make himself a nuisance to other people.
On Liberty (1859), ch.3

3 When the land is cultivated entirely by the spade and no horses are kept, a cow is kept for every three acres of land.
Principles of Political Economy (1848). **A Treatise on Flemish Husbandry**

4 The most important thing women have to do is to stir up the zeal of women themselves.
Letter to Alexander Bain, 14 July 1869

EDNA ST. VINCENT MILLAY 1892–1950

5 Gently they go, the beautiful, the tender, the kind;
Quietly they go, the intelligent, the witty, the brave.
I know. But I do not approve. And I am not resigned.
The Buck in the Snow, III, **Dirge without Music**

6 Childhood is the kingdom where nobody dies.

Nobody that matters, that is.
Childhood is the Kingdom where Nobody dies

7 Man has never been the same since God died.
He has taken it very hard.
Conversation at Midnight, IV

8 My candle burns at both ends;
  It will not last the night;
But ah, my foes, and oh my friends—
  It gives a lovely light!
A Few Figs from Thistles (1920). **First Fig**

9 Was it for this I uttered prayers,
And sobbed and cursed and kicked the stairs,
That now, domestic as a plate,
I should retire at half-past eight?
Grown-up

10 After all, my erstwhile dear,
  My no longer cherished,

Need we say it was not love,
  Just because it perished?
Passer Mortuus Est

WILLIAM MILLER 1810–1872

1 Wee Willie Winkie rins through the town,
Up stairs and down stairs in his nicht-gown,
Tirling at the window, crying at the lock,
Are the weans in their bed, for it's now ten o'clock?
Willie Winkie (1841)

A.A. MILNE 1882–1956

2 They're changing guard at Buckingham Palace—
Christopher Robin went down with Alice.
Alice is marrying one of the guard.
'A soldier's life is terrible hard,'
          Says Alice.
When We Were Very Young (1924). **Buckingham Palace**

3 You must never go down to the end of the town if you don't go down with me.
Disobedience

4 I do like a little bit of butter to my bread!
The King's Breakfast

5 Little Boy kneels at the foot of the bed,
Droops on the little hands, little gold head;
Hush! Hush! Whisper who dares!
Christopher Robin is saying his prayers.
Vespers

6 I am a Bear of Very Little Brain, and long words Bother me.
Winnie-the-Pooh (1926), ch.4

7 Time for a little something.
ch.6

8 When I was young, we *always* had mornings like this.
Toad of Toad Hall (1929), II.3. Milne's dramatization of Kenneth Grahame's *The Wind in the Willows*.

LORD MILNER 1854–1925

1 If we believe a thing to be bad, and if we have a right to prevent it, it is our duty to try to prevent it and to damn the consequences. [The Peers and the Budget.]
Speech at Glasgow, 26 Nov. 1909

JOHN MILTON 1608–1674

2 Come, knit hands, and beat the ground,
In a light fantastic round.
Comus (1634), l.143

3 That I incline to hope rather than fear,
And gladly banish squint suspicion.
l.412

4 How charming is divine philosophy!
l.476

5 Hence, vain deluding joys,
The brood of Folly without father bred.
Il Penseroso (1632), l.1

6 Far from all resort of mirth,
Save the cricket on the hearth.
l.81

7 Hence, loathed Melancholy,
Of Cerberus, and blackest Midnight born.
L'Allegro (1632), l.1

8 So buxom, blithe, and debonair.
l.24

9 Nods, and becks, and wreathed smiles.
l.28

10 Come, and trip it as ye go
On the light fantastic toe.
l.33

11 Of herbs, and other country messes,
Which the neat-handed Phyllis dresses.
l.85

12 Or sweetest Shakespeare, Fancy's child,
Warble his native wood-notes wild.
l.133

1 To sport with Amaryllis in the shade.
Lycidas (1637), 1.68

2 Fame is the spur that the clear spirit doth raise
(That last infirmity of noble mind).
1.70

3 Their lean and flashy songs
Grate on their scrannel pipes of wretched straw,
The hungry sheep look up, and are not fed.
1.123

4 Look homeward, Angel, now, and melt with ruth.
1.163

5 At last he rose, and twitch'd his mantle blue;
To-morrow to fresh woods, and pastures new.
1.192

6 It was the winter wild
While the Heav'n-born child
All meanly wrapt in the rude manger lies.
On the Morning of Christ's Nativity (1629), 1.29

7 Ring out ye crystal spheres,
Once bless our human ears.
1.125

8 Time will run back, and fetch the age of gold
And speckled Vanity
Will sicken soon and die.
1.135

9 Of Man's first disobedience, and the fruit
Of that forbidden tree, whose mortal taste
Brought death into the world, and all our woe,
With loss of Eden.
Paradise Lost (1667), 1668 edn. bk.i, 1.1

10 Things unattempted yet in prose or rhyme.
1.16

11 I may assert eternal Providence,
And justify the ways of God to Men.
1.25

12 Better to reign in hell, than serve in heav'n.
1.263

1 And when night
Darkens the streets, then wander forth the sons
Of Belial, flown with insolence and wine.
l.500

2 Who overcomes
By force, hath overcome but half his foe.
l.648

3 Let none admire
That riches grow in hell; that soil may best
Deserve the precious bane.
l.690

4 From morn
To noon he fell, from noon to dewy eve,
A summer's day; and with the setting sun
Dropt from the zenith like a falling star.
l.742

5 With ruin upon ruin, rout on rout,
Confusion worse confounded.
bk.ii, l.995

6 So on this windy sea of land, the Fiend
Walked up and down alone bent on his prey.
bk.iii, l.440

7 He for God only, she for God in him.
bk.iv, l.299

8 These two
Imparadised in one another's arms,
The happier Eden.
l.505

9 With thee conversing I forget all time.
l.639

10 But wherefore thou alone? Wherefore with thee
Came not all hell broke loose?
l.917

11 Best image of myself and dearer half.
bk.v, l.95

12 Drive far off the barb'rous dissonance
Of Bacchus and his revellers.
bk.vii, l.32

1 Necessity and chance
Approach not me, and what I will is fate.
l.172

2 And feel that I am happier than I know?
bk.viii, l.282

3 Yet I shall temper so
Justice with mercy.
bk.x, l.77

4 The world was all before them, where to choose
Their place of rest, and Providence their guide:
They hand in hand with wandering steps and slow
Through Eden took their solitary way.
bk.xii, l.646

5 Of whom to be dispraised were no small praise.
Paradise Regained (1671), bk.iii, l.56

6 A little onward lend thy guiding hand
To these dark steps, a little further on.
Samson Agonistes (1671), l.1

7 Eyeless in Gaza, at the mill with slaves.
l.41

8 O dark, dark, dark, amid the blaze of noon,
Irrecoverably dark, total eclipse
Without all hope of day!
l.80

9 For evil news rides post, while good news baits.
l.1538

10 Nothing is here for tears.
l.1721

11 And calm of mind all passion spent.
l.1755

12 How soon hath Time, the subtle thief of youth
Stoln on its wing my three and twentieth year.
Sonnet ii. **On his having arrived at the age of twenty-three**

13 Avenge, O Lord, thy slaughtered saints, whose bones
Lie scattered on the Alpine mountains cold.
xv. **On the late Massacre in Piedmont**

14 When I consider how my light is spent,
E're half my days, in this dark world and wide,

And that one Talent which is death to hide,
Lodg'd with me useless.
xvi. **On His Blindness**

1 Thousands at his bidding speed
And post o'er Land and Ocean without rest:
They also serve who only stand and wait.

2 For what can war but endless war still breed?
On the Lord General Fairfax

3 Peace hath her victories
No less renowned than war.
To the Lord General Cromwell, May 1652

4 As good almost kill a man as kill a good book.
Areopagitica (1644)

5 A good book is the precious life-blood of a master spirit.

6 I cannot praise a fugitive and cloistered virtue, unexercised and unbreathed, that never sallies out and sees her adversary, but slinks out of the race, where that immortal garland is to be run for, not without dust and heat.

7 Let not England forget her precedence of teaching nations how to live.
The Doctrine and Discipline of Divorce (1643)

8 I owe no light or leading received from any man in the discovery of this truth.
The Judgement of Martin Bucer Concerning Divorce

MISSAL

9 *O felix culpa, quae talem ac tantum meruit habere Redemptorem.*
O happy fault, which has deserved to have such and so mighty a Redeemer.
'Exsultet' on Holy Saturday

MARGARET MITCHELL 1900–1949

10 After all, tomorrow is another day.
Gone with the Wind (1936), closing words.

NANCY MITFORD 1904–1973

1 When the loo paper gets thicker and the writing paper thinner it's always a bad sign, at home.
Love in a Cold Climate, pt.2, ch.2

2 Abroad is unutterably bloody and foreigners are fiends.
The Pursuit of Love, ch.15

EMILIO MOLA d. 1937

3 *La quinta columna.*
The fifth column.
Reported in *Mundo Obrero* in the first week of Oct. 1936

MOLIÈRE (J.-B. POQUELIN) 1622–1673

4 *Il faut manger pour vivre et non pas vivre pour manger.*
One should eat to live, and not live to eat.
L'Avare (1668), III.v

5 *Par ma foi! il y a plus de quarante ans que je dis de la prose sans que j'en susse rien.*
Good heavens! For more than forty years I have been speaking prose without knowing it.
Le Bourgeois Gentilhomme (1670), II.iv

6 *Tout ce qui n'est point prose est vers; et tout ce qui n'est point vers est prose.*
All that is not prose is verse; and all that is not verse is prose.

7 *Que diable allait-il faire dans cette galère?*
What the devil would he be doing in this gang?
Les Fourberies de Scapin (1671), II.vii

8 *Oui, cela était autrefois ainsi, mais nous avons changé tout cela.*
Yes, in the old days that was so, but we have changed all that.
Le Médecin malgré lui (1666), II.iv

9 *Assassiner c'est le plus court chemin.*
Assassination is the quickest way.
Le Sicilien (1668), XIII

LADY MARY WORTLEY MONTAGU 1689–1762

1 People wish their enemies dead—but I do not; I say give them the gout, give them the stone!
Letter from Horace Walpole to the Earl of Harcourt, 17 Sept. 1778

MONTAIGNE 1533–1592

2 *Il faut noter, que les jeux d'enfants ne sont pas jeux: et les faut juger en eux, comme leurs plus sérieuses actions.*
It should be noted that children at play are not playing about; their games should be seen as their most serious-minded activity.
Essais, xxiii

3 *Si on me presse de dire pourquoi je l'aimais, je sens que cela ne se peut s'exprimer, qu'en répondant: 'Parce que c'était lui; parce que c'était moi.'*
If I am pressed to say why I loved him, I feel it can only be expressed by replying: 'Because it was he; because it was me.'
[Of his friend Étienne de la Boétie.] xxviii

4 *Pour être les occupations domestiques moins importantes, elles n'en sont pas moins importunes.*
Domestic business is no less importunate for being less important.
xxxix

5 *L'homme est bien insensé. Il ne saurait forger un ciron, et forge des Dieux à douzaines.*
Man is quite insane. He cannot create a maggot, and he creates Gods by the dozen.
II.xii

6 *J'ai seulement fait ici un amas de fleurs étrangères.*
In this book I have only made up a bunch of other men's flowers.
III.xii

CASIMIR, COMTE DE MONTROND 1768–1843

7 *Défiez-vous des premiers mouvements parce qu'ils sont bons.*

Have no truck with first impulses as they are always generous ones.
Attr., Comte J. d'Estournel, *Derniers Souvenirs*. Also attr. Talleyrand. See Corneille.

EDWARD MOORE 1712–1757

1 This is adding insult to injuries.
The Foundling (1747–8), V.ii

2 I am rich beyond the dreams of avarice.
The Gamester (1753), II.ii

MARIANNE MOORE 1887–1972

3 My father used to say
'Superior people never make long visits.'
Silence

THOMAS MOORE 1779–1852

4 The harp that once through Tara's halls
The soul of music shed,
Now hangs as mute on Tara's walls
As if that soul were fled.
Irish Melodies (1807). **The Harp that Once**

5 No, there's nothing half so sweet in life
As love's young dream.
Love's Young Dream

6 'Tis the last rose of summer
Left blooming alone;
All her lovely companions
Are faded and gone.
'Tis the Last Rose

7 I never nurs'd a dear gazelle,
To glad me with its soft black eye,
But when it came to know me well,
And love me, it was sure to die!
Lalla Rookh (1817). **The Fire-Worshippers,** i, l.283

THOMAS OSBERT MORDAUNT 1730–1809

8 One crowded hour of glorious life
Is worth an age without a name.
Verses Written During the War, 1756–1763. The Bee, 12 Oct. 1791

THOMAS MORELL 1703–1784

1 See, the conquering hero comes!
Sound the trumpets, beat the drums!
Joshua (1748), pt.iii (Libretto for Handel's oratorio)

GENERAL GEORGE POPE MORRIS 1802–1864

2 Woodman, spare that tree!
Touch not a single bough!
In youth it sheltered me,
And I'll protect it now.
Woodman, Spare That Tree (1830)

WILLIAM MORRIS 1834–1896

3 And ever she sung from noon to noon,
'Two red roses across the moon.'
Two Red Roses Across the Moon

4 Have nothing in your houses that you do not know to be useful, or believe to be beautiful.
Hopes and Fears for Art (1882), p.108

THOMAS MORTON 1764?–1838

5 Approbation from Sir Hubert Stanley is praise indeed.
A Cure for the Heartache (1797), V.ii

6 Always ding, dinging Dame Grundy into my ears—what will Mrs Grundy zay? What will Mrs Grundy think?
Speed the Plough (1798), I.i

JOHN LOTHROP MOTLEY 1814–1877

7 As long as he lived, he was the guiding-star of a whole brave nation, and when he died the little children cried in the streets. [William of Orange.]
Rise of the Dutch Republic (1856), pt.vi, ch.vii

8 Give us the luxuries of life, and we will dispense with its necessities.
O.W. Holmes, *Autocrat of the Breakfast-Table*, ch.6

ALFRED DE MUSSET 1810–1857

9 *Malgré moi l'infini me tourmente.*
I can't help it, the idea of the infinite torments me.
***Premières Poésies.* L'Espoir en Dieu**

NAPOLEON I 1769–1821

1 *Du sublime au ridicule il n'y a qu'un pas.*
There is only one step from the sublime to the ridiculous.
To De Pradt, Polish ambassador, after the retreat from Moscow in 1812. De Pradt, *Histoire de l'Ambassade dans le grand-duché de Varsovie en 1812*, 1815 edn., p.215. See Paine.

2 *Quant au courage moral, il avait trouvé fort rare, disait-il, celui de deux heures après minuit; c'est-à-dire le courage de l'improviste.*
As to moral courage, I have very rarely met with two o'clock in the morning courage: I mean instantaneous courage.
Las Cases, Mémorial de Ste-Hélène, 4–5 Dec. 1815

3 *La carrière ouverte aux talents.*
The career open to talents.
O'Meara, *Napoleon in Exile* (1822), vol.i, p.103

4 *L'Angleterre est une nation de boutiquiers.*
England is a nation of shopkeepers.
Attr. by B.E. O'Meara, *Napoleon at St. Helena*, vol.ii. See Adam Smith.

5 An army marches on its stomach.
Attr. See, e.g., *Windsor Magazine*, 1904, p.268. Probably condensed from a long passage in Las Cases, *Mémorial de Ste-Hélène* (Nov. 1816). Also attr. to Frederick the Great

OGDEN NASH 1902–1971

6 One would be in less danger
From the wiles of a stranger
If one's own kin and kith
Were more fun to be with.
Family Court

7 Candy
  Is dandy
  But liquor
  Is quicker.
Reflections on Ice-Breaking

8 The turtle lives 'twixt plated decks
Which practically conceal its sex.
I think it clever of the turtle
In such a fix to be so fertile.
The Turtle

1 Sure, deck your lower limbs in pants;
Yours are the limbs, my sweeting.
You look divine as you advance—
Have you seen yourself retreating?
What's the Use?

THOMAS NASHE 1567–1601

2 Brightness falls from the air;
Queens have died young and fair;
Dust hath closed Helen's eye.
I am sick, I must die.
In Time of Pestilence

HORATIO, LORD NELSON 1758–1805

3 I have only one eye,—I have a right to be blind sometimes: ... I really do not see the signal!
At the battle of Copenhagen. Southey, *Life of Nelson*, ch. 7

4 England expects that every man will do his duty.
At the battle of Trafalgar

5 Thank God, I have done my duty.

6 Kiss me, Hardy.

EMPEROR NERO A.D. 37–68

7 *Qualis artifex pereo!*
What an artist dies with me!
Suetonius, *Life of Nero*, xlix.1

SIR HENRY NEWBOLT 1862–1938

8 Admirals all, for England's sake,
  Honour be yours, and fame!
And honour, as long as waves shall break,
  To Nelson's peerless name!
Admirals All, i

9 There's a breathless hush in the Close to-night—
  Ten to make and the match to win.
The Island Race. **Vitaï Lampada**

10 Play up! play up! and play the game!'

1 Now the sunset breezes shiver,
And she's fading down the river,
But in England's song for ever
She's the Fighting Téméraire.
The Fighting Téméraire

CARDINAL NEWMAN 1801–1890

2 It is very difficult to get up resentment towards persons whom one has never seen.
Apologia pro Vita Sua (1864). **Mr. Kingsley's Method of Disputation**

3 It is almost a definition of a gentleman to say that he is one who never inflicts pain.
The Idea of a University (1852). **Knowledge and Religious Duty**

4 It is as absurd to argue men, as to torture them, into believing.
Sermon at Oxford, 11 Dec. 1831

5 *We can believe what we choose*. We are answerable for what we choose to believe.
Letter to Mrs. William Froude, 27 June 1848

SIR ISAAC NEWTON 1642–1727

6 I do not know what I may appear to the world, but to myself I seem to have been only like a boy playing on the sea-shore, and diverting myself in now and then finding a smoother pebble or a prettier shell than ordinary, whilst the great ocean of truth lay all undiscovered before me.
L.T. More, *Isaac Newton* (1934), p.664

EMPEROR NICHOLAS I OF RUSSIA 1796–1855

7 *Nous avons sur les bras un homme malade—un homme gravement malade*.
We have on our hands a sick man—a very sick man.
[The sick man of Europe, the Turk.]
Parliamentary Papers. Accounts and Papers, vol.lxxi, pt.5. Eastern Papers, p.2. Sir G.H. Seymour to Lord John Russell, 11 Jan. 1853

1 Russia has two generals in whom she can confide—Generals Janvier and Février.
Attr. See *Punch*, 10 Mar. 1853.

FRIEDRICH NIETZSCHE 1844–1900

2 *Ich lehre euch den Übermenschen. Der Mensch ist Etwas, das überwunden werden soll.*
I teach you the superman. Man is something to be surpassed.
Also Sprach Zarathustra. Prologue (1883)

3 *Lachende Löwen müssen kommen.*
Laughing lions must come.
IV, **Die Begrüssung**

4 *Gott ist tot.*
God is dead.
Die fröhliche Wissenschaft, III.108

5 *Der christliche Entschluss, die Welt hässlich und schlecht zu finden, hat die Welt hässlich und schlecht gemacht.*
The Christian resolution to find the world ugly and bad has made the world ugly and bad.
130

6 *Gefährlich leben!*
Live dangerously!
IV.283

7 *Wenn du lange in einen Abgrund blickst, blickt der Abgrund auch in dich hinein.*
If you gaze for long into an abyss, the abyss gazes also into you.
Jenseits von Gut und Böse, IV.146

GENERAL R.-G. NIVELLE 1856–1924

8 *Ils ne passeront pas.*
They shall not pass.
Used as a slogan throughout the defence of Verdun and often attributed to Marshal Pétain. Nivelle's Order of the Day dated 26 Feb. 1916 read '*Vous ne les laisserez pas passer.*' Taken up by the Republicans in the Spanish Civil War as '*No pasarán!*'

ALFRED NOYES 1880–1958

1 Go down to Kew in lilac-time (it isn't far from London!)
Barrel Organ

2 The wind was a torrent of darkness among the gusty trees,
The moon was a ghostly galleon tossed upon cloudy seas,
The road was a ribbon of moonlight over the purple moor,
And the highwayman came riding—
Riding—riding—
The highwayman came riding, up to the old inn-door.
The Highwayman

SEAN O'CASEY 1884–1964

3 The whole counthry's in a state of chassis. [Boyle.]
Juno and the Paycock (1924), II. Meaning 'a state of chaos'. In Act I and Act III (last line) used of the whole world.

WILLIAM OCCAM c.1280–1349

4 *Entia non sunt multiplicanda praeter necessitatem.*
No more things should be presumed to exist than are absolutely necessary.
'Occams's Razor'. Ancient philosophical principle, often attributed to Occam, but used by many earlier thinkers. Not found in this form in his writings, though he frequently used similar expressions, e.g. *Pluralitas non est ponenda sine necessitate* (***Quodlibeta,*** c.1324, V, Q.i)

ADOLPH S. OCHS 1858–1935

5 All the news that's fit to print.
Motto of the *New York Times*

DANIEL O'CONNELL 1775–1847

6 [Sir Robert] Peel's smile: like the silver plate on a coffin.
Quoting J.P. Curran (1750–1817), Irish politician and lawyer. See *Hansard*, 26 Feb. 1835.

JOHN O'KEEFFE 1747–1833

7 Fat, fair and forty were all the toasts of the young men.
Irish Mimic (1795), ii

1 You should always except the present company.
London Hermit (1793), I.ii

DENNIS O'KELLY 1720?–1787

2 Eclipse first, the rest nowhere.
Epsom, 3 May 1769. *Annals of Sporting*, vol.ii, p.271. *D.N.B.* gives the occasion as the Queen's Plate at Winchester, 1769.

FRANK WARD O'MALLEY 1875–1932

3 Life is just one damned thing after another.
Attr. See *Literary Digest*, 5 Nov. 1932. Also attr. Elbert Hubbard

BARONESS ORCZY 1865–1947

4 We seek him here, we seek him there,
Those Frenchies seek him everywhere.
Is he in heaven?—Is he in hell?
That demmed, elusive Pimpernel?
The Scarlet Pimpernel (1905), ch.12

GEORGE ORWELL 1903–1950

5 All animals are equal but some animals are more equal than others.
Animal Farm (1945), ch.10

6 I'm fat, but I'm thin inside. Has it ever struck you that there's a thin man inside every fat man, just as they say there's a statue inside every block of stone?
Coming Up For Air (1939), Part I, ch.3. See Connolly.

7 Big Brother is watching you.
1984 (1949), p.1

8 *Doublethink* means the power of holding two contradictory beliefs in one's mind simultaneously, and accepting both of them.
pt.II, ch.9

9 If you want a picture of the future, imagine a boot stamping on a human face— for ever.
pt.III, ch.3

JOHN L. O'SULLIVAN 1813–1895

1 The best government is that which governs least.
Introduction to *The United States Magazine and Democratic Review* (1837)

JAMES OTIS 1725–1783

2 Taxation without representation is tyranny.
Watchword (coined 1761?) of the American Revolution. See Samuel Eliot Morison, *Dict. Am. Biog.*, xiv.102.

OVID 43 B.C–A.D. 17

3 *Iuppiter ex alto periuria ridet amantum.*
Jupiter from on high laughs at lovers' perjuries.
Ars Amatoria, i.633

4 *Video meliora, proboque;*
Deteriora sequor.
I see the better way, and approve it; I follow the worse.
Metamorphoses, vii.20

5 *Principiis obsta.*
Stop it at the start.
Remedia Amoris, 91

6 *Sponte sua carmen numeros veniebat ad aptos,*
Et quod temptabam dicere versus erat.
Of its own accord my song would come in the right rhythms, and what I was trying to say was poetry.
Tristia, IV.x.25

WILFRED OWEN 1893–1918

7 Above all, this book is not concerned with Poetry.
The subject of it is War, and the Pity of War.
The Poetry is in the pity.
Poems (1920), Preface

8 All the poet can do today is to warn.

9 What passing-bells for these who die as cattle?
Anthem for Doomed Youth

10 Red lips are not so red
As the stained stones kissed by the English dead.
Greater Love

1 I went hunting wild
After the wildest beauty in the world.
Strange Meeting

2 I am the enemy you killed, my friend.

TOM PAINE 1737–1809

3 Infidelity does not consist in believing, or in disbelieving, it consists in professing to believe what one does not believe.
The Age of Reason (1794), pt.i

4 The sublime and the ridiculous are often so nearly related, that it is difficult to class them separately.
pt.ii (1795), p.20

5 These are the times that try men's souls. The summer soldier and the sunshine patriot will, in this crisis, shrink from the service of their country.
The Crisis, Intro. (Dec. 1776)

JOSÉ DE PALAFOX 1780–1847

6 War to the knife.
On 4 Aug. 1808, at the siege of Saragossa.

LORD PALMERSTON 1784–1865

7 Die, my dear Doctor, that's the last thing I shall do!
Attr. last words

DOROTHY PARKER 1893–1967

8 Oh, life is a glorious cycle of song,
A medley of extemporanea;
And love is a thing that can never go wrong,
And I am Marie of Roumania.
Comment

9 Four be the things I'd been better without:
Love, curiosity, freckles, and doubt.
Inventory

10 Men seldom make passes
At girls who wear glasses.
News Item

1 Guns aren't lawful;
Nooses give;
Gas smells awful;
You might as well live.
Résumé

2 She ran the whole gamut of the emotions from A to B.
Of Katharine Hepburn in a Broadway play

3 How could they tell?
[On being told of the death of President Coolidge.]
John Keats, *You might as well live* (1971), Foreword

C. NORTHCOTE PARKINSON 1909–

4 Work expands so as to fill the time available for its completion.
Parkinson's Law (1958), I, opening words

BLAISE PASCAL 1623–1662

5 *Tout le malheur des hommes vient d'une seule chose, qui est de ne savoir pas demeurer en repos dans une chambre.*
All the misfortunes of men derive from one single thing, which is their inability to be at ease in a room [at home].
Pensées, ed. L. Brunschivicg (5th edn. 1909), ii.139

6 *Le nez de Cléopâtre: s'il eût été plus court, toute la face de la terre aurait changé.*
Had Cleopatra's nose been shorter, the whole face of the world would have changed.
162

7 *Le silence éternel de ces espaces infinis m'effraie.*
The eternal silence of these infinite spaces [the heavens] terrifies me.
iii.206

8 *On mourra seul.*
We shall die alone.
211

9 *Le coeur a ses raisons que la raison ne connaît point.*
The heart has its reasons which reason knows nothing of.
iv.277

1 *Je n'ai fait celle-ci plus longue que parce que je n'ai pas eu le loisir de la faire plus courte.*
I have made this letter longer than usual, only because I have not had the time to make it shorter.
Lettres Provinciales (1657), xvi

LOUIS PASTEUR 1822–1895

2 *Dans les champs de l'observation le hasard ne favorise que les esprits préparés.*
Where observation is concerned, chance favours only the prepared mind.
Address given on the inauguration of the Faculty of Science, University of Lille, 7 Dec. 1854.

WALTER PATER 1839–1894

3 She is older than the rocks among which she sits.
Studies in the History of the Renaissance (1873), **Leonardo da Vinci**

4 All art constantly aspires towards the condition of music.
The School of Giorgione

5 To burn always with this hard, gemlike flame, to maintain this ecstasy, is success in life.
Conclusion

MARK PATTISON 1813–1884

6 In research the horizon recedes as we advance.
Isaac Casaubon (1875), ch.10

JAMES PAYN 1830–1898

7 I had never had a piece of toast
Particularly long and wide,
But fell upon the sanded floor,
And always on the buttered side.
Chambers's Journal, 2 Feb. 1884. See Thomas Moore.

J.H. PAYNE 1791–1852

8 Mid pleasures and palaces though we may roam,
Be it ever so humble, there's no place like home.
Clari, the Maid of Milan (1823), **Home, Sweet Home**

THOMAS LOVE PEACOCK 1785–1866

1 The mountain sheep are sweeter,
  But the valley sheep are fatter;
We therefore deemed it meeter
  To carry off the latter.

The Misfortunes of Elphin (1823), ch.11. **The War-Song of Dinas Vawr**

1ST EARL OF PEMBROKE 1501?–1570

2 Out ye whores, to work, to work, ye whores, go spin.

Aubrey, *Brief Lives*. Commonly quoted as 'Go spin, you jades, go spin'. See Sir W. Scott, *Journal*, 19 Feb. 1826.

2ND EARL OF PEMBROKE c.1534–1601

3 A parliament can do any thing but make a man a woman, and a woman a man.

Quoted in Speech made by his son, the 4th Earl on 11 Apr. 1648, proving himself Chancellor of Oxford. *Harleian Miscellany* (1810), Vol.5, p.113

WILLIAM PENN 1644–1718

4 The taking of a Bribe or Gratuity, should be punished with as severe Penalties as the defrauding of the State.

Some Fruits of Solitude, in Reflections and Maxims relating to the conduct of Humane Life (1693), pt.i, No.384

SAMUEL PEPYS 1633–1703

5 And so to bed.

Diary, 20 Apr. 1660

6 Music and women I cannot but give way to, whatever my business is.

9 Mar. 1665–6

7 And mighty proud I am (and ought to be thankful to God Almighty) that I am able to have a spare bed for my friends.

8 Aug. 1666

PERICLES c.495–429 B.C.

8 For famous men have the whole earth as their memorial.

Funeral Oration, Athens, 430 B.C., as reported by Thucydides, *Histories*, ii.43, 3. Trans. Rex Warner

PETRONIUS A.D. 1st cent.

1 *Cave canem.*
Beware of the dog.
Satyricon: Cena Trimalchionis, 29.1

2 *Abiit ad plures.*
He's gone to join the majority.
42.5. Meaning the dead.

EDWARD JOHN PHELPS 1822–1900

3 The man who makes no mistakes does not usually make anything.
Speech at Mansion House, 24 Jan. 1899

WENDELL PHILLIPS 1811–1884

4 Every man meets his Waterloo at last.
Speeches (1880), Lecture at Brooklyn, N.Y., 1 Nov. 1859

WILLIAM PITT, EARL OF CHATHAM 1708–1778

5 The atrocious crime of being a young man ... I shall neither attempt to palliate nor deny.
House of Commons, 27 Jan. 1741

WILLIAM PITT 1759–1806

6 England has saved herself by her exertions, and will, as I trust, save Europe by her example.
Guildhall, 1805

7 Roll up that map; it will not be wanted these ten years.
On a map of Europe, after hearing the news of the Battle of Austerlitz Dec. 1805. Lord Stanhope, *Life of the Rt. Hon. William Pitt* (1862), vol.iv, p.369

PLATO c.429–347 B.C.

8 But, my dearest Agathon, it is truth which you cannot contradict; you can without any difficulty contradict Socrates.
Symposium, 201

PLAUTUS d. c.184 B.C.

1 *Lupus est homo homini, non homo, quom qualis sit non novit.*
A man is a wolf rather than a man to another man, when he hasn't yet found out what he's like.
Asinaria, 495. Often cited simply as ***Homo homini lupus*** (A man is a wolf to another man)

2 *Dictum sapienti sat est.*
What's been said is enough for anyone with sense.
Persa, 729. Proverbially later, *Verbum sapienti sat est*, A word is enough for the wise.

PLUTARCH c.50–c.120

3 He who cheats with an oath acknowledges that he is afraid of his enemy, but that he thinks little of God.
Lives: **Lysander, 18**

EDGAR ALLAN POE 1809–1849

4 I was a child and she was a child,
In this kingdom by the sea;
But we loved with a love which was more than love—
I and my Annabel Lee.
Annabel Lee (1849)

5 The fever call'd 'Living'
Is conquer'd at last.
For Annie

6 Quoth the Raven, 'Nevermore'.
The Raven (1845), xvii

7 The glory that was Greece
And the grandeur that was Rome.
To Helen, l.9

MADAME DE POMPADOUR 1721–1764

8 *Après nous le déluge.*
After us the deluge.
Madame de Hausset, *Mémoires*, p.19

ALEXANDER POPE 1688–1744

9 Stretch'd on the rack of a too easy chair.
The Dunciad, bk.iv, l.342

1 On all the line a sudden vengeance waits,
And frequent hearses shall besiege your gates.
Elegy to the Memory of an Unfortunate Lady, l.37

2 You beat your pate, and fancy wit will come;
Knock as you please, there's nobody at home.
Epigram

3 I am his Highness' dog at Kew;
Pray, tell me sir, whose dog are you?
Epigram Engraved on the Collar of a Dog which I gave to his Royal Highness

4 Sir, I admit your gen'ral rule
That every poet is a fool;
But you yourself may serve to show it,
That every fool is not a poet.
Epigram from the French

5 As yet a child, nor yet a fool to fame,
I lisp'd in numbers, for the numbers came.
Epistle to Dr. Arbuthnot, l.127. See Ovid.

6 Damn with faint praise, assent with civil leer,
And, without sneering, teach the rest to sneer.
l.201. See Wycherley.

7 Satire or sense, alas! can Sporus feel?
Who breaks a butterfly upon a wheel?
l.307

8 'Tis Education forms the common mind,
Just as the twig is bent, the tree's inclin'd.
Epistles to Several Persons Ep.i. **To Lord Cobham,** l.149

9 You purchase pain with all that joy can give,
And die of nothing but a rage to live.
Ep.ii. **To a Lady,** l.99

10 Still round and round the ghosts of beauty glide,
And haunt the places where their honour died.
l.241

11 The ruling passion, be it what it will,
The ruling passion conquers reason still.
Ep.iii. **To Lord Bathurst,** l.153

12 Consult the genius of the place in all.
Ep.iv. **To Lord Burlington,** l.57

1 Nature, and Nature's laws lay hid in night:
God said, *Let Newton be!* and all was light.
Epitaphs. **Intended for Sir Isaac Newton.** See Squire.

2 Some have at first for wits, then poets pass'd,
Turn'd critics next, and prov'd plain fools at last.
An Essay on Criticism, l.36

3 A little learning is a dang'rous thing;
Drink deep, or taste not the Pierian spring:
There shallow draughts intoxicate the brain,
And drinking largely sobers us again.
l.215

4 True wit is nature to advantage dress'd,
What oft was thought, but ne'er so well express'd.
l.297

5 A needless Alexandrine ends the song,
That, like a wounded snake, drags its slow length along.
l.356

6 To err is human, to forgive, divine.
l.525

7 All seems infected that th'infected spy,
As all looks yellow to the jaundic'd eye.
l.558

8 The bookful blockhead, ignorantly read,
With loads of learned lumber in his head.
l.612

9 For fools rush in where angels fear to tread.
l.625

10 Hope springs eternal in the human breast;
Man never Is, but always To be blest.
An Essay on Man. Epistle i, l.95

11 Know then thyself, presume not God to scan,
The proper study of mankind is man.
Ep.ii, l.1. See Charron.

12 A wit's a feather, and a chief a rod;
An honest man's the noblest work of God.
Ep.iv, l.247

13 Thou wert my guide, philosopher, and friend.
l.390

1 There St John mingles with my friendly bowl
The feast of reason and the flow of soul.
Imitations of Horace. Hor.II, Sat.1. **To Mr. Fortescue,** l.127

2 Welcome the coming, speed the parting guest.
Odyssey, xv.83

3 Where'er you walk, cool gales shall fan the glade.
Pastorals, Summer, l.73

4 They shift the moving Toyshop of their heart.
The Rape of the Lock, c.i, l.100

5 Fair tresses man's imperial race insnare,
And beauty draws us with a single hair.
l.27

6 At ev'ry word a reputation dies.
c.iii, l.16

7 This is the Jew
That Shakespeare drew.
Of Macklin's performance of Shylock, 14 Feb. 1741. Baker, Reed & Jones, *Biographia Dramatica* (1812), vol.I, pt.ii, p.469

8 A man should never be ashamed to own he has been in the wrong, which is but saying, in other words, that he is wiser to-day than he was yesterday.
Thoughts on Various Subjects (1706)

BEILBY PORTEUS 1731–1808

9 War its thousands slays, Peace its ten thousands.
Death (1759), l.179

10 Teach him how to live,
And, oh! still harder lesson! how to die.
l.319

EZRA POUND 1885–1972

11 Winter is icummen in,
Lhude sing Goddamm,
Raineth drop and staineth slop,
And how the wind doth ramm!
Sing: Goddamm.
Ancient Music. See Anon.

1 There died a myriad,
And of the best, among them,
For an old bitch gone in the teeth,
For a botched civilization.
Hugh Selwyn Mauberley, V

2 I had over-prepared the event,
that much was ominous.
With middle-ageing care
I had laid out just the right books.
I had almost turned down the pages.
Villanelle: the psychological hour

WINTHROP MACKWORTH PRAED 1802–1839

3 My own Araminta, say 'No!'
A Letter of Advice

PRAYER BOOK 1662

4 We have erred, and strayed from thy ways like lost sheep. We have followed too much the devices and desires of our own hearts.
General Confession

5 We have left undone those things which we ought to have done; And we have done those things which we ought not to have done; And there is no health in us.

6 That we may hereafter live a godly, righteous, and sober life.

7 Give peace in our time, O Lord.
Versicle

8 In Quires and Places where they sing.
Rubric after Third Collect

9 Lighten our darkness, we beseech thee, O Lord.
Evening Prayer. Third Collect

10 Have mercy upon us miserable sinners.
The Litany

11 All sorts and conditions of men.
Collect or Prayer for all Conditions of Men

12 A happy issue out of all their afflictions.

1 Hear them read, mark, learn, and inwardly digest them.
Collects. 2nd Sunday in Advent

2 An open and notorious evil liver.
Holy Communion. Introductory rubric

3 I should renounce the devil and all his works.
Catechism

4 To keep my hands from picking and stealing, and my tongue from evil-speaking, lying, and slandering.

5 An outward and visible sign of an inward and spiritual grace.

6 If any of you know cause, or just impediment, why these two persons should not be joined together in holy Matrimony, ye are to declare it.
Solemnization of Matrimony. The Banns

7 Not by any to be enterprised, nor taken in hand, unadvisedly, lightly, or wantonly.
Exhortation

8 Let him now speak, or else hereafter for ever hold his peace.

9 Forsaking all other, keep thee only unto her, so long as ye both shall live?
Betrothal

10 To have and to hold from this day forward, for better for worse, for richer for poorer, in sickness and in health, to love, cherish, and to obey, till death us do part.

11 With this Ring I thee wed, with my body I thee worship, and with all my worldly goods I thee endow.
Wedding

12 Those whom God hath joined together let no man put asunder.

13 In the midst of life we are in death.
Burial of the Dead. First anthem

14 Earth to earth, ashes to ashes, dust to dust.
Interment

15 Why do the heathen so furiously rage together?
Psalms 2:1

1 Out of the mouth of very babes and sucklings hast thou ordained strength.
8:2

2 The fool hath said in his heart: There is no God.
14:1

3 The heavens declare the glory of God: and the firmament sheweth his handy-work.
19:1

4 Some put their trust in chariots, and some in horses.
20:7

5 The Lord is my shepherd: therefore can I lack nothing. He shall feed me in a green pasture: and lead me forth beside the waters of comfort.
23:1

6 Yea, though I walk through the valley of the shadow of death, I will fear no evil: for thou art with me; thy rod and thy staff comfort me.
Thou shalt prepare a table before me against them that trouble me: thou hast anointed my head with oil, and my cup shall be full.
But thy loving-kindness and mercy shall follow me all the days of my life: and I will dwell in the house of the Lord for ever.
4

7 The earth is the Lord's, and all that therein is: the compass of the world, and they that dwell therein.
24:1

8 Lift up your heads, O ye gates, and be ye lift up, ye everlasting doors: and the King of glory shall come in.
7

9 Heaviness may endure for a night, but joy cometh in the morning.
30:5

10 Sing unto the Lord a new song: sing praises lustily unto him with a good courage.
33:3

11 I have been young, and now am old: and yet saw I never the righteous forsaken, nor his seed begging their bread.
37:25

1 I myself have seen the ungodly in great power: and flourishing like a green bay-tree.
36

2 Lord, let me know mine end, and the number of my days: that I may be certified how long I have to live.
39:5

3 The King's daughter is all glorious within.
45:14

4 God is our hope and strength: a very present help in trouble.
46:1

5 O that I had wings like a dove: for then would I flee away, and be at rest.
55:6

6 Which refuseth to hear the voice of the charmer: charm he never so wisely.
58:5

7 Let them fall upon the edge of the sword: that they may be a portion for foxes.
63:11

8 The zeal of thine house hath even eaten me.
69:9

9 Thy rebuke hath broken my heart; I am full of heaviness.
21

10 For promotion cometh neither from the east, nor from the west: nor yet from the south.
75:7

11 O how amiable are thy dwellings: thou Lord of hosts!
84:1

12 They will go from strength to strength.
7

13 I had rather be a door-keeper in the house of my God: than to dwell in the tents of ungodliness.
11

14 Lord, thou hast been our refuge: from one generation to another.
90:1

1 For a thousand years in thy sight are but as yesterday: seeing that is past as a watch in the night.
4

2 The days of our age are threescore years and ten.
10

3 Thou shalt not be afraid for any terror by night: nor for the arrow that flieth by day;
For the pestilence that walketh in darkness: nor for the sickness that destroyeth in the noon-day.
91:5

4 For he shall give his angels charge over thee.
11

5 O come, let us sing unto the Lord: let us heartily rejoice in the strength of our salvation.
95:1

6 O sing unto the Lord a new song.
98:1

7 Man goeth forth to his work, and to his labour: until the evening.
104:23

8 The iron entered into his soul.
105:18

9 They that go down to the sea in ships: and occupy their business in great waters;
These men see the works of the Lord: and his wonders in the deep.
107:23

10 I will lift up mine eyes unto the hills: from whence cometh my help.
My help cometh even from the Lord: who hath made *heaven and earth.*
He will not suffer thy foot to be moved: and he that keepeth thee will not sleep.
Behold, he that keepeth Israel: shall neither slumber nor sleep.
121:1

11 The Lord shall preserve thy going out, and thy coming in: from this time forth for evermore.
8

1 I was glad when they said unto me: We will go into the house of the Lord.
122:1

2 Except the Lord build the house: their labour is but lost that build it.
Except the Lord keep the city: the watchman waketh but in vain.
127:1

3 Thy wife shall be as the fruitful vine: upon the walls of thine house.
Thy children like the olive-branches: round about thy table.
128:3

4 Out of the deep have I called unto thee, O Lord: Lord, hear my voice.
130:1

5 O give thanks unto the Lord, for he is gracious: and his mercy endureth for ever.
136:1

6 By the waters of Babylon we sat down and wept: when we remembered thee, O Sion.
137:1

7 How shall we sing the Lord's song: in a strange land?
If I forget thee, O Jerusalem: let my right hand forget her cunning.
4

8 Such knowledge is too wonderful and excellent for me: I cannot attain unto it.
139:5

9 I will give thanks unto thee, for I am fearfully and wonderfully made.
13

10 O put not your trust in princes, nor in any child of man: for there is no help in them.
146:2

11 To bind their kings in chains: and their nobles with links of iron.
149:8

1 Holy Scripture containeth all things necessary to salvation.
Articles of Religion (1562). 6

2 It is lawful for Christian men, at the commandment of the Magistrate, to wear weapons, and serve in the wars.
37

MATTHEW PRIOR 1664–1721

3 For as our diff'rent ages move,
'Tis so ordained, would Fate but mend it,
That I shall be past making love,
When she begins to comprehend it.
To a Child of Quality of Five Years Old

4 No, no; for my virginity,
When I lose that, says Rose, I'll die:
Behind the elms last night, cried Dick,
Rose, were you not extremely sick?
A True Mind

ALEXANDRE PRIVAT D'ANGLEMONT
1820?–1859

5 *Je les ai épatés, les bourgeois.*
I flabbergasted them, the *bourgeois*.
Attr. Also attr. to Baudelaire, in the form *Il faut épater le bourgeois*.

PROTAGORAS c.481–411 B.C.

6 Man is the measure of all things.
Plato, *Theaetetus*, 160d

PIERRE-JOSEPH PROUDHON 1809–1865

7 *La propriété c'est le vol.*
Property is theft.
Qu'est-ce que la Propriété? (1840), ch.1

MARCEL PROUST 1871–1922

8 *Longtemps je me suis couché de bonne heure.*
For a long time I used to go to bed early.
A la Recherche du Temps Perdu, tr. C.K. Scott-Moncrieff and S. Hudson (1922–31), **Du côté de chez Swann**, opening sentence

1 *Ces dépêches dont M. de Guermantes avait spirituellement fixé le modèle: 'Impossible venir, mensonge suit.'*
One of those telegrams of which M. de Guermantes had wittily fixed the formula: 'Cannot come, lie follows'.
Le Temps Retrouvé, vol.I, ch.1. See Beresford.

2 *Les vrais paradis sont les paradis qu'on a perdus.*
The true paradises are paradises we have lost.
vol.II, ch.3

PUBLILIUS SYRUS 1st cent. B.C.

3 *Inopi beneficium bis dat qui dat celeriter.*
He gives the poor man twice as much good who gives quickly.
Sententiae, 274. J.W. and A.M. Duff, *Minor Latin Poets*, Loeb edn. (1934). Proverbially *Bis dat qui cito dat* (He gives twice who gives soon)

4 *Necessitas dat legem non ipsa accipit.*
Necessity gives the law without itself acknowledging one.
444. Proverbially *Necessitas non habet legem* (Necessity has no law)

JOHN PUDNEY 1909–1977

5 Do not despair
For Johnny head-in-air;
He sleeps as sound
As Johnny underground.
For Johnny

PUNCH

6 Advice to persons about to marry.—'Don't.'
vol.viii, p.1. 1845

7 Never do to-day what you can put off till to-morrow.
vol.xvii, p.241. 1849

8 Who's 'im, Bill?
A stranger!
'Eave 'arf a brick at 'im.
vol.xxvi, p.82. 1854

1 Go directly—see what she's doing, and tell her she mustn't.
vol. lxiii, p.202. 1872

2 It's worse than wicked, my dear, it's vulgar.
Almanac. 1876

3 I used your soap two years ago; since then I have used no other.
vol.lxxxvi, p.197. 1884

4 Don't look at me, Sir, with—ah—in that tone of voice.
vol.lxxxvii, p.38. 1884

5 I'm afraid you've got a bad egg, Mr Jones.
Oh no, my Lord, I assure you! Parts of it are excellent!
vol.cix, p.222. 1895

ISRAEL PUTNAM 1718–1790

6 Men, you are all marksmen—don't one of you fire until you see the whites of their eyes.
Bunker Hill, 1775. Frothingham, *History of the Siege of Boston* (1873), ch.5, note. Also attributed to William Prescott (1726–95)

PYRRHUS 319–272 B.C

7 One more such victory and we are lost.
Plutarch, *Pyrrhus*. After defeating the Romans at Asculum, 279 B.C.

FRANCIS QUARLES 1592–1644

8 Our God and soldiers we alike adore
Ev'n at the brink of danger; not before:
After deliverance, both alike requited,
Our God's forgotten, and our soldiers slighted.
Epigram

9 My soul, sit thou a patient looker-on;
Judge not the play before the play is done:
Her plot hath many changes; every day
Speaks a new scene; the last act crowns the play.
Epigram. Respice Finem

FRANÇOIS QUESNAY 1694–1774

1 *Laisser passer et laisser faire.*
Free passage and freedom of action.
Salleron, *François Quesnay et la Physiocratie* (1958), II.940. See Argenson.

FRANÇOIS RABELAIS 1494?–c.1553

2 *L'appétit vient en mangeant.*
The appetite grows by eating.
Gargantua (1534), I.v

3 *Fay ce que vouldras.*
Do what you like.
lvii

4 *Je vais quérir un grand peut-être.*
I am going to seek a great perhaps.
Attr. last words. See Jean Fleury, *Rabelais et ses oeuvres* (1877), vol.I, ch.3, pt.15, p.130.

5 *Tirez le rideau, la farce est jouée.*
Bring down the curtain, the farce is played out.

JEAN RACINE 1639–1699

6 *Elle flotte, elle hésite; en un mot, elle est femme.*
She floats, she hesitates; in a word, she's a woman.
Athalie (1691), iii.3

7 *C'est Vénus tout entière à sa proie attachée.*
It's Venus entire and whole fastening on her prey.
Phèdre (1677), I.iii

8 *Point d'argent, point de Suisse, et ma porte était close.*
No money, no service, and my door stayed shut.
Les Plaideurs (1668), I.i

SIR WALTER RALEGH 1552?–1618

9 If all the world and love were young,
And truth in every shepherd's tongue,
These pretty pleasures might me move
To live with thee, and be thy love.
Answer to Marlow

10 Only we die in earnest, that's no jest.
On the Life of Man

1 Give me my scallop-shell of quiet,
My staff of faith to walk upon,
My scrip of joy, immortal diet,
My bottle of salvation,
My gown of glory, hope's true gage,
And thus I'll take my pilgrimage.
The Passionate Man's Pilgrimage

SIR WALTER RALEIGH 1861–1922

2 I wish I loved the Human Race;
I wish I loved its silly face;
I wish I liked the way it walks;
I wish I liked the way it talks;
And when I'm introduced to one
I wish I thought *What Jolly Fun!*
Laughter from a Cloud (1923), p.228. **Wishes of an Elderly Man**

JULIAN RALPH 1853–1903

3 News value.
Lecture to Brander Matthews's English Class, Columbia, 1892. Thomas Beer, *Mauve Decade*

TERENCE RATTIGAN 1911–1977

4 *Brian:* Elle a des idées au-dessus de sa gare. *Kenneth:* You can't do it like that. You can't say au-dessus de sa gare. It isn't that sort of station.
French Without Tears (1937), Act I

CHARLES READE 1814–1884

5 Sow an act, and you reap a habit. Sow a habit, and you reap a character. Sow a character, and you reap a destiny.
Attr. See *N. & Q.*, 9th series, vol.12, p. 377.

HENRY REED 1914–

6 To-day we have naming of parts. Yesterday
We had daily cleaning. And tomorrow morning,
We shall have what to do after firing. But to-day,
To-day we have naming of parts.
Naming of Parts (1946)

GENERAL JOSEPH REED 1741–1785

1 I am not worth purchasing, but such as I am, the King of Great Britain is not rich enough to do it.
U.S. Congress, 11 Aug. 1878. Reed understood himself to have been offered a bribe on behalf of the British Crown.

JULES RENARD 1864–1910

2 *Les bourgeois, ce sont les autres.*
The bourgeois are other people.
Journal, 28 Jan. 1890

DR. MONTAGUE JOHN RENDALL 1862–1950

3 Nation shall speak peace unto nation.
Written as the motto of the BBC in 1927 by Dr. Rendall, one of the first Governors of the Corporation

FREDERIC REYNOLDS 1764–1841

4 How goes the enemy? [Said by Mr. Ennui, 'the time-killer'.]
The Dramatist (1789), I.i

GRANTLAND RICE 1880–1954

5 For when the One Great Scorer comes
To write against your name,
He marks—not that you won or lost—
But how you played the game.
Alumnus Football

MANDY RICE-DAVIES 1944–

6 He would, wouldn't he?
When told that Lord Astor had denied her allegations. Trial of Stephen Ward, 29 June 1963

RAINER MARIA RILKE 1875–1926

7 *So leben wir und nehmen immer Abschied.*
Thus we live, forever taking leave.
Duineser Elegien, VIII

1 The love which consists in this, that two solitudes protect and limit and greet each other.
Briefe an einem jungen Dichter (1929), 14 May 1904

MARTIN RINKART 1586–1649

2 *Nun danket alle Gott.*
Now thank you all your God.
Das Danklied (1636). Sung as a hymn to the tune by Johann Crüger (1598–1662) composed in 1649

ANTOINE DE RIVAROL 1753–1801

3 *Ce qui n'est pas clair n'est pas français.*
What is not clear is not French.
Discours sur l'Universalité de la Langue Française (1784)

JOHN WILMOT, EARL OF ROCHESTER 1647–1680

4 What vain, unnecessary things are men!
How well we do without 'em!
Fragment

5 'Is there then no more?'
She cries. 'All this to love and rapture's due;
Must we not pay a debt to pleasure too?'
The Imperfect Enjoyment

6 Here lies a great and mighty king
  Whose promise none relies on;
He never said a foolish thing,
  Nor ever did a wise one.
The King's Epitaph

SAMUEL ROGERS 1763–1855

7 Think nothing done while aught remains to do.
Human Life (1819), l.49. See Lucan, *Works*, II.657.

8 But there are moments which he calls his own,
Then, never less alone than when alone,
Those whom he loved so long and sees no more,
Loved and still loves—not dead—but gone before,
He gathers round him.
l.755

1 By mahy a temple half as old as Time.
Italy. A Farewell (1828), ii.5

2 It doesn't much signify whom one marries, for one is sure to find next morning that it was someone else.
Table Talk (ed. Alexander Dyce, 1860)

MME ROLAND 1754–1793

3 *O liberté! O liberté! que de crimes on commet en ton nom!*
O liberty! O liberty! what crimes are committed in thy name!
Lamartine, *Histoire des Girondins* (1847), livre li, ch.8

PIERRE DE RONSARD 1524–1585

4 *Quand vous serez bien vieille, au soir, à la chandelle,*
Assise auprès du feu, dévidant et filant,
Direz, chantant mes vers, en vous émerveillant,
Ronsard me célébrait du temps que j'étais belle.
When you are very old, and sit in the candle-light at evening spinning by the fire, you will say, as you murmur my verses, a wonder in your eyes, 'Ronsard sang of me in the days when I was fair'.
Sonnets pour Hélène (1578), ii.43

PRESIDENT FRANKLIN D. ROOSEVELT 1882–1945

5 I pledge you—I pledge myself—to a new deal for the American people.
Chicago Convention, 2 July 1932. (See also *N. & Q.*, cxciv, p.529.)

6 Let me assert my firm belief that the only thing we have to fear is fear itself.
First Inaugural Address, 4 Mar. 1933

7 In the field of world policy; I would dedicate this nation to the policy of the good neighbour.

PRESIDENT THEODORE ROOSEVELT 1858–1919

8 Every reform movement has a lunatic fringe.
Speaking of the Progressive Party, in 1913

ALAN C. ROSS 1907–

1 'U' and 'Non-U'.
***Upper Class English Usage**, Bulletin de la Société Neo-Philologique de Helsinki* (1954). Reprinted in *Noblesse Oblige* (1956), ed. Nancy Mitford

CHRISTINA ROSSETTI 1830–1894

2 My heart is like a singing bird
Whose nest is in a watered shoot;
My heart is like an apple-tree
Whose boughs are bent with thickset fruit;
My heart is like a rainbow shell
That paddles in a halcyon sea;
My heart is gladder than all these
Because my love is come to me.
A Birthday

3 Come to me in the silence of the night;
Come in the speaking silence of a dream;
Come with soft rounded cheeks and eyes as bright
As sunlight on a stream;
Come back in tears,
O memory, hope, love of finished years.
Echo

4 Better by far you should forget and smile
Than that you should remember and be sad.
Remember

5 When I am dead, my dearest,
Sing no sad songs for me.
Song: 'When I am Dead'

6 And if thou wilt, remember,
And if thou wilt, forget.

DANTE GABRIEL ROSSETTI 1828–1882

7 I have been here before,
But when or how I cannot tell:
I know the grass beyond the door,
The sweet keen smell,
The sighing sound, the lights around the shore.
Sudden Light, i

GIOACCHINO ROSSINI 1792–1868

1 *Monsieur Wagner a de beaux moments, mais de mauvais quart d'heures.*
Wagner has lovely moments but awful quarters of an hour.
Said to Emile Naumann, April 1867. Naumann, *Italienische Tondichter* (1883), IV, 541

EDMOND ROSTAND 1868–1918

2 *Le seul rêve intéresse,*
Vivre sans rêve, qu'est-ce?
Et j'aime la Princesse
Lointaine.
The dream, alone, is of interest. What is life, without a dream? And I love the Distant Princess.
La Princesse Lointaine, I.iv

LEO C. ROSTEN 1908–

3 Any man who hates dogs and babies can't be all bad.
Of W.C. Fields, and often attributed to him. Speech at Masquers' Club dinner, 16 Feb. 1939. See letter, *T.L.S.*, 24 Jan. 1975.

NORMAN ROSTEN

4 Soldiers who wish to be a hero
Are practically zero
But those who wish to be civilians
Jesus they run into millions.
The Big Road (1946), pt.V

C.-J. ROUGET DE LISLE 1760–1836

5 *Allons, enfants de la patrie,*
Le jour de gloire est arrivé.
Come, children of our country, the day of glory has arrived.
La Marseillaise (25 Apr. 1792)

JEAN-JACQUES ROUSSEAU 1712–1778

6 *L'homme est né libre, et partout il est dans les fers.*
Man was born free, and everywhere he is in chains.
Du Contrat Social, ch.1

DR. ROUTH 1755–1854

1 You will find it a very good practice always to verify your references, sir!

Burgon, *Quarterly Review*, July 1878, vol.cxlvi, p.30, and *Lives of Twelve Good Men* (1888 edn.), vol I, p.73

NICHOLAS ROWE 1674–1718

2 Is this that haughty, gallant, gay Lothario?

The Fair Penitent (1703), V.i

DAMON RUNYON 1884–1946

3 More than somewhat.

Phrase used frequently in Runyon's work, and adopted as book-title in 1937.

JOHN RUSKIN 1819–1900

4 I have seen, and heard, much of Cockney impudence before now; but never expected to hear a coxcomb ask two hundred guineas for flinging a pot of paint in the public's face.

[On Whistler's 'Nocturne in Black and Gold'] ***Fors Clavigera*** letter lxxix, 18 June 1877

5 All violent feelings ... produce in us a falseness in all our impressions of external things, which I would generally characterize as the 'Pathetic Fallacy'.

Modern Painters (1888), vol.iii

6 Which of us ... is to do the hard and dirty work for the rest—and for what pay? Who is to do the pleasant and clean work, and for what pay?

Sesame and Lilies (1865), Lecture i. **Of King's Treasuries,** 30, note

7 There is really no such thing as bad weather, only different kinds of good weather.

Quoted by Lord Avebury

BERTRAND RUSSELL 1872–1970

8 Mathematics, rightly viewed, possesses not only truth, but supreme beauty—a beauty cold and austere, like that of sculpture.

Mysticism and Logic (1918), ch.4

SIR WILLIAM HOWARD RUSSELL 1820–1907

1 They dashed on towards that *thin red line tipped with steel.*

The British Expedition to the Crimea (1877), p.156. Of the Russians charging the British.

LORD RUTHERFORD 1871–1937

2 We haven't the money, so we've got to think.

Attr. in Prof. R.V. Jones, 1962 Brunel Lecture, 14 Feb. 1962

GILBERT RYLE 1900–1976

3 The dogma of the Ghost in the machine.

The Concept of Mind (1949), passim

CHARLES-AUGUSTIN SAINTE-BEUVE 1804–1869

4 *Et Vigny plus secret,*
Comme en sa tour d'ivoire, avant midi rentrait.
And Vigny more reserved,
Returned ere noon, within his ivory tower.

Les Pensées d'Août, à M. Villemain, p.152

'SAKI' (H.H. MUNRO) 1870–1916

5 There are so many things to complain of in this household that it would never have occurred to me to complain of rheumatism.

The Chronicles of Clovis (1911). **The Quest**

6 Never be a pioneer. It's the Early Christian that gets the fattest lion.

Reginald (1904), **Reginald's Choir Treat**

7 The cook was a good cook, as cooks go; and as cooks go she went.

Reginald on Besetting Sins

LORD SALISBURY 1830–1903

8 If you believe the doctors, nothing is wholesome: if you believe the theologians, nothing is innocent: if you believe the soldiers, nothing is safe.

Letter to Lord Lytton, 15 June 1877. Lady Gwendolen Cecil, *Life of Robert, Marquis of Salisbury*, vol.II, ch.4

1 By office boys for office boys.
Of the Daily Mail. See H. Hamilton Fyfe, *Northcliffe, an Intimate Biography*, ch.4.

JEAN-PAUL SARTRE 1905–1980

2 *L'Enfer, c'est les Autres.*
Hell is other people.
Huis Clos, sc.v

3 *Trois heures, c'est toujours trop tard ou trop tôt pour tout ce qu'on veut faire.*
Three o'clock is always too late or too early for anything you want to do.
La Nausée, **Vendredi**

SIEGFRIED SASSOON 1886–1967

4 Does it matter?—losing your legs? ...
For people will always be kind.
Does it Matter?

5 Does it matter?—losing your sight? ...
There's such splendid work for the blind.

6 You are too young to fall asleep for ever;
And when you sleep you remind me of the dead.
The Dug-Out

7 Everyone suddenly burst out singing.
Everyone Sang

8 In me the tiger sniffs the rose.
The Heart's Journey, VIII

GEORGE SAVILE, MARQUIS OF HALIFAX
see HALIFAX

FRIEDRICH VON SCHELLING 1775–1854

9 Architecture in general is frozen music.
Philosophie der Kunst (1809)

FRIEDRICH VON SCHILLER 1759–1805

10 *Freude, schöner Götterfunken,*
Tochter aus Elysium,
Wir betreten feuertrunken,
Himmlische, dein Heiligtum.

Deine Zauber binden wieder,
Was die Mode streng geteilt,
Alle Menschen werden Brüder
Wo dein sanfter Flügel weilt.

Joy, beautiful radiance of the gods, daughter of Elysium, we set foot in your heavenly shrine dazzled by your brilliance. Your charms re-unite what common use has harshly divided: all men become brothers under your tender wing.

An die Freude (1786)

1 *Die Weltgeschichte ist das Weltgericht.*
The world's history is the world's judgement.
First lecture as Prof. of History, Jena. 26 May 1789

PROFESSOR E.F. SCHUMACHER 1911–1977

2 Small is beautiful.
Title of book (1973)

CARL SCHURZ 1829–1906

3 Our country, right or wrong! When right, to be kept right; when wrong, to be put right!
Speech, U.S. Senate, 1872. See Decatur.

C.P. SCOTT 1846–1932

4 Comment is free but facts are sacred.
Manchester Guardian, 6 May 1926

5 Television? The word is half Latin and half Greek. No good can come of it.
Attr.

CAPTAIN ROBERT FALCON SCOTT 1868–1912

6 For God's sake look after our people.
Journal, 25 Mar. 1912

7 Had we lived, I should have had a tale to tell of the hardihood, endurance, and courage of my companions which would have stirred the heart of every Englishman.
Message to the Public

SIR WALTER SCOTT 1771–1832

1 Hail to the Chief who in triumph advances!
The Lady of the Lake (1810), c.II.xix

2 The way was long, the wind was cold,
The Minstrel was infirm and old;
His wither'd cheek and tresses grey,
Seem'd to have known a better day.
The Lay of the Last Minstrel (1805), introd. l.1

3 Breathes there the man, with soul so dead,
Who never to himself hath said,
  This is my own, my native land!
c.VI.i

4 To the vile dust, from whence he sprung,
Unwept, unhonour'd, and unsung.

5 O, young Lochinvar is come out of the west,
Through all the wide Border his steed was the best.
Marmion (1808), c.V.xii

6 So faithful in love, and so dauntless in war,
There never was knight like the young Lochinvar.

7 O what a tangled web we weave,
When first we practise to deceive!
c.VI.xvii

8 O Woman! in our hours of ease,
Uncertain, coy, and hard to please.
xxx

9 When pain and anguish wring the brow,
A ministering angel thou!

10 'Charge, Chester, charge! On, Stanley, on!'
Were the last words of Marmion.
xxxii

11 The play-bill, which is said to have announced the tragedy of Hamlet, the character of the Prince of Denmark being left out.
The Talisman (1825), introd.

ALAN SEEGER 1888–1916

1 I have a rendezvous with Death
At some disputed barricade.

I Have a Rendezvous with Death (*North American Review*, Oct. 1916)

JOHN SELDEN 1584–1654

2 Ignorance of the law excuses no man.

Table Talk (1689), 1892 edn. p.99. **Law**

3 Pleasure is nothing else but the intermission of pain, the enjoying of something I am in great trouble for till I have it.

p.132. **Pleasure**

W.C. SELLAR 1898–1951 and R.J. YEATMAN 1898?–1968

4 The Roman Conquest was, however, a *Good Thing*.

1066, And All That (1930), ch.1

5 The Cavaliers (Wrong but Wromantic) and the Roundheads (Right but Repulsive).

ch.35

6 The National Debt is a very Good Thing and it would be dangerous to pay it off for fear of Political Economy.

ch.38

SENECA 4 B.C./A.D. 1–65

7 Anyone can stop a man's life, but no one his death; a thousand doors open on to it.

Phoenissae, 152

ROBERT W. SERVICE 1874–1958

8 Ah! the clock is always slow;
It is later than you think.

Ballads of a Bohemian. **Spring,** ii

EDWARD SEXBY d. 1658

9 Killing no Murder Briefly Discourst in Three Questions.

Title of Pamphlet, 1657

ANNE SEXTON 1928–1974

1 In a dream you are never eighty.
Old

WILLIAM SHAKESPEARE 1564–1616

The line number is given without brackets where the scene is all verse up to the quotation and the line number is certain, and in square brackets where prose makes it variable. All references are to the Oxford Standard Authors Shakespeare in one volume.

2 A young man married is a man that's marred.
All's Well That Ends Well, II.iii.[315]

3 My salad days,
When I was green in judgment.
Anthony and Cleopatra, I.v.73

4 The barge she sat in, like a burnish'd throne,
Burn'd on the water.
II.ii. [199]

5 Age cannot wither her, nor custom stale
Her infinite variety.
[243]

6 Let's have one other gaudy night: call to me
All my sad captains.
III.xi.182

7 To business that we love we rise betime,
And go to 't with delight.
IV.iv.20

8 Finish, good lady; the bright day is done,
And we are for the dark.
V.ii.192

9 Give me my robe, put on my crown; I have
Immortal longings in me.
[282]

10 Now boast thee, death, in thy possession lies
A lass unparallel'd.
[317]

11 Sweet are the uses of adversity,
Which like the toad, ugly and venomous,
Wears yet a precious jewel in his head.
As You Like It, II.i.12

1 Sermons in stones, and good in everything.
17

2 As true a lover
As ever sigh'd upon a midnight pillow.
iv.[26]

3 Under the greenwood tree
Who loves to lie with me,
And turn his merry note
Unto the sweet bird's throat,
Come hither, come hither, come hither.
v.1

4 All the world's a stage,
And all the men and women merely players.
vii.139

5 And then the whining schoolboy, with his satchel,
And shining morning face, creeping like snail
Unwillingly to school.
145

6 Seeking the bubble reputation
Even in the cannon's mouth.
152

7 Second childishness, and mere oblivion,
Sans teeth, sans eyes, sans taste, sans everything.
165

8 Blow, blow, thou winter wind,
Thou art not so unkind
As man's ingratitude.
174

9 Down on your knees,
And thank heaven, fasting, for a good man's love.
III.v.57

10 I pray you, do not fall in love with me,
For I am falser than vows made in wine.
[72]

11 It was a lover and his lass,
With a hey, and a ho, and a hey nonino.
V.iii.[18]

12 My gracious silence, hail!
Coriolanus, II.i.[194]

1 Despising,
For you, the city, thus I turn my back:
There is a world elsewhere.
III.iii.131

2 Boldness be my friend!
Arm me, audacity.
Cymbeline, I.vi.18

3 Hark! hark! the lark at heaven's gate sings,
And Phoebus 'gins arise.
II.iii.[22]

4 Fear no more the heat o' the sun,
Nor the furious winter's rages.
IV.ii.258

5 Golden lads and girls all must,
As chimney-sweepers, come to dust.
262

6 For this relief much thanks; 'tis bitter cold
And I am sick at heart.
Hamlet, I.i.8

7 But, look, the morn, in russet mantle clad,
Walks o'er the dew of yon high eastern hill.
166

8 A little more than kin, and less than kind.
ii.65

9 Seems, madam! Nay, it is; I know not 'seems'.
76

10 O! that this too too solid flesh would melt,
Thaw, and resolve itself into a dew.
129

11 *How* weary, *stale*, flat, and unprofitable
Seem to me all the uses of this world.
133

12 Frailty, thy name is woman!
146

13 O God! a beast, that wants discourse of reason,
Would have mourn'd longer.
150

1 Thrift, thrift, Horatio! the funeral bak'd meats
Did coldly furnish forth the marriage tables.
180

2 He was a man, take him for all in all,
I shall not look upon his like again.
187

3 The friends thou hast, and their adoption tried,
Grapple them to thy soul with hoops of steel.
iii.62

4 Neither a borrower, nor a lender be.
75

5 This above all: to thine own self be true,
And it must follow, as the night the day,
Thou canst not then be false to any man.
78

6 It is a custom
More honour'd in the breach than the observance.
iv.15

7 Angels and ministers of grace defend us!
39

8 Something is rotten in the state of Denmark.
90

9 Leave her to heaven,
And to those thorns that in her bosom lodge,
To prick and sting her.
v.86

10 My tables,—meet it is I set it down,
That one may smile, and smile, and be a villain.
105

11 There are more things in heaven and earth, Horatio,
Than are dreamt of in your philosophy.
166

12 The time is out of joint; O cursed spite,
That ever I was born to set it right!
188

13 Brevity is the soul of wit.
II.ii.90

1 Though this be madness, yet there is method in't.
[211]

2 There is nothing either good or bad, but thinking makes it so.
[259]

3 O God! I could be bounded in a nut-shell, and count myself a king of infinite space, were it not that I have bad dreams.
[264]

4 What a piece of work is a man!
[323]

5 He that plays the king shall be welcome.
[341]

6 I know a hawk from a handsaw.
[406]

7 The play, I remember, pleased not the million; 'twas caviare to the general.
[465]

8 Use every man after his desert, and who should 'scape whipping?
[561]

9 What's Hecuba to him or he to Hecuba
That he should weep for her?
[593]

10 The play's the thing
Wherein I'll catch the conscience of the king.
[641]

11 To be, or not to be: that is the question:
Whether 'tis nobler in the mind to suffer
The slings and arrows of outrageous fortune,
Or to take arms against a sea of troubles,
And by opposing end them?
III.i.56

12 To sleep: perchance to dream: ay, there's the rub;
For in that sleep of death what dreams may come
When we have shuffled off this mortal coil,
Must give us pause.
65

1 The undiscover'd country from whose bourn
No traveller returns.
79

2 Thus conscience doth make cowards of us all;
And thus the native hue of resolution
Is sicklied o'er with the pale cast of thought.
83

3 Get thee to a nunnery: why wouldst thou be a breeder of sinners?
[124]

4 The glass of fashion, and the mould of form.
162

5 Speak the speech, I pray you, as I pronounced it to you, trippingly on the tongue.
ii.1

6 Suit the action to the word, the word to the action.
[20]

7 To hold, as 'twere, the mirror up to nature.
[26]

8 Give me that man
That is not passion's slave, and I will wear him
In my heart's core.
[76]

9 The lady doth protest too much, methinks.
[242]

10 My words fly up, my thoughts remain below:
Words without thoughts never to heaven go.
iii.97

11 Thou wretched, rash, intruding fool, farewell!
iv.31

12 A king of shreds and patches.
102

13 I must be cruel only to be kind.
178

14 How all occasions do inform against me,
And spur my dull revenge!
IV.iv.32

1 When sorrows come, they come not single spies,
But in battalions.
v.[78]

2 There's rosemary, that's for remembrance; pray, love, remember: and there is pansies, that's for thoughts.
[174]

3 O! you must wear your rue with a difference.
[181]

4 There is a willow grows aslant a brook,
That shows his hoar leaves in the glassy stream;
There with fantastic garlands did she come.
vii.167

5 Alas, poor Yorick. I knew him, Horatio; a fellow of infinite jest, of most excellent fancy.
V.i.[201]

6 Sweets to the sweet: farewell!
[265]

7 There's a divinity that shapes our ends,
Rough-hew them how we will.
ii.10

8 If it be now, 'tis not to come; if it be not to come, it will be now; if it be not now, yet it will come: the readiness is all.
[232]

9 A hit, a very palpable hit.
[295]

10 The rest is silence.
[372]

11 Now cracks a noble heart. Good-night, sweet prince,
And flights of angels sing thee to thy rest!
[373]

12 *Rosencrantz* and Guildenstern are dead.
[385]

13 If all the year were playing holidays,
To sport would be as tedious as to work.
Henry IV, Part 1, I.ii.[226]

14 Falstaff sweats to death
And lards the lean earth as he walks along.
II.ii.[119]

1 Out of this nettle, danger, we pluck this flower, safety.
iii.[11]

2 I am not only witty in myself, but the cause that wit is in other men.
Henry IV, Part 2, I.ii.[10]

3 Shall pack-horses,
And hollow pamper'd jades of Asia,
Which cannot go but thirty miles a day,
Compare with Caesars, and with Cannibals,
And Trojan Greeks?
II.iv.[176]. See Marlowe.

4 Is it not strange that desire should so many years outlive performance?
[283]

5 Then, happy low, lie down!
Uneasy lies the head that wears a crown.
III.i.30

6 We have heard the chimes at midnight.
ii.[231]

7 I care not; a man can die but once; we owe God a death.
[253]

8 Thy wish was father, Harry, to that thought.
IV.v.91

9 My father is gone wild into his grave.
V.ii.123

10 Under which king, Bezonian? speak, or die!
iii.[116]

11 O! for a Muse of fire, that would ascend
The brightest heaven of invention.
Henry V, Chorus, 1

12 Can this cockpit hold
The vasty fields of France? or may we cram
Within this wooden O the very casques
That did affright the air at Agincourt?
11

13 Now all the youth of England are on fire,
And silken dalliance in the wardrobe lies.
II. Chorus, 1

1 Once more unto the breach, dear friends, once more;
Or close the wall up with our English dead!
III.i.1

2 But when the blast of war blows in our ears,
Then imitate the action of the tiger.
5

3 I see you stand like greyhounds in the slips,
Straining upon the start.
31

4 A little touch of Harry in the night.
IV. Chorus, 47

5 I think the king is but a man, as I am: the violet smells to him as it doth to me.
i.[106]

6 If we are mark'd to die, we are enow
To do our country loss; and if to live,
The fewer men, the greater share of honour.
iii.20

7 Then will he strip his sleeve and show his scars,
And say, 'These wounds I had on Crispin's day.'
Old men forget: yet all shall be forgot,
But he'll remember with advantages
What feats he did that day.
47

8 We few, we happy few, we band of brothers.
60

9 The naked, poor, and mangled Peace,
Dear nurse of arts, plenties, and joyful births.
V.ii.34

10 Expect Saint Martin's summer, halcyon days.
Henry VI, Part 1, I.ii.131

11 She's beautiful and therefore to be woo'd;
She is a woman, therefore to be won.
V.iii.78. See also *Titus Andronicus*, II.1.82.

12 Is this the government of Britain's isle?
Henry VI, Part 2, I.iii.[47]

13 Thrice is he arm'd that hath his quarrel just.
III.ii.233

1 If I chance to talk a little wild, forgive me;
I had it from my father.
Henry VIII, I.iv.26

2 Orpheus with his lute made trees,
And the mountain-tops that freeze,
Bow themselves when he did sing.
III.i.3

3 I shall fall
Like a bright exhalation in the evening,
And no man see me more.
ii.226

4 And when he falls, he falls like Lucifer,
Never to hope again.
372

5 Cromwell, I charge thee, fling away ambition:
By that sin fell the angels.
441

6 Had I but serv'd my God with half the zeal
I serv'd my king, he would not in mine age
Have left me naked to mine enemies.
456

7 Beware the ides of March.
Julius Caesar, I.ii.18

8 I had as lief not be as live to be
In awe of such a thing as I myself.
95

9 Why, man, he doth bestride the narrow world
Like a Colossus.
134

10 The fault, dear Brutus, is not in our stars,
But in ourselves, that we are underlings.
139

11 Let me have men about me that are fat;
Sleek-headed men and such as sleep o' nights;
Yond' Cassius has a lean and hungry look;
He thinks too much: such men are dangerous.
191

1 Cowards die many times before their deaths;
The valiant never taste of death but once.
II.ii.32

2 I am constant as the northern star,
Of whose true-fix'd and resting quality
There is no fellow in the firmament.
III.i.60

3 *Et tu, Brute?*
77

4 Cry, 'Havoc!' and let slip the dogs of war.
273

5 Not that I loved Caesar less, but that I loved Rome more.
ii.[22]

6 Friends, Romans, countrymen, lend me your ears;
I come to bury Caesar, not to praise him.
The evil that men do lives after them,
The good is oft interred with their bones.
[79]

7 For Brutus is an honourable man;
So are they all, all honourable men.
[88]

8 If you have tears, prepare to shed them now.
[174]

9 This was the most unkindest cut of all.
[188]

10 O! what a fall was there, my countrymen;
Then I, and you, and all of us fell down,
Whilst bloody treason flourish'd over us.
[195]

11 There is a tide in the affairs of men,
Which, taken at the flood, leads on to fortune.
IV.iii.217

12 This was the noblest Roman of them all;
All the conspirators save only he
Did that they did in envy of great Caesar.
V.v.68

1 His life was gentle, and the elements
So mix'd in him that Nature might stand up
And say to all the world, 'This was a man!'
73

2 Bell, book, and candle shall not drive me back,
When gold and silver becks me to come on.
***King John*,** III.iii.12

3 Grief fills the room up of my absent child,
Lies in his bed, walks up and down with me.
iv.93

4 Life is as tedious as a twice-told tale,
Vexing the dull ear of a drowsy man.
108

5 To gild refined gold, to paint the lily,
To throw a perfume on the violet ...
Is wasteful and ridiculous excess.
IV.ii.11

6 Heaven take my soul, and England keep my bones!
iii.10

7 This England never did, nor never shall,
Lie at the proud foot of a conqueror.
V.vii.112

8 Come the three corners of the world in arms,
And we shall shock them: nought shall make us rue,
If England to itself do rest but true.
116

9 Nothing will come of nothing: speak again.
***King Lear*,** I.i.[92]

10 I grow, I prosper;
Now, gods, stand up for bastards!
ii.21

11 How sharper than a serpent's tooth it is
To have a thankless child!
iv.[312]

12 O! let me not be mad, not mad, sweet heaven;
Keep me in temper; I would not be mad!
v.[51]

1 Blow, winds, and crack your cheeks! rage! blow!
III.ii.1

2 I am a man
More sinned against than sinning.
[59]

3 The prince of darkness is a gentleman.
iv.[148]

4 Poor Tom's a-cold.
[151]

5 Child Roland to the dark tower came,
His word was still, Fie, foh, and fum,
I smell the blood of a British man.
[185]

6 The worst is not,
So long as we can say, 'This is the worst.'
IV.i.27

7 As flies to wanton boys, are we to the gods;
They kill us for their sport.
36

8 Thou must be patient; we came crying hither.
vi.[183]

9 I am a very foolish, fond old man.
vii.60

10 Men must endure
Their going hence, even as their coming hither:
Ripeness is all.
V.ii.9

11 Her voice was ever soft,
Gentle and low, an excellent thing in woman.
iii.[274]

12 *Study is like the heaven's glorious sun,*
That will not be deep-search'd with saucy looks.
Love's Labour's Lost, I.i.84

13 A wightly wanton with a velvet brow,
With two pitch balls stuck in her face for eyes.
III.i.[206]

14 When daisies pied and violets blue
And lady-smocks all silver-white

And cuckoo-buds of yellow hue
Do paint the meadows with delight,
The cuckoo then, on every tree,
Mocks married men; for thus sings he,
Cuckoo;
Cuckoo, cuckoo; O, word of fear,
Unpleasing to a married ear!
V.ii.[902]

1 When icicles hang by the wall,
And Dick the shepherd, blows his nail,
And Tom bears logs into the hall,
And milk comes frozen home in pail,
When blood is nipp'd and ways be foul,
Then nightly sings the staring owl,
Tu-who;
Tu-whit, tu-who—a merry note,
While greasy Joan doth keel the pot.
[920]

2 The words of Mercury are harsh after the songs of Apollo. You, that way: we, this way.
[938]

3 Fair is foul, and foul is fair:
Hover through the fog and filthy air.
Macbeth, I.i.9

4 Nothing in his life
Became him like the leaving it.
iv.7

5 There's no art
To find the mind's construction in the face.
12

6 Yet I do fear thy nature;
It is too full o' the milk of human kindness.
v.[16]

7 The raven himself is hoarse
That croaks the fatal entrance of Duncan
Under my battlements.
[38]

8 If it were done when 'tis done, then 'twere well
It were done quickly.
vii.1

1 We but teach
Bloody instructions.
8

2 Letting 'I dare not' wait upon 'I would,'
Like the poor cat i' the adage.
44

3 I dare do all that may become a man;
Who dares do more is none.
46

4 But screw your courage to the sticking-place,
And we'll not fail.
60

5 Is this a dagger which I see before me,
The handle toward my hand?
II.i.33

6 That which hath made them drunk hath made me bold.
ii.1

7 The attempt and not the deed,
Confounds us.
12

8 Methought I heard a voice cry, 'Sleep no more!
Macbeth does murder sleep,' the innocent sleep,
Sleep that knits up the ravell'd sleave of care.
36

9 Give me the daggers. The sleeping and the dead
Are but as pictures; 'tis the eye of childhood
That fears a painted devil.
55

10 Will all great Neptune's ocean wash this blood
Clean from my hand? No, this my hand will rather
The multitudinous seas incarnadine,
Making the green one red.
61

11 A little water clears us of this deed.
68

12 The labour we delight in physics pain.
iii.[56]

1 Who can be wise, amazed, temperate, and furious,
Loyal and neutral, in a moment? No man.
[115]

2 Look to the lady.
[125]

3 We have scotch'd the snake, not killed it.
III.ii.13

4 After life's fitful fever he sleeps well.
23

5 Light thickens, and the crow
Makes wing to the rooky wood.
50

6 Now I am cabin'd, cribb'd, confin'd, bound in
To saucy doubts and fears.
iv.24

7 Stand not upon the order of your going,
But go at once.
119

8 It will have blood, they say; blood will have blood.
122

9 Double, double toil and trouble;
Fire burn and cauldron bubble.
IV.i.10

10 By the pricking of my thumbs,
Something wicked this way comes.
44

11 But yet, I'll make assurance double sure.
83

12 What! will the line stretch out to the crack of doom?
117

13 Stands Scotland where it did?
iii.164

14 What! all my pretty chickens and their dam,
At one fell swoop?
220

15 Out, damned spot! out, I say!
V.i.[38]

1 Yet who would have thought the old man to have had so much blood in him?
[41]

2 What! will these hands ne'er be clean?
[47]

3 Here's the smell of the blood still: all the perfumes of Arabia will not sweeten this little hand.
[55]

4 What's done cannot be undone. To bed, to bed, to bed.
[74]

5 The devil damn thee black, thou cream-faced loon!
Where gott'st thou that goose look?
iii.11

6 She should have died hereafter;
There would have been a time for such a word.
To-morrow, and to-morrow, and to-morrow,
Creeps in this petty pace from day to day,
To the last syllable of recorded time;
And all our yesterdays have lighted fools
The way to dusty death. Out, out, brief candle!
Life's but a walking shadow, a poor player,
That struts and frets his hour upon the stage,
And then is heard no more; it is a tale
Told by an idiot, full of sound and fury,
Signifying nothing.
v.16

7 Lay on, Macduff;
And damn'd be him that first cries, 'Hold, enough!'
vii.62

8 Be absolute for death; either death or life
Shall thereby be the sweeter.
Measure for Measure, III.i.5

9 Ay, but to die, and go we know not where;
To lie in cold obstruction and to rot.
116

10 The weariest and most loathed worldly life
That age, ache, penury, and imprisonment

Can lay on nature, is a paradise
To what we fear of death.
127

1 By my troth, Nerissa, my little body is aweary of this great world.
The Merchant of Venice, I.ii.1

2 They are as sick that surfeit with too much, as they that starve with nothing.
[5]

3 God made him, and therefore let him pass for a man.
[59]

4 The devil can cite Scripture for his purpose.
iii.[99]

5 For sufferance is the badge of all our tribe.
[111]

6 It is a wise father that knows his own child.
II.ii.[83]

7 Hath not a Jew eyes? hath not a Jew hands, organs, dimensions, senses, affections, passions?
III.i.[63]

8 If you prick us, do we not bleed? if you tickle us, do we not laugh? if you poison us, do we not die? and if you wrong us, shall we not revenge?
[69]

9 I would not have given it for a wilderness of monkeys.
[130]

10 Tell me where is fancy bred.
Or in the heart or in the head?
ii.63

11 A harmless necessary cat.
IV.i.55

12 I am a tainted wether of the flock.
114

13 The quality of mercy is not strain'd,
It droppeth as the gentle rain from heaven
Upon the place beneath.
[184]

1 And earthly power doth then show likest God's
When mercy seasons justice.
[196]

2 A Daniel come to judgment!
[223]

3 He is well paid that is well satisfied.
[416]

4 How sweet the moonlight sleeps upon this bank!
Here will we sit, and let the sounds of music
Creep in our ears.
V.i.54

5 I am never merry when I hear sweet music.
69

6 The man that hath no music in himself,
Nor is not mov'd with concord of sweet sounds,
Is fit for treasons, stratagems, and spoils.
79

7 How far that little candle throws his beams!
So shines a good deed in a naughty world.
90

8 Peace, ho! the moon sleeps with Endymion,
And would not be awak'd!
109

9 Why, then the world's mine oyster.
The Merry Wives of Windsor, II.ii.2

10 To live a barren sister all your life,
Chanting faint hymns to the cold fruitless moon.
A Midsummer Night's Dream, I.i.72

11 The course of true love never did run smooth.
134

12 Love looks not with the eyes, but with the mind,
And therefore is wing'd Cupid painted blind.
234

13 I will roar you as gently as any sucking dove.
ii.[85]

14 Over hill, over dale,
Thorough bush, thorough brier,

Over park, over pale,
Thorough flood, thorough fire.
II.i.2

1 Ill met by moonlight, proud Titania.
60

2 The nine men's morris is filled up with mud.
98

3 In maiden meditation, fancy-free.
164

4 I'll put a girdle round about the earth
In forty minutes.
175

5 I know a bank whereon the wild thyme blows.
249

6 Out of this wood do not desire to go.
III.i.[159]

7 Lord, what fools these mortals be!
ii.115

8 The lunatic, the lover, and the poet,
Are of imagination all compact.
V.i.7

9 The poet's eye, in a fine frenzy rolling,
Doth glance from heaven to earth, from earth to heaven;
And, as imagination bodies forth
The forms of things unknown, the poet's pen
Turns them to shapes, and gives to airy nothing
A local habitation and a name.
12

10 If we shadows have offended,
Think but this, and all is mended,
That you have but slumber'd here
While these visions did appear.
ii.54

11 Speak low, if you speak love.
Much Ado About Nothing, II.i.[104]

12 No, sure, my lord, my mother cried; but then there was a star danced, and under that was I born.
[350]

1 Sigh no more, ladies, sigh no more,
  Men were deceivers ever.
iii.[65]

2 For look where Beatrice, like a lapwing, runs
Close by the ground, to hear our counsel.
III.1.24

3 Benedick, love on; I will requite thee,
  Taming my wild heart to thy loving hand.
111

4 Comparisons are odorous.
v.[18]

5 I do love nothing in the world so well as you: is not that strange?
IV.i.[271]

6 Your daughter and the Moor are now making the beast with two backs.
Othello, I.i.[117]

7 Keep up your bright swords, for the dew will rust them.
ii.59

8   Yet, by your gracious patience,
I will a round unvarnish'd tale deliver.
iii.89

9 Put money in thy purse.
[345]

10   If it were now to die,
'Twere now to be most happy.
II.i.[192]

11 Silence that dreadful bell!
iii.[177]

12 Reputation, reputation, reputation! O! I have lost my reputation.
[264]

13 O God! that men should put an enemy in their mouths to steal away their brains.
[293]

14 Excellent wretch! Perdition catch my soul
But I do love thee!
III.iii.90

1 Who steals my purse steals trash; 'tis something, nothing;
'Twas mine, 'tis his, and has been slave to thousands;
But he that filches from me my good name
Robs me of that which not enriches him,
And makes me poor indeed.
157

2 O! beware, my lord, of jealousy;
It is the green-ey'd monster which doth mock
The meat it feeds on.
165

3 I humbly do beseech you of your pardon
For too much loving you.
212

4 Trifles light as air
Are to the jealous confirmations strong
As proofs of holy writ.
323

5 Othello's occupation's gone!
358

6 But yet the pity of it, Iago! O! Iago, the pity of it, Iago!
IV.i.[205]

7 The poor soul sat sighing by a sycamore tree,
Sing all a green willow.
iii.[41]

8 It is the cause, it is the cause, my soul.
V.ii.1

9 Put out the light, and then put out the light.
7

10 May his pernicious soul
Rot half a grain a day!
153

11 I have done the state some service.
338

12 Speak of me as I am; nothing extenuate,
Nor set down aught in malice: then, must you speak
Of one that lov'd not wisely but too well.
341

1 Teach thy necessity to reason thus;
There is no virtue like necessity.
Richard II, I.iii.277

2 The setting sun, and music at the close.
II.i.12

3 Methinks I am a prophet new inspir'd.
31

4 This royal throne of kings, this scepter'd isle,
This earth of majesty, this seat of Mars,
This other Eden, demi-paradise.
40

5 This happy breed of men, this little world,
This precious stone set in the silver sea.
45

6 This blessed plot, this earth, this realm, this England.
50

7 This land of such dear souls, this dear, dear land,
Dear for her reputation through the world.
57

8 That England, that was wont to conquer others,
Hath made a shameful conquest of itself.
65

9 I count myself in nothing else so happy
As in a soul remembering my good friends.
iii.46

10 Grace me no grace, nor uncle me no uncle.
87

11 O! call back yesterday, bid time return.
III.ii.69

12 Let's choose executors, and talk of wills.
148

13 For God's sake, let us sit upon the ground
And tell sad stories of the death of kings.
155

14 What must the king do now? Must he submit?
The king shall do it.
iii.143

15 A little little grave, an obscure grave.
154

1 I wasted time, and now doth time waste me.
V.v.49

2 Now is the winter of our discontent
Made glorious summer by this sun of York.
Richard III, I.i.1

3 I am not in the giving vein to-day.
IV.ii.115

4 A horse! a horse! my kingdom for a horse!
V.iv.7

5 O! she doth teach the torches to burn bright.
Romeo and Juliet, I.v.[48]

6 He jests at scars, that never felt a wound.
But, soft! what light through yonder window breaks?
It is the east, and Juliet is the sun.
II.ii.1

7 O Romeo, Romeo! wherefore art thou Romeo?
33

8 What's in a name? that which we call a rose
By any other name would smell as sweet.
43

9 How silver-sweet sound lovers' tongues by night,
Like softest music to attending ears!
165

10 Good-night, good-night! parting is such sweet sorrow
That I shall say good-night till it be morrow.
185

11 No, 'tis not so deep as a well, nor so wide as a church door; but 'tis enough, 'twill serve.
III.i.[100]

12 A plague o' both your houses!
[112]

13 O! I am Fortune's fool.
[142]

14 Night's candles are burnt out, and jocund day
Stands tiptoe on the misty mountain tops.
v.9

15 This is the way to kill a wife with kindness.
The Taming of the Shrew, IV.i.[211]

1 What seest thou else
In the dark backward and abysm of time?
The Tempest, I.ii.49

2 You taught me language; and my profit on't
Is, I know how to curse.
363

3 Come unto these yellow sands,
And then take hands.
375

4 Full fathom five thy father lies;
Of his bones are coral made:
Those are pearls that were his eyes:
Nothing of him that doth fade,
But doth suffer a sea-change
Into something rich and strange.
394

5 When they will not give a doit to relieve a lame beggar, they will lay out ten to see a dead Indian.
II.ii.[33]

6 Be not afeard: the isle is full of noises,
Sounds and sweet airs, that give delight, and hurt not.
III.ii.[147]

7 We are such stuff
As dreams are made on, and our little life
Is rounded with a sleep.
IV.i.156

8 This rough magic
I here abjure.
V.i.50

9 Where the bee sucks, there suck I
In a cowslip's bell I lie.
88

10 How beauteous mankind is! O brave new world,
That has such people in't.
183

11 The strain of man's bred out
Into baboon and monkey.
Timon of Athens, I.i.[260]

1 Time hath, my lord, a wallet at his back,
Wherein he puts alms for oblivion.
Troilus and Cressida, III.iii.145

2 One touch of nature makes the whole world kin.
175

3 If music be the food of love, play on;
Give me excess of it, that, surfeiting,
The appetite may sicken, and so die.
Twelfth Night, I.i.1

4 Make me a willow cabin at your gate,
And call upon my soul within the house.
v.[289]

5 O mistress mine! where are you roaming?
O! stay and hear; your true love's coming.
II.iii.[42]

6 Trip no further, pretty sweeting;
Journeys end in lovers meeting.
[45]

7 Present mirth hath present laughter.
[49]

8 Then come kiss me, sweet and twenty,
Youth's a stuff will not endure.
[52]

9 Dost thou think, because thou art virtuous, there shall be no more cakes and ale?
[124]

10 Let still the woman take
An elder than herself.
iv.29

11 Come away, come away, death,
And in sad cypress let me be laid.
51

12 She never told her love,
But let concealment, like a worm i' the bud,
Feed on her damask cheek: she pin'd in thought;
And with a green and yellow melancholy,
She sat like patience on a monument,
Smiling at grief.
[111]

1 Some men are born great, some achieve greatness, and some have greatness thrust upon them.
v.[158]

2 Thus the whirligig of time brings in his revenges.
V.i.[388]

3 When that I was and a little tiny boy,
With hey, ho, the wind and the rain;
A foolish thing was but a toy,
For the rain it raineth every day.
[401]

4 O! how this spring of love resembleth
The uncertain glory of an April day.
The Two Gentlemen of Verona, I.iii.84

5 Who is Sylvia? what is she,
That all our swains commend her?
IV.ii.40

6 *Exit, pursued by a bear.*
The Winter's Tale, III.iii. Stage Direction.

7 A snapper-up of unconsidered trifles.
IV.ii.[26]

8 For you there's rosemary and rue; these keep
Seeming and savour all the winter long.
iii.74

9 Daffodils,
That come before the swallow dares, and take
The winds of March with beauty.
118

10 Though I am not naturally honest, I am so sometimes by chance.
[734]

11 Crabbed age and youth cannot live together:
Youth is full of pleasance, age is full of care.
The Passionate Pilgrim, xii

12 To the onlie begetter of these insuing sonnets, Mr. W.H.
Sonnets, Dedication (also attr. Thomas Thorpe)

13 Shall I compare thee to a summer's day?
Thou art more lovely and more temperate:

Rough winds do shake the darling buds of May,
And summer's lease hath all too short a date.
18

1 When in disgrace with fortune and men's eyes
I all alone beweep my outcast state.
29

2 But if the while I think on thee, dear friend,
All losses are restor'd and sorrows end.
30

3 Full many a glorious morning have I seen
Flatter the mountain-tops with sovereign eye.
33

4 Why didst thou promise such a beauteous day,
And make me travel forth without my cloak
To let base clouds o'ertake me in my way,
Hiding thy bravery in their rotten smoke?
34

5 What is your substance, whereof are you made,
That millions of strange shadows on you tend?
53

6 Being your slave, what should I do but tend
Upon the hours and times of your desire?
57

7 No longer mourn for me when I am dead
Than you shall hear the surly sullen bell.
71

8 Bare ruin'd choirs, where late the sweet birds sang.
73

9 Farewell! thou art too dear for my possessing,
And like enough thou know'st thy estimate.
87

10 Thus have I had thee, as a dream doth flatter,
In sleep a king, but, waking, no such matter.

11 For sweetest things turn sourest by their deeds;
Lilies that fester smell far worse than weeds.
94

12 How like a winter hath my absence been
From thee, the pleasure of the fleeting year!
97

1 From you have I been absent in the spring,
When proud-pied April, dress'd in all his trim,
Hath put a spirit of youth in everything.
98

2 When in the chronicle of wasted time
I see descriptions of the fairest wights,
And beauty making beautiful old rime,
In praise of ladies dead and lovely knights.
106

3 Alas! 'tis true I have gone here and there,
And made myself a motley to the view.
110

4 Let me not to the marriage of true minds
Admit impediments.
116

5 Love's not Time's fool, though rosy lips and cheeks
Within his bending sickle's compass come;
Love alters not with his brief hours and weeks,
But bears it out even to the edge of doom.
  If this be error, and upon me prov'd,
I never writ, nor no man ever lov'd.

6 The expense of spirit in a waste of shame
Is lust in action.
129

7 Whoever hath her wish, thou hast thy *Will*,
And *Will* to boot, and *Will* in over-plus.
135

8 When my love swears that she is made of truth,
I do believe her, though I know she lies.
138

9 Two loves I have of comfort and despair,
Which like two spirits do suggest me still:
The better angel is a man right fair,
The worser spirit a woman colour'd ill.
144

10 And Death once dead, there's no more dying then.
146

11 Item, I give unto my wife my second best bed, with the furniture.
Will, 1616

GEORGE BERNARD SHAW 1856–1950

1 I never resist temptation, because I have found that things that are bad for me do not tempt me.
The Apple Cart (1929), Act II

2 You can always tell an old soldier by the inside of his holsters and cartridge boxes. The young ones carry pistols and cartridges: the old ones, grub.
Arms and the Man (1898), Act I

3 I'm only a beer teetotaller, not a champagne teetotaller.
Candida (1898), Act III

4 The British soldier can stand up to anything except the British War Office.
The Devil's Disciple, (1897), Act III

5 All professions are conspiracies against the laity.
The Doctor's Dilemma (1906), Act I

6 The one point on which all women are in furious secret rebellion against the existing law is the saddling of the right to a child with the obligation to become the servant of a man.
Getting Married (1908), Preface

7 The greatest of evils and the worst of crimes is poverty.
Major Barbara (1907), Preface

8 You darent handle high explosives; but youre all ready to handle honesty and truth and justice and the whole duty of man, and kill one another at that game.
Act III

9 Nothing is ever done in this world until men are prepared to kill one another if it is not done.

10 A lifetime of happiness! No man alive could bear it: it would be hell on earth.
Man and Superman (1903), Act I

11 Vitality in a woman is a blind fury of creation.

12 The true artist will let his wife starve, his children go barefoot, his mother drudge for his living at seventy, sooner than work at anything but his art.

13 Very nice sort of place, Oxford, I should think, for people that like that sort of place.
Act II

1 It is a woman's business to get married as soon as possible, and a man's to keep unmarried as long as he can.

2 You can be as romantic as you please about love, Hector; but you mustnt be romantic about money.

3 Hell is full of musical amateurs.
Act III

4 An Englishman thinks he is moral when he is only uncomfortable.

5 There are two tragedies in life. One is not to get your heart's desire. The other is to get it.
Act IV

6 The Golden Rule is that there are no golden rules.
Maxims for Revolutionists (by 'John Tanner'): **'The Golden Rule'**

7 He who can, does. He who cannot teaches.
'Education'

8 Marriage is popular because it combines the maximum of temptation with the maximum of opportunity.
'Marriage'

9 Every man over forty is a scoundrel.
'Stray Sayings'

10 Youth, which is forgiven everything, forgives itself nothing: age, which forgives itself anything, is forgiven nothing.

11 It is impossible for an Englishman to open his mouth, without making some other Englishman despise him.
Pygmalion (1912), Preface

12 Gin was mother's milk to her.
Act III

13 Walk! Not bloody likely. I am going in a taxi.

LORD SHAWCROSS 1902–

14 We are the masters at the moment, and not only at the moment, but for a very long time to come.
House of Commons, 2 Apr. 1946. Often misquoted as 'We are the masters now'.

PERCY BYSSHE SHELLEY 1792–1822

1 From the contagion of the world's slow stain
He is secure.
Adonais (1821), XL

2 The One remains, the many change and pass;
Heaven's light forever shines, Earth's shadows fly;
Life, like a dome of many-coloured glass,
Stains the white radiance of Eternity,
Until Death tramples it to fragments.
LII

3 I never was attached to that great sect,
Whose doctrine is that each one should select
Out of the crowd a mistress or a friend,
And all the rest, though fair and wise, commend
To cold oblivion.
Epipsychidion (1821), l.149

4 I met Murder in the way—
He had a mask like Castlereagh.
The Mask of Anarchy (1819), II

5 O wild West Wind, thou breath of Autumn's being,
Thou, from whose unseen presence the leaves dead
Are driven, like ghosts from an enchanter fleeing.
Ode to the West Wind (1819), l.1

6 Oh, lift me as a wave, a leaf, a cloud!
I fall upon the thorns of life! I bleed!
l.53

7 Be through my lips to unawakened earth
The trumpet of a prophecy! O, Wind,
If Winter comes, can Spring be far behind?
l.68

8 I met a traveller from an antique land.
Ozymandias

9 'My name is Ozymandias, king of kings:
Look on my works, ye Mighty, and despair!'

10 Rarely, rarely, comest thou,
Spirit of Delight!
Song

1 Men of England, wherefore plough
For the lords who lay you low?
Song to the Men of England

2 Lift not the painted veil which those who live
Call Life.
Sonnet

3 Hail to thee, blithe Spirit!
Bird thou never wert.
To a Skylark (1819)

4 Swiftly walk over the western wave,
Spirit of Night!
To Night

5 And like a dying lady, lean and pale,
Who totters forth, wrapped in a gauzy veil.
The Waning Moon

6 Poets are the unacknowledged legislators of the world.
A Defence of Poetry

PHILIP HENRY SHERIDAN 1831–1888

7 The only good Indian is a dead Indian.
Attr., at Fort Cobb, Jan. 1869

RICHARD BRINSLEY SHERIDAN 1751–1816

8 O Lord, sir, when a heroine goes mad she always goes into white satin.
The Critic (1779), III.i

9 I was struck all of a heap.
The Duenna (1775), II.ii

10 A nice derangement of epitaphs!
The Rivals (1775), III.iii

11 She's as headstrong as an allegory on the banks of the Nile.

12 I'm called away by particular business. But I leave my character behind me.
The School for Scandal (1777), II.ii

13 Here's to the maiden of bashful fifteen;
Here's to the widow of fifty;

Here's to the flaunting, extravagant quean;
And here's to the housewife that's thrifty.
III.iii. Song

1 An unforgiving eye, and a damned disinheriting countenance.
IV.i

JAMES SHIRLEY 1596–1666

2 Only the actions of the just
Smell sweet, and blossom in their dust.
The Contention of Ajax and Ulysses (1659), I.iii

SIR PHILIP SIDNEY 1554–1586

3 My true love hath my heart and I have his,
By just exchange one for the other giv'n;
I hold his dear, and mine he cannot miss,
There never was a better bargain driv'n.
The Arcadia (1590), bk.iii

4 'Fool,' said my Muse to me, 'look in thy heart and write'.
Astrophel and Stella (1591), Sonnet 1

5 Thy necessity is yet greater than mine.
On giving his water-bottle to a dying soldier on the battle-field of Zutphen, 1586. Sir Fulke Greville, *Life* (1652). The word 'necessity' is more often quoted as 'need'

ABBÉ EMMANUEL JOSEPH SIEYÈS 1748–1836

6 *J'ai vécu.*
I survived.
When asked what he had done during the French Revolution. V. Mignet, 'Notice Historique sur la Vie et les Travaux de M. le Comte de Sieyès'. *Recueil des Lectures ... 28 Déc. 1836.*

SIMONIDES c.556–468 B.C.

7 Go, tell the Spartans, thou who passest by,
That here obedient to their laws we lie.
Herodotus, *Histories*, vii, 228.

GEORGE R. SIMS 1847–1922

8 It is Christmas Day in the Workhouse.
The Dagonet and Other Poems (1903)

B.F. SKINNER 1904–

1 Education is what survives when what has been learnt has been forgotten.
Education in 1984. *New Scientist*, 21 May 1964, p.484

CHRISTOPHER SMART 1722–1771

2 For I will consider my Cat Jeoffry.
For he is the servant of the Living God, duly and daily serving Him.
Jubilate Agno, XIX.51

3 For he counteracts the Devil, who is death, by brisking about the Life.
XX.15

SAMUEL SMILES 1812–1904

4 A place for everything, and everything in its place.
Thrift (1875), ch.5

ADAM SMITH 1723–1790

5 People of the same trade seldom meet together, even for merriment and diversion, but the conversation ends in a conspiracy against the public, or in some contrivance to raise prices.
Wealth of Nations (ed. Todd, 1976), I.x.c.27

6 To found a great empire for the sole purpose of raising up a people of customers, may at first sight appear a project fit only for a nation of shopkeepers. It is, however, a project altogether unfit for a nation of shopkeepers; but extremely fit for a nation whose government is influenced by shopkeepers.
IV.vii.c.63. See Napoleon.

7 There is no art which one government sooner learns of another than that of draining money from the pockets of the people.
V.ii.h.12

8 Be assured, my young friend, that there is a great deal of *ruin* in a nation.
Correspondence of Sir John Sinclair (1831), i.390–1

ALFRED EMANUEL SMITH 1873–1944

1 No matter how thin you slice it, it's still baloney.
Speech, 1936

F.E. SMITH see BIRKENHEAD

LOGAN PEARSALL SMITH 1865–1946

2 There is more felicity on the far side of baldness than young men can possibly imagine.
Afterthoughts (1931), ch.2. **Age and Death**

3 Married women are kept women, and they are beginning to find it out.
ch.3. **Other People**

4 To suppose, as we all suppose, that we could be rich and not behave as the rich behave, is like supposing that we could drink all day and keep absolutely sober.
ch.4. **In the World**

5 Thank heavens, the sun has gone in, and I don't have to go out and enjoy it.
Last Words (1933)

SAMUEL FRANCIS SMITH 1808–1895

6 My country, 'tis of thee,
Sweet land of liberty,
  Of thee I sing.
America (1831)

STEVIE SMITH 1902–1971

7 Oh I am a cat that likes to
Gallop about doing good.
The Galloping Cat

8 Nobody heard him, the dead man,
But still he lay moaning:
I was much further out than you thought
And not waving but drowning.
Not Waving But Drowning

REVD. SYDNEY SMITH 1771–1845

1 Take short views, hope for the best, and trust in God.
Lady Holland, *Memoir* (1st edn. 1855), vol.I, ch.6, p.48

2 Looked as if she had walked straight out of the Ark.
ch.7, p.157

3 Madam, I have been looking for a person who disliked gravy all my life; let us swear eternal friendship.
ch.9, p.257

4 As the French say, there are three sexes—men, women, and clergymen.
p.262

5 Marriage ... resembles a pair of shears, so joined that they cannot be separated; often moving in opposite directions, yet always punishing anyone who comes between them.
ch.11, p.363

6 He [Macaulay] has occasional flashes of silence, that make his conversation perfectly delightful.

7 I never read a book before reviewing it; it prejudices a man so.
H. Pearson, *The Smith of Smiths* (1934), ch.iii, p.54

8 —'s idea of heaven is, eating *pâtés de foie gras* to the sound of trumpets.
ch.10, p.236

9 Where etiquette prevents me from doing things disagreeable to myself, I am a perfect martinet.
Letters. To Lady Holland, 6 Nov. 1842

10 I have no relish for the country; it is a kind of healthy grave.
To Miss G. Harcourt, 1838

C.P. SNOW 1905–1980

11 The official world, the corridors of power.
Homecomings (1956), ch.22

SOCRATES 469–399 B.C.

12 The unexamined life is not worth living.
Plato, *Apology*, 38a

SOLON c.630–c.555 B.C.

1 Laws are like spider's webs: if some poor weak creature come up against them, it is caught; but a bigger one can break through and get away.
Diogenes Laertius, *Lives of the Eminent Philosophers*, I.58

2 I grow old ever learning many things.
Poetae Lyrici Graeci (ed. Bergk), Solon, 18

3 Call no man happy till he dies, he is at best but fortunate.
Herodotus, *Histories*, i.32

SOPHOCLES 496–406 B.C.

4 There are many wonderful things, and nothing is more wonderful than man.
Antigone, 332

5 Not to be born is, past all prizing, best.
Oedipus Coloneus, 1224. Tr. R.W. Jebb

JOHN L.B. SOULE 1815–1891

6 Go West, young man, go West!
Editorial, *Terre Haute* (Indiana) *Express* (1851)

ROBERT SOUTHEY 1774–1843

7 It was a summer evening,
  Old Kaspar's work was done.
The Battle of Blenheim

8 But what they fought each other for,
  I could not well make out.

9 'But what good came of it at last?'
  Quoth little Peterkin.
'Why that I cannot tell,' said he,
'But 'twas a famous victory.'

10 You are old, Father William, the young man cried
  And pleasures with youth pass away,
And yet you lament not the days that are gone,
  Now tell me the reason, I pray.
The Old Man's Comforts, and how he Gained them

1 She has made me half in love with a cold climate.
Letter to his brother Thomas, 28 Apr. 1797

ROBERT SOUTHWELL 1561?–1595

2 Times go by turns, and chances change by course,
From foul to fair, from better hap to worse.
Times go by Turns. See Anon.

HERBERT SPENCER 1820–1903

3 People are beginning to see that the first requisite to success in life is to be a good animal.
Education (1861), ch.2

4 This survival of the fittest implies multiplication of the fittest.
Principles of Biology (1865), pt.iii, ch.12, **Indirect Equilibration,** 164

STEPHEN SPENDER 1909–

5 I think continually of those who were truly great—
The names of those who in their lives fought for life,
Who wore at their hearts the fire's centre.
I Think Continually of Those

6 What I had not foreseen
Was the gradual day
Weakening the will
Leaking the brightness away.
Preludes, 12

EDMUND SPENSER 1552?–1599

7 Triton blowing loud his wreathed horn.
Colin Clout's Come Home Again (1595), l.245

8 Ah! when will this long weary day have end,
And lend me leave to come unto my love?
Epithalamion (1595), l.278

9 A gentle knight was pricking on the plain.
The Faerie Queen (1596), bk.I, c.I.i

10 Sleep after toil, port after stormy seas,
Ease after war, death after life does greatly please.
c.IX.xl

1 And all for love, and nothing for reward.
bk,II, c.VIII.ii

2 Sweet Thames, run softly, till I end my Song.
Prothalamion (1596), l.54

3 At length they all to merry London came,
To merry London, my most kindly nurse,
That to me gave this life's first native source.
l.127

4 To be wise and eke to love,
Is granted scarce to God above.
The Shepherd's Calendar (1579), **March. Willy's Emblem**

5 So now they have made our English tongue a gallimaufry or hodgepodge of all other speeches.
***The Shepard's Calendar*.** **Letter to Gabriel Harvey**

SIR CECIL ARTHUR SPRING-RICE 1858–1918

6 I vow to thee, my country—all earthly things above—
Entire and whole and perfect, the service of my love.
Last Poem

J.C. (SIR JOHN) SQUIRE 1884–1958

7 God heard the embattled nations sing and shout
'Gott strafe England!' and 'God save the King!'
God this, God that, and God the other thing—
'Good God', said God, 'I've got my work cut out.'
Epigrams, no.1, **'The Dilemma'**

8 It did not last: the Devil howling 'Ho!
Let Einstein be!' restored the status quo.
Answer to Pope's Epitaph on Newton.

MME DE STAËL 1766–1817

9 *Tout comprendre rend très indulgent.*
To be totally understanding makes one very indulgent.
Corinne (1807), lib.iv, ch.2

JOSEPH STALIN 1879–1953

10 The Pope! How many divisions has *he* got?
When asked by Laval to encourage Catholicism in Russia to conciliate the Pope, 13 May 1935. Churchill, *The Second World War*, vol.i, 'The Gathering Storm', ch.8

SIR HENRY MORTON STANLEY 1841–1904

1 Dr Livingstone, I presume?
How I found Livingstone (1872), ch.11

COLONEL C.E. STANTON 1859–1933

2 Lafayette, we are here!
Address delivered at the grave of Lafayette, Paris, 4 July 1917. Often attr. to General John J. Pershing, but disclaimed by him

SIR RICHARD STEELE 1672–1729

3 There are so few who can grow old with a good grace.
The Spectator, No.263

4 Reading is to the mind what exercise is to the body.
The Tatler, No.147

LINCOLN STEFFENS 1866–1936

5 I have seen the future, and it works.
After visiting Moscow in 1919. J. Kaplan, *Lincoln Steffens* (1975), ch.13, ii

GERTRUDE STEIN 1874–1946

6 Rose is a rose is a rose is a rose.
Sacred Emily

7 What *is* the answer? ... In that case, what is the question?
Last words. Donald Sutherland, *Gertrude Stein, A Biography of her Work* (1951), ch.6

J.K. STEPHEN 1859–1892

8 Two voices are there: one is of the deep ...
And one is of an old half-witted sheep ...
And, Wordsworth, both are thine.
Lapsus Calami (1896). **A Sonnet**

9 When the Rudyards cease from kipling
And the Haggards Ride no more.
To R.K.

LAURENCE STERNE 1713–1768

1 They order, said I, this matter better in France.
A Sentimental Journey (1768), I.1

2 'I can't get out,—I can't get out,' said the starling.
The Passport. The Hotel at Paris

3 I wish either my father or my mother, or indeed both of them, as they were in duty both equally bound to it, had minded what they were about when they begot me.
Tristram Shandy (1760–7), bk.I, ch.1, opening words

4 The nonsense of the old women (of both sexes) throughout the kingdom.
bk.v, ch.16

5 Said my mother, 'what is all this story about?'—
'A Cock and a Bull,' said Yorick.
bk.ix, ch.33

WALLACE STEVENS 1879–1955

6 The only emperor is the emperor of ice-cream.
The Emperor of Ice-Cream

ROBERT LOUIS STEVENSON 1850–1894

7 I regard you with an indifference closely bordering on aversion.
The New Arabian Nights (1882). **The Rajah's Diamond. Story of the Bandbox**

8 Fifteen men on the dead man's chest
Yo-ho-ho, and a bottle of rum!
Drink and the devil had done for the rest—
Yo-ho-ho, and a bottle of rum!
Treasure Island (1883), ch.1

9 Tip me the black spot.
ch.3

10 Many's the long night I've dreamed of cheese—toasted, mostly. [Ben Gunn.]
ch.15

11 Marriage is like life in this—that it is a field of battle, and not a bed of roses.
Virginibus Puerisque (1881), I.i

1 To travel hopefully is a better thing than to arrive, and the true success is to labour.
VI. **El Dorado**

2 What hangs people ... is the unfortunate circumstance of guilt.
The Wrong Box (with Lloyd Osbourne, 1889), ch.7

3 The world is so full of a number of things,
I'm sure we should all be as happy as kings.
A Child's Garden of Verses (1885). XXIV. **Happy Thought**

4 Give to me the life I love,
Let the lave go by me.
Songs of Travel (1896). I. **The Vagabond**

5 Bright is the ring of words
When the right man rings them,
Fair the fall of songs
When the singer sings them.
XIV

6 Trusty, dusky, vivid, true,
With eyes of gold and bramble-dew,
Steel-true and blade-straight,
The great artificer
Made my mate.
XXV. **My Wife**

7 Under the wide and starry sky
Dig the grave and let me lie.
Underwoods (1887), bk.I.xxi. **Requiem**

8 Here he lies where he longed to be;
Home is the sailor, home from sea,
And the hunter home from the hill.

HARRIET BEECHER STOWE 1811–1896

9 'Do you know who made you?' 'Nobody, as I knows on,' said the child, with a short laugh ... 'I 'spect I grow'd.'
Uncle Tom's Cabin (1852), ch.20

LORD STOWELL 1745–1836

10 The elegant simplicity of the three per cents.
Lord Campbell, *Lives of the Lord Chancellors* (1857), vol.x, ch.212, p.218

SIR JOHN SUCKLING 1609–1642

1 Why so pale and wan, fond lover?
Prithee, why so pale?
Will, when looking well can't move her,
Looking ill prevail?
Prithee, why so pale?
Aglaura (1637), IV.i. Song

2 Her feet beneath her petticoat,
Like little mice, stole in and out,
As if they fear'd the light.
A Ballad upon a Wedding (1646), viii

3 Out upon it, I have loved
Three whole days together;
And am like to love three more,
If it prove fair weather.
A Poem with the Answer

SUETONIUS c.69–c.130

4 *Festina lente.*
Make haste slowly.
Augustus, 25

MAXIMILIEN DE BÉTHUNE, DUC DE SULLY 1559–1641

5 *Les Anglais s'amusent tristement selon l'usage de leur pays.*
The English take their pleasures sadly after the fashion of their country.
Memoirs, c.1630

SU TUNG-P'O 1036–1101

6 Families, when a child is born
Want it to be intelligent.
I, through intelligence,
Having wrecked my whole life,
Only hope the baby will prove
Ignorant and stupid.

Then he will crown a tranquil life
By becoming a Cabinet Minister.

On the Birth of his Son, tr. Arthur Waley, *170 Chinese Poems* (1918), p.98

R.S. SURTEES 1803–1864

1 Where the M.F.H. dines he sleeps, and where the M.F.H. sleeps he breakfasts.

Handley Cross (1843), ch.15

2 Hellish dark, and smells of cheese!

ch.50

HANNEN SWAFFER 1879–1962

3 Freedom of the press in Britain is freedom to print such of the proprietor's prejudices as the advertisers don't object to.

In conversation with Tom Driberg, c.1928

JONATHAN SWIFT 1667–1745

4 Instead of dirt and poison we have rather chosen to fill our hives with honey and wax; thus furnishing mankind with the two noblest of things, which are sweetness and light.

The Battle of the Books (1704), preface

5 And he gave it for his opinion, that whoever could make two ears of corn or two blades of grass to grow upon a spot of ground where only one grew before, would deserve better of mankind, and do more essential service to his country than the whole race of politicians put together.

Gulliver's Travels (1726). **Voyage to Brobdingnag,** ch.7

6 I told him ... that we ate when we were not hungry, and drank without the provocation of thirst.

A Voyage to the Houyhnhnms, ch.6

7 Will she pass in a crowd? Will she make a figure in a country church?

Journal to Stella, 9 Feb. 1711

8 I hate and detest that animal called man; although I heartily love John, Peter, Thomas, and so forth.

Letter to Pope, 29 Sept. 1725

1 A young healthy child well nursed is at a year old a most delicious, nourishing, and wholesome food, whether stewed, roasted, baked, or boiled, and I make no doubt that it will equally serve in a fricassee, or a ragout.
A Modest Proposal for Preventing the Children of Ireland from being a Burden to their Parents or Country (1729)

2 When a true genius appears in the world, you may know him by this sign, that the dunces are all in confederacy against him.
Thoughts on Various Subjects (1706)

3 So, naturalists observe, a flea
Hath smaller fleas that on him prey;
And these have smaller fleas to bite 'em,
And so proceed *ad infinitum*.
On Poetry (1733), l.337

4 In Church your grandsire cut his throat;
To do the job too long he tarry'd,
He should have had my hearty vote,
To cut his throat before he marry'd.
Verses on the Upright Judge

5 *Ubi saeva indignatio ulterius cor lacerare nequit.*
Where fierce indignation can no longer tear his heart.
Swift's Epitaph

ALGERNON CHARLES SWINBURNE 1837–1909

6 When the hounds of spring are on winter's traces,
The mother of months in meadow or plain
Fills the shadows and windy places
With lisp of leaves and ripple of rain.
Atalanta in Calydon (1865). Chorus

7 For winter's rains and ruins are over.

8 Blossom by blossom the spring begins.

9 Change in a trice
The lilies and languors of virtue
For the raptures and roses of vice.
Dolores (1866), ix

10 Glory to Man in the highest! for Man is the master of things.
Hymn of Man

1 Thou hast conquered, O pale Galilean; the world has grown grey from Thy breath.
Hymn to Proserpine. See Julian.

2 And the best and the worst of this is
That neither is most to blame,
If you have forgotten my kisses
And I have forgotten your name.
An Interlude

TACITUS 55 or 56–c.120

3 *Solitudinem faciunt pacem appellant.*
They make a wilderness and call it peace.
Agricola, 30

4 *Elegantiae arbiter.*
The authority on taste.
Annals, xvi.18. Of Petronius

CHARLES-MAURICE DE TALLEYRAND 1754–1838

5 *Surtout, Messieurs, point de zèle.*
Above all, gentlemen, not the slightest zeal.
P. Chasles, *Voyages d'un critique à travers la vie et les livres* (1868), vol.2, p.407

6 *Ils n'ont rien appris, ni rien oublié.*
They have learnt nothing, and forgotten nothing.
Attributed to Talleyrand by the Chevalier de Panat in a letter to Mallet du Pan, Jan. 1796. See Dumouriez.

NAHUM TATE 1652–1715 and NICHOLAS BRADY 1659–1726

7 As pants the hart for cooling streams
When heated in the chase.
New Version of the Psalms (1696). **As Pants the Hart**

8 Through all the changing scenes of life.
Through all the Changing

9 While shepherds watch'd their flocks by night,
All seated on the ground,
The Angel of the Lord came down,
And glory shone around.
Supplement to the New Version of the Psalms (1700). **While Shepherds Watched**

JANE TAYLOR 1783–1824

1 Twinkle, twinkle, little star,
How I wonder what you are!
Up above the world so high,
Like a diamond in the sky!
The Star

ARCHBISHOP WILLIAM TEMPLE 1881–1944

2 In place of the conception of the Power-State we are led to that of the Welfare-State.
Citizen and Churchman (1941), ch.II

SIR JOHN TENNIEL 1820–1914

3 Dropping the pilot.
Caption of a cartoon and title of a poem in *Punch*, 29 March 1890, referring to the departure from office of Bismark

ALFRED, LORD TENNYSON 1809–1892

4 Break, break, break,
  On thy cold gray stones, O Sea!
And I would that my tongue could utter
  The thoughts that arise in me.
Break, Break, Break

5 I come from haunts of coot and hern,
I make a sudden sally
And sparkle out among the fern,
To bicker down a valley.
The Brook, l.23

6 For men may come and men may go,
  But I go on for ever.
l.33

7 Half a league, half a league,
  Half a league onward.
The Charge of the Light Brigade

8 'Forward the Light Brigade!'
Was there a man dismay'd?
Not tho' the soldier knew
  Some one had blunder'd:

Their's not to make reply,
Their's not to reason why,
Their's but to do and die:
Into the valley of Death
Rode the six hundred.

Cannon to right of them
Cannon to left of them,
Cannon in front of them
Volley'd and thunder'd.

1 Sunset and evening star,
And one clear call for me!
And may there be no moaning of the bar
When I put out to sea.
Crossing the Bar

2 A daughter of the gods, divinely tall
And most divinely fair. [Iphigenia.]
A Dream of Fair Women, l.87

3 More black than ashbuds in the front of March.
The Gardener's Daughter, l.28

4 Before a thousand peering littlenesses,
In that fierce light which beats upon a throne.
The Idylls of the King, Dedication, l.25

5 Clothed in white samite, mystic, wonderful.
The Coming of Arthur, l.284, and **The Passing of Arthur**, l.199

6 We needs must love the highest when we see it.
Guinevere, l.655

7 God make thee good as thou art beautiful.
The Holy Grail, l.136

8 His honour rooted in dishonour stood,
And faith unfaithful kept him falsely true.
Lancelot and Elaine, l.871

9 Unfaith in aught is want of faith in all.
Merlin and Vivien, l.387

10 It is the little rift within the lute,
That by and by will make the music mute.
l.388

11 So all day long the noise of battle roll'd
Among the mountains by the winter sea.
The Passing of Arthur, l.170

1 The old order changeth, yielding place to new,
And God fulfils himself in many ways,
Lest one good custom should corrupt the world.
l.408

2 Pray for my soul. More things are wrought by prayer
Than this world dreams of.
l.415

3 Never morning wore
To evening, but some heart did break.
In Memoriam A.H.H., vi

4 And ghastly thro' the drizzling rain
On the bald street breaks the blank day.
vii

5 'Tis better to have loved and lost
Than never to have loved at all.
xxvii

6 And Time, a maniac scattering dust,
And Life, a Fury slinging flame.
l

7 Oh yet we trust that somehow good
Will be the final goal of ill.
liv

8 An infant crying for the light:
And with no language but a cry.

9 Nature, red in tooth and claw.
lvi

10 So many worlds, so much to do,
So little done, such things to be.
lxxiii

11 There lives more faith in honest doubt,
Believe me, than in half the creeds.
xcvi

12 He seems so near and yet so far.
xcvii

13 Ring out, wild bells, to the wild sky,
The flying cloud, the frosty light:
The year is dying in the night;
Ring out, wild bells, and let him die.
cvi

1 Kind hearts are more than coronets,
And simple faith than Norman blood.
Lady Clara Vere de Vere, vi

2 Out flew the web and floated wide;
The mirror crack'd from side to side;
'The curse is come upon me,' cried
The Lady of Shalott.
The Lady of Shalott, pt.iii

3 In the Spring a young man's fancy lightly turns to thoughts of love.
Locksley Hall, l.20

4 As the husband is, the wife is.
l.47

5 For I dipt into the future, far as human eye could see,
Saw the Vision of the world, and all the wonder that would be.
l.119

6 Till the war-drum throbb'd no longer, and the battle-flags were furl'd
In the Parliament of man, the Federation of the world.
l.127

7 Knowledge comes, but wisdom lingers.
l.143

8 Forward, forward let us range,
Let the great world spin for ever down the ringing grooves of change.
l.181

9 Better fifty years of Europe than a cycle of Cathay.
l.184

10 'Courage!' he said, and pointed toward the land,
'This mounting wave will roll us shoreward soon.'
In the afternoon they came unto a land
In which it seemed always afternoon.
The Lotos-Eaters

11 Music that gentlier on the spirit lies,
Than tir'd eyelids upon tir'd eyes.
Choric Song, i

1 She only said, 'My life is dreary,
He cometh not,' she said;
She said, 'I am aweary, aweary.
I would that I were dead!'
Mariana

2 Faultily faultless, icily regular, splendidly null.
Maud, Pt.I.ii

3 Come into the garden, Maud,
For the black bat, night, has flown.
xxii.1

4 And blessings on the falling out
That all the more endears,
When we fall out with those we love
And kiss again with tears!
The Princess, ii. Song

5 Sweet and low, sweet and low,
Wind of the western sea.
iii. Song

6 The splendour falls on castle walls
And snowy summits old in story:
The long light shakes across the lakes,
And the wild cataract leaps in glory.
iv. Song (1)

7 O sweet and far from cliff and scar
The horns of Elfland faintly blowing!

8 Tears, idle tears, I know not what they mean.
Song (2)

9 Bright and fierce and fickle is the South,
And dark and true and tender is the North.
Song (3)

10 Man is the hunter; woman is his game:
The sleek and shining creatures of the chase.
v, l.147

11 Home they brought her warrior dead.
She nor swoon'd, nor utter'd cry:
All her maidens, watching said,
'She must weep or she will die.'
vi. Song

1 Now sleeps the crimson petal, now the white.
vii. Song (2)

2 Now lies the Earth all Danaë to the stars,
And all thy heart lies open unto me.

3 The moan of doves in immemorial elms,
And murmuring of innumerable bees.
Song (3)

4 Sink me the ship, Master Gunner—sink her, split her in twain!
Fall into the hands of God, not into the hands of Spain.
The Revenge, xi

5 And they praised him to his face with their courtly foreign grace.
xiii

6 My strength is as the strength of ten,
Because my heart is pure.
Sir Galahad

7 The woods decay, the woods decay and fall ...
And after many a summer dies the swan.
Tithonus, 1.1

8 Far on the ringing plains of windy Troy.
Ulysses, 1.17

9 How dull it is to pause, to make an end,
To rust unburnish'd, not to shine in use!
As tho' to breathe were life.
1.22

10 Death closes all: but something ere the end,
Some work of noble note, may yet be done,
Not unbecoming men that strove with gods.
1.51

11 It may be we shall touch the Happy Isles,
And see the great Achilles, whom we knew.
1.63

12 To strive, to seek, to find, and not to yield.
1.70

13 Every moment dies a man,
Every moment one is born.
The Vision of Sin, IV.ix

TERENCE c.190–159 B.C.

1 *Hinc illae lacrimae.*
Hence all those tears shed.
Andria, 126

2 *Homo sum; humani nil a me alienum puto.*
I am a man, I count nothing human foreign to me.
Heauton Timorumenos, 77

3 *Quot homines tot sententiae: suo' quoique mos.*
There are as many opinions as there are people: each has his own correct way.
Phormio, 454

TERTULLIAN c.160–c.225

4 *Certum est quia impossibile est.*
It is certain because it is impossible.
De Carne Christi, 5. Often quoted as, *Credo quia impossibile.*

WILLIAM MAKEPEACE THACKERAY 1811–1863

5 If a man's character is to be abused, say what you will, there's nobody like a relation to do the business.
Vanity Fair, ch.19

6 There's no sweeter tobacco comes from Virginia, and no better brand than the Three Castles.
The Virginians, ch.1

LOUIS ADOLPHE THIERS 1797–1877

7 [*Le roi*] *règne et le peuple se gouverne.*
The king reigns, and the people govern themselves.
Le National, 20 Jan. 1830

THOMAS À KEMPIS c.1380–1471

8 *O quam cito transit gloria mundi.*
Oh how quickly the world's glory passes away!
Of the Imitation of Christ, I.iii.6. See Anon.

9 *Nam homo proponit, sed Deus disponit.*
For man plans, but God arranges.
xix.2

ST. THOMAS AQUINAS c.1225–1274

1 *Pange, lingua, gloriosi*
Corporis mysterium.
Sing, my tongue, of the mystery of the glorious Body.
Pange Lingua Gloriosi. Corpus Christi hymn

BRANDON THOMAS 1856–1914

2 I'm Charley's aunt from Brazil—where the nuts come from.
Charley's Aunt (1892), Act 1

DYLAN THOMAS 1914–1953

3 Do not go gentle into that good night,
Old age should burn and rave at close of day;
Rage, rage against the dying of the light.
Do not go gentle into that good night

4 It was my thirtieth year to heaven
Woke to my hearing from harbour and neighbour wood
And the mussel pooled and the heron
Priested shore.
Poem in October

5 There could I marvel
My birthday
Away but the weather turned around.

6 After the first death, there is no other.
A refusal to mourn the death, by fire, of a child in London

7 And before you let the sun in, mind it wipes its shoes.
Under Milk Wood

8 Gomer Owen who kissed her once by the pig-sty when she wasn't looking and never kissed her again although she was looking all the time.

9 Nothing grows in our garden, only washing. And babies.

EDWARD THOMAS 1878–1917

10 Yes. I remember Adlestrop—
The name, because one afternoon

Of heat the express train drew up there
Unwontedly. It was late June.
Adlestrop

1 The past is the only dead thing that smells sweet.
Early One Morning

2 I have come to the borders of sleep,
The unfathomable deep
Forest where all must lose
Their way.
Lights Out

3 Out in the dark over the snow
The fallow fawns invisible go.
Out in the Dark

FRANCIS THOMPSON 1859–1907

4 It is little I repair to the matches of the Southron folk,
Though my own red roses there may blow.
At Lord's

5 O my Hornby and my Barlow long ago!

6 I fled Him, down the nights and down the days;
I fled Him, down the arches of the years.
The Hound of Heaven

7 Yea, faileth now even dream
The dreamer, and the lute the lutanist.

8 Lo, all things fly thee, for thou fliest Me!

9 O world invisible, we view thee,
O world intangible, we touch thee,
O world unknowable, we know thee,
Inapprehensible, we clutch thee!
In No Strange Land

10 'Tis ye, 'tis your estrangèd faces,
That miss the many-splendoured thing.

11 Wake! for the Ruddy Ball has taken flight
That scatters the slow Wicket of the Night;
And the swift Batsman of the Dawn has driven
Against the Star-spiked Rails a fiery Smite.
Wake! for the Ruddy Ball has Taken Flight. J.C. Squire, *Apes and Parrots*. See Fitzgerald.

WILLIAM HEPWORTH THOMPSON 1810–1886

1 We are none of us infallible—not even the youngest of us.
Remark referring to G.W. Balfour, then Junior Fellow of Trinity. G.W.E. Russell, *Collections and Recollections*, ch.18

2 What time he can spare from the adornment of his person he devotes to the neglect of his duties.
Of Sir Richard Jebb, afterwards Professor of Greek at Cambridge. M.R. Bobbit, *With Dearest Love to All*, ch.7

JAMES THOMSON 1700–1748

3 Rule, Britannia, rule the waves;
Britons never will be slaves.
Alfred: a Masque (1740), Act II, Scene the last

4 Delightful task! to rear the tender thought,
To teach the young idea how to shoot.
The Seasons (1728), **Spring**, l.1152

JAMES THOMSON 1834–1882

5 The City is of Night; perchance of Death,
But certainly of Night.
The City of Dreadful Night

LORD THOMSON OF FLEET 1894–1977

6 It's just like having a licence to print your own money.
(After the opening of Scottish commercial television.) Braddon, *Roy Thomson of Fleet Street*, p.240

HENRY DAVID THOREAU 1817–1862

7 Under a government which imprisons any unjustly, the true place for a just man is also a prison.
Civil Disobedience

8 As if you could kill time without injuring eternity.
Walden (1854). **Economy**

9 The mass of men lead lives of quiet desperation.

10 There are now-a-days professors of philosophy but not philosophers.

1 Our life is frittered away by detail ... Simplify, simplify.
Where I lived, and what I lived for

2 It takes two to speak the truth,—one to speak, and another to hear.
A Week on the Concord and Merrimack Rivers (1849). **Wednesday**

3 Some circumstantial evidence is very strong, as when you find a trout in the milk.
Journal, 11 Nov. 1850 (pub. 1903)

4 It were treason to our love
And a sin to God above
One iota to abate
Of a pure impartial hate.
Indeed, Indeed I Cannot Tell (1852)

JAMES THURBER 1894–1961

5 It's a Naïve Domestic Burgundy, Without Any Breeding, But I Think You'll be Amused by its Presumption.
Men, Women and Dogs. Cartoon caption

EDWARD, FIRST BARON THURLOW 1731–1806

6 Corporations have neither bodies to be punished, nor souls to be condemned, they therefore do as they like.
Poynder, *Literary Extracts* (1844), vol.I. Usually quoted as 'Did you ever expect a corporation to have a conscience, when it has no soul to be damned, and no body to be kicked?'

LEO TOLSTOY 1828–1910

7 All happy families resemble one another, but each unhappy family is unhappy in its own way.
Anna Karenina (1875–7), pt.i, ch.1. Tr. Maude

8 It is amazing how complete is the delusion that beauty is goodness.
The Kreutzer Sonata, 5. Tr. Maude

9 I sit on a man's back, choking him and making him carry me, and yet assure myself and others that I am very sorry for him and wish to ease his lot by all possible means—except by getting off his back.
What Then Must We Do? (1886), ch.16. Tr. Maude

THOMAS TRAHERNE 1637?–1674

1 The corn was orient and immortal wheat.
Centuries of Meditations. Cent.iii, 3

JOSEPH TRAPP 1679–1747

2 The King, observing with judicious eyes
The state of both his universities,
To Oxford sent a troop of horse, and why?
That learned body wanted loyalty;
To Cambridge books, as very well discerning
How much that loyal body wanted learning.
On George I's Donation of the Bishop of Ely's Library to Cambridge University. Nichols, *Literary Anecdotes*, vol.iii, p.330. For the reply see W. Browne.

ANTHONY TROLLOPE 1815–1882

3 Of all the needs a book has the chief need is that it be readable.
Autobiography (1883), ch.19

4 Nobody holds a good opinion of a man who has a low opinion of himself.
Orley Farm (1862), ch.22

5 A fainéant government is not the worst government that England can have. It has been the great fault of our politicians that they have all wanted to do something.
Phineas Finn (1869), ch.13

6 Mr Turnbull had predicted evil consequences ... and was now doing the best in his power to bring about the verification of his own prophecies.
ch.25

LEV TROTSKY 1879–1940

7 *Old* age is the most unexpected of all the things that happen to a man.
Diary in Exile, 8 May 1935

HARRY S. TRUMAN 1884–1972

8 The buck stops here.
Hand-lettered sign on President Truman's desk. Phillips, *The Truman Presidency*, ch.12

1 If you can't stand the heat, get out of the kitchen.
Mr. Citizen, ch.15.

WALTER JAMES REDFERN TURNER 1889–1946

2 Chimborazo, Cotopaxi,
They had stolen my soul away!
Romance, vii

MARK TWAIN 1835–1910

3 There was things which he stretched, but mainly he told the truth.
The Adventures of Huckleberry Finn (1884), ch.1

4 Hain't we got all the fools in town on our side? and ain't that a big enough majority in any town?
ch.26

5 It is by the goodness of God that in our country we have those three unspeakably precious things: freedom of speech, freedom of conscience, and the prudence never to practise either of them.
Following the Equator (1897), heading of ch.20

6 Man is the only animal that blushes. Or needs to.
heading of ch.27

7 When angry, count four; when very angry, swear.
Pudd'nhead Wilson's Calendar, March

8 The report of my death was an exaggeration.
Cable from Europe to the Associated Press

9 A verb has a hard time enough of it in this world when its all together. It's downright inhuman to split it up. But that's just what those Germans do. They take part of a verb and put it down here, like a stake, and they take the other part of it and put it away over yonder like another stake, and between these two limits they just shovel in German.
Address at dinner of the Nineteenth Century Club, New York, 20 Nov. 1900, to the toast, 'The Disappearance of Literature'

SIR JOHN VANBRUGH 1664–1726

10 Much of a muchness.
The Provok'd Husband (1728), I.i

HENRY VAUGHAN 1622–1695

1 Man is the shuttle, to whose winding quest
And passage through these looms
God order'd motion, but ordain'd no rest.
Silex Scintillans **(1650–5), Man**

2 Happy those early days, when I
Shin'd in my angel-infancy.
The Retreat, l.1

3 They are all gone into the world of light,
And I alone sit lingering here.
They Are All Gone

4 I saw Eternity the other night,
Like a great ring of pure and endless light,
All calm, as it was bright.
The World

THORSTEIN VEBLEN 1857–1929

5 Conspicuous consumption of valuable goods is a means of reputability to the gentleman of leisure.
The Theory of the Leisure Class (1899), ch.iv

VEGETIUS 4th–5th cent. A.D.

6 *Qui desiderat pacem, praeparet bellum.*
Let him who desires peace, prepare for war.
De Re Mil. 3, prol. Usually cited in the form ***Si vis pacem, para bellum*** (If you want peace, prepare for war.)

PIERRE VERGNIAUD 1753–1793

7 *Il a été permis de craindre que la Révolution, comme Saturne, dévorât successivement tous ses enfants.*
There was reason to fear that the Revolution, like Saturn, might devour in turn each one of her children.
Lamartine, *Histoire des Girondins* (1847), bk.xxxviii, ch.20

PAUL VERLAINE 1844–1896

8 *Les sanglots longs*
Des violons
De l'automne
Blessent mon coeur
D'une langueur
Monotone.

The drawn-out sobs of the violins of autumn wound my heart with a monotonous languor.
Chanson de l'automne

1 *Et, Ô ces voix d'enfants chantants dans la coupole!*
And oh those children's voices, singing beneath the dome!
Parsifal, A Jules Tellier

EMPEROR VESPASIAN 9–79

2 *Pecunia non olet.*
Money has no smell.
Traditional summary of Suetonius, *Vespasian*, 23,3

QUEEN VICTORIA 1819–1901

3 I will be good.
To Baroness Lehzen, 11 Mar. 1830. Martin, *The Prince Consort* (1875), vol.i, p.13

4 This mad, wicked folly of 'Woman's Rights'.
Letter to Sir Theodore Martin, 29 May 1870

5 We are not amused.
Attr. *Notebooks of a Spinster Lady*, 2 Jan. 1900

6 We are not interested in the possibilities of defeat; they do not exist.
To A.J. Balfour, in 'Black Week', Dec. 1899

PHILIPPE-AUGUSTE VILLIERS DE L'ISLE-ADAM 1838–1889

7 *Vivre? les serviteurs feront cela pour nous.*
Living? The servants will do that for us.
Axël (1890), IV, sect 2

FRANÇOIS VILLON b. 1431

8 *Mais où sont les neiges d'antan?*
But where are the snows of yesteryear?
Le Grand Testament (1461). **Ballade des Dames du Temps Jadis.** Tr. D.G. Rossetti

VIRGIL 70–19 B.C.

1 *Arma virumque cano.*
I sing of arms and the man.
Aeneid, i.1

2 *Forsan et haec olim meminisse iuvabit.*
Maybe one day we shall be glad to remember even these things.
203

3 *Et vera incessu patuit dea.*
And in her walk it showed, she was in truth a goddess.
405

4 *Sunt lacrimae rerum.*
There are tears shed for things.
462

5 *Timeo Danaos et dona ferentis.*
I fear the Greeks even when they bring gifts.
ii.49

6 *Dis aliter visum.*
The gods thought otherwise.
428

7 *Varium et mutabile semper*
Femina.
Fickle and changeable always is woman.
iv.569. Richard Stanyhurst's translation (1582):
A windfane changabil huf puffe
Always is a woomman.

8 *Bella, horrida bella,*
Et Thybrim multo spumantem sanguine cerno.
I see wars, horrible wars, and the Tiber foaming with much blood.
vi.86

9 *Facilis descensus Averno.*
Easy is the way down to the Underworld.
126

10 *Procul, o procul este, profani.*
Far off, Oh keep far off, you uninitiated ones.
258

1 *Experto credite.*
Trust one who has gone through it.
xi.283

2 *Latet anguis in herba.*
There's a snake hidden in the grass.
Eclogue, iii.93

3 *Omnia vincit Amor: et nos cedamus Amori.*
Love conquers all things: let us too give in to Love.
x.69

4 *Ultima Thule.*
Farthest Thule.
Georgics, i.30

5 *Felix qui potuit rerum cognoscere causas.*
Lucky is he who has been able to understand the causes of things.
ii.490

VOLTAIRE 1694–1778

6 *Si nous ne trouvons pas des choses agréables, nous trouverons du moins des choses nouvelles.*
If we do not find anything pleasant, at least we shall find something new.
Candide (1759), ch.17

7 *Dans ce pays-ci il est bon de tuer de temps en temps un amiral pour encourager les autres.*
In this country [England] it is thought well to kill an admiral from time to time to encourage the others.
ch.23

8 *Tout est pour le mieux dans le meilleur des mondes possibles.*
All is for the best in the best of possible worlds.
ch.30

9 *Il faut cultiver notre jardin.*
We must cultivate our garden. (We must attend to our own affairs.)

10 *Le mieux est l'ennemi du bien.*
The best is the enemy of the good.
Dict. Philosophique (1764). **Art Dramatique**

1 *Si Dieu n'existait pas, il faudrait l'inventer.*
If God did not exist, it would be necessary to invent him.
Épîtres, xcvi. **A l'Auteur du Livre des Trois Imposteurs**

2 *En effet, l'histoire n'est que le tableau des crimes et des malheurs.*
Indeed, history is nothing more than a tableau of crimes and misfortunes.
L'Ingénu (1767), ch.10

3 *Écrasez l'infâme.*
Stamp out abuses.
Letter to M. d'Alembert, 28 Nov. 1762

4 *Dieu n'est pas pour les gros bataillons, mais pour ceux qui tirent le mieux.*
God is on the side not of the heavy batallions, but of the best shots.
The Piccini Notebooks, p.547. See Bussy-Rabutin.

5 *On doit des égards aux vivants; on ne doit aux morts que la vérité.*
We owe respect to the living; to the dead we owe only truth.
Oeuvres (1785), vol.I, p.15n. (**Première Lettre sur Oedipe**)

6 I disapprove of what you say, but I will defend to the death your right to say it.
Attr. in S.G. Tallentyre, *The Friends of Voltaire* (1907), p.199

WILLIAM ROSS WALLACE d. 1881

7 The hand that rocks the cradle
Is the hand that rules the world.
J.K. Hoyt, *Cyclopedia of Practical Quotations* (1896), 402

GRAHAM WALLAS 1858–1932

8 The little girl had the making of a poet in her who, being told to be sure of her meaning before she spoke, said: 'How can I know what I think till I see what I say?'
The Art of Thought

EDMUND WALLER 1606–1687

9 Go, lovely Rose!
Tell her, that wastes her time and me,

That now she knows,
When I resemble her to thee,
How sweet and fair she seems to be.
Song: 'Go Lovely Rose!'

HORACE WALPOLE, FOURTH EARL OF ORFORD 1717–1797

1 Every drop of ink in my pen ran cold.
Letters. To Montagu, 3 July 1752

2 The way to ensure summer in England is to have it framed and glazed in a comfortable room.
To Cole, 28 May 1774

3 This world is a comedy to those that think, a tragedy to those that feel.
To the Countess of Upper Ossory, 16 Aug. 1776

4 I do not dislike the French from the vulgar antipathy between neighbouring nations, but for their insolent and unfounded airs of superiority.
To Hannah More, 14 Oct. 1787

SIR ROBERT WALPOLE, FIRST EARL OF ORFORD 1676–1745

5 They now *ring* the bells, but they will soon *wring* their hands.
On the declaration of war with Spain, 1739. W. Coxe, *Memoirs of Sir Robert Walpole* (1798), vol.i, p.618

6 The balance of power.
House of Commons, 13 Feb. 1741

BISHOP WILLIAM WARBURTON 1698–1779

7 Orthodoxy is my doxy; heterodoxy is another man's doxy.
To Lord Sandwich. Priestley, *Memoirs* (1807), vol.i, p.372

MRS. HUMPHRY WARD 1851–1920

8 'Propinquity does it'—as Mrs Thornburgh is always reminding us.
Robert Elsmere (1888), bk.i, ch.2

GEORGE WASHINGTON 1732–1799

1 Father, I cannot tell a lie, I did it with my little hatchet.
Attr. Mark Twain, *Mark Twain as George Washington*

WILLIAM WATSON 1559?–1603

2 *Fiat justitia et ruant coeli.*
Let justice be done though the heavens fall.
A Decacordon of Ten Quodlibeticall Questions Concerning Religion and State (1602). First citation in an English work of a famous maxim. See Ferdinand.

ISAAC WATTS 1674–1748

3 Birds in their little nests agree.
Divine Songs for Children, xvii. **Love between Brothers and Sisters**

4 How doth the little busy bee
Improve each shining hour!
xx. **Against Idleness and Mischief**

5 For Satan finds some mischief still
For idle hands to do.

6 'Tis the voice of the sluggard; I heard him complain,
'You have wak'd me too soon, I must slumber again'.
Moral Songs, i. **The Sluggard**

EVELYN WAUGH 1903–1966

7 Feather-footed through the plashy fen passes the questing vole.
Scoop (1938), bk.I, ch.1

8 Up to a point, Lord Copper.
Meaning 'No'. *passim*

DANIEL WEBSTER 1782–1852

9 There is always room at the top.
When advised not to become a lawyer as the profession was overcrowded

JOHN WEBSTER 1580?–1625?

10 Vain the ambition of kings
Who seek by trophies and dead things,

To leave a living name behind,
And weave but nets to catch the wind.

The Devil's Law-Case, V.iv

1 I am Duchess of Malfi still.

The Duchess of Malfi, IV.ii.146

2 Cover her face; mine eyes dazzle: she died young.

267

3 But keep the wolf far thence that's foe to men,
For with his nails he'll dig them up again.

The White Devil, V.iv.108

4 We think caged birds sing, when indeed they cry.

128

5 I have caught
An everlasting cold; I have lost my voice
Most irrecoverably.

vi.270

THOMAS EARLE WELBY 1881–1933

6 'Turbot, Sir,' said the waiter, placing before me two fishbones, two eyeballs, and a bit of black mackintosh.

The Dinner Knell

DUKE OF WELLINGTON 1769–1852

7 The battle of Waterloo was won on the playing fields of Eton.

See Montalembert, *De l'Avenir Politique de l'Angleterre* (1856). The attribution was refuted by the 7th Duke.

8 I always say that, next to a battle lost, the greatest misery is a battle gained.

Frances, Lady Shelley, *Diary*, p.102

9 In my situation as Chancellor of the University of Oxford, I have been much exposed to authors.

G.W.E. Russell, *Collections and Recollections*, ch.2.

10 Ours [our army] is composed of the scum of the earth—the mere scum of the earth.

Stanhope, *Notes of Conversations with the Duke of Wellington*, 4 Nov. 1831

1 Up Guards and at them again!
Letter from Captain Batty 22 June 1815. Booth, *Battle of Waterloo*. See also Croker, *Correspondence and Diaries* (1884), III, 280

2 Publish and be damned.
Attr. According to legend, Wellington wrote these words across a blackmailing letter from Stockdale, publisher of Harriette Wilson's *Memoirs*, and posted it back to him. See Elizabeth Pakenham, *Wellington: The Years of the Sword* (1969), ch.10.

H.G. WELLS 1866–1946

3 Human history becomes more and more a race between education and catastrophe.
The Outline of History, ch.40 of the 1951 edn.

CHARLES WESLEY 1707–1788

4 Gentle Jesus, meek and mild,
  Look upon a little child;
Pity my simplicity,
  Suffer me to come to thee.
Hymns and Sacred Poems (1742), **Gentle Jesus, Meek and Mild**

REVD. SAMUEL WESLEY 1662–1735

5 Style is the dress of thought; a modest dress,
Neat, but not gaudy, will true critics please.
An Epistle to a Friend concerning Poetry (1700)

MAE WEST 1892?–1980

6 'Goodness, what beautiful diamonds.'
'Goodness had nothing to do with it, dearie.'
Night After Night (1932), script by Vincent Lawrence

7 Why don't you come up sometime, see me?
She Done Him Wrong (1933). Commonly misquoted as 'Come up and see me sometime'.

RICHARD BETHELL, LORD WESTBURY 1800–1873

8 Then, sir, you will turn it over once more in what you are pleased to call your mind.
T.A. Nash, *Life of Lord Westbury* (1888), bk.2, ch.12

JOHN FANE, LORD WESTMORLAND 1759–1841

1 *Merit*, indeed! ... We are come to a pretty pass if they talk of *merit* for a bishopric.

Noted in Lady Salisbury's diary, 9 Dec. 1835. C. Oman, *The Gascoyne Heiress* (1968), V

SIR CHARLES WETHERELL 1770–1846

2 Then there is my noble and biographical friend who has added a new terror to death.

Of Lord Campbell. Lord St. Leonards, *Misrepresentations in Campbell's Lives of Lyndhurst and Brougham* (1869), p.3. See Lyndhurst.

EDITH WHARTON 1862–1937

3 Mrs Ballinger is one of the ladies who pursue Culture in bands, as though it were dangerous to meet it alone.

Xingu (1916), ch.1

WILLIAM WHEWELL 1794–1866

4 Hence no force however great can stretch a cord however fine into an horizontal line which is accurately straight.

Elementary Treatise on Mechanics, (1819), ch.IV, prob.ii. An example of accidental metre and rhyme, changed in later editions.

JAMES McNEILL WHISTLER 1834–1903

5 I am not arguing with you—I am telling you.

The Gentle Art of Making Enemies (1890)

6 [Answering Oscar Wilde's 'I wish I had said that']
You will, Oscar, you will.

L.C. Ingleby, *Oscar Wilde*, p.67

WILLIAM WHITING 1825–1878

7 O hear us when we cry to Thee
For those in peril on the sea.

Eternal Father Strong to Save

WALT WHITMAN 1819–1892

8 Silent and amazed even when a little boy.

A Child's Amaze

1 O Captain! my Captain! our fearful trip is done.
O Captain! My Captain!, i

2 I think I could turn and live with animals, they are so placid and self-contain'd.
Song of Myself, 32

3 They do not sweat and whine about their condition,
They do not lie awake in the dark and weep for their sins,
They do not make me sick discussing their duty to God.

4 Not one is respectable or unhappy over the whole earth.

5 Do I contradict myself?
Very well then I contradict myself,
(I am large, I contain multitudes.)
51

JOHN GREENLEAF WHITTIER 1807–1892

6 'Shoot, if you must, this old gray head,
But spare your country's flag,' she said.
Barbara Frietchie, l.35

7 For all sad words of tongue or pen,
The saddest are these: 'It might have been!'
Maud Muller, l.105

CORNELIUS WHURR c.1845

8 What lasting joys the man attend
Who has a polished female friend.
The Accomplished Female Friend

ELLA WHEELER WILCOX 1855–1919

9 Laugh and the world laughs with you;
  Weep, and you weep alone;
For the sad old earth must borrow its mirth,
  But has trouble enough of its own.
Solitude

OSCAR WILDE 1854–1900

10 Yet each man kills the thing he loves,
  By each let this be heard,

Some do it with a bitter look,
  Some with a flattering word.
The coward does it with a kiss,
  The brave man with a sword!
The Ballad of Reading Gaol (1898), I.vii

1 For he who lives more lives than one
  More deaths than one must die.
III.xxxvii

2 As long as war is regarded as wicked, it will always have its fascination. When it is looked upon as vulgar, it will cease to be popular.
The Critic as Artist, Part 2

3 The truth is rarely pure, and never simple.
The Importance of Being Earnest (1895), Act 1

4 In married life three is company and two none.

5 To lose one parent, Mr Worthing, may be regarded as a misfortune; to lose both looks like carelessness.

6 All women become like their mothers. That is their tragedy. No man does. That's his.

7 The good ended happily, and the bad unhappily. That is what Fiction means. [Miss Prism on her novel.]
Act II

8 On an occasion of this kind it becomes more than a moral duty to speak one's mind. It becomes a pleasure.

9 I couldn't help it. I can resist everything except temptation.
Lady Windermere's Fan (1891), Act I

10 We are all in the gutter, but some of us are looking at the stars.
Act III

11 A man who knows the price of everything and the value of nothing.
Definition of a cynic

12 There is no such thing as a moral or an immoral book. Books are well written, or badly written.
The Picture of Dorian Gray (1891), preface

1 The nineteenth century dislike of Realism is the rage of Caliban seeing his own face in the glass.

2 There is only one thing in the world worse than being talked about, and that is not being talked about.
ch.1

3 A cigarette is the perfect type of a perfect pleasure. It is exquisite, and it leaves one unsatisfied. What more can one want?
ch.6

4 The English country gentleman galloping after a fox—the unspeakable in full pursuit of the uneatable.
A Woman of No Importance (1893), Act I

5 *Lord Illingworth:* The Book of Life begins with a man and a woman in a garden.
Mrs Allonby: It ends with Revelations.

6 Children begin by loving their parents; after a time they judge them; rarely, if ever, do they forgive them.

7 I have put my genius into my life; all I've put into my works is my talent.
To André Gide. Gide, *Oscar Wilde: In Memoriam*

8 [At the New York Custom House]
I have nothing to declare except my genius.
F. Harris, *Oscar Wilde* (1918), p.75

9 Work is the curse of the drinking classes.
H. Pearson, *Life of Oscar Wilde* (1946), ch.12

10 [A huge fee for an operation was mentioned]
'Ah, well, then, I suppose that I shall have to die beyond my means.'
R.H. Sherard, *Life of Oscar Wilde* (1906), p.421

JOHN WILKES 1727–1797

11 'Wilkes,' said Lord Sandwich, 'you will die either on the gallows, or of the pox.'
'That,' replied Wilkes blandly, 'must depend on whether I embrace your lordship's principles or your mistress.'
Charles Chenevix-Trench, *Portrait of a Patriot* (1962), ch.3. But see H. Brougham, *Statesmen of George III*, third series (1843), p.189. Also attr. Samuel Foote.

WENDELL WILLKIE 1892–1944

1 The Constitution does not provide for first and second class citizens.
New York Herald Tribune, 13 June 1944

CHARLES ERWIN WILSON 1890–1961

2 For many years I thought what was good for our country was good for General Motors, and vice versa.
Testimony before the Senate Armed Services Committee, Jan. 1953

SIR HAROLD WILSON 1916–

3 That doesn't mean, of course, that the pound here in Britain—in your pocket or purse or in your bank—has been devalued.
Ministerial Broadcast, 19 Nov. 1967

4 A week is a long time in politics.
Phrase used a number of times in 1965–6

PRESIDENT WOODROW WILSON 1856–1924

5 There is such a thing as a man being too proud to fight.
Address at Philadelphia, 10 May 1915

6 The world must be made safe for democracy.
Address to Congress, 2 Apr. 1917

7 Open covenants of peace openly arrived at.
Address to Congress, 8 Jan. 1918. First of *Fourteen Points.*

OWEN WISTER 1860–1938

8 When you call me that, *smile.*
The Virginian (1902), ch.2

LUDWIG WITTGENSTEIN 1889–1951

9 *Die Welt ist alles, was der Fall ist.*
The world is everything that is the case.
Tractatus Logico-Philosophicus (1922), 1

10 *Die Logik muss für sich selber sorgen.*
Logic must take care of itself.
5.473

1 *Wovon man nicht sprechen kann, darüber muss man schweigen.*
Whereof one cannot speak, thereon one must remain silent.
7

P.G. WODEHOUSE 1881–1975

2 Jeeves shimmered out and came back with a telegram.
Carry on Jeeves (1925). **Jeeves Takes Charge**

3 He spoke with a certain what-is-it in his voice, and I could see that, if not actually disgruntled, he was far from being gruntled.
The Code of the Woosters (1938)

4 What with excellent browsing and sluicing and cheery conversation and what-not the afternoon passed quite happily.
My Man Jeeves (1919). **Jeeves and the Unbidden Guest**

5 Ice formed on the butler's upper slopes.
Pigs Have Wings (1952), ch.5. pt.i

6 The Right Hon was a tubby little chap who looked as if he had been poured into his clothes and had forgotten to say 'When!'
Very Good Jeeves (1930). **Jeeves and the Impending Doom**

CHARLES WOLFE 1791–1823

7 Not a drum was heard, not a funeral note,
As his corse to the rampart we hurried.
The Burial of Sir John Moore at Corunna, i

8 But he lay like a warrior taking his rest,
With his martial cloak around him.
iii

9 We carved not a line, and we raised not a stone—
But we left him alone with his glory.
viii

HUMBERT WOLFE 1886–1940

10 You cannot hope
to bribe or twist,
thank God! the
British journalist.

But, seeing what
  the man will do
unbribed, there's
  no occasion to.

The Uncelestial City, Bk.I. ii.2. **Over the Fire**

MARY WOLLSTONECRAFT 1759–1797

1 A king is always a king—and a woman always a woman: his authority and her sex ever stand between them and rational converse.

A Vindication of the Rights of Woman (1792), ch.4

2 I do not wish them [women] to have power over men; but over themselves.

CARDINAL WOLSEY 1475?–1530

3 Had I but served God as diligently as I have served the King, he would not have given me over in my gray hairs.

Cavendish, *Negotiations of Thomas Woolsey* (1641), p.113

MRS. HENRY WOOD 1814–1887

4 Dead! and ... never called me mother.

East Lynne (dramatized version by T.A. Palmer, 1874). These words do not occur in the novel

ELIZABETH WORDSWORTH 1840–1932

5 If all the good people were clever,
And all clever people were good,
The world would be nicer than ever
We thought that it possibly could.

But somehow, 'tis seldom or never
The two hit it off as they should;
The good are so harsh to the clever,
The clever so rude to the good!

St. Christopher and Other Poems: **Good and Clever**

WILLIAM WORDSWORTH 1770–1850

6 The light that never was, on sea or land.

Elegiac Stanzas (on a picture of Peele Castle in a storm, 1807)

1 Bliss was it in that dawn to be alive,
But to be young was very heaven!
French Revolution, as it Appeared to Enthusiasts (1809), and ***The Prelude,*** bk.xi, l.108

2 The moving accident is not my trade.
Hart-leap Well (1800), pt.2, l.1

3 I wandered lonely as a cloud
That floats on high o'er vales and hills,
When all at once I saw a crowd,
A host, of golden daffodils.
I wandered Lonely as a Cloud (1807)

4 For oft, when on my couch I lie
In vacant or in pensive mood,
They flash upon that inward eye
Which is the bliss of solitude;
And then my heart with pleasure fills,
And dances with the daffodils.

5 His little, nameless, unremembered, acts
Of kindness and of love.
Lines composed a few miles above Tintern Abbey (1798), l.34

6 The still, sad music of humanity.
l.91

7 My heart leaps up when I behold
A rainbow in the sky.
My Heart Leaps Up

8 The Child is father of the Man.

9 The rainbow comes and goes,
And lovely is the rose.
Ode. Intimations of Immortality (1807), ii

10 But yet I know, where'er I go,
That there hath passed away a glory from the earth.

11 Whither is fled the visionary gleam?
Where is it now, the glory and the dream?
v

12 Trailing clouds of glory do we come
From God, who is our home:
Heaven lies about us in our infancy!
Shades of the prison-house begin to close
Upon the growing boy.

1 Though nothing can bring back the hour
Of splendou in the grass, of glory in the flower.

ix

2 To me the meanest flower that blows can give
Thoug that do often lie too deep for tears.

ose by a river's brim
3 A w primrose was to him,
A was nothing more.
Bell (1819), pt.i, l.249

osopher!—a fingering slave,
that would peep and botanize
on his mother's grave?
Poet's Epitaph

The harvest of a quiet eye,
That broods and sleeps on his own heart.

6 All things have second birth;
The earthquake is not satisfied at once.
The Prelude, bk.x, l.83

7 Still glides the Stream, and shall for ever glide;
The Form remains, the Function never dies.
The River Duddon, xxxiv. **After-Thought**

8 We feel that we are greater than we know.

9 She dwelt among the untrodden ways
Beside the springs of Dove,
A maid whom there were none to praise
And very few to love.
She Dwelt Among the Untrodden Ways

10 But she is in her grave, and, oh,
The difference to me!

11 She was a phantom of delight
When first she gleamed upon my sight.
She was a Phantom of Delight

12 A perfect woman, nobly planned,
To warn, to comfort, and command.

13 Earth has not anything to show more fair.
Sonnets. **Composed upon Westminster Bridge**

1 This City now doth, like a garment, wear
The beauty of the morning.

2 Dear God! the very houses seem asleep;
And all that mighty heart is lying still!

3 It is a beauteous evening, calm and free,
The holy time is quiet as a nun,
Breathless with adoration.
It is a beauteous evening

4 Milton! thou shouldst be living at this hour:
England hath need of thee.
Milton! thou shouldst

5 Plain living and high thinking are no more:
The homely beauty of the good old cause
Is gone.
O friend! I know not

6 Surprised by joy—impatient as the Wind
I turned to share the transport—Oh! with whom
But Thee, deep buried in the silent tomb.
Surprised by joy

7 Give all thou canst; high Heaven rejects the lore
Of nicely-calculated less or more.
Tax not the royal Saint

8 Two Voices are there; one is of the sea,
One of the mountains; each a mighty Voice,
In both from age to age thou didst rejoice,
They were thy chosen music, Liberty!
Two Voices are there

9 The world is too much with us; late and soon,
Getting and spending, we lay waste our powers.
The world is too much with us

10 Our meddling intellect
Misshapes the beauteous forms of things:—
We murder to dissect.
The Tables Turned

11 Close up these barren leaves.

12 I've measured it from side to side:
'Tis three feet long and two feet wide.
The Thorn (1798), iii [early reading]

1 O Cuckoo! Shall I call thee bird,
Or but a wandering voice?
To the Cuckoo

2 Spade! with which Wilkinson hath tilled his lands.
To the Spade of a Friend

3 Poetry is the spontaneous overflow of powerful feelings: it takes its origin from emotion recollected in tranquillity.
Lyrical Ballads, preface to 2nd edn. (1802)

4 Every great and original writer, in proportion as he is great and original, must himself create the taste by which he is to be relished.
Letter to Lady Beaumont, 21 May 1807

SIR HENRY WOTTON 1568–1639

5 He first deceas'd; she for a little tri'd
To live without him: lik'd it not, and di'd.
Death of Sir Albertus Moreton's Wife

6 You meaner beauties of the night,
That poorly satisfy our eyes,
More by your number, than your light;
You common people of the skies,
What are you when the moon shall rise?
On His Mistress, the Queen of Bohemia

7 An ambassador is an honest man sent to lie abroad for the good of his country.
Written in the Album of Christopher Fleckmore (1604). Izaak Walton, *Life*

SIR THOMAS WYATT 1503?–1542

8 And wilt thou leave me thus?
Say nay, say nay, for shame.
An Appeal

9 They flee from me, that sometime did me seek
With naked foot, stalking in my chamber.
Remembrance

10 When her loose gown from her shoulders did fall,
And she me caught in her arms long and small,
Therewith all sweetly did me kiss
And softly said, 'Dear heart how like you this?'

WILLIAM WYCHERLEY 1640?–1716

1 You [drama critics] who scribble, yet hate all who write ...
And with faint praises one another damn.
The Plain Dealer (1677), prologue

XENOPHON c.428/7–c.354 B.C.

2 The sea! the sea!
Anabasis, IV.vii.24

AUGUSTIN, MARQUIS DE XIMÉNÈZ 1726–1817

3 *Attaquons dans ses eaux*
La perfide Albion!
Let us attack in her own waters perfidious Albion!
L'Ère des Français (Oct. 1793). *Poésies Révolutionnaires et contre-révolutionnaires* (Paris, 1821), I, p.160. See Bossuet.

THOMAS RUSSELL YBARRA b. 1880

4 A Christian is a man who feels
Repentance on a Sunday
For what he did on Saturday
And is going to do on Monday.
The Christian (1909)

W.F. YEAMES 1835–1918

5 And when did you last see your father?
Title of painting (1878) now in the Walker Art Gallery, Liverpool

W.B. YEATS 1865–1939

6 O body swayed to music, O brightening glance,
How can we know the dancer from the dance?
Among School Children, VIII

7 That dolphin-torn, that gong-tormented sea.
Byzantium

8 Now that my ladder's gone,
I must lie down where all the ladders start,
In the foul rag-and-bone shop of the heart.
The Circus Animals' Desertion, III

1 Down by the salley gardens my love and I did meet;
She passed the salley gardens with little snow-white feet.
She bid me take love easy, as the leaves grow on the tree;
But I, being young and foolish, with her would not agree.
Down by the Salley Gardens

2 All changed, changed utterly:
A terrible beauty is born.
Easter 1916

3 Too long a sacrifice
Can make a stone of the heart.

4 Only God, my dear,
Could love you for yourself alone
And not your yellow hair.
For Anne Gregory

5 The years to come seemed waste of breath,
A waste of breath the years behind
In balance with this life, this death.
An Irish Airman Forsees his Death

6 I will arise and go now, and go to Innisfree,
And a small cabin build there, of clay and wattles made:
Nine bean-rows will I have there, a hive for the honey-bee,
And live alone in the bee-loud glade.
The Lake Isle of Innisfree

7 A shudder in the loins engenders there
The broken wall, the burning roof and tower
And Agamemnon dead.
Leda and the Swan

8 That is no country for old men.
Sailing to Byzantium, I

9 The salmon-falls, the mackerel-crowded seas,
Fish, flesh, or fowl, commend all summer long
Whatever is begotten, born, and dies.

10 An aged man is but a paltry thing,
A tattered coat upon a stick, unless
Soul clap its hands and sing, and louder sing
For every tatter in its mortal dress.
II

1 And therefore I have sailed the seas and come
To the holy city of Byzantium.

2 Turning and turning in the widening gyre
The falcon cannot hear the falconer;
Things fall apart; the centre cannot hold.
The Second Coming

3 The best lack all conviction, while the worst
Are full of passionate intensity.

4 And what rough beast, its hour come round at last,
Slouches towards Bethlehem to be born?

5 Irish poets, learn your trade,
Sing whatever is well made,
Scorn the sort now growing up
All out of shape from toe to top.
***Under Ben Bulben*, V**

6 *Cast a cold eye*
On life, on death.
Horseman, pass by!
VI

EDWARD YOUNG 1683–1765

7 Procrastination is the thief of time.
***The Complaint: Night Thoughts*,** Night i, l.393

8 Man wants but little; nor that little, long.
Night iv, l.122

GEORGE W. YOUNG 1846–1919

9 Your lips, on my own, when they printed 'Farewell',
Had never been soiled by the 'beverage of hell';
But they come to me now with the bacchanal sign,
And the lips that touch liquor must never touch mine.
The Lips That Touch Liquor Must Never Touch Mine; also attr., in a different form, to Harriet A. Glazebrook

ÉMILE ZOLA 1840–1902

10 *J'accuse.*
I accuse.
Title of an open letter to the President of the French Republic, in connection with the Dreyfus case, published in *L'Aurore*, 13 Jan. 1898

INDEX

NOTE. The order of the index both in the keywords and in the entries following each keyword is strictly alphabetical. Singular and plural nouns (including their possessive forms) are grouped separately: for 'some old lover's ghost' see 'lover'; for 'at lovers' perjuries' see 'lovers'. Eccentric, archaic, and dialect spellings have been changed to the normal modern English equivalent in most cases; foreign words appear in the general alphabetical scheme, but in italic type. To save space, the definite and indefinite articles and words such as but, and, for, as, oh, have been dropped from the beginning of entries, and the alphabetical order may be affected: 'and did those feet' is given as 'did those feet'. In many cases the entries themselves have been elided in a similar manner, giving the sense of the quotation referred to, not an exact transcript of it. References are in the form 'page : quotation number': 311:10=quotation 10 on page 311.

aiming at a million 83:2
air that kills 197:8
castles built with a. 208:1
fire-folk sitting in the a. 193:4
pinions skim the a. 167:10
aired: morning well-a. 85:5
airs: sounds and sweet a. 318:6
alarms: confused a. 13:2
alas: may say a. 16:10
albatross: I shot the a. 123:4
Albion: *perfide A.* 374:3
ale: cakes and a. 319:9
drink your a. 198:5
alexandrine: needless a. 270:5
alibi: vy worn't there a a. 140:11
Alice is marrying 246:2
A., where art thou 86:6
alien: amid the a. corn 213:1
alienum: *humani nil a.* 347:2
aliter: *dis a. visum* 356:6
alive: as if a. 83:11
dawn to be a. 370:1
dead, and is a. again 60:3
officiously to keep a. 121:8
still a. at twenty-two 216:5
all for love 333:1
a. for one 151:4
a. for the best 357:8
a. hell broke loose 249:10
a. human beings born free 4:1
a. human life 203:2
a. our yesterdays 310:6
a. places hell 237:4
a.'s right with the world 84:6
a. the conspirators 304:12
a. the world is young 215:9
a. things bright and beautiful 2:6
a. things lawful for me 65:2
a. things to a. men 65:1
for a. in a. 297:2
allegiance to any master 194:3
victim demands a. 179:5
allegory on banks of Nile 326:11
alles: *Welt ist a.* 367:9
alley: lives in our a. 102:2
alliteration's artful aid 117:4
allons, *enfants* 287:5
Allsopp: Guinness, A., Bass 99:3
alluring: little scorn a. 127:3
almighty dollar 7:4
almost thou persuadest me 63:16
alms for oblivion 319:1
when thou doest a. 51:4
aloft: now he's gone a. 137:7
alone and palely loitering 211:9
a. on wide wide sea 123:8
a., poor maid 244:8
a. went she 215:6
blindfold and a. 217:5
never less a. 284:8
want to be a. 170:5
when wholly a. 119:9
Alph the sacred river 124:6
Alpha and Omega 69:8
alway: with you a. 57:7
always mornings like this 246:8
a. verify references 288:1
am: here I a. 234:2
think, therefore I a. 137:3
yet what I a. 120:6
amantum: *periuria ridet a.* 262:3
Amaryllis: sport with A. 248:1
amateurs: artistic temperament afflicts a. 116:5
hell full of musical a. 324:3
amaze: cogitations still a. 154:2
amazed: silent and a. 363:8
ambassador an honest man 373:7
ambition, distraction 105:10
fling away a. 303:5
amemus: *vivamus atque a.* 108:2
America: o my A. 144:7
Americans: good A. 11:5
ignorant A. 242:6
amiable are thy dwellings 275:11
a. weakness 161:5
amicus *Plato* 12:7
amis: *adversité des a.* 223:6
amitié *de la connaissance* 92:10
ammunition: pass the a. 165:3
amo: *non a. te* 239:1
odi et a. 108:5
amor: *omnia vincit a.* 357:3

amour *dans la société* 110:7
a. vient de l'aveuglement 92:10
faire l'a. en tout temps 25:1
amused by its presumption 351:5
we are not a. 355:5
ancestors: look backward to a. 79:3
ancestral voices 124:8
ancestry: trace my a. 174:1
ancient mariner 123:1
anders: *kann nicht a.* 231:3
Anderson: John A. my jo 91:1
angel of death abroad 79:5
a. of death spread wings 96:4
a. of the Lord came 58:4; 340:9
ape or a. 142:9
better a. 322:9
ministering a. thou 292:9
white as an a. 74:4
angeli: *non Angli sed a.* 179:7
angels and ministers 297:7
a. fear to tread 270:9
a. of God ascending 34:14
entertained a. unawares 68:11
flights of a. 300:11
give his a. charge 276:4
nore life, nor a. 64:6
side of a. 142:9
tongues of men and a. 65:5
anger makes dull witty 156:9
a. one of sinews 169:8
some rich a. shows 212:7
telegrams and a. 165:7
Anglais *s'amusent tristement* 337:5
angle: every a. greet 239:5
Angles: not A. but angels 179:7
Angleterre: *perfide A.* 77:1
Anglo-Saxon *attitudes* 107:8
angry and sin not 66:16
a. with me 81:6
a. young men 160:3
proud and a. dust 198:5
very a., swear 353:7
animal called man 338:8
be a good a. 332:3
man a noble a. 82:2
not to, a. 168:8
political a. 12:3
this a. is very bad 8:5
tool-making a. 167:3
animal *est très méchant* 8:5
omne a. triste 10:6
animals never kill for sport 168:11
live with a. 364:2
anguis *in herba* 357:2
anguish: pain and a. 292:9
angusta: *res a. domi* 210:2
Annabel Lee 268:4
annals of the poor 178:7
annihilating all that's made 239:6
annoy: does it to a. 105:6
annual income twenty pounds 138:8
anointed my head 274:6
another country 238:3
members one of a. 66:15
answer a fool 42:3
a. to 'Hi' 104:1
dusty a. 244:4
soft a. turneth 41:9
what is the a. 334:7
answered three questions 105:4
no one a. 136:7
ant: go to the a. 40:12
antan: *neiges d'a.* 355:8
antic: dance an a. hay 237:9
Antichrist: look'st like A. 207:9
anybody: is there a. there 136:6
no one's a. 173:3
anxiety: taboo'd by a. 173:9
apart: thing a. 96:7
ape *or* angel 142:9
apes, peacocks 38:10; 240:9
for dogs and a. 83:1
aphorism: corroboration of a. 72:2
aphrodisiac: circumambulating a. 169:4
Apollo: burnèd is A.'s laurel 237:8
songs of A. 307:2
apostle: rank as an a. 174:12

awful quarters of hour 287:1
awoke and found myself famous 98:3
axe: Lizzie Borden took an a. 5:6
babes and sucklings 274:1
babies: hates dogs and b. 287:3
washing and b. 348:9
baboon and monkey 318:11
baby: first b. laughed 23:6
Babylon: waters of B. 277:6
Bacchus and revellers 249:12
back: at my b. always hear 239:9
b. in the closet 162:5
before cried 'b.' 232:6
sit on a man's b. 351:9
wife looked b. 34:10
backing into the limelight 31:2
backs to the wall 180:2
beast with two b. 314:6
backward: look b. to ancestors 89:3
bacon nat fet for hem 112:14
b. not only thing 216:6
bauble: take away fool's b. 132:7
bay: flourishing like green b. 275:1
bad: either good or b. 298:2
mad, b., dangerous 222:1
no b. weather 288:7
sad, b., mad it was 82:10
this is animal is very b. 8:5
when she was b. 229:3
badge of our tribe 311:5
badgers: when b. fight 120:2
badly: worth doing b. 116:8
bag: eggs inside paper b. 202:5
baked me too brown 106:1
balance of power 359:6
b. with this life 375:5
bald and unconvincing 174:9
baldness: far side of b. 329:2
ball no question makes 162:6
ruddy b. 349:11
ballad: met with a b. 99:2
ballads, songs and snatches 173:10
permitted to make all b. 163:8
balm in Gilead 47:11
baloney: it's still b. 329:1
band of brothers 302:8
high aesthetic b. 174:12
bane: precious b. 249:3
bang: not with a b. 154:11
banish squint suspicion 247:3
bank: all the way to b. 226:4
I know a b. 313:5
upon this b. 312:4
banker: saw a b.'s clerk 104:6
banks and braes 92:3
banner over me was love 44:4
b. with strange device 227:7
freedom! yet thy b. 95:9
star-spangled b. 214:8
banners: confusion on thy b. 178:3
bar: moaning of b. 342:1
Barabbas a publisher 101:6
B. was a robber 62:9
***barajar**: paciencia y b.* 109:7
barbarians: his young b. 95:10
without any b. 108:6
bards of passion 212:3
bare ruin'd choirs 321:8
barefoot friars singing vespers 172:2
bare-legg'd son of a gun 99:5
barge she sat in 294:4
Barkis is willin' 138:7
Barlow long ago 349:5
barren: live a b. sister 312:10
these b. leaves 372:11
barricade: disputed b. 293:1
bars: through same b. 223:2
baser: fellows of the b. sort 63:7
bashful fifteen 326:13
basia mille 108:3
basically I'm viable 31:6
basin: stare in the b. 15:3
Basingstoke: like B. 175:8
Bass: Guinness, Allsopp, B. 99:3
bassoon: heard the loud b. 123:3
bastards: stand up for b. 305:10
bat: black b., night 345:3

batallions: not for heavy b. 358:4
Bath: ever be tired of B. 18:5
baton: field marshal's b. 229:9
batsman and bat 222:10
b. of the dawn 349:11
batter my heart 145:5
battle-flags furl'd 344:6
b. to the strong 43:9
far-flung b.-line 219:3
marriage field of b. 335:11
next to a b. lost 361:8
noise of b. 342:11
smelleth the b. 40:7
battledores: lawyers the b. 140:7
be: to b., or not 298:11
beach: only pebble on b. 78:4
beaches: fight on the b. 117:10
Beachy Head: by way of B. 115:10
beaded bubbles 212:9
beaker full of warm South 212:9
Beale: Miss Buss and Miss B. 6:1
beam in thine own 52:3
beamish nephew 104:2
my b. boy 106:5
beams: candle throws b. 312:7
bean: home of b. and cod 76:8
nine b.-rows 375:6
bear of little brain 246:6
b. them we can 198:5
b. the yoke in youth 48:2
b. with sore head 238:9
eaten by the b. 199:7
Puritan hated b.-baiting 233:5
pursued by a b. 320:6
still less the b. 167:10
beard: by thy grey b. 123:1
singeing King of Spain's b. 148:5
beareth all things 65:8
bears: dancing dogs and b. 190:2
beast that wants discourse 296:13
b. with two backs 314:6
what rough b. 376:4
beastie: tim'rous b. 91:12
beasties: long-leggety b. 4:10
beat as one 181:1
b. on my door 202:2
b. swords into plowshares 44:13
b. your pate 269:2
that ye b. my people 45:1
beating: charity and b. 164:2
hear b. of his wings 79:5
beats upon a throne 342:4
***beatus** vir qui timet* 70:6
***beauté**: qu'ordre et b.* 24:5
beauteous: how b. mankind 318:9
beauties: you meaner b. 373:6
beautiful: against b. and clever 179:4
all things bright and b. 2:6
b. railway bridge 233:9
b., tender, kind 245:5
b. upon the mountains 46:14
believe to be b. 255:4
entirely b. 16:3
good as b. 342:7
more b. daughter 194:10
she's b. 302:11
small is b. 291:2
when woman isn't b. 113:12
beauty cold and austere 288:8
b. draws us 271:5
b. is truth 212:6
b. must be truth 213:12
delusion b. is goodness 351:8
dreamed life was b. 192:5
England, home, b. 78:3
ghosts of b. glide 269:10
homely b. 372:5
no b. hath not strangeness 19:7
principal b. in building 169:7
she walks in b. 97:9
simply order and b. 24:5
terrible b. is born 375:2
thing of b. 211:4
wildest b. 263:1
winds of March with b. 320:9
because it is there 235:7
b. it was he 253:3

bells (cont.):
ring out, wild b. 343:13
what passing-b. 262:9
bellum: *preparet b.* 354:6
beloved: my b. Son 50:4
below: between, above, b. 144:7
belted you an' flayed you 217:10
bends: though she b. him 228:8
benison of hot water 80:6
bent: as twig is b. 269:8
bereav'd of light 74:4
Berliner: *Ich bin ein B.* 214:7
berry: made a better b. 95:1
best and the worst 340:2
b. be still 13:5
b. enemy of good 357:10
b. government governs least 262:1
b. lack all conviction 376:3
b. of actions tend 93:8
b. of dark and bright 97:9
b. of possible worlds 98:4; 357:8
b. of times 141:2
b. words in b. order 125:3
b. ye breed 219:11
b. yet to be 84:10
have b. trousers on 201:7
loveliest and b. 162:1
other person's b. 183:6
past prizing, b. 331:5
bestride the narrow 303:9
best-seller sold well 76:3
betray: guts to b. my country 165:9
that men b. 177:4
betrayed by what is false 244:2
better by far 286:4
b. *in France* 335:1
b. man than I am 217:10
b. marry than burn 64:15
b. than arrive 336:1
b. than light 183:2
b. to have loved 94:8; 343:5
far, far b. thing 141:3
for b. for worse 273:10
getting b. and b. 129:9
he is not b. 4:4
I'm kent the b. 91:8
known a b. day 292:2
knows of a b. 'ole 21:11
made a b. berry 95:1
make a b. mouse-trap 158:6
no b. than you should 25:3
see b. way 262:4
between: before, behind, b. 144:7
who comes b. 330:5
betwixt the stirrup 100:3
beware of the dog 267:1
b. the ides 303:7
beweep: all alone b. 321:1
beyond: not b. conjecture 82:1
Bible an opium-dose 216:1
words only fit for B. 169:3
bicker down a valley 341:5
bien: *l'ennemi du b.* 357:10
big: awfully b. adventure 23:8
B. Brother is watching 261:7
fear those b. words 209:5
side of the b. squadrons 93:2
bigger they come 163:4
Billy: poke poor B. 178:1
bind another to its delight 74:2
b. kings in chains 277:11
biography is about chaps 30:2
history the b. of great men 103:1
no history only b. 157:10
bird thou never wert 326:3
call thee b. 373:1
dromedary a cheerful b. 27:2
like a singing b. 286:2
rare b. 210:3
stirred for a b. 193:7
birds have nests 53:1
b. in little nests 360:3
nest of singing b. 204:4
no b. sing 211:9
time of singing of b. 44:6
Birmingham by way of Beachy Head 115:10
no great hopes from B. 18:1
birth: rainbow gave thee b. 135:3
birthday: marvel my b. 348:5

birth-rate: into a rising b. 169:4
birthright for mess of potage 34:12
bis dat 279:3
bishop, elect, of Vermont 221:3
bishopric: merit for b. 363:1
bitch-goddess success 203:4
old b. gone in teeth 272:1
bite hand that fed 89:8
b. other generals 172:1
bites: man b. dog 75:10
biting: more than b. Time 155:10
bitter: makes misfortunes more b. 20:8
bitterness of life 104:4
no hatred or b. 108:7
black as the pit 185:7
b. but comely 44:2
b. merciless things 203:1
b. swan 210:3
b. than ashbuds 342:3
I am b. 74:4
looking for b. hat 77:6
tip me the b. spot 335:9
blackbirds: full of b. 1:9
blade-straight 336:6
blast of war 302:2
blaze: amid b. of noon 250:8
bleed: do we not b. 311:8
I b. 325:6
blemish: without fear without b. 8:6
bless our human ears 248:7
b. squire and his relations 138:4
God b. us every one 138:5
blessed: bed be b. 5:7
b. are the poor 50:8
b. art thou among women 57:15
b. be the name 39:7
call her b. 42:9
more b. to give 63:12
none b. before death 49:5
this b. plot 316:6
blessing: boon and a b. 7:6
blessings in disguise 188:10
glass of b. 187:11
blight man born for 193:3
blind guides 55:12
b. lead the b. 54:8
b. man in dark room 77:6
Cupid painted b. 312:12
maimed, halt, b. 59:12
though she be b. 20:2
work for b. 290:5
blindfold and alone 217:5
bliss of solitude 370:4
b. was it 370:1
deprived of everlasting b. 237:2
where ignorance is b. 179:3
blithe spirit 326:3
buxom, b. 247:8
no lark more b. 71:7
block: big black b. 174:6
blockhead ever wrote 205:8
bookful b. 270:8
blood is nipp'd 307:1
b. of patriots 203:5
b., toil, tears 117:9
b. will have b. 309:8
Christ's b. streams 237:6
flesh and b. so cheap 192:4
life-b. of master spirit 251:5
not against flesh and b. 67:2
ocean wash this b. 308:10
smell of b. still 310:3
smell the b. 306:5
so much b. 310:1
Tiber foaming b. 356:8
when the moon was b. 115:4
without shedding of b. 68:5
young b. have its course 215:9
bloody but unbowed 185:8
b. instructions 308:1
not b. likely 324:13
bloom in the spring 174:10
b. on a woman 23:9
b. sae fresh 92:3
hung with b. 196:1
piece in b. 186:2
blossom as the rose 46:7
b. by b. 339:8
b. in their dust 327:2

consumption: conspicuous c. 354:5
contact de deux épidermes 110:7
contagion of the world 325:1
content: land of lost c. 197:8
contention: long c. cease 13:5
continency: chastity and c. 17:2
you impose c. 17:4
continentiam: *imperas nobis c.* 17:4
continents: three separate c. 147:13
continuing: no c. city 68:12
contradict myself 364:5
c. Socrates 267:8
contradictions: bundle of c. 126:6
contrairy: everythink goes c. 138:6
contrive: nature always does c. 173:6
conversation: religion no proper c. 114:9
conversations: without pictures or c. 104:7
conversing: with thee c. 249:9
converted: except ye be c. 54:13
conviction: lack all c. 376:3
convincing myself I am right 19:2
cook a little unnerved 31:7
good c. 289:7
cool of the day 33:12
coot and hern 341:5
coral: bones are c. 318:4
cord: silver c. be loosed 43:15
cormorant or shag 202:5
corn: amid the alien c. 213:1
breast high amid the c. 192:2
c. in Egypt 35:3
treadeth out the c. 36:10
corner of a foreign field 80:13
corners: earth's imagined c. 145:1
three c. of world 305:8
Cornish: twenty thousand C. men 183:3
coronets: more than c. 344:1
corporations have neither 351:6
c. have no souls 122:11
corpore sano 210:6
corporis mysterium 348:1
corpse: make a lovely c. 139:4
correct: present and c. 4:2
each his c. way 347:3
correcteth: Lord loveth he c. 40:9
corridors of power 330:11
corroboration of this aphorism 72:2
corroborative detail 174:9
corrupt the world 343:1
equally wicked and c. 88:2
corrupts: absolute power c. 1:3
Cortez: like stout C. 213:6
cottage: love and a c. 126:1
couché de bonne heure 278:8
couched in white bosom 131:10
coucher sous les ponts 166:1
counsellor: wonderful, c. 45:10
count myself in nothing else 316:9
c. the ways 82:5
countenance: cheerful c. 41:10
c. divine 73:4
disinheriting c. 327:1
knight of doleful c. 109:4
lift up his c. 36:2
of a beautiful c. 37:14
counter: all things c. 193:1
counteracts the Devil 328:3
counties: coloured c. 197:1
country: ask not what your c. 214:6
c. a healthy grave 330:10
c. diversion 127:4
c. in town 239:3
c., right or wrong 135:5; 291:3
c. that has 265 kinds of cheese 135:6
died to save their c. 115:7
die for one's c. 195:4
every c. but his own 101:9
fight for its King and c. 7:3
fit c. for heroes 171:10
from yon far c. 197:8

cypress: in sad c. 319:11
D: big, big D 175:1
da *mi basia mille* 108:3
d. mihi castitatem 17:2
daffodils, that come 320:9
fair d. 188:7
host of golden d. 370:3
in the west wind, d. 241:5
dagger: is this a d. 308:5
daggers: give me the d. 308:9
dahin! *dahin!* 176:5
daily: our d. bread 51:5
daintily: things d. served 31:7
daisies pied 306:14
dalliance: silken d. 301:13
damages: first d. his mind 9:7
Dame: belle D. sans Merci 212:2
damn her at venture 222:5
d. the consequences 247:1
d. with faint praise 269:6
d. you, Jack 76:1
devil d. thee black 310:5
damned be him 310:7
d. from here 217:7
d. lies and statistics 143:10
one d. thing 261:3
those d. dots 117:6
your d. flower-pots 84:12
damning those no mind to 93:4
damp souls of housemaids 155:8
damsel with a dulcimer 124:9
Danaë to the stars 346:2
Danaos: *timeo D.* 356:5
dance: dancer from the d. 374:6
join the d. 105:13
on with the d. 95:8
danced by light of moon 225:3
dancer from the dance 374:6
dances with daffodils 370:4
danceth without musick 187:4
dancing: manners of d. master 204:6
dandelions: drooping d. 32:5
dandy: candy is d. 256:7
danger: at brink of d. 280:8
be in less d. 256:6
this nettle, d. 301:1
dangerous remedy 160:2
d. to know 222:1
d. to meet it alone 363:3
if right, d. precedent 129:2
such men are d. 303:11
dangerously: live d. 259:6
Daniel come to judgement 312:2
danket: *nun d. alle Gott* 284:2
dapple-dawn-drawn falcon 193:6
dappled: for d. things 192:10
dare not speak 146:10
letting 'I d. not' 308:2
none d. call it treason 182:4
you who d. 244:5
darent handle explosives 323:8
dares: who d. do more 308:3
Darien: peak in D. 213:6
dark: as children fear d. 19:10
as good i' th' d. 188:5
blind man in d. room 77:6
d. and true 345:9
d. backward and abysm 318:1
d., dark, dark 250:8
d. Satanic mills 73:4
d. world of sin 71:10
hellish d. 338:2
leap in the d. 190:1
out in the d. 349:3
real d. night of soul 163:2
to the d. tower 306:5
we are for the d. 294:8
darkening like a stain 16:11
darkest day (live till tomorrow) 130:9
darkling: on a d. plain 13:2
darkly: through a glass, d. 65:11
darkness at noon-day 130:12
d. comprehended it not 60:16
d. deepens 232:2
lie where shades of d. 136:3
lighten our d. 272:9
prince of d. gentleman 306:3
that walked in d. 45:9
to d. and to me 178:5
darling buds of May 320:13
d. of my heart 102:2
dastards: commands, and d. me 81:6
dat: *bis d.* 279:3

Dieb: *er war ein D.* 184:10
died a myriad 272:1
d. before god of love 145:7
d. for our lands 217:3
d. hereafter 310:6
d. in good old age 39:5
d. to save their country 115:7
dog it was that d. 177:2
I had d. for thee 38:7
since God d. 245:7
sweet dove d. 213:4
dies fighting has increase 179:10
d. rich d. disgraced 103:7
every moment d. a man 19:3; 346:13
gods love d. young 243:8
kingdom where nobody d. 245:6
until he d. 331:3
dies irae 109:1
diet: immortal d. 282:1
Dieu *n'a que dix* 121:1
D. pour les gros escadrons 93:2
differemus: *negabimus aut d.* 235:4
difference to me 371:10
made all the d. 168:5
rue with a d. 300:3
different from home life 5:3
d. from us 6:1
rich are d. 163:3
difficult and left untried 116:7
d. to get up resentment 258:2
d. to speak 89:2
d. we do immediately 99:1
diffugere *nives* 195:7
dig the grave 336:7
d. them up again 361:3
I cannot d. 60:4
digest: *inwardly* d. them 273:1
digested: chewed and d. 20:11
diggeth a pit shall fall 43:10
dignity: in d. and rights 4:1
dilectione *hominum* 17:7
dilige *et quod vis* 17:6
diminished: ought to be d. 152:1
diminishes: death d. me 146:8
dimittis: *nunc d.* 70:11
dine: go to inns to d. 116:2
if this should stay to d. 104:6
to d. with some men 30:5
dines: where M.F.H. d. 338:1
dinner: ask him to d. 103:5
d. of herbs 41:11
gat ye to your d. 22:5
direct: going d. to heaven 141:2
House pleased to d. 226:2
directions: in all d. 224:7
direful in the sound 18:1
dirt: poverty, hunger, and d. 192:3
dirty British coaster 240:10
do hard d. work 288:6
Dis *aliter visum* 356:6
disagreeable to myself 330:9
tell d. truths 86:5
disappeared with curious perfume 15:1
disappointment all I endeavour 193:5
disapprove of what you say 358:6
disaster: meet triumph and d. 218:2
disbelief: willing suspension of d. 125:1
discharge: no d. in that war 43:5
discontent: winter of our d. 317:2
discontents: more d. I never had 188:4
disdain not amiss 127:3
disease: desperate d. 160:2
no cure for this d. 27:6
diseases: cure of all d. 81:7
disgrace: when in d. 321:1
disgraced: rich dies d. 103:7
disguise: blessings in d. 188:10
dish: lordly d. 37:1
disinheriting countenance 327:1
dismal: professors of d. science 103:2
with a d. headache 173:9
dismayed: was there a man d. 341:8

disobedience: man's first d. 248:9
disorder: sweet d. 188:3
dispense with necessities 255:8
displeasing: something not d. 223:6
disponit: Deus d. 347:9
dispraised no small praise 250:5
disputations: doubtful d. 64:12
dissect: murder to d. 372:10
dissimulate their instability 199:8
dissociation of sensibility 156:8
dissolve, and quite forget 212:10
dissonance: barb'rous d. 249:12
distance is nothing 151:1
d. lends enchantment 101:5
distance n'y fait rien 151:1
distinguished thing 203:3
distraction: ambition, d. 105:10
dit: peine d'être d. 24:6
ditch: both fall into d. 54:8
ditchwater: dull as d. 140:3
dive: for pearls must d. 149:11
divided into three parts 98:5
house d. 57:9
in death not d. 38:3
divine: countenance d. 73:4
d. as you advance 257:1
human form d. 74:5
makes drudgery d. 187:7
to forgive, d. 270:6
what form d. 222:7
divinely fair 342:2
divinest: two d. things 200:8
divinity that shapes 300:7
piece of d. in us 81:9
division is as bad 6:2
divisions: how many d. 333:10
dixerunt: ante nos d. 143:11
do and die 341:8
d. as you would be done by 114:2
d. lovely things 215:4
d. something today 125:6
d. to be saved 63:6
d. what you like 281:3
d. what you will 17:6
d. ye even unto them 52:7
know not what they d. 60:13
revolts me, but I d. it. 174:2
too little to d. 218:7
wanted to d. something 352:5
whatever you d. 10:7
Doasyouwouldbedoneby 216:3
doctors: if you believe d. 289:8
doctrine: every wind of d. 66:14
doctrines: all d. plain 93:6
documents: sign d. not read 201:1
dog: beware of the d. 267:1
d. did nothing 147:10
d. has his day 76:6
d. it was that died 177:2
d. on hinder legs 205:3
d. returneth to vomit 42:4
every d. his day 215:9
living d. better 43:6
man bites d. 75:10
thy servant a d. 39:3
whose d. are you 269:3
your heart to a d. 219:2
dogs: but as straw d. 223:3
dancing d. and bears 190:2
d. of war 304:4
hates d. and babies 287:3
lame d. over stiles 215:5
mad d. and Englishmen 130:4
now for d. and apes 83:1
doileys: soiling the d. 31:8
doing something for posterity 2:2
see what she's d. 280:1
what everyone is d. 187:2
what was he d. 82:4
worth d. badly 116:8
doleful: knight of d. countenance 109:4
doll: sweet little d. 215:8
dollar: almighty d. 7:4
dolphin-torn 374:7
domestic as a plate 245:9
d. business no less 253:4
domi: *res angusta d.* 210:2
dominion: no more d. 64:2
Dominus *illuminatio mea* 70:5

don: remote and ineffectual d. 28:6
dona nobis pacem 242:4
et d. ferentis 356:5
done cannot be undone 310:4
d. it unto me 56:10
d. one braver thing 146:5
d. state some service 315:11
d. those things 272:5
d. well out of the war 22:3
find it d. at all 205:3
gone and d. 172:7
have d. with you 132:8
if it were d. 307:8
nothing is ever d. 323:9
possible, consider d. 99:1
seen to be d. 188:11
something d. 229:1
Don John of Austria 115:8
don't let anyone bomb 32:3
marry – 'D.' 279:6
doom: edge of doom 322:5
regardless of their d. 179:2
to crack of d. 309:12
Doon: bonny D. 92:3
door: beat on my d. 202:2
d. stayed shut 281:8
grass beyond the d. 286:7
I stand at the d. 69:10
knocking on moonlit d. 136:6
men come through a d. 111:1
out by the same d. 162:3
wide as church d. 317:11
door-keeper in house of God 275:13
doors: death a thousand d. 293:7
d. of perception 75:5
everlasting d. 274:8
dots: damned d. 117:6
double, double 309:9
made error d. 120:4
doublethink 261:8
doubt: faith in honest d. 343:11
freckles, and d. 263:9
never, never d. 28:10
no possible d. 173:1
doubted: Christian religion d. 94:5
never cheated, never d. 31:5
doubtful disputations 64:12
doubtless God never did 95:1
doubts: saucy d. 309:6
***douzaines**: Dieux à d.* 253:5
Dove: springs of D. 371:9
dove: all the d. 131:7
any sucking d. 312:13
sweet d. died 213:4
wings like a d. 275:5
doves eyes within thy locks 44:8
harmless as d. 53:9
moan of d. 346:3
down among dead men 152:4
d. by salley gardens 375:1
d. in lovely muck 198:4
d. on your knees 295:9
d. the rushy glen 3:1
d. these mean streets 111:2
d. to seas again 241:1
d. to the sea 276:9
d. with defeated 227:3
d. with me 246:3
easy way d. 356:9
soft young d. 244:8
downhearted: are we d.? 4:7
we are not d. 110:1
downwards: no way but d. 87:5
doxy: another man's d. 359:7
dragons: brother to d. 40:3
d. in pleasant palaces 46:1
drags its slow length 270:5
drains: democracy and proper d. 32:4
drama's laws 207:3
drank without thirst 338:6
gloried and d. deep 161:9
draw but twenty miles 238:7
d. out leviathan 40:8
drawers of water 36:14
dream doth flatter 321:10
d. of joye in vayne 113:4
d. of peace 200:5
faileth now d. 349:7
glory and the d. 370:11
if you can d. 218:1
I have a d. 215:3
in d. never eighty 294:1

entsichere ich 207:6
envieth: charity e. not 65:7
envy of brilliant men 26:7
épatés, les bourgeois 278:5
Ephesians: Diana of the E. 63:11
épidermes: contact de deux e. 110:7
epigram a dwarfish whole 124:3
epitaph drear 219:1
epitaphs: derangement of e. 326:10
epitome: all mankind's e. 149:7
eppur si muove 170:4
equal: all men created e. 7:9
all men e. 165:6
born free and e. 4:1
e. upstairs 23:5
some more e. 261:5
equality: never e. in servants' hall 23:5
erecteth: where Christ e. his church 23:3
err: to e. is human 168:8; 270:6
erred and strayed 272:4
e. exceedingly 38:1
error: if this be e. 322:5
errors like straws 149:11
erst kommt das Fressen 78:8
erstwhile: my e. dear 245:10
es: ce que tu e. 79:7
Esau my brother 34:13
escadrons: pour les gros e. 93:2
escalier: esprit de l'e. 142:2
escape me? never 83:6
ten guilty e. 72:7
espaces infinis m'effraie 264:7
esprit de l'escalier 142:2
esprits préparés 265:2
essentially I integrate 31:6
estate: fourth e. 232:10
order'd their e. 2:7
estimate: know'st thy e. 321:9
État c'est moi 229:7
eternal vigilance 133:4
energy is e. delight 74:7
e. silence 264:7
e. triangle 7:5
grant e. rest 241:8
eternity: deserts of vast e. 239:9
e. in an hour 72:8
e. is in love 74:11
from here to e. 217:7
injuring e. 350:8
I saw e. 354:4
radiance of e. 325:2
etherized upon a table 154:12
Ethiopian change skin 47:12
etiquette prevents me 330:9
Eton: playing fields of E. 361:7
étonne-moi 137:5
étrangères: fleurs é. 253:6
étrangers: plus je vis d'é. 29:5
et tu, Brute 304:3
eureka 11:9
Europe: all over E. 180:1
fifty years of E. 344:9
Europeans: you are learned E. 242:6
evangelical vicar 221:3
eve: noon to dewy e. 249:4
even as you and I 219:9
evening: beauteous e. 372:3
e. and the morning 33:5
e. spread out 154:12
exhalation in the e. 303:3
winter e. settles 155:13
event: over-prepared e. 272:2
events: coming e. cast shadows 101:3
everlasting: caught e. cold 361:5
e. day 143:12
have e. life 61:7
evermore: name liveth e. 49:12
every day, in e. way 129:9
e. moment dies 346:13
e.-single-one 218:5
God bless us e. one 138:5
everyone suddenly 290:7
everything before us 141:2
e. by starts 149:7
e. like something 165:4
laugh at e. 24:7
place for e. 328:4
sans e. 295:7
smattering of e. 141:1

fall (cont.):
do not f. in love 295:10
f. into the hands 49:4; 68:6; 346:4
f. into the ocean 237:7
f. in with marriage-procession 121:4
f. like rain 16:11
f. upon thorns 325:6
fear no f. 87:6
haughty spirit before a f. 41:12
I shall f. 303:3
meditated on the F. 32:2
not f. without your Father 53:10
things f. apart 376:2
what a f. 304:10
when we f. out 345:4
Fallacy: Pathetic F. 288:5
fallen: lot has f. to me 219:8
mighty f. 38:4
falling: by oft f. 224:1
here f. houses 207:2
fallow fawns invisible 349:3
falls like Lucifer 303:4
false: betrayed by what is f. 244:2
beware f. prophets 52:10
f., ere I come 145:12
f. to any man 297:5
falsehood: truth with f. 230:6
falseness: violent feelings produce f. 288:5
falser: I am f. 295:10
fame is the spur 248:2
fool to f. 269:5
physicians of the utmost f. 27:6
familiar: old f. faces 222:4
families: happy f. resemble 351:7
mothers of large f. 27:4
family pride inconceivable 174:1
I am the f. face 181:4
famous have whole earth 266:8
f. victory 331:9
found myself f. 98:3
praise f. men 49:10
fancy-free 313:3
let f. roam 211:8
most excellent f. 300:5
where is f. bred 311:10
young man's f. 344:3
fantasies: exchange of two f. 110:7
fantastic: horrible, f., incredible 110:3
light f. round 247:2
light f. toe 247:10
far above rubies 42:8
f. and few 225:1
f.-away country 110:3
f., f. better thing 141:3
f.-flung battle-line 219:3
f. from madding crowd 178:11
keep f. off 356:10
near yet so f. 343:12
farce est jouée 281:5
farewell my bok 113:3
f., rewards and fairies 128:5
f! thou art too dear 321:9
farrow: old sow eats her f. 209:4
farthing: two sparrows for a f. 53:10
fashion: faithful in my f. 146:12
glass of f. 299:4
marriage ever out of f. 93:5
fashions: this year's f. 185:2
faster than light 86:2
walk on a little f. 105:12
fasting: thank heaven, f. 295:9
fat, fair and forty 260:7
f. of the land 35:5
f. ox with evil 41:11
f. white woman 129:1
in every f. mare 127:10; 261:6
that are f. 303:11
fatal: so f. to my suit 170:6
strange and f. interview 144:5
fate: hostages to f. 230:8
master of my f. 186:1
time and f. 162:1
what I will is f. 250:1
with f. conspire 163:1
father: cometh unto the f. 62:6
either f. or mother 335:3
everlasting f. 45:10

flesh (cont.):
f. perishes 181:4
make your f. creep 140:5
not against f. and blood 67:2
set our f. upright 144:6
thorn in the f. 66:11
too solid f. 296:10
word was made f. 61:3
fleurs étrangères 253:6
flies to wanton boys 306:7
murmurous haunt of f. 212:12
flight: alarms of struggle and f. 13:2
fling away ambition 303:5
f. the ringleaders 14:3
flirtation: innocent f. 97:2
flock: feed f. like a shepherd 46:12
watch over their f. 58:4
flog the rank and file 14:3
flood: taken at the f. 304:11
floods: neither f. drown it 44:11
floor: fell on sanded f. 265:7
flotte: *elle f.* 281:6
flourishing like green bay-tree 275:1
flow gently, sweet Afton 90:9
f. of soul 271:1
flower of cities all 151:8
forth like a f. 39:12
full many a f. 178:9
glory in the f. 371:1
glory of man as f. 68:16
heaven in a wild f. 72:8
meanest f. that blows 371:2
this f., safety 301:1
flower-pots: your damned f. 84:12
flowers *appear on the* earth 44:6
f. of the forest 157:2
f. that bloom 174:10
hundred f. blossom 236:5
it won't be f. 16:11
other men's f. 253:6
flowing with milk and honey 35:8
flown with insolence 249:1
flows: everything f. 186:9
flushed and confident 202:1
fly: all things f. thee 349:8
sparks f. upward 39:10
flying-fishes play 218:11
snow came f. 79:3
foe was folly 192:6
fog in my throat 84:9
f. that rubs its back 155:1
London particular . . . f. 138:1
foil: shining from shook f. 192:8
fold tents like Arabs 227:6
wolf on the f. 96:3
folded: ocean f. and hung up 15:2
folding of the hands 40:13
follow me 50:7
f. the worse 262:4
I ought to f. 225:5
folly: brood of f. 247:5
ends in f. 125:5
foe was f. 192:6
f. to be wise 179:3
fool according to f. 42:3
fool persist in f. 74:12
fool returneth to his f. 42:4
mad, wicked f. 355:4
woman stoops to f. 156:3; 177:4
fond: foolish, f. old man 306:9
font: second-hand f. 221:3
food of love 319:3
wholesome f. 339:1
fool: every f. not a poet 269:4
f. according to folly 42:3
f. all the people 226:5
f. hath said 274:2
f. lies here 219:1
f. persist in folly 74:12
f. returneth to his folly 42:4
'f.' said my Muse 327:4
f. sees not same tree 74:10
f. there was 219:9
f., this night thy soul 59:9
f. to fame 269:5
I have played the f. 38:1
laughter of a f. 43:3
rash, intruding f. 299:11
take away f.'s bauble 132:7

forty (cont.):
man over f. scoundrel 324:9
forty-three: pass for f. 175:9
forward, f. let us range 344:8
look f. to posterity 89:3
fox knows many things 11:8
foxes have holes 53:1
little f. 44:7
portion for f. 275:7
fou: wasna f. 90:8
fou qui se croyait 122:9
fought a good fight 68:3
f. each other for 331:8
f. for life 332:5
foul is fair 307:3
ways be f. 307:1
foul-mouthed nation 184:3
found my sheep 59:13
f. myself famous 98:3
f. out by accident 222:3
lost, and is f. 60:3
not yet f. a role 1:2
when f., make a note 138:13
foundation of morals 29:9
foundations: earth's f. stay 198:8
fountain: healing f. start 16:1
fourteen? Lord has only ten 121:1
fourth estate 232:10
frabjous day 106:5
fragments have I shored 156:6
tramples it to f. 325:2
frailty, thy name is woman 296:12
frame thy fearful symmetry 73:7
framed: have it f. 359:2
***français**: n'est pas f.* 284:3
France: vasty fields of F. 301:12
wind for F. 148:7
frankincense: gold, f., myrrh 50:1
freckled: fickle, f. 193:1
freckles, and doubt 263:9
free: born f. 287:6
born f. and equal 4:1
comment is f. 291:4
f. as nature 150:1
f. speech, f. passes 32:4
Greece still be f. 96:11
land of the f. 214:8
teach the f. man 16:1
thou art f. 13:8
truth shall make you f. 61:11
wholly slaves or wholly f. 150:5
who would be f. 95:7
writing f. verse 168:9
freedom: cure for evils of f. 233:2
fight for f. 201:7
f. and whisky 90:5
f. of press 338:3
f. of speech 353:5
f. yet thy banner 95:9
my life for f. 159:5
freeing any slave 226:6
French: dislike the F. 359:4
F. of Parys 112:2
not clear not F. 284:3
speak F. when can't think of English 106:7
frenzy: fine f. rolling 313:9
frequent hearses 269:1
fresh as month of May 112:1
f. woods 248:5
***Fressen**: erst kommt das F.* 78:8
fret: weariness, fever, and f. 212:10
frets: ferments and f. 93:9
struts and f. 310:6
fretted pigmy body 149:4
***Freude**, schöner Götterfunken* 290:10
friars: barefoot f. singing vespers 172:2
fricassee or ragout 339:1
friend: betraying my f. 165:9
f., go up higher 59:10
f. of every country 101:9
f. tell disagreeable truths 86:5
f. that sticketh closer 41:13
from the candid f. 101:10
guide, philosopher, f. 270:13
not use a f. 188:1
to have f. be one 157:9
friends, Romans 304:6
f. thou hast 297:3

garden (cont.):
glory of the g. 217:8
God first planted a g. 20:3
God the first g. made 130:8
God walking in the g. 33:12
grows in our g. 348:9
man and woman in g. 366:5
value my g. more 1:9
gardener: Adam was a g. 217:9
gardens: closing time in the g. 127:11
gare: au-dessus de sa g. 282:4
garland briefer 196:8
immortal g. run for 251:6
garment: like a g. wear 372:1
garments: dyed g. from Bozrah 47:7
garnished: empty, swept, and g. 54:3
Garter; no merit in it 243:1
gas: all g. and gaiters 139:11
g. smells awful 264:1
gasp: at the last g. 49:13
g. and stretch one's eyes 27:11
gate: dreams out of ivory g. 81:5
poor man at his g. 2:7
wide is the g. 52:8
gates of hell not prevail 54:10
o ye g. 274:8
Gath: tell it not in G. 38:2
gather the lambs 46:12
g. ye rosebuds 188:8
gathered: where two or three are g. 55:1
gaudeamus *igitur* 10:3
gaudy night 294:6
neat not g. 362:5
Gaul divided into three 98:5
Gaunt: seige of city of G. 22:6
gave his only begotten 61:7
Lord g. 39:7
gay deceiver 126:4
Gaza: eyeless in G. 250:7
gaze not in my eyes 196:6
g. out from land 231:2
gazelle: nurs'd a dear g. 254:7
Gedanke: *zwei Seelen ein G.* 181:1
geese are swans 13:5
gefährlich *leben* 259:6
gem of all joy 151:8
general: caviare to the g. 298:7
generals: bite other g. 172:1
G. Janvier and Février 259:1
generation: chosen g. 69:1
g. of vipers 50:3
generations: no hungry g. 212:14
generous: first impulses g. 253:7
génie *aptitude à la patience* 86:1
vous croyez un grand g. 25:2
genius: believe yourself a g. 25:2
declare except my g. 366:8
g. aptitude for patience 86:1
g. better discerning 177:3
g. capacity for getting into pains 94:1
g. capacity of taking trouble 102:7
g. into my life 366:7
g. of the place 269:12
g. one per cent inspiration 152:6
ramp up my g. 208:4
talent recognizes g. 148:2
true g. appears 339:2
genteely: cheat g. 77:2
gentil: parfit g. knyght 111:9
gentle: do not go g. 348:3
g. Jesus, meek 362:4
g. rain from heaven 311:13
his life was g. 305:1
gentleman: cannot make a g. 89:6
definition of a g. 258:3
g.-rankers out on spree 217:7
mariner with g. 148:6
prince of darkness g. 306:3
very gallant g. 14:7
gentlemen go by 219:7
not forget we are g. 88:3
gently they go 245:5
roar you as g. 312:13
geography is about maps 30:2
George the Third 30:6
German: shovel in G. 353:9
Gesang: *ewige G.* 176:1

Weib und G. 231:4
get me to England 80:9
g. thee behind me 54:11
getting and spending 372:9
ghastly good taste 32:9
g. thro' drizzling rain 343:4
ghost in machine 289:3
some old lover's g. 145:7
ghosties: ghoulies and g. 4:10
ghosts from an enchanter 325:5
g. of beauty glide 269:10
ghoulies and ghosties 4:10
giant leap for mankind 12:8
giants in the earth 34:7
on the shoulders of g. 31:1
***giberne**: dans sa g.* 229:9
giftie gie us 91:11
gifts: presented unto him g. 50:1
they bring g. 356:5
gild refined gold 305:5
Gilead: balm in G. 47:11
gin mother's milk 324:12
gird up thy loins 40:5
girdle: put a g. 313:4
girl: garland briefer than g.'s 196:8
g. like I 229:4
no g. wants to laugh 229:6
girls and boys I sing 195:3
g. that are so smart 102:2
g. who wear glasses 263:10
lads for the g. 197:3
girt: loins g. with truth 67:3
Gitche Gumee 228:6
give all thou canst 372:7
g., and it shall be given 58:11
g. crowns and pounds 196:4
g. me back my heart 97:8
g. me the sun 201:8
g. me your tired 224:6
g. to me the life 336:4
g. to the poor 55:3
g. up their liberties 89:1
g. us the tools 118:3
g. us this day 51:5
more blessed to g. 63:12
such as I have g. I 62:15
given me over 369:3
that hath shall be g. 56:7
unto us a son is g. 45:10
giver: loveth a cheerful g. 66:9
gives quickly 279:3
g. to airy nothing 313:9
giving: not in g. vein 317:3
glad that you won 32:7
I was g. 277:1
too soon made g. 84:1
wise son g. a father 41:2
gladder than all these 286:2
glade: bee-loud g. 375:6
gladly wolde he lerne 112:4
glass is falling 234:8
g. of blessings 187:11
g. of fashion 299:4
many-coloured g. 325:2
own face in the g. 366:1
sound of broken g. 29:1
through a g., darkly 65:11
glasses: girls who wear g. 263:10
two g. two chairs 235:1
gleamed upon my sight 371:11
gleaned: before my pen has g. 213:9
glen: down the rushy g. 3:1
glittering prizes 72:4
his g. eye 123:2
globule: atomic g. 174:1
***gloire**: jour de g.* 287:5
***gloria** in excelsis* 242:1
***gloriam**: majorem Dei g.* 9:9
nomini tuo g. 70:7
gloried: where Jamshyd g. 161:9
glorious: all g. within 275:3
burns in g. Araby 134:3
glory: alone with his g. 368:9
die in their g. 197:4
earth full of his g. 45:4
eyes have seen g. 200:1
g. and the dream 370:11
g. be to God 192:10
g. of man as the flower 68:16
g. of the garden 217:8
g. of the Lord revealed 46:11
g. of the Lord shone 58:4
g. shone around 340:9
g. that was Greece 268:7

gone (cont.):
g. into world of light 354:3
g. to-morrow 26:10
g. with the wind 146:11
haste I can to be g. 132:9
gong-tormented sea 374:7
gongs: strong g. groaning 115:8
struck regularly, like g. 130:3
good: all g. people clever 369:5
all things work for g. 64:5
be a g. animal 332:3
be g., sweet maid 215:4
best enemy of g. 357:10
bored with g. wine 143:7
do g. to them which hate 58:10
either g. or bad 298:2
filches my g. name 315:1
gallop about doing g. 329:7
ghastly g. taste 32:9
go about doing g. 132:1
God saw that it was g. 33:6
g. action by stealth 222:3
g. Americans 11:5
g. and faithful servant 56:6
g. as beautiful 342:7
g. cook 289:7
g. ended happily 365:7
g. fences make 168:4
g. for General Motors 367:2
g. hunting 219:12
g. in everything 295:1
g. minute goes 85:3
g. news baits 250:9
g. of the people 119:8
g. oft interr'd 304:6
g. that I would 64:4
g. thing 293:4
g. to be out on road 241:4
he wos wery g. 138:3
I am the g. shepherd 61:14
I will be g. 355:3
likes that little g. 94:3
never had it so g. 234:3
only g. Indian 326:7
overcome evil with g. 64:9
policy of g. neighbour 285:7
see your g. works 50:10
shines g. deed 312:7
sun rise on evil and g. 51:2
trust somehow g. 343:7
what g. came of it 331:9
whatsoever things are of g. report 67:6
when she was g. 229:3
goodly to look to 37:14
goodness: delusion beauty is g. 351:8
g. nothing to do 362:6
good-night sweet prince 300:11
g. till morrow 317:10
goods: all my worldly g. 273:11
goodwill toward men 58:6
goose: every g. a swan 215:9
that g. look 310:5
gossip a sort of smoke 153:4
got a little list 174:4
***Gott** ist tot* 259:4
G. würfelt nicht 153:2
nun danket alle G. 284:2
***Gottesmühlen** mahlen* 227:4
gout: give them g. 253:1
***gouverne**: peuple se g.* 347:7
***gouvernement** qu'elle mérite* 235:5
govern New South Wales 27:10
people g. themselves 347:7
governed: nation not g. 88:7
government: best g. governs least 262:1
fainéant g. 352:5
g. influenced by shopkeepers 328:6
g. it deserves 235:5
g. of Britain's isle 302:12
g. upon his shoulder 45:10
worst form of g. 118:7
governs: best government g. least 262:1
gown: her loose g. 373:10
grace: but for g. of God 77:8
courtly foreign g. 346:5
g. may abound 64:1
g. me no g. 316:10
inward and spiritual g. 273:5
ministers of g. 297:7
old with good g. 334:3

gracious: he is g. 277:5
gradual day 332:6
grain: world in a g. of sand 72:8
gramina: *iam g. campis* 195:7
grammar, nonsense, learning 177:3
grammatici *certant* 193:9
grandeur of God 192:8
g. that was Rome 268:7
grandsire cut his throat 339:4
grapes: fathers eaten sour g. 48:4
g. of thorns 52:11
g. of wrath 200:1
vine and g. in gold 163:7
grapeshot: whiff of g. 102:9
grapple them 297:3
grasp: reach should exceed g. 82:7
grass: all flesh is g. 68:16
g. beyond the door 286:7
g. returns to fields 195:7
snake in the g. 357:2
gratuity: taking bribe or g. 266:4
grave: dig the g. 336:7
g. not its goal 228:4
g.'s a fine and private 240:1
g., thy victoree 6:4
g., where is thy victory 66:5
healthy g. 330:10
in ev'ry g. make room 134:7
in her g. 371:10
lead but to g. 178:8
little little g. 316:15
pompous in the g. 82:2
pot of honey on g. 244:1
upon his mother's g. 371:4
wild into his g. 301:9
with sorrow to the g. 35:4
graves: voluntarie g. 187:10
watch from their g. 83:8
gravy: abominated g. 30:3
disliked g. 330:3
greasy: grey-green, g. Limpopo 220:3
great: behind g. possessions 203:1
creatures g. and small 2:6
g. book g. evil 98:10
g. gulf fixed 60:7
g. is Diana 63:11
g. is misunderstood 158:3
g. things are done 73:6
g. things from valley 116:4
g. wits to madness 149:5
lives of g. men 228:5
no force however g. 363:4
those truly g. 332:5
Great Britain: Graces not natives of G. 114:5
greater love hath no man 62:7
g. than mine 327:5
g. than we know 371:8
greatest happiness for g. numbers 201:2
g. happiness of g. number 29:9
g. of these is charity 65:12
greatness thrust upon them 320:1
Greece: for G. a tear 96:12
glory that was G. 268:7
G. still be free 96:11
isles of G. 96:10
Greek: less G. 208:5
questioned him in G. 104:5
study of G. literature 170:1
Greeks: for G. a blush 96:12
I fear the G. 356:5
when G. joined G. 225:7
green: colourless g. ideas 116:9
die when trees were g. 120:3
feed in g. pasture 274:5
g. and pleasant land 73:4
g.-ey'd monster 315:2
g. in judgement 294:3
g. thought in g. shade 239:6
making g. one red 308:10
not quite so g. 220:6
shore-sea g. 163:7
wearin' of the g. 5:5
greenery-yallery 174:13
greenness: recovered g. 187:8
greenwood: under g. tree 295:3
grey: bring down my g. hairs 35:4

grey (cont.):
g. widow-maker 217:11
lend me your g. mare 23:2
grey-green: great g., greasy 220:3
greyhounds in the slips 302:3
grief: acquainted with g. 47:2
g. fills the room 305:3
grieve: what could it g. for 213:4
grieving: Margaret, are you g. 193:2
grievous: my most g. fault 241:6
grind exceeding small 227:4
g. faces of the poor 45:1
groan: hear each other g. 212:10
grocer: God made the wicked g. 116:2
grooves of change 344:8
***gros**: pour les g. escadrons* 93:2
Grosvenor Gallery 174:13
grotesque to horrible 147:12
so g. a blunder 30:6
ground: in a fair g. 219:8
lays lads under g. 198:1
sit upon the g. 316:13
stirrup and the g. 100:3
groves of Academe 194:8
grow old with me 84:10
growed: 'spect I g. 336:9
grows in our garden 348:9
grub: old ones, g. 323:2
Grundy: what will Mrs G. think 255:6
gruntled: far from g. 368:3
guard: changing g. at Buckingham Palace 246:2
g. the guards 210:4
Guards die not surrender 100:1
up G. 362:1
***guerre**: n'est pas la g.* 76:7
guest: speed parting g. 271:2
guide, philosopher, friend 270:13
guides: blind g. 55:12
guile: packed with g. 80:10
guilt: circumstance of g. 336:2
dwell on g. and misery 18:4
sign of g. or ill breeding 127:2
wash her g. away 177:4
guilty of dust 187:9
mortal, g. 16:3
ten g. escape 72:7
guinea: rank but g.'s stamp 90:10
guineas: pounds and g. 196:4
Guinness, Allsopp, Bass 99:3
gulf: great g. fixed 60:7
gull's way 241:3
gun: got the Maxim g. 28:9
g. in his hand 111:1
power out of a g. 236:6
son of a g. 99:5
Gunga Din 217:10
gunpowder, printing, Protestant religion 102:5
g. treason and plot 6:9
guns aren't lawful 264:1
g. before butter 175:11
g. boom far 115:8
gutta cavat lapidem 224:1
gutter: all in the g. 365:10
gypsy: time, you old g. 190:3
vagrant g. life 241:3
gyre and gimble 106:4
habit: sow a h. 282:5
habitation: local h. 313:9
***habiter**: machine à h.* 225:4
hadn't ought to be 182:7
Haggards Ride 334:9
Hail Caesar 9:10
H. Mary 10:1
H., thou art highly favoured 57:15
H. to the Chief 292:1
H. to thee 326:3
hair: colour of his h. 199:5
combed their h. 198:7
drew long black h. 156:5
h. become very white 105:3
h. so charmingly curled 215:8
hank of h. 219:9
her eyes, her h. 244:8
language make your h. curl 175:7
long h. a glory 65:4
man have long h. 65:4

not your yellow h. 375:4
pleasant mazes of h. 130:6
smoothes her h. 156:3
such h., too 85:2
sugar my h. 106:1
vine leaves in his h. 202:1
with a single h. 271:5
hairless as an egg 188:6
hairs: bring down my gray h. 35:4
h. of your head are numbered 53:11
set our h. upright 144:6
hairy: brother a h. man 34:13
halcyon days 302:10
h. sea 286:2
half: but h. his foe 249:2
dearer h. 249:11
h. a league 341:7
h. as old as time 285:1
h. dead and h. alive 31:4
h. Latin h. Greek 291:5
h. that's got my keys 177:9
h. was not told 38:9
half-a-dozen of the other 238:11
hall: never equality in servants' h. 23:5
pram in the h. 127:8
hallowed be thy name 51:5
halls: dwelt in marble h. 86:7
halo: what is a h. 169:2
halt: poor, maimed, h., blind 59:12
***hambre*:** *mejor salsa es el h.* 109:5
hamlet: forefathers of the h. 178:6
hand: adorable tennis-girl's h. 32:8
bite h. that fed 89:8
emprison her soft h. 212:7
fear thy skinny h. 123:7
h. findeth to do 43:8
h. forget her cunning 277:7
h. for hand 35:11
h. into h. of God 183:2
h. rocks cradle 358:7
h. that wrote 131:6
h. to the plough 58:13
h. will rather 308:10
hold infinity in your h. 72:8
imprison her soft h. 212:7
into h. of physician 49:9
in your medieval h. 174:12
kissing your h. 229:5
lend thy guiding h. 250:6
let not thy left h. know 51:4
like a man's h. 38:12
my h. a needle 78:2
sweeten little h. 310:3
sword sleep in my h. 73:4
time's devouring h. 78:7
what immortal h. 73:7
written with my own h. 66:13
handed: neat-h. Phyllis 247:11
handful: fear in h. of dust 156:1
for a h. of silver 83:7
handle honesty and truth 323:8
handles: every thing hath two h. 92:6
handmaid to religion 19:4
hands: any h., however lowly 174:3
before rude h. 208:8
fall into h. of the Lord 49:4
folding of the h. 40:13
h. are blue 225:1
h. ne'er be clean 310:2
h. of the living God 68:6
house not made with h. 66:8
into thy h. 60:14
my roving h. 144:7
not into h. of Spain 346:4
pale h. I loved 192:7
plunge your h. in water 15:3
warmed both h. 222:6
handsaw: hawk from a h. 298:6
handsome: my h. young man 22:5
hang: all h. together 167:2
hanged in a fortnight 205:11
not h. for stealing horses 180:6
hanging from a string 216:6
h. men an' women there 5:5
h. too good 87:4
hangs: what h. people 336:2

hank of hair 219:9
happen: poetry makes nothing h. 15:8
happens anywhere 223:4
happier Eden 249:8
h. than I know 250:2
happiness: best recipe for h. 18:3
h. for greatest numbers 201:2
h. of greatest number 29:9
lifetime of h. 323:10
pursuit of h. 7:9
result h. 138:8
secret of h. 78:1
take away h. 202:3
happy: be h. while y'er leevin 4:8
be most h. 314:10
call no man h. 331:3
h. as kings 336:3
h. families resemble 351:7
h. issue 272:12
h. is that city 5:1
h. low 301:5
h. man who fears 70:6
h. people whose annals blank 102:8
h. those early days 354:2
h. with either 171:6
in nothing else so. h. 316:9
misfortune to have been h. 75:8
old woman h. 166:6
this h. breed 316:5
those h. highways 197:8
touch the H. Isles 346:11
winter or summer when h. 113:11
harder they fall 163:4
hard-faced: a lot of h. men 22:3
hardly ever 174:14
hares: little hunted h. 190:2
hark h! the lark 296:3
harlot: prerogative of the h. 220:12
harm: do so much h. 132:1
fear we'll come to h. 22:8
harmless as doves 53:9
h. great thing 145:8
h. necessary cat 311:11
harmony: from heavenly h. 150:9
harp that once 254:4
harrow the house of the dead 16:5
Harry: touch of H. 302:4
hart: as pants the h. 340:7
harvest of a quiet eye 371:5
hasard ne favorise 265:2
***hässlich**: Welt h.* 259:5
haste away so soon 188:7
h. I can to be gone 132:9
hat: looking for black h. 77:6
that lewd h. 207:9
hate: do good to them which h. 58:10
h. and detest man 338:8
h. and love 108:5
h. anyone we know 184:4
let them hate 1:1
pure impartial h. 351:4
time to h. 43:1
hates dogs and babies 287:3
hateth his brother 69:7
h. his son 41:8
hath: unto every one that h. 56:7
hatless: young man lands h. 31:5
hatred: love to h. turn'd 127:1
no h. or bitterness 108:7
stalled ox and h. 41:11
haughty spirit before a fall 41:12
haunted by woman wailing 124:7
haunts of coot and hern 341:5
have and to hold 273:10
other folks h. 161:3
till I h. it 293:3
haves and have-nots 109:6
havoc: cry 'H.' 304:4
hawk from a handsaw 298:6
hay: dance an antic h. 237:9
he: because it was h. 253:3
h. for God only 249:7
head: bear with sore h. 238:9
God be in my h. 4:11

hairs of your h. numbered 53:11
h. of a traveller 199:6
Johnny h.-in-air 279:5
keep your h. 217:12
King Charles's h. 138:10
lay your sleeping h. 16:2
my h. is bloody 185:8
not where to lay his h. 53:1
off with his h. 119:5
one small h. 176:10
stand on your h. 105:3
uneasy lies the h. 301:5
headache: with a dismal h. 173:9
heads are green 225:1
lift up your h. 274:8
headstrong as allegory 326:11
healing fountain start 16:1
health: in sickness in h. 273:10
no h. in us 272:5
this h. deny 152:4
healthy grave 330:10
heap: struck all of a h. 326:9
hear: at my back always h. 239:9
ears to h. 57:10
h. each other groan 212:10
h. O Israel 36:6
h. them read 273:1
h. us when we cry 363:7
I h. you 197:2
read music but can't h. 26:1
you will h. me 142:4
heard: ain't h. nothin' 207:7
h. melodies are sweet 212:5
heareth: thy servant h. 37:8
hearses: frequent h. 269:1
heart: batter my h. 145:5
bury my h. 29:7
'Calais' in my h. 240:8
change of h. 16:5
cracks a noble h. 300:11
darling of my h. 102:2
deserts of the h. 16:1
get your h.'s desire 324:5
give me back my h. 97:8
God be in my h. 4:11
h. and voice would fail 120:8
h. be troubled 62:4
h. go pit-a-pat 84:4
h. has its reasons 264:9
h. in my breast 199:4
h. is deceitful 47:13
h. is pure 346:6
h. leaps up 370:7
h. lies open 346:2
h.'s in the Highlands 91:5
h. still as loving 97:10
h. the keener 7:8
h. too soon made glad 84:1
it dooth myn h. boote 113:1
look in thy h. 327:4
make stone of h. 375:3
man after his own h. 37:11
mercy has a human h. 74:5
merry h. 41:10
my h. aches 212:8
my h. in hiding 193:7
my h. is heavy 176:2
my h. is like 286:2
my shrivel'd h. 187:8
nation had the lion's h. 118:9
nearer to h.'s desire 163:1
not your h. away 196:4
pure in h. 50:8
rebuke broken my h. 275:9
said to h. 28:2
sick at h. 296:6
softer pillow than my h. 98:1
some h. did break 343:3
taming my wild h. 314:3
tear his h. 339:5
that mighty h. 372:2
there will your h. be 51:7
toyshop of their h. 271:4
true love hath my h. 327:3
wine with merry h. 43:7
with rue my h. 198:2
your h. to a dog 219:2
heart-break in the heart 172:6
hearth: cricket on the h. 247:6
hearts: first in h. 225:6
h. that have lost 198:10
keep your h. and minds 67:5
kind h. are more 344:1
stout h. and sharp swords 72:4

human (cont.):
step aside is h. 89:10
to err is h. 168:8; 270:6
***humani** nil alienum* 347:2
humanity: crooked timber of h. 211:1
sad music of h. 370:6
treat h. as an end 210:8
humans: isn't fit for h. 32:6
humble: be it ever so h. 265:8
humbled: maintains I am h. 128:7
humbleth: that h. himself 59:11
Humiliation: valley of H. 87:2
hump we get 218:7
***humus**: nos habebit h.* 10:3
hundred flowers blossom 236:5
h.'s soon hit 83:2
same h. years hence 139:8
hung: ocean folded and h. up 15:2
hunger allows no choice 16:6
h. and thirst 50:8
h. best sauce 109:5
poverty, h., and dirt 192:3
hungred, and ye gave me meat 56:9
hungry: ate when not h. 338:6
filled the h. 58:2
h. sheep look up 248:3
lean and h. 303:11
no h. generations 212:14
hunter home from hill 336:8
Nimrod the mighty h. 34:9
hunting: good h. 219:12
I'm weary wi' h. 22:5
went h. wild 263:1
huntress: *queen and h.* 207:10
hurly-burly of the chaise-longue 100:6
hurt: power to h. us 25:6
husband: as h. is 344:4
crown to her h. 41:4
life her h. makes 153:7
husbands at chirche dore 112:6
hush: breathless h. 257:9
hustle the East 219:1
hymns: chanting faint h. 312:10
***hypocrite** lecteur* 24:4
I am batsman 222:10
ice formed on butter 368:5
over thin i. 158:1
ice-cream: emperor of i. 335:6
icicles hang by wall 307:1
icumen: sumer is i. in 7:2
icummen: winter is i. in 271:11
idea: invasion by an i. 200:3
pain of a new i. 21:10
teach young i. 350:4
ideas: colourless green i. 116:9
***ideés**: invasion des i.* 200:3
identity presses upon me 214:3
ides of March 303:7
idiot: tale told by i. 310:6
idle: be not i. 92:8
for i. hands 360:5
i. as a painted ship 123:5
when wholly i. 119:9
world calls i. 131:3
idleness refuge of weak minds 114:6
idolatry: this side i. 208:7
if it was so 106:9
i. not now 189:4
i. there be a God 6:5
i. you can keep 217:12
ignorance, madam 204:7
i. of the law 293:2
keeping women in i. 221:4
no sin but i. 237:10
where i. is bliss 179:3
ignorant armies clash 13:2
i. prescribed to learned 152:3
ill: goal of i. 343:7
guilt or i. breeding 127:2
i. fares the land 176:6
i. met by moonlight 313:1
illiberal and ill-bred 113:13
ill-tempered and queer 224:8
***illuminatio**: Dominus i. mea* 70:5
image: best i. of myself 249:11
scatter'd his Maker's i. 149:2
images: garden of bright i. 78:6
imagination all compact 313:8
i. bodies forth 313:9
i. resembled wings 232:9

irrevocably: word takes wing i. 194:6
Ishmael: call me I. 243:6
island: no man an i. 146:7
snug little i. 137:8
this i. now 16:4
Zuleika, on a desert i. 26:6
islands: favourite i. 15:5
isle: fairest i. 150:6
i. full of noises 318:6
this scepter'd i. 316:4
isles of Greece 96:10
isn't: as it i. 106:9
Israel loved Joseph 35:1
isst: *Mensch ist was er i.* 160:5
issue: happy i. 272:12
it: it's just i. 220:9
iudice: *sub i. lis est* 193:9
Iuppiter *ex alto* 262:3
iurare *in verba magistri* 194:3
iuvabit: *meminisse i.* 356:2
ivoire: *tour d'i.* 289:4
ivory, apes, peacocks 38:10; 240:9
i. tower 289:4
out of i. gate 81:5
Jabberwock 106:5
Jack: damn you, J. 76:1
jades: pampered j. 238:7; 301:3
jail: ship is being in j. 204:10
jam: never j. to-day 107:2
Janvier: Generals J. and Février 259:1
jardin: *cultiver notre j.* 357:9
jasper of jocunditie 151:8
jaundic'd: yellow to the j. 270:7
jawbone of an ass 37:6
jaw-jaw better than war-war 118:8
jealous: art a j. mistress 157:8
j. confirmations 315:4
thy God a j. God 36:7
jealousy: beware of j. 315:2
Jehu: driving of J. 39:4
jelly-bellied flag-flapper 220:8
Jenny kissed me 200:6
Jerusalem: daughters of J. 44:2
from the east to J. 49:14
J. to Jericho 59:2
till we have built J. 73:4
Jesse: stem of J. 45:11
jest: life is a j. 171:9
of infinite j. 300:5
jests at scars 317:6
Jesus: come, Lord J. 70:4
J. wept 62:1
Jesus Christ were to come 103:5
jeunesse: *si j. savoit* 158:10
jeux *d'enfants pas j.* 253:2
Jew: hath not a J. 311:7
J. that Shakespeare drew 271:7
jewel in his head 294:11
j. I should tine 90:6
Jews: born King of the J. 49:14
choose the J. 159:6
spurn the J. 81:4
jigging veins 238:5
jingo: by j. if we do 200:4
Joan: greasy J. 307:1
Miss J. Hunter Dunn 32:7
Job: patience of J. 68:14
John Anderson my jo 91:1
Johnny head-in-air 190:4; 279:5
join house to house 45:2
joined: what God hath j. 55:2
whom God hath j. 273:12
joint: out of j. 297:12
jokes: my little j. 168:3
jollity: my yowthe and j. 113:1
jolly boating weather 129:4
there was a j. miller 71:7
Joseph: Israel loved J. 35:1
jostle: Philistines may j. 174:12
jostling in the street 73:6
journalist: British j. 368:10
journalists say a thing 29:8
journey: going on a j. 184:2
when j.'s over 196:2
journeys end 319:6
joy: dreme of j. in vayne 113:4
j., beautiful radiance 290:10
j. cometh in morning 274:9
j. for ever 211:4
j. shall be in heaven 59:14
let j. be unconfined 95:8
scrip of j. 282:1

joy (cont.):
shouted for j. 40:6
snatch fearful j. 179:1
surprised by j. 372:6
tidings of great j. 58:5
joys in another's loss 74:2
vain deluding j. 247:5
judge none blessed 49:5
j. not 52:2
j. not the play 280:9
judgement: critical j. so exquisite 169:1
Daniel come to j. 312:2
history world's j. 291:1
not industry only, but j. 88:5
Judy: Colonel's Lady and J. O'Grady 218:10
Jumblies: where J. live 225:1
June: it was late J. 348:10
***Jupiter** vult perdere* 152:2
just: actions of the j. 327:2
art indeed j. 193:5
his quarrel j. 71:11; 302:13
j. and lasting peace 226:8
j. as it comes 31:8
j. enough of learning 97:5
ninety and nine j. persons 59:14
place for a j. man 350:7
rain on j. and unjust 51:2; 77:5
whatsoever things are j. 67:6
justice not only done 188:11
j. open to all 242:8
kind of wild j. 20:9
let j. be done 160:4; 360:2
mercy seasons j. 312:1
right or j. 235:4
temper j. with mercy 250:3
justifies: ends j. means 92:9
justify God's ways 198:3
j. ways of God 248:11
***justitia**: fiat j.* 160:4
***justitiam**: rectum aut j.* 235:4
***juvenes** dum sumus* 10:3
***juventutem**: post jucundam j.* 10:3
***kann** nicht anders* 231:3
***kategorisch**: Imperativ ist k.* 210:7
Keats: porridge had John K. 84:7
who killed John K. 97:7
keel the pot 307:1
keep a hold of Nurse 27:8
k., and pass 157:3
k. saying it enough 29:8
k. shutters up 139:5
k. the bridge with me 232:5
k. the wolf thence 361:3
k. up appearances 117:3
k. your head 217:12
k. your hearts and minds 67:5
to k. the goal 197:5
keeper: my brother's k. 34:4
keepeth: that k. Israel 276:10
***kenne** mich auch nicht* 175:12
***kennst** du das Land* 176:4
k. du es wohl 176:5
Kent – apples, cherries 140:4
kent: I'm k. the better 91:8
Kentish Town: courts of K. 32:5
kept the faith 68:3
Kew: go down to K. 260:1
Highness' dog at K. 269:3
key: turn the k. deftly 213:8
keys: half that's got my k. 177:9
Khatmandu: north of K. 183:5
kick against the pricks 63:3
kicked the stairs 245:9
k. up stairs 180:7
no body to be k. 351:6
kid in his mother's milk 35:13
leopard lie down with k. 45:12
kiddies have crumpled 31:7
kill: animals never k. for sport 168:11
k. a good book 251:4
k. an admiral 357:7
k. sick people 238:2
k. us for sport 306:7
k. wife with kindness 317:15
k. you if you quote 87:12
prepared to k. 323:9
thou shalt not k. 121:8
when you have to k. 119:1
killed: effort very nearly k. 27:11

kissing (cont.):
k. had to stop 85:1
k. your hand 229:5
kitchen: out of k. 353:1
kith: own kin and k. 256:6
Kitty, fair but frozen 170:6
knapsack the field marshal's baton 229:9
knaves: bold k. thrive 150:3
world of fools and k. 85:7
knees: body between your k. 129:5
done upon his k. 217:9
live on your k. 201:5
knell of parting day 178:5
knew: carry all he k. 176:10
God and I both k. 220:13
knife: smylere with the k. 112:8
war to the k. 263:6
knight: gentle k. was pricking 332:9
k. of doleful countenance 109:4
k. without fear 8:6
parfit gentil k. 111:9
knits: sleep that k. up 308:8
knock, and it shall be opened 52:5
k. as you please 269:2
k. me down with the butt 119:4
right to k. him down 206:3
stand at the door, and k. 69:10
yet but k. 145:5
knocking on moonlit door 136:6
know: all ye need to k. 212:6
do not k. myself 175:12
hate anyone we k. 184:4
how pleasant to k. 224:8
k. *mine* end 275:2
k. my redeemer liveth 40:1
k. myself a man 135:2
k. not what they do 60:13
k. not where 310:9
k. then thyself 270:11
k. thyself 9:5
k. to be useful 255:4
k. what work 103:4
k. you the land 176:4
no one to k. what 3:5
now I k. it 171:9
we k. in part 65:9
who only England k. 217:4
knowest how busy 14:6
knoweth not God 69:5
knowing: for lust of k. 163:5
misfortune of k. anything 18:6
knowledge comes 344:7
k. increaseth sorrow 42:13
k. itself is power 21:6
k. of good and evil 33:9
k. of London 140:8
k. of nothing 141:1
k. too wonderful 277:8
known for well-knownness 76:2
k. unto God 220:11
safer than k. way 183:2
should not be k. 163:5
knows: Gawd k. 220:10
God alone k. 220:13
he k. – he k. 162:6
k. own child 311:6
none cares or k. 120:6
Krieg *eine Fortsetzung* 120:10
krummem: *aus so k. Holze* 211:1
Kubla Khan: in Xanadu did K. 124:6
Kultur: *wenn ich K. höre* 207:6
Kurd: same about the K. 27:2
Kurtz: Mistah K. – he dead 127:12
kyrie eleison 241:7
labour: all ye that l. 53:15
Chinese cheap l. 182:8
l. against cure 81:7
l. is but lost 277:2
l. we delight in 308:12
success is to l. 336:1
labourer worthy of hire 59:1
labouring: sleep of l. man 43:2
labours: children sweeten l. 20:8
labyrinthical soul 146:9
lacessit: *me impune l.* 10:4
lachende *Löwen* 259:3
lacrimae: *hinc illae l.* 347:1
sunt l. rerum 356:4

wear l. like your watch 114:4
whence thy l. 171:8
learnt nothing 151:5; 340:6
lease: summer's l. 320:13
least: best government governs l. 262:1
unto the l. of my brethren 56:10
leather: attired in l. boots 199:6
leave: forever taking l. 283:7
intreat me not to l. thee 37:7
l. her to heaven 297:9
l. living name 360:10
l. me thus 373:8
l. off first 49:7
leaving his country 161:6
like l. of it. 307:4
leaves dead are driven 325:5
l. him out so late 168:6
l. to the trees 195:7
l. world to darkness 178:5
lisp of l. 339:6
sewed fig l. 33:12
snow the l. 197:6
these barren l. 372:11
***leben**: so l. wir* 283:7
led: Carlyle l. into desert 122:7
l. regiment from behind 172:8
left him alone 368:9
l. your souls 212:3
leg: Julia's dainty l. 188:6
legacy work wonders 72:3
***lege**: tolle l.* 17:3
***legem**: necessitas dat l.* 279:4
legion: my name is l. 57:11
legislation: morals and l. 29:9
legislators: unacknowledged l. 326:6
legs: cannon-ball took off his l. 191:6
losing your l. 290:4
lemon-trees: where l. bloom 176:4
lend me your ears 304:6
l. me your grey mare 23:2
little onward l. 250:6
lender: nor a l. be 297:4
leopard change his spots 47:12
l. lie down with kid 45:12
***Lesbia**: vivamus, mea L.* 108:2
less: about l. and l. 93:3
far l. brilliant pen 26:4
l. Greek 208:5
loved Caesar l. 304:5
lessen from day to day 105:11
lesson: still harder l. 271:10
lessons: reason they're called l. 105:11
lest we forget 219:5
l. we should be 2:5
let my people go 35:9
l. sounds of music 312:4
l. them eat cake 237:1
l. there be light 33:4
l. the sun in 348:7
l. who can be clever 215:4
Lethe: wharf of Lethe 199:1
letter: how large a l. 66:13
l. from his wife 104:4
l. killeth 66:7
letters mingle souls 145;6
leviathan: draw out l. 40:8
lewd: certain l. fellows 63:7
that l. hat 207:9
***lex**: suprema est l.* 119:8
lexicographer escape reproach 206:8
l. writer of dictionaries 204:8
liaison: partly a l. man 31:6
liar and father of it 61:12
Liberal: either a little L. 173:6
Liberté! Egalité! Fraternité! 9:1
liberties: give up their l. 89:1
liberty: condition of l. eternal vigilance 133:4
give me l. 186:7
land of l. 329:6
l. thus far limited 245:2
l. to the captives 47:6
life, l., pursuit of happiness 7:9
o l.! what crimes 285:3
people contend for l. 180:5
poverty destroys l. 206:4
seek power and lose l. 20:4
this is L.-Hall 177:5
thy chosen music, l. 372:8

marriage from l. 96:9
mess of pottage with l. 41:11
my l. is come 286:2
my l. swears 322:8
never told her l. 319:12
O lyric l. 84:11
passing l. of women 38:5
past making l. 278:3
say it was not l. 245:10
see her was to l. 90:1
separate us from l. of God 64:6
service of my l. 333:6
sports of l. 208:9
swear thou think'st I l. 146:3
this spring of l. 320:4
thoughts of l. 344:3
time to l. 43:1
true l. hath my heart 327:3
true l.'s coming 319:5
vegetable l. should grow 239:8
very few to l. 371:9
where people make l. 100:5
wilder shores of l. 75:6
wise and eke l. 333:4
loved: did till we l. 144:9
God so l. the world 61:7
Israel l. Joseph 35:1
l. and lost 94:8; 343:5
l. not honour more 230:3
l. Rome more 304:5
l. the time 120:3
l. three whole days 337:3
more I l. my homeland 29:5
never l., never liv'd 171:7
never l. sae kindly 90:2
she l. much 58:12
they l. each other 184:10
time, place, l. one 84:2
we l., sir 82:10
loveliest and best 162:1
l. of trees 196:1
loveliness: its l. increases 211:4
lovely: all things l. 136:4
gives a l. light 245:8
l. and pleasant 38:3
l. is the rose 370:9
l. woman stoops 156:3
thou art more l. 320:13
whatsoever things are l. 67:6
when l. woman 177:4
your have l. hair 113:12
lover: as true a l. 295:2
ex-wife searching for new l. 127:9
l. and his lass 295:11
lunatic, l., poet 313:8
some old l.'s ghost 145:7
wailing for her demon-l. 124:7
lovers: at l. perjuries 262:3
l. fled away 211:7
l. meeting 319:6
loves: as lines so l. 239:5
kills thing he l. 364:10
l. to lie 295:3
lovesome thing 81:3
loveth a cheerful giver 66:9
l. he correcteth 40:9
made and l. all 124:1
that l. not 69:5
whom the Lord l. 68:10
loving: heart still as l. 97:10
l., and saying so 146:4
l. himself better 124:11
l. longest 18:9
l. that old arm-chair 128:3
night made for l. 97:11
too much l. you 315:3
low: exalted them of l. degree 58:2
he that is l. 87:6
l. man adding 83:2
l. opinion of himself 352:4
Lowells talk only to Cabots 76:8
***Löwen**: lachende L.* 259:3
lower than vermin 32:10
loyal, neutral 309:1
loyalties: impossible l. 13:11
loyalty: Oxford wanted l. 352:2
Lucifer: falls like L. 303:4
L. son of morning 46:2
lucrative: so l. to cheat 122:1
lucre: filthy l. 67:11
Luke, beloved physician 67:8
lullaby: dreamy l. 173:10
lumber: loads of learned l. 270:8

man (cont.):
study of m. 111:7
style is the m. 85:9
this was a m. 305:1
whan God maked m. 112:10
when a m. should marry 20:7
when I became a m. 65:10
wise m. will make more 19:9
with one m. mann'd 144:7
work is a m. 298:4
you'll be a m. 218:4
Mandalay: road to M. 218:11
manger: in rude m. lies 248:6
laid him in a m. 58:3
***manger** pour vivre* 252:4
***manges**: ce que tu m.* 79:7
maniac scattering dust 343:6
man-in-the-street: to the m. 16:8
mankind: giant leap for m. 12:8
how beauteous m. 318:9
proper study of m. 270:11
ride m. 157:5
spectator of m. 1:7
survey m. 207:4
manner: all m. of thing 209:9
manners: evil communications corrupt m. 66:2
for m. sake 49:7
m. of a dancing master 204:6
m. of a Marquis 175:6
oh, the m. 119:10
mansions: many m. 62:5
mantle: morn in russet m. 296:7
twitch'd his m. blue 248:5
manure: its natural m. 203:5
many a good tune 94:7
m. are called 55:9
m. change and pass 325:2
m.-splendoured thing 349:10
so m. to so few 118:2
we are m. 57:11
map: roll up that m. 267:7
maps: geography about m. 30:2
Marathon looks on the sea 96:11
marble: dwelt in m. halls 86:7
left it m. 17:9
m. to retain 95:4
March: droghte of M. 111:8
ides of M. 303:7
mad M. days 240:10
that highte M. 112:10
winds of M. 320:9
marches: army m. on stomach 256:5
mare: lend me your grey m. 23:2
Margaret you mourn for 193:3
***Maria**: Ave M.* 10:1
***mariages**: de bons m.* 223:7
Marie Seaton, Marie Beaton 22:7
mari magno turbantibus 231:2
mariner: ancient m. 123:1
draw with m. 148:6
mark, learn 273:1
m. upon Cain 34:5
marquis: manners of a m. 175:6
marred: married is m. 294:2
marriage: fall in with m.-procession 121:4
furnish forth m. tables 297:1
m. ever out of fashion 93:5
m. field of battle 335:11
m. from love 96:9
m. has pains 207:1
m. is popular 324:8
m. of true minds 322:4
m. pair of shears 330:5
marry nor given in m. 55:11
marriages: there are good m. 223:7
married: as if not m. 127:5
before he m. 339:4
business to get m. 324:1
if we had been m. 171:4
m. ear 306:14
m. is marred 294:2
m. past redemption 150:7
m. women kept women 329:3
reader, I m. him 79:8
marries: signify whom one m. 285:2
marry: better m. than burn 64:15

meet: hope to m. my Maker 128:7
infinite can never m. 239:5
make ends m. 169:6
men and mountains m. 73:6
used to m. 82:10
meeting: lovers m. 319:6
meets his Waterloo 267:4
more than m. the eye 217:8
melancholy: green and yellow m. 319:12
hence, loathed m. 247:7
rare recipe for m. 222:2
soothe her m. 177:4
meliora: *video m.* 262:4
melodies: heard m. are sweet 212:5
member of parliament 88:6
members one of another 66:15
meminisse *iuvabit* 356:2
memorial longer lasting 195:5
some have no m. 49:11
whole earth as m. 266:8
men: all things to all m. 65:1
delight in proper young m. 91:3
fishers of m. 50:7
for fear of little m. 3:1
form Christian m. 14:2
match the m. 153:3
m. about me 303:11
m. and mountains meet 73:6
m. created equal 7:9
m. decay 176:6
m. for pieces 162:5
m. like satyrs 237:9
m. may come 341:6
m. must work 215:7
m. of England 326:1
m. of large fortune 18:2
m. seldom make passes 263:10
m. were deceivers 314:1
m. with oaths 232:1
m., woman, clergymen 330:4
mice an' m. 92:1
other m.'s flowers 253:6
power over m. 369:2
purgatory of m. 164:4
rejected of m. 47:2
sorts and conditions of m. 272:11
that m. betray 177:4
tongues of m. and angels 65:5
unnecessary things are m. 284:4
wars begin in minds of m. 7:1
ways of God to m. 248:11
when m. all asleep 79:3
words m.'s daughters 235:3
mend electric light 28:7
seek to m. 145:5
mendier *dans les rues* 166:1
mene, tekel, upharsin 48:9
mens *sana* 210:6
Menschen *werden Brüder* 290:10
mental: cease from m. fight 73:4
mercies: tender m. of wicked 41:5
merciful: blessed are m. 50:8
God be m. to me 60:10
m. eclipse 173:2
merciless: black m. things 203:1
Mercury: words of M. 307:2
mercy: his m. endureth 277:5
m. has human heart 74:5
m. I asked 100:3
m. seasons justice 312:1
m. shall follow me 274:6
m. upon us 272:10
quality of m. 311:13
temper justice with m. 250:3
they shall obtain m. 50:8
merde 100:2
merit: Garter; no m. in it 243:1
m. for bishopric 363:1
mérite: *gouvernement qu'elle m.* 235:5
mermaids: heard m. singing 155:5
merriment: scheme of m. 206:12
merry: I am never m. 312:5
m. heart 41:10
merrygoround: no go m. 234:7
meruit: *palmam qui m.* 209:1
mess of potage 34:12
m. of pottage with love 41:11

message: medium is the m. 234:1
messe: *Paris vaut une m.* 186:4
messing about in boats 178:2
met: never m. with again 104:2
method in 't 298:1
Methodist: morals of a M. 175:6
methods: know my m. 147:7
methought I heard a voice 308:8
métier: *c'est son m.* 185:1
metuant: *oderint, dum m.* 1:1
mezzo del cammin 133:6
M.F.H.: where M. dines 338:1
mice: like little m. 337:2
m. an' men 92:1
Michelangelo: talking of M. 155:1
middle: companions for m. age 20:6
into the m. 193:11
m. of next week 104:5
m. of road of life 133:6
middle-ageing care 272:2
Midlands: living in the M. 29:2
midnight: blackest m. born 247:7
cease upon the m. 212:13
chimes at m. 301:6
consum'd m. oil 171:8
m. pillow 295:2
troubled m. 154:2
visions before m. 81:5
midst: in m. of life 273:13
mieux: *de m. en m.* 129:9
tout pour le m. 357:8
might: as our m. lessens 7:8
do it with thy m. 43:8
it m. have been 182:7; 364:7
m. as well live 264:1
mightier than sword 86:4
mighty fallen 38:4
put down the m. 58:2
miles: hundred m. away 182:1
m. to go 168:7
military: too serious to be left to m. 121:2
milk: drunk m. of Paradise 124:10
flowing with m. and honey 35:8
gin mother's m. 324:12
kid in his mother's m. 35:13
m. and then just 31:8
m. comes frozen 307:1
m. of human kindness 307:6
trout in the m. 351:3
milkiness of infancy 88:2
Mill: John Stuart M. 30:4
mille: *basia m.* 108:3
miller: there was a jolly m. 71:7
millions of strange shadows 321:5
run into m. 287:4
mills: dark Satanic m. 73:4
m. of God 227:4
millstone hanged about his neck 54:14
Milton: malt does more than M. 198:3
M.! thou shouldst 372:4
M. was for us 83:8
M. wrote in fetters 74:8
mute inglorious M. 178:10
mimsy were the borogoves 106:4
mince: dined on m. 225:3
mind: calm of m. 250:11
clothed, and in his right m. 57:12
first damages his m. 9:7
how little m. employed 205:6
laugh spoke vacant m. 176:8
m. has mountains 192:9
m.'s construction 307:5
my m.'s unsworn 159:2
out of m. 122:6
pleased to call m. 362:8
reading is to m. 334:4
sound m. 210:6
minds: hobgoblins of little m. 158:2
idleness refuge of weak m. 114:6
keep your hearts and m. 67:5
little things affect little m. 143:8
marriage of true m. 322:4

minds (cont.):
wars begin in m. of men 7:1
mine: 'twas m., 'tis his 315:1
minion: morning's m. 193:6
Minister: becoming Cabinet M. 337:6
M. that meddles with art 243:4
ministering angel thou 292:9
ministers of grace defend 297:7
Minnehaha, Laughing Water 228:7
minority always right 201:6
minstrel was infirm 292:2
wandering m. I 173:10
mintage of man 197:4
minute: cage the m. 235:2
good m. goes 85:3
sucker born every m. 23:4
unforgiving m. 218:4
minutes: take care of m. 114:3
miracles do not happen 13:12
Miranda: remember an inn, M. 29:3
mirror crack'd 344:2
m. up to nature 299:7
mirth: passion and of m. 212:3
present m. 319:7
resort of m. 247:6
miscarriages: at least four m. 26:2
mischief: Satan finds m. 360:5
miserable comforters 39:13
m. sinners 272:10
only two people m. 94:10
young girl m. 166:6
misery: dwell on guilt and m. 18:4
m. to distribute 230:4
misfortune of friends 223:6
m. of knowing any thing 18:6
m. to have been happy 75:8
misfortunes: all the m. 264:5
make m. more bitter 20:8
misquote: enough learning to m. 97:5
missed: never would be m. 174:4
wonder what you've m. 15:3
misses an unit 83:2
missing so much 129:1
Mississippi muddy water 89:9
mist in my face 84:9
mistake to theorize 147:6
mistaken: you may be m. 132:5
mistakes: makes no m. 267:3
mistress: art a jealous m. 157:8
m. rich anger shows 212:7
O m. mine 319:5
principles or your m. 366:11
mistresses: young men's m. 20:6
mists: season of m. 213:10
misunderstood: great is m. 158:3
***Mittel**: Einmischung anderer M.* 120:10
niemals bloss als M. 210:8
Mizpah 34:15
moan of doves 346:3
moanday, tearsday 209:3
moaning: no m. of bar 342:1
mobs: suppose two m. 140:6
mock on, Voltaire 73:5
mocked: God is not m. 66:12
mocker: wine is a m. 41:14
mocks married men 306:14
model of a modern Major-General 175:4
moderately: if drunk m. 49:8
moderation: astonished at own m. 121:3
m. a sort of treason 88:9
modern Major-General 175:4
***Möglichen**: die Lehre vom M.* 72:5
mome raths 106:4
moment: every m. dies a man 19:3; 346:13
m. mercifully gave 244:3
moments: Wagner has lovely m. 287:1
monarch of all I survey 131:5
monarchy: under constitutional m. 21:8
Monday: do on M. 374:4
money: draining m. from pockets 328:7
except for m. 205:8

morning: always three o'clock in the m. 163:2
awake! for m. 161:7
beauty of the m. 372:1
evening and the m. 33:5
find next m. 285:2
glad confident m. 83:9
joy cometh in m. 274:9
Lucifer, son of m. 46:2
many a glorious m. 321:3
m. after death 141:5
m.'s minion 193:6
m. stars sang 40:6
m. well-aired 85:5
m. wore to evening 343:3
up early in the m. 45:3
mornings: always m. like this 246:8
morris: nine men's m. 313:2
morrow: no thought for the m. 52:1
mors stupebit 109:2
mortal: laugh at any m. thing 97:1
m. coil 298:12
m., guilty 16:3
mortality: old m. 81:10
urns and sepulchres of m. 132:3
mortals: fools these m. be 313:7
'tis not in m. 1:5
mortis: *timor m. conturbat* 151:6
mortuus: *passer m. est* 108:1
Moscow: if I lived in M. 113:11
mot de Cambronne 100:2
mote in thy brother's eye 52:3
moth and rust corrupt 51:6
mother: as m., daughter 48:3
beautiful m. 194:10
church for his m. 133:5
either father or m. 335:3
m. forty whacks 5:6
m. of months 339:6
m. of Parliaments 79:6
m. of sciences 21:5
my m. cried 313:12
never called me m. 369:4
sorrowing m. 202:7
their Dacian m. 95:10
mothers: become like their m. 365:6
m. of large families 27:4
motion: God order'd m. 354:1
motley to the view 322:3
mould: broke the m. 12:2
mountain: flatter the m.-tops 321:3
if the m. will not 19:8
m. and hill made low 46:11
m. sheep are sweeter 266:1
tiptoe on misty m. 317:14
up the airy m. 3:1
mountains: beautiful upon m. 46:14
could remove m. 65:6
men and m. meet 73:6
m. look on Marathon 96:11
m. will heave 193:10
mourir: *partir c'est m.* 181:2
mourn: countless thousands m. 91:4
Margaret you m. for 193:3
no longer m. 321:7
they that m. 50:8
mourned: would have m. longer 296:13
mourra: *on m. seul* 264:8
mouse: silly little m. 193:10
mouse-trap: make a better m. 158:6
moustache: wax his m. 220:7
mouth: Englishman open his m. 324:11
God be in my m. 4:11
m. of babes 274:1
m. of Lord hath spoken 46:11
out of the m. of God 50:5
mouths: enemy in their m. 314:13
moutons: *revenons à m.* 9:3
mouvement: *premier m. jamais* 128:6
mouvements: *premiers m. bons* 253:7
move: feel earth m. 185:6
in him we live, and m. 63:10

it does m. 170:4
moves: God m. mysterious way 130:10
moving accident 370:2
m. finger writes 162:7
m. toyshop 271:4
stopped the m. stairs 235:1
MPs: in that House M. divide 173:7
mss as drunkards lamp-posts 199:8
much of a muchness 353:10
so m. owed 118:2
so m. to do 343:10
won't be m. for us 104:6
muck: down in lovely m. 198:4
money is like m. 20:10
muckrake in his hand 87:5
mud: me name is m. 136:9
one sees m. 223:2
muddied oafs at goals 218:6
multiplicanda: *non sunt m.* 260:4
multiplication is vexation 6:2
multiply: be fruitful and m. 33:8
multitude: giddy m. 242:7
m. of sins 69:3
multitudes: I contain m. 364:5
m. in valley of decision 49:1
mundi: *gloria m.* 10:8; 347:8
mundus: *pereat m.* 160:4
muove: *eppur si m.* 170:4
murder: I met m. 325:4
killing no m. 293:9
love and m. will out 126:8
m. one of the fine arts 137:2
m. sleep 308:8
m. to dissect 372:10
m. wol out 112:11
sooner m. an infant 75:3
murex: fished the m. 84:7
murmuring of innumerable 346:3
murmurous haunt of flies 212:12
mus: *ridiculus m.* 193:10
muscular: Christianity m. 143:5
muse of fire 301:11
music: condition of m. 265:4
danceth without m. 187:4
fiddled whisper m. 156:5
fled is that m. 213:3
frozen m. 290:9
hear sweet m. 312:5
how potent cheap m. 130:2
let sounds of m. 312:4
m. and women 266:6
m. at the close 316:2
m. be food of love 319:3
m. has charms 126:10
m. that gentlier 344:11
m. to attending ears 317:9
read m., can't hear it 26:1
still, sad m. 370:6
that hath no m. 312:6
thou hast thy m. too 213:11
uproar's your only m. 214:2
musical: full of m. amateurs 324:3
musician: lady is a m. 147:11
musicologist can read music 26:1
muss es sein 26:9
mussel pooled 348:4
must: forget because we m. 12:9
if we can we m. 198:5
m. addressed to princes 156:12
m. it be 26:9
mustard: grain of m. seed 54:5
mutabile *semper femina* 356:7
mutamur: *nos m. in illis* 11:3
mute inglorious Milton 178:10
mutter: peep and m. 45:8
muzzle the ox 36:10
myriad: died a m. 272:1
myrrh: gold, frankincense, m. 50:1
myrtle and turkey part 18:3
myself: as I m. 303:8
do not know m. 175:12
if not for m. 189:4
m. when young 162:3
mysterious: God moves m. way 130:10
mystery inside enigma 117:8
m. of body 348:1
nail: for want of a n. 167:1
nails: with his n. 361:3
naître: *peine de n.* 25:2

occasions how all o. 299:14
occupation: Othello's o.'s gone 315:5
occupations: love our o. 138:4
occupations domestiques moins 253:4
occurred: actually o. 216:8
ocean: dark blue o. 96:2
make the mighty o. 103:8
o. of truth 258:6
o. wash this blood 308:10
till the o. is folded 15:2
upon a painted o. 123:5
odd: exceedingly o. 221:2
not so o. 81:4
o. of God 159:6
odds: facing fearful o. 232:4
oderint, dum metuant 1:1
odi et amo 108:5
odio vitiorum 17:7
odorous: comparisons are o. 314:4
Odyssey: surge and thunder of O. 222:9
off with his head 119:5
offend one of these little ones 54:14
offended: shadows have o. 313:10
offenders: society o. 174:4
office: for o. boys 290:1
o. boy to an attorney 175:2
officiously to keep alive 121:8
oft: what o. was thought 270:4
oil: boiling o. in it 174:8
consum'd midnight o. 171:8
oiled: deftly in o. wards 213:8
old: chilly and grown o. 85:2
grow not o. 72:1
grow o. with me 84:10
half as o. as time 285:1
I grow o. 155:4
lads never be o. 197:3, 4
more virtue than o. men 205:2
no country for o. men 375:8
now am o. 274:11
o. age most unexpected 352:7
o. age should burn 348:3
o. as she looks 125:8
o. ever learning 331:2
o., Father William 105:3; 331:10
o. Kaspar's work 331:7
o. lamps for new 11:6
o. man in dry month 154:8
o. men dream dreams 48:13
o. men's nurses 20:6
o. men who never cheated 31:5
o. mortality 81:10
o. order changeth 343:1
o. with good grace 334:3
o. wives' fables 67:12
o. woman happy 166:6
o. women of both sexes 335:4
say I'm growing o. 200:6
tell an o. soldier 323:2
tiresomeness of o. age 10:3
when you are very o. 285:4
older than the rocks 265:3
richer still the o. 93:9
'ole: knows of a better o. 21:11
olive: children like o.-branches 277:3
Omega: Alpha and O. 69:8
ominous: that much was o. 272:2
omnia vincit amor 357:3
on Stanley 292:10
Onaway! awake 228:9
once: die but o. 1:6
o. to every man 230:6
o. was a man 182:3
one: God is o. Lord 36:6
members o. of another 66:15
o. damned thing 261:3
o. grew before 338:5
o. remains 325:2
o. small step 12:8
procession of o. 139:6
sixty religions, o. sauce 102:1
one-eyed yellow idol 183:5
only: he for God o. 249:7
o. begetter 320:12
open and notorious 273:2
o. covenants 367:7
o. that Pandora's Box 33:2

perception: doors of p. 75:5
perchance to dream 298:12
perdere: Jupiter vult p. 152:2
perdition catch my soul 314:14
perdu fors l'honneur 166:2
perdus: paradis p. 279:2
pereant qui ante nos 143:11
pereat mundus 160:4
perennius: aere p. 195:5
perfect: be ye p. 51:3
p. love casteth out 69:6
p. woman 371:12
perfection of a kind 15:6
perfide Albion 374:3
p. Angleterre 77:1
perfidious Albion 374:3
perform: wonders to p. 130:10
performance: desire outlive p. 301:4
perfume: curious p. 15:1
p. on the violet 305:5
perfumes of Arabia 310:3
perhaps: great p. 281:4
peril on the sea 363:7
periphrastic study 154:6
perish: nation p. not 62:2
p. with the sword 57:4
should not p. 61:7
perished: because it p. 245:10
perishes: everything p. 9:4
periuria ridet amantum 262:3
perjuries: at lovers' p. 262:3
pernicious: his p. soul 315:10
perpetual light shine 241:8
p. night 208:10
perpetually to be conquered 88:7
persecutest: why p. thou me 63:2
Persians: Medes and P. 48:10
persist: fool p. in folly 74:12
person: adornment of his p. 350:2
cheek of young p. 140:2
not the sort of p. 102:3
p. from Porlock 124:5
persons: no respecter of p. 63:4
p. never seen 258:2
perspiration: ninety-nine per cent p. 152:6
persuadest to be Christian 63:16
pessimist fears this true 98:4
pestilence that walketh 276:3
petal: sleeps crimson p. 346:1
Peter: shock-headed P. 190:5
thou art P. 54:10
petits: contre les p. 93:2
petticoat: feet beneath p. 337:2
petty: creeps in p. pace 310:6
petulance not sarcasm 142:7
peuple se gouverne 347:7
peur: sans p., sans reproche 8:6
peut-être: un grand p. 281:4
pews and steeples 114:11
phantom of delight 371:11
phenomenon: infant p. 139:10
Philip: from P. drunk 4:6
Philistines may jostle 174:12
philosopher: guide, p., friend 270:13
p! fingering slave 371:4
some p. has said 119:7
tried to be a p. 153:1
philosophers interpreted 240:6
philosophical: poetry more p. 12:5
philosophy: charming is divine p. 247:4
in your p. 297:11
little p. inclineth man 19:6
p. but an handmaid 19:4
p. from examples 142:3
professors of p. 350:10
phone for the fish-knives 31:7
Phyllis: neat-handed P. 247:11
physician: into hand of p. 49:9
Luke, the beloved p. 67:8
p. heal thyself 58:9
physicians: incident to p. 204:5
p. of the utmost fame 27:6
pianist: do not shoot the p. 6:8
Piccadilly: walk down P. 174:12
pick: scruple to p. a pocket 136:10
picking and stealing 273:4

pretty (cont.):
post-chaise with p. woman 205:10
p. women to deserve them 18:2
prevails: it p. 71:6
prevent: try to p. it. 247:1
prevented: timely compliance p. 161:1
previous: returned p. night 86:2
prey: bent on his p. 249:6
fastening on her p. 281:7
price: pearl of great p. 54:6
p. of everything 365:11
prices: contrivance to raise p. 328:5
prick: if you p. us 311:8
pricking of my thumbs 309:10
p. on the plain 332:9
prickly: round the p. pear 154:10
pricks: kick against the p. 63:3
pride: family p. inconceivable 174:1
low no p. 87:6
p. goeth before destruction 41:12
priest who slew slayer 232:8
turbulent p. 186:8
priestcraft: ere p. 149:1
priesthood: royal p. 69:1
Prime Minister: next P. but three 27:9
primordial atomic globule 174:1
primrose by river's brim 371:3
prince: good-night, sweet p. 300:11
great p. in prison 144:8
p. being left out 292:11
p. of darkness gentleman
princes: trust in p. 277:10
princesse lointaine 287:2
principalities: against p. 67:2
p., nor powers 64:6
principe de tous progrès 165:10
principiis obsta 262:5
principle: don't believe in p. 230:5
p. of English constitution 72:6
p. of social progress 165:10
principles or your mistress 366:11
wrote 'P. of Political Economy' 30:4
print: fit to p. 260:5
licence to p. money 350:6
printed in a book 39:15
printing: gunpowder, p. 102:5
p. house in hell 75:4
prism: prunes and p. 139:2
prison: great prince in p. 144:8
in p., and ye came 56:9
not a p. make 230:2
opening of the p. 47:6
p. of his days 16:1
shades of the p.-house 370:12
taking him to p. 199:5
private faces in public places 16:7
fine and p. place 240:1
religion invade p. life 243:2
privilege I claim 18:9
power which stands on p. 28:4
privilèges des femmes 165:10
prizes: glittering p. 72:4
P.R.O.: partly P. 31:6
probable impossibilities 12:6
problem: three-pipe p. 147:3
proceedings: subsequent p. 182:9
procession of one 139:6
procrastination thief of time 376:7
productions of time: 74:11
profani: procul este, p. 356:10
profession: discharge of any p. 205:6
ornament to her p. 87:7
professions are conspiracies 323:5
professors of dismal science 103:2
p. of philosophy 350:10
profit by their example 186:6
profited: what is a man p. 54:12
profound: turbid look p. 222:8

profundis: *de p. clamavi* 70:8
progrès: *tous p. sociaux* 165:10
progress: no summer p. 3:4
proie: *à sa p. attachée* 281:7
proletariat: dictatorship of p. 240:7
promise none relies on 284:6
why didst thou p. 321:4
promises to keep 168:7
promotion cometh neither 275:10
proofs of holy writ 315:4
proper gardener's work 217:9
p. study of mankind 270:11
religion no p. conversation 114:9
p. young men 91:3
property: little snug p. 152:5
p. has its duties 148:9
p. is theft 278:7
public p. 203:6
prophecies: verification of his p. 352:6
prophecy: trumpet of p. 325:7
prophesy: sons and daughters p. 48:13
we p. in part 65:9
prophesying war 124:8
prophet new inspir'd 316:3
p. not without honour 54:7
prophets: beware of false p. 52:10
propinquity does it 359:8
proponit: *homo p.* 347:9
proportion: strangeness in the p. 19:7
propre: *moins p. à la société* 110:6
propriété *c'est le vol* 278:7
proprietor's prejudices 338:3
propriety: evince its p. 19:1
prose: all not p. is verse 252:6
in p. or rhyme 248:10
only p. 82:8
p. when lines go on 30:1
p. words in best order 125:3
speaking p. without knowing 252:5
prospect: every p. pleases 184:7
noblest p. Scotchman sees 205:1
prosper: I p. 305:10
sinners' ways p. 193:5
protest: lady doth p. 299:9
Protestant: printing, P. religion 102:5
protoplasmal primordial 174:1
proud: death be not p. 145:2
p. and angry dust 198:5
p. and yet wretched 135:2
too p. to fight 367:5
prove: let us p. 208:9
proved: to be p. 159:1
Providence their guide 250:4
way P. dictates 189:6
provokes me with impunity 10:4
proximus: *paries cum p. ardet* 194:7
prudenter *agas* 10:7
prunes and prism 139:2
pruninghooks into spears 48:14
spears into p. 44:13
public: paint in p.'s face 288:4
private faces in p. places 16:7
p. schools nurseries of vice 161:2
p. trust 203:6
publicans and sinners 53:3
publish and be damned 362:2
p. it not in the streets 38:2
publisher: Barabbas a p. 101:6
puerisque: *virginibus p. canto* 195:3
puero: *se p.* 194:1
puffed: charity not p. up 65:7
pulchrior: *filia p.* 194:10
pulse like a soft drum 215:1
with one p. 235:1
pun: so vile a p. 136:10
punctuality politeness of kings 230:1
punishment fit the crime 174:7
purchase: you p. pain 269:9
purchasing: not worth p. 283:1
Pure: real Simon P. 109:3
pure: heart is p. 346:6

record on the gramophone 156:3
recording, not thinking 202:6
recte: si possis r. 194:4
rectum aut justitiam 235:4
recurret: tamen usque r. 194:5
red: like a r. r. rose 91:6
making green r. 308:10
never blows so r. 161:10
r. flag flying 127:7
r. in tooth and claw 343:9
r. lips not so r. 262:10
thin r. line 289:1
wine when it is r. 41:16
redeemer: my r. liveth 40:1
redemption: married past r. 150:7
reed shaken with the wind 53:14
reeds by the river 82:4
references: always verify r. 288:1
refreshment: accept r. at any hands 174:3
refuge: been our r. 275:14
last r. of scoundrel 205:7
refusal: great r. 134:1
regardless of their doom 179:2
regiment: led r. from behind 172:8
monstrous r. 221:1
regret: one thing I r. 104:5
r. I have but one life 180:3
regular: icily r. 345:2
reign: better r. in hell 248:12
rejected of men 47:2
rejoice: desert shall r. 46:7
heartily r. 276:5
let us then r. 10:3
r. in the Lord alway 67:4
relation: nobody like a r. 347:5
relations: squire and his r. 138:4
relaxes: bless r. 75:2
relief: for this r. 296:6
religion: about to r. 19:6
handmaid to r. 19:4
r. but a toy 237:10
r. invade private life 243:2
r. no proper conversation 114:9
r. opium of the people 240:5
r. powerless to bestow 165:1
some of r. 152:5
superstition r. of feeble 89:5
true meaning of r. 13:13
religions: sixty r., one sauce 102:1
***rem**: quocumque modo r.* 194:4
remains: one r. 325:2
while aught r. 284:7
remarks: said our r. before 143:11
remedy: dangerous r. 160:2
remember: glad to r. 356:2
if thou wilt, r. 286:6
I r., I r. 191:8
r. and be sad 286:4
r. an inn 29:3
r. how they go 99:4
r. now thy Creator 43:14
r. fifth of November 6:9
r. with advantages 302:7
we will r. them 72:1
remembered: blue r. hills 197:8
r. for a very long time 233:9
remembering my good friends 316:9
remembrance: rosemary for r. 300:2
remembreth: whan it r. me 113:1
remind me of dead: 290:6
remission: without blood no r. 68:5
remote and ineffectual don 28:6
re-mould it nearer 163:1
***rend**: ne se r. pas* 100:1
render unto Caesar 55:10
rendezvous with death 293:1
renounce the devil 273:3
repair: friendship in constant r. 204:9
repay: I will r. 64:8
tiger well r. 27:4
repentance on Sunday 374:4
sinners to r. 53:4
repented: much r. 96:6
repenteth: one sinner that r. 59:14

roaming: where are you r. 319:5
roar: give the r. 118:9
r. their ribs out 175:10
r. you as gently 312:13
roast beef of England 160:8
robbed: love, that had r. us 244:3
robber: Barabbas was a r. 62:9
robe: give me my r. 294:9
robin redbreast in a cage 73:1
rock: on the sea-wet r. 198:7
upon this r. I build 54:10
rocks: older than the r. 265:3
rod: lightning and lashed r. 193:8
r. and thy staff 274:6
r. out of stem of Jesse 45:11
spares the r. 191:9
spareth his r. 41:8
rode madly off 224:7
roes: like two young r. 44:10
Roland: Child R. 306:5
role: not yet found a r. 1:2
roll on 96:2
r. up that map 267:7
roller, pitch, stumps 222:10
rolling English road 115:9
***Roma** locuta est* 17:8
***Romae**: si fueris R.* 3:2
Roman: before R. came 115:9
I am a R. citizen 119:11
live in the R. style 3:2
make a R. holiday 95:10
noblest R. 304:12
R. conquest good thing 293:4
romantic about money 324:2
***Romanus**: civis R. sum* 119:11
Rome: grandeur that was R. 268:7
if you are at R. 3:2
loved R. more 304:5
R. has spoken 17:8
when R. falls 96:1
Ronsard sang of me 285:4
room: in ev'ry grave make r. 134:7
no r. in the inn 58:3
riches in little r. 238:1
r. at the top 360:9
root of all evil 68:2
Rose extremely sick 278:4
rose: blossom as the r. 46:7
English unofficial r. 80:8
fayre as r. in May 113:2
go, lovely r. 358:9
I pluck the r. 85:3
last r. of summer 254:6
like a red red r. 91:6
lovely is the r. 370:9
r. by any other name 317:8
r. is a r. 334:6
r. of Sharon 44:3
roves back the r. 136:1
tiger sniffs r. 290:8
Rose Aylmer, all were thine 222:7
rosebuds: gather ye r. 188:8
rosemary and rue 320:8
r. for remembrance 300:2
Rosencrantz and Guildenstern 300:12
rose-red city 87:13
roses: my own red r. 349:4
not bed of r. 335:11
raptures and r. 339:9
r., all the way 84:3
r. and white lilies 101:7
time of r. 191:5
two red r. 255:3
wine and r. 147:1
rot half a grain 315:10
rotten: something is r. 297:8
rough: more r. diamond 114:5
r.-hew them 300:7
r. places plain 46:11
r. winds do shake 320:13
this r. magic 318:8
what r. beast 376:4
Roumania: I am Marie of R. 263:8
round unvarnish'd tale 314:8
roundabouts: lost upon the r. 109:8
rounded with a sleep 318:7
Roundheads (Right) 293:5
Rousseau: Voltaire, R. 73:5

service: done state some s. 315:11
s. of my love 333:6
serviettes: crumpled the s. 31:7
serving: cumbered about much s. 59:5
six honest s.-men 218:8
set: race s. before us 68:9
s. before you life 36:12
setting: time is s. 91:7
seven maids with s. mops 106:10
s. sleepers den 144:9
seventh seal 69:14
sever: nothing in life s. 129:6
severity: set in with usual s. 125:2
Severn: thick on S. 197:6
sex: conceal its s. 256:8
privilege I claim for my s. 18:9
talk on 'S. and Civics' 32:2
sexes: three s. 330:4
sexton toll'd the bell 191:7
shabby tigers 190:2
shade: in a green s. 239:6
shades of night 227:7
s. of the prison-house 370:12
where s. of darkness 136:3
shadow: fleeth as a s. 39:12
life's a walking s. 310:6
s. at morning 156:1
valley of the s. 274:6
shadows: coming events cast s. 101:3
millions of strange s. 321:5
s. have offended 313:10
shake dust of your feet 53:8
Shakespeare was of us 83:8
sweetest S. 247:12
shallow draughts intoxicate 270:3
shame: keep from s. 197:7
live and s. the land 199:3
waste of s. 322:6
shameful conquest 316:8
share: greater s. of honour 302:6
s. the transport 372:6
Sharon: rose of S. 44:3
sharper than serpent's tooth 140:3; 305:11
she: not impossible s. 131:11
s. for God in him 249:7
shed them now 304:8
shedding: without s. of blood 68:5
sheep: half-witted s. 334:8
hungry s. look up 248:3
in s.'s clothing 52:10
like lost s. 272:4
like s. gone astray 47:3
mountain s. are sweeter 266:1
s. in s.'s clothing 177:7
s. on his right hand 56:8
s. which was lost 59:13
sheer no-man-fathomed 192:9
sheet: wet s., flowing sea 133:3
sheets: kindliness of s. 80:5
shell: rainbow s. 286:2
Shelley: Burns, S., were with us 83:8
see S. plain 83:10
shepherd: Dick the s. 307:1
every s.'s tongue 281:9
feed flock like a s. 46:12
I am the good s. 61:14
Lord is my s. 274:5
they call you, s. 13:6
shepherds abiding in fields 58:4
while s. watched 340:9
shimmered: Jeeves s. out 368:2
shine: face s. upon thee 36:2
light so s. 50:10
s. in use 346:9
shineth: light s. in darkness 60:16
shining Big-Sea-Water 228:6
s. from shook foil 192:8
s. morning face 295:5
ship: idle as a painted s. 123:5
s. is being in jail 204:10
sink me the s. 346:4
tall s. and a star 241:1
way of a s. 42:7
whither, O splendid s. 79:4
ships: launch'd a thousand s. 237:5

silence (cont.):
s. in heaven 69:14
s. that dreadful bell 314:11
s. virtue of fools 19:5
to be in s. 67:10
silent: her s. throat 172:4
impossible to be s. 89:2
must remain s. 368:1
s. and amazed 363:8
s. upon a peak 213:6
silken dalliance 301:13
silks: whenas in s. 188:9
sillier: nothing s. 108:4
silly: its s. face 282:2
lovely to be s. 195:8
silvas Academi 194:8
silver: for a handful of s. 83:7
gold and s. becks 305:2
in a s. tassie 90:12
in her s. shoon 136:8
s. and gold have I none 62:15
s. cord be loosed 43:15
s., ivory, apes 38:10
s. or small change 110:6
s. plate on a coffin 260:6
s. swan 172:4
thirty pieces of s. 56:11
Simon: real S. Pure 109:3
simple: rarely pure, never s. 365:3
simplicitas: *sancta s.* 203:7
simplicity: elegant s. 336:10
holy s. 203:7
pity my s. 362:4
simplify, s. 351:1
sin: angry, s. not 66:16
continue in s. 64:1
dark world of s. 71:10
go, s. no more 61:10
hate the s. 17:7
no s. but ignorance 237:10
s. find you out 36:5
s. is behovely 209:9
s. to God above 351:4
taketh away the s. 61:5
wages of s. 64:3
without s. among you 61:9
would you like to s. 8:3
sinecure: love no s. 98:2
sinews of the soul 169:8
s. of war 120:1
sing: cannot s. old songs 99:4; 120:8
clap hands, and s. 375:10
come, let us s. 276:5
die before they s. 124:4
not s. to me 155:5
of thee I s. 329:6
places where they s. 272:8
s. Lord's song 277:7
s. no sad songs 286:5
s. unto the Lord 274:10; 276:5, 6
think caged birds s. 361:4
singeing King of Spain's beard 148:5
singer: sans s. 162:2
when s. sings them 336:5
singing: burst out s. 290:7
nest of s. birds 204:4
s. in the wilderness 161:8
single: not s. spies 300:1
sink me the ship 346:4
sinks: it s. 222:6
sinned: more s. against 306:2
s. against heaven 60:1
sinner: love the s. 17:7
merciful to me a s. 60:10
one s. that repenteth 59:14
sinners: breeder of s. 299:3
miserable s. 272:10
publicans and s. 53:3
s. to repentance 53:4
s. ways prosper 193:5
sinneth before his Maker 49:9
sins: her s. are forgiven 58:12
multitude of s. 69:3
s. be as scarlet 44:12
s. inclin'd to 93:4
s. were scarlet 28:3
weep for their s. 364:3
sirens: song s. sang 82:1
sister: live a barren s. 312:10
sisters under their skins 218:10
sit: I shall s. here 105:5
s. and look at it 203:9

s. first punishment 131:6
s. fools gladly 66:10
s. little children 57:14
s. me to come 362:4
s. thy foot 276:10
sufferance is the badge 311:5
sufficient unto the day 52:1
sugar my hair 106:1
suis: *j'y s.* 234:2
Suisse: *point de S.* 281:8
suit action to word 299:6
suitably attired 199:6
suits: than s. a man 199:2
suivre: *fallait les s.* 225:5
sultry: where climate's s. 96:5
sum of things 198:8
sum: *cogito, ergo s.* 137:3
summer: after many a s. 346:7
last rose of s. 254:6
Saint Martin's s. 302:10
spring nor s. beauty 144:4
s. has set in 125:2
s. is icumen in 7:2
s.'s lease 320:13
s. soldier 263:5
to a s.'s day 320:13
to ensure s. 359:2
was a s. evening 331:7
winter or s. when happy 113:11
summertime on Bredon 196:9
sun: give me the s. 201:8
going down of s. 72:1
heaven's glorious s. 306:12
Juliet is the s. 317:6
let the s. in 348:7
place in the s. 86:3
setting s. 316:2
s. go down on wrath 66:16
s. has gone in 329:5
s. of York 317:2
s. rise on evil and good 51:2
under the s. 42:11
unruly s. 146:1
Sunday: of a S. morning 197:1
rainy S. in London 137:1
repentance on S. 374:4
sundial: I am a s. 28:5
sunlight on the garden 235:2
suns that set 208:10
sunset and evening star 342:1
s. breezes shiver 258:1
s. of life 101:3
sunshine patriot 263:5
sunt *lacrimae rerum* 356:4
superior people never 254:3
superiority: airs of s. 359:4
superman: teach the s. 259:2
superstition in avoiding s. 20:13
s. religion of feeble 89:5
superstitions: end as s. 201:4
support me in the wrong 243:5
supports with insolence 206:11
suprema *est lex* 119:8
sure: nobody is s. 28:10
s. to die 254:7
surfeit: sick that s. 311:2
surge and thunder of Odyssey 222:9
surmise: with a wild s. 213:6
surprised by joy 372:6
surrender: die but not s. 100:1
we shall never s. 117:10
survey: monarch of all I s. 131:5
s. mankind 207:4
survival of fittest 332:4
survived: I s. 327:6
suspension of disbelief 125:1
suspicion: above s. 98:9
banish squint s. 247:3
Sussex by the sea 219:8
swaddling: wrapped him in s. 58:3
swallow: before s. dares 320:9
s. a camel 55:12
swallowed: others to be s. 20:11
swan: black s. 210:3
dies the s. 346:7
silver s. 172:4
s. sail with her young 244:3
swans: like s. asleep 163:6
s. are geese 13:5
s. sing before they die 124:4
swear no where 145:11
s. thou think'st I love 146:3
very angry, s. 353:7
sweat: blood, toil, tears, s. 117:9

unwritten: custom, that u. law 134:6
up guards 362:1
u. the airy mountain 3:1
u. to a point 360:8
u. with which 119:3
upharsin: mene, tekel, u. 48:9
upper: like many of u. class 29:1
upright: our flesh u. 144:6
uproar your only music 214:2
upside: world u. down 63:8
upstairs: equal u. 23:5
kicked u. 180:7
urban, squat 80:10
urbe: *rus in u.* 239:3
urge for destruction 22:1
urgent: bosom of u. west 79:4
urns and sepulchres 132:3
us: not unto u. 70:7
use: as I u. thee 188:1
u. any language 173:9
u. every man 298:8
u. of a book 104:7
u. of new-born child 167:7
used no other 280:3
useful: know to be u. 255:4
useless each without other 228:8
usurp authority over man 67:10
utter: in all they u. 95:5
vacant: laugh spoke v. mind 176:8
v. or pensive mood 370:4
vadis: *quo v.* 71:2
vae *victis* 227:3
vain unnecessary things 284:4
watchman waketh in v. 277:2
valet: hero to his v. 129:3
valiant never taste death 304:1
valley: bicker down a v. 341:5
every v. be exalted 46:11
great things from v. 116:4
into v. of death 341:8
v. full of bones 48:6
v. of decision 49:1
v. of humiliation 87:2
v. of the shadow 274:6
v. sheep are fatter 266:1
valleys: lily of the v. 44:3
valour: mighty man of v. 37:2
true v. see 87:8
value my garden more 1:9
v. of nothing 365:11
vanish: softly and suddenly v. 104:2
vanitas *vanitatum* 70:9
vanity: lighter than v. 87:3
speckled v. 248:8
v. and vexation 42:12
v. of vanities 42:10; 70:9
Vanity-Fair 87:3
variety: infinite v. 294:5
v.'s the very spice 131:2
various: how v. his employments 131:3
man so v. 149:7
varium *et mutabile* 356:7
vaster than empires 239:8
vécu: *j'ai v.* 327:6
vegetable love should grow 239:8
veil: painted v. 326:2
vein: not in giving v. 317:3
veins: jigging v. 238:5
vendemus: *nulli v.* 235:4
vengeance: sudden v. waits 269:1
v. is mine 64:8
veni, *vidi, vici* 98:7
vent: *au feu le v.* 93:1
enflamment au v. 166:3
venture: bow at a v. 39:1
damn her at a v. 222:5
Vénus *toute entière* 281:7
verb has hard time 353:9
verba: *iurare in v.* 194:3
verbosity: exuberance of v. 143:3
not crude v. 203:7
verbrennt: *wo man Bücher v.* 184:9
verbum *sapienti* 268:2
volat irrevocabile v. 194:6
verification of his prophecies 352:6
verify: always v. references 288:1

wasted: chronicle of w. time 322:2
I w. time 317:1
w. his substance 59:15
wasteful and ridiculous 305:5
w., blundering, low 134:5
wastes her time 358:9
watch: done better by a w. 28:5
Lord w. between 34:15
w. and pray 57:3
w. in the night 276:1
w. over their flock 58:4
w. therefore 56:5
w. the wall 219:7
w. with me one hour 57:2
wear learning like w. 114:4
watcher of the skies 213:6
watchman: passed by the w. 168:1
w. waketh in vain 277:2
w., what of the night 46:3
water: benison of hot w. 80:6
care where w. goes 116:3
drawers of w. 36:14
little drops of w. 103:8
name writ in w. 214:4
plunge your hands in w. 15:3
shining Big-Sea-W. 228:6
w. clears us 308:11
w. of affliction 38:14
w., w., every where 123:6
w. your damned flower-pots 84:12
wetter w. 80:7
Waterloo: meets his W. 267:4
W. won on playing fields 361:7
watermen that row one way 92:4
waters: beside w. of comfort 274:5
bread upon the w. 43:13
business in great w. 276:9
pour the w. of the Nile 105:1
stolen w. sweet 41:1
w. cannot quench love 44:11
w. of Babylon 277:6
w. to a thirsty soul 42:2
wattles: of clay and w. 375:6
wave: behind white w. 91:7
lift me as a w. 325:6
Waverley: Pickwick, Owl, and W. 7:6
waves: wild w. saying 103:9
waving: not w. but drowning 329:8
wax to receive 95:4
way: broad is the w. 52:8
not pass this w. 179:8
prepare ye the w. 50:2
to his own w. 47:3
w. for Billy and me 190:6
w. of an eagle 42:7
w. of putting it 154:6
w. of transgressors 41:7
w. Providence dictates 189:6
w., the truth, the life 62:6
w. the world ends 154:11
w. to dusty death 310:6
w. was long 292:2
woman has her w. 191:3
you, that w. 307:2
ways: count the w. 82:5
nine and sixty w. 218:5
w. of God to men 248:11
w. of pleasantness 40:10
wayside: fell by the w. 54:4
weak: flesh is w. 57:3
idleness refuge of w. minds 114:6
weakening the will 332:6
weaker vessel 69:2
weakness: amiable w. 161:5
wealth: where w. accumulates 176:6
wealthy: business of the w. 28:7
weaned: not w. till then 144:9
weapon: his w. wit 192:6
weapons: lawful to wear w. 278:2
wear: better w. than rust 133:1
w. your rue 300:3
weariest most loathed 310:10
weariness: not go for w. 145:9
study is a w. 44:1
w., fever, and fret 212:10
wearing of the green 5:5
weary: age shall not w. 72:1

wine (cont.):
vows made in w. 295:10
when w. is in 25:9
w. as good as life 49:8
w. for stomach's sake 67:13
w. is a mocker 41:14
w. maketh merry 43:12
w. when it is red 41:16
w. with merry heart 43:7
woman, w. and song 231:4
wings: angel of death spread w. 96:4
hear beating of his w. 79:5
w. like a dove 275:5
w. of an ostrich 232:9
winners: no w., all losers 110:2
winter: Christmas in middle of w. 1:8
English w. 97:3
how like a w. 321:12
if w. comes 325:7
it was the w. wild 248:6
savour all w. 320:8
very dead of w. 3:4
w. is icummen 271:11
w. is past 44:6
w. of despair 141:2
w. of our discontent 317:2
w. or summer when happy 113:11
w.'s rains and ruins 339:7
wipe away all tears 69:13
wire: along the electric w. 4:4
wisdom: get w. 40:11
palace of w. 74:9
what bettre than w. 112:9
w. above rubies 40:2
w. lingers 344:7
w. shall die 39:11
wise: all things w. 2:6
be w. 40:12
folly to be w. 179:3
heard a w. man 196:4
never did w. one 284:6
that's the w. thrush 83:4
tree the w. man sees 74:10
w., amazed 309:1
w. and eke love 333:4
w. as serpents 53:9
w. father knows 311:6
w. in his own conceit 42:3
w. man will make more 19:9
w. men from the east 49:14
w. son glad father 41:2
word enough for w. 268:2
wisely: not w. 315:12
wiser: sadder and w. man 124:2
w. to-day 271:8
wisest fool in Christendom 186:5
wish: hath her w. 322:7
who would w. to die 76:5
w. enemies dead 253:1
w. father to thought 301:8
w. I loved 282:2
wit: accepted w. but to say 175:10
brevity soul of w. 297:13
his weapon w. 192:6
true w. is nature 270:4
whetstone to sharpen w. 14:4
w. is out 25:9
w. its soul 124:3
w.'s a feather 270:12
witch: suffer a w. to live 35:12
with you alway 57:7
wither: age cannot w. 294:5
withers away 158:8
within: kingdom of God w. 60:8
never went w. 130:7
w. would fain go out 135:1
without: been better w. 263:9
he that is w. sin 61:9
nor w. you 239:2
w. would fain go in 135:1
witnesses: cloud of w. 68:8
wits: great w. to madness 149:5
rhyming mother-w. 238:5
stolen his w. away 136:2
witty: intelligent, w. 245:5
not only w. 301:2
wives: old w. fables 67:12
w. young men's mistresses 20:6
wizards that peep 45:8
woe: see another's w. 74:6
w. is me 45:5
w. to thee, O land 43:11

w. unto them that join 45:2
w. unto them that rise up 45:3
w. unto you, lawyers 59:8
wolf: keep the w. thence 361:3
man is w. 268:1
w. on the fold 96:3
w. dwell with lamb 45:12
wolves: inwardly ravening w. 52:10
woman: bloom on a w. 23:9
born of a w. 39:12
changeable always w. 356:7
excellent thing in w. 306:11
fat white w. 129:1
find a virtuous w. 42:8
frailty, thy name is w. 296:12
lovely w. in rural spot 200:8
lovely w. stoops 156:3; 177:4
make man w. 266:3
perfect w. 371:12
post-chaise with pretty w. 205:10
rib made he a w. 33:10
she's a w. 281:6; 302:11
so unto man is w. 228:8
suffer not a w. 67:10
support of w. I love 152:7
virtuous w. a crown 41:4
vitality in a w. 323:11
weak and feeble w. 156:11
what bettre than good w. 112:9
what is a w. 217:11
when a w. isn't beautiful 113:12
w. always a w. 369:1
w. among all those 43:4
w. colour'd ill 322:9
w. drew long black hair 156:5
w. especially 18:6
w. has her way 191:3
w. have long hair 65:4
w. his game 345:10
w. in hours of ease 292:8
w. is only a w. 216:9
w. old as she looks 125:8
w.'s business to get married 324:1
w. scorn'd 127:1
w.'s desire for desire 125:4
w.'s preaching 205:3
w.'s whole existence 96:7
w. take an elder 319:10
w. true and fair 145:11
w. wailing 124:7
w., wine and song 231:4
worthy w. al hir lyve 112:6
women: blessed among w. 57:15
bridge, w., champagne 28:4
cherries, hops, w. 140:4
dear dead w. 85:2
experience of w. 147:13
extension of w.'s rights 165:10
happiest w. 153:9
keeping w. in ignorance 221:4
learn about w. 218:9
let us have wine and w. 96:8
married w. kept w. 329:3
men, w., clergymen 330:4
music and w. 266:6
old w. of both sexes 335:4
paradise of w. 164:4
passing the love of w. 38:5
pretty w. to deserve them 18:2
regiment of w. 221:1
sorrows of w. averted 153:6
stir the zeal of w. 245:4
when hid among w. 82:1
w. are foolish 153:3
w. become like mothers 365:6
w. come and go 155:1
w. in secret rebellion 323:6
w. must weep 215:7
w. not so young as painted 26:3
w. should be struck 130:3
won: therefore to be w. 302:11
w. or lost 283:5
you have w., Galilean 209:8
wonder: I w. by my troth 144:9
still the w. grew 176:10
w. and wild desire 84:11
w. grew 196:7
w. that would be 344:5
w. what you've missed 15:3
wonderful: love to me was w. 38:5

wrestle not against flesh and blood 67:2
wretch: excellent w. 314:14
wretched: proud yet w. 135:2
w. child expires 27:7
w., rash 299:11
wring: soon w. hands 359:5
writ: name w. in water 214:4
write: restraint with which they w. 100:7
writers: clear w., like fountains 222:8
writing an exact man 20:12
w. paper thinner 252:1
w. that was written 48:9
written: adversary w. a book 40:4
what I have w. 62:10
words were now w. 39:15
w. with mine own hand 66:13
w. without effort 206:7
wrong: absent always w. 137:4
always in the w. 149:7
fear I may be w. 19:2
if you w. us 311:8
king can do no w. 72:6
own he has been w. 271:8
right deed w. reason 155:11
support me in the w. 243:5
w. but wromantic 293:5
w. forever on throne 230:7
wrote: blockhead ever w. 205:8
sorry I w. it 87:12
wrought: what hath God w. 36:4
***würfelt**: Gott w. nicht* 153:2
Wynken, Blynken 160:6
Xanadu: in X. did Kubla 124:6
yarn: merry y. 241:3
yea, y.; nay, nay 50:12
your y. be yea 68:15
year: pleasure of fleeting y. 321:12
y. is dying 343:13
yearning to breathe free 224:6
years: arches of the y. 349:6
forty y. on 77:7
love of finished y. 286:3
nor the y. condemn 72:1
threescore y. and ten 276:2
y. locust hath eaten 48:12
y. slipping by 195:2
y. to come 375:5
yellow: these y. sands 318:3
y. god forever gazes 183:5
y. to the jaundic'd 270:7
yes: I did say y. 193:8
y. I said y. 209:7
yesterday: but as y. 276:1
call back y. 316:11
dead y. 162:4
give me y. 207:8
no tomorrow, nor y. 143:12
pomp of y. 219:6
yesterdays: all our y. 310:6
yesteryear: snows of y. 355:8
yet: continency – but not y. 17:2
young man not y. 20:7
yew: that y.-tree's shade 178:6
yield: just y. to it 177:8
not to y. 346:12
yo-ho-ho 335:8
yoke: bear y. in youth 48:2
my y. is easy 54:1
Yorick: alas, poor Y. 300:5
young: crime of being y. 267:5
delight in proper y. men 91:3
gods love dies y. 243:8
I have been y. 274:11
lead those with y. 46:12
love's y. dream 254:5
love were y. 281:9
myself when y. 162:3
not so y. as painted 26:3
no y. man believes 184:5
she died y. 361:2
tomorrow for the y. 16:9
too y. to fall asleep 290:6
when I was y. 246:8
while we are y. 10:3
y., fresshe folkes 113:9
y. girl miserable 166:6
y. have more virtue 205:2
y. man lands hatless 31:5
y. man not yet 20:7
y. man's fancy 344:3
y. men see visions 48:13

NOTES

NOTES

NOTES

NOTES

NOTES

NOTES

NOTES

NOTES

NOTES

NOTES

NOTES

NOTES

NOTES

NOTES

NOTES

NOTES

NOTES

NOTES

NOTES

NOTES

NOTES

NOTES

NOTES

NOTES